The Battle of Vimy Ridge

Wall of Fire

Michael Krawchuk

Detselig Enterprises Ltd.

Calgary, Alberta, Canada

The Battle of Vimy Ridge

Library and Archives Canada Cataloguing in Publication Data

Krawchuk, Michael J

   The battle of Vimy Ridge : wall of fire / Michael J. Krawchuk.

Includes bibliographical references.

ISBN 978-1-55059-372-3

   1. Vimy Ridge, Battle of, France, 1917. 2. World War, 1914-1918 – Campaigns – France. 3. Canada. Canadian Army – History – World War, 1914-1918. 4. World War, 1914-1918 – Canada. I. Title.

D545.V5K73 2009   940.4'31   C2009-902251-6

DETSELIG
ENTERPRISES LTD

Detselig Enterprises Ltd.

210 - 1220 Kensington Road NW

Calgary, Alberta T2N 3P5

Phone: 403-283-0900   Fax: 403-283-6947

email: temeron@telusplanet.net

www.temerondetselig.com

We acknowledge the financial support of the Government of Canada through the Book Publishing Industry Development Program (BPIDP) for our publishing activities.

We also acknowledge the support of the Alberta Foundation for the Arts for our publishing program.

978-1-55059-372-3   SAN 113-0234   Printed in Canada

This book is dedicated to my sister, Stephanie, whose creativity, drive and passion inspired me to look inside myself for my own.

Acknowledgments

At many times when I was researching and writing this book, I felt like an outsider. I am not an academic with university degrees in history, nor have I served in the military. I am just a guy with a life-long, passionate interest in military history. Nevertheless, with sufficient drive and energy, along with the help of others, even an outsider can make a contribution.

I do not believe that my project would have been possible twenty years ago, at least not without the need to expend a tremendous amount of personal resources. The internet has changed all that. I was able to do a lot of my research "in my pajamas."

In particular, I am grateful for the excellent on-line resource offered by Library and Archives Canada. They have reproduced, on-line, the War Diaries of the Canadian Corps for the entire Great War. This was a priceles resource that was available "at my finger tips." They should be commended for their contribution to the preservation of Canadian history and making it available to the public.

The Government of Canada is not the only one to utilize the internet as a means to offer history to the world. One website, in particular, that I found very useful was *The Canadian Images & Letters Project.* They offer a vast collection of letters, diaries, etc., of Canadian soldiers from not just the Great War, but throughout Canada's history. It is a brilliant project.

I was fortunate that I reside in the city of my *alma mater*, the University of Saskatchewan in Saskatoon. Whenever I could not purchase research material on my own or locate it on-line, I was usually able to find it at the U of S. With my alumni library card providing me access to the U of S's on-line catalog and the help of the library staff, I was able to fill in many gaps.

While I did a lot of my research on the internet, just as much was done the "traditional way," reading books. Much has been written on the Great War over the years and I cannot claim originality in many of the ideas found within my book. Although I have included many works in my Bibliography, I would be remiss if I did not make special mention of certain books, collections and authors that were particularly helpful and influential.

The history of the Great War has been clouded by a great many myths that have arisen since the War ended. Gary Sheffield's *Forgotten Victory: The First World War: Myths and Realities* and Gordon Corrigan's *Mud, Blood and Poppycock,* at least in my mind, comprehensively shattered many of the old myths. I would recommend them to anyone who wants to learn more about the true nature of the Western Front in the Great War.

For those with an interest in how the Great War was actually fought by the Canadians and British, the "must reads" are Bill Rawling's *Surviving Trench Warfare: Technology and the Canadian Corps, 1914-1918,* Paddy Griffith's *Battle Tactics of the Western Front: The British Army's Art of Attack 1916-18* and, of course, Robin Prior and Trevor Wilson's classic, *Command on the Western Front: The Military Career of Sir Henry Rawlinson 1914-1918.*

History is not, of course, only the "big picture." There is much to learn from the personal accounts of those who were actually there. While there are many publishers who offer Canadian soldiers' stories to the public, I must mention the collection available from Norm Christie's CEF Books. If you want to read a memoir or diary from a Canadian who served in the Great War, his collection is a good place to start.

In terms of style, I found the works of Lyn MacDonald and Peter Hart influential. Their use of soldiers' accounts with the "big picture" produces a brilliant combination. I would recommend any of their works.

As an outsider, I took inspiration from Martin Middlebrook, the poultry farmer who wrote the classic *The First Day on the Somme*. Similar with Jonathan Nicholls, this police officer wrote *the* book on the Battle of Arras, *Cheerful Sacrifice: The Battle of Arras 1917.* I can only hope to make a contribution like theirs.

Finally, I must mention Pierre Berton. His *Vimy* sparked my interest in the Great War and the Canadian Corps many years ago.

Although I feel like an outsider, no man is an island, and I had the help and support of many people along the way. I am a lawyer by training and for years I tried to balance the demands of private practice and writing a book. Before work, after work, on weekends and during my holidays I tried to get as much done on my book as possible. However, something "had to give" and I decided to quit my job to dedicate myself to my book. So I did.

The law firm I work at, Wallace Meschishnick Clackson Zawada, were amazing. Rather than having us go our separate ways, they offered to turn my quitting into a sabbatical. So I accepted and, on my return to practicing law, they allowed me to work on reduced time while I pursued publishing. I thank the directors of the firm for their generosity, support and patience.

While everyone at Wallace Meschishnick Clackson Zawada, past and present, have been great to me, I must mention three people in particular. Thank you to Craig Zawada for his interest in my project, his facilitating my use of firm office equipment when needed and his legal advice on intellectual property issues. I also appreciated the support and encouragement I received from Lorne Jamieson, especially during the early years of my project. Finally, of course, Marnie Wandler. Not only was she my "military history assistant" when it came to the "nuts and bolts" of putting together submissions and my manscript, but she was always a source of support and encouragement. Along the way she discovered her own interest in the Great War.

While my sister, Stephanie Krawchuk, did not make any actual direct contribution to my book, she was an influence. Indeed, she is an inspiration. She is an artist and, being a writer, I always felt that she knew "where I was coming from." Only she could understand the creative process, its motivation, the risks inherent, the stresses and the joys of it all.

Finally, last but certainly not least to receive special mention, is my mother, Jan Krawchuk. She has always been my biggest fan and supporter, but there is more. She is my "military history buddy." We have travelled the route of the Great War together, taking the journey to Ypres, Arras and Vimy Ridge. She has developed her own interest in the Great War and has read quite a few of the books listed in my Bibliography. If I want to talk to someone about the Great War, she is the one I turn to. I thank her for her support, encouragement and interest she developed in the Great War.

Throughout the researching and writing of my book my close friends and family were always there for me. They all helped in their own way: Don Krawchuk, Jordan Krawchuk, Mandy Krawchuk, John Krawchuk, Olga Krawchuk, Elaine Shabaga, Judi Cherry, Clint Cherry, Joel Cherry, Harley Rivet and Christy Bell.

Contents

Introduction

Perhaps no war is more controversial than the First World War. Why the War was fought, how it was fought and the War's consequences have been endlessly debated by generations since its conclusion. Despite the passage of time, fascination with the conflict remains.

Some of this interest finds its roots in the horrific human casualties the First World War (or the Great War as it was known at the time) produced. Although there are no firm figures, approximately 10 million people lost their lives to the conflict during the years 1914 to 1918 with about 20 million more wounded. Added to these gruesome totals were the millions who were mentally maimed by their experience. Sparsely inhabited Canada, with a pre-war population of only 7.2 million, suffered almost 60 000 dead and a further 175 000 wounded.[1] The toll in Canadian dead exceeds those suffered by the behemoth United States in the long Vietnam War.

In human terms, the Great War had a more profound impact on the populations of the Western Powers, such as Great Britain, than the Second World War. This impact may be measured by the monuments to the dead erected in many of the Allied countries. Be it in London, Paris, Rome or a small Canadian prairie town, the lists of the fallen from the Great War on these monuments always outnumber the names of the slain from the Second World War.

The casualties inflicted by the Great War were suffered by people from all corners of the earth. While at first glance the combatants of the Great War appear to be limited to Europeans, this is misleading. Not only were the United States, the Turkish Empire and Japan involved, but a closer look at the make-up of the European armies shows a vast collection of nationalities. Looking at the British Army, it was made up of soldiers from all across the globe: Canada, Australia, Ireland, New Zealand, South Africa, India and Bermuda to name a few. The French Army was multi-national too, including units from Morocco, Algeria, Tunisia and Indo-China. Although the battlefields of the Great War were largely confined to Europe and the Middle East, it truly was a world war.

Along with the tremendous casualties, the Great War changed the political face of the world, providing another source of fascination for later generations. Gone were the long-standing Russian, Austro-Hungarian and Turkish Empires by War's end. In their place Communist Russia was born, a myriad of Eastern European countries were created and the Arab world was cast onto the long and troubled road that it is still wandering to this date.

For other historic powers such as Britain, France and Germany, their strength was not broken, but it had been badly battered. Although it would take a second world war to complete the task, the Great War began a decline in influence for these nations that lead to the destruction of their empires and ensured that they could not become super-powers in the latter half of the twentieth century.

The Great War also marked the rise of a new player in world affairs; the United States. Prior to the War, the United States was not involved in world matters to a great extent, however, the Great War changed this, thrusting the United States onto the world stage. Following the War its power grew so that, at the conclusion of the Second World War, it emerged as a super-power.

These massive political changes had, and still have, far reaching effects. In addition to helping shape the context of the Second World War, the Great War also saw the rise of Communism, which sowed the seeds for the dominant conflict of the 20th Century, the Cold War. Into the 21st Century, the present troubles in the Middle East have roots in the fall of the Ottoman Empire and the Allies' handling of this event. Arguably, the Great War created the framework within which subsequent major world events have occurred.

For Canada, no event is more important to its history than the Great War. Although technically an independent nation in 1867, Canada had virtually no foreign recognition as an entity separate from the British Empire, and its foreign policy was dictated by the British in the years leading up to the Great War. It was as a result of Canada's excellent military performance and significant contribution during the Great War that Canada became recognized as a nation on its own on the world stage.

Within the Great War, the most important military achievement for Canada was the successful capture of Vimy Ridge in April of 1917. Although the Canadian Corps experienced many successes during the Great War, the Battle of Vimy Ridge stands out amongst the rest. It was the first battle in which all four Divisions of the Corps were united, a development that was maintained through all successive battles. Canadians would serve and fight with Canadians. Some say that once Vimy Ridge was seized, Canada was born.

In recognition of the important contribution Canada made in the Great War and the significance of Vimy Ridge to Canadians, France has granted, in perpetuity, 110 hectares of land on Vimy Ridge to Canada. For the Canadian citizen, to walk this land is to walk Canadian soil.

Although home, in a sense, to Canadian soldiers in 1917, much of the battlefield today would be unrecognizable to a soldier from then. Where once existed the shell-torn wasteland of No Man's Land and the labyrinth of opposing trenches, now grows a healthy forest. The Ridge, so important to the Allies at the time, is obscured from vision by this living presence. Near the asphalt roads that lead the traveller to sad and lonely, but beautifully tended, cemeteries, sheep graze peacefully on fresh grass, shielded from the sun by the shade provided by the forest's leaves. Crowning the Ridge is another post-war addition; the magnificent Vimy Memorial with its twin columns reaching towards the heavens and its base inscribed with the names of approximately 10 000 Canadian soldiers killed in the Great War for whom there is no known grave.

However, co-existing with these more recent additions, the scars of battle do remain. The land has retained the pock-marks created by the massive amounts of explosive material the combatants hurled at each other, more resembling an ocean in a storm than a piece of *terra firma*. For this reason the battlefield remains a dangerous place, and much of the terrain is blocked from passage lest a visitor become a modern casualty of the Great War. Amongst these old shell craters can be barely discerned the traces of what at the time composed the vast web of trenches that cut into Vimy Ridge. Below this broken ground, tunnels and mine galleries still honeycomb the Ridge. Although resilient, mother nature, like humankind, retains the imprint of war.

. . . .

This book is a military history written with a main character and a theme. The main character is the Battle of Vimy Ridge and the theme is the offensive in the Great War. In the writer's view, to understand the significance of the Battle of Vimy Ridge, one needs first to have a grasp on the inherent difficulties facing any attacker on the Western Front. The Western Front was an imposing and deadly battleground. A continuous line of fortified trenches stretched across Western Europe, held by millions of soldiers armed with high powered rifles, machine guns and artillery. While opinion appears to be changing, for years after the Great War, the trench stalemate that persisted for most of the War has been seen in popular opinion as evidence of a military bankrupt of ideas. However, nothing is ever quite so simple.

The trench system that developed during the Great War was the result of the interplay of several factors that influence how any war is fought: firepower, mobility, communications and manpower. The tremendous firepower that the technology of the day had developed, the mobile firepower and instantaneous communications that technology could not provide and the enormous reserves of manpower available to the combatants created a lethal, but relatively static battlefield. This situation quite naturally transformed itself into trench stalemate across western Belgium and north-eastern and eastern France. The same factors that influenced the trench system's development also made it extremely difficult for an attacker to breakthrough the stalemate. It was a situation no one anticipated before the War.

Much of the controversy that surrounds the Great War to this day has to do with the offensive operations undertaken to break the stalemate. Any offensive on the Western Front was handicapped by the fact that an attack had to be a frontal assault; the most difficult and dangerous type of operation. The massive trench system had no vulnerable flanks to turn. That so many frontal assaults failed with heavy casualties has been seen by many since as, if not criminal, at least futile.

There is an element of hindsight to this viewpoint though. While, in retrospect, some of the assaults made in the Great War may appear futile, this was not the anticipated result at the time. Once trench warfare began, the combatants did not intentionally waste their soldiers in fruitless attempts to break the stalemate. Instead, the Great War was an ever-evolving process through which the combatants tried to learn from their mistakes, apply new technology and try new tactics and techniques. Unfortunately, in war, a learning process such as this is going to be costly in lives.

The Battle of Vimy Ridge that took place in April of 1917 was an offensive operation. The Battle will be examined in the context of the inherent difficulties any attacker faced on the Western Front. How the Canadian Corps was able to surmount these difficulties at Vimy Ridge is key to the historical importance of the Battle and is the story of this book. In placing Vimy Ridge within this larger context, it is hoped that a better understanding of the Canadians' achievement will be reached.

· · · ·

To explain the Western Front, the problems facing the attacker and the Battle of Vimy Ridge, this book is divided into Parts. Part I "The Great War Battlefield" is, in a sense, introductory. There are chapters describing the trench system, life in the trenches, the weapons of war and the experience of battle on the Western Front. Emphasis is on how dangerous the Great War battlefield was, with the lethality of the weapons used and the power of the defence.

Part II "The Offensive in the Great War" is also, to an extent, introductory. There are chapters explaining why breaking through the trench system was so difficult, the particular problems experienced in the beginning of the War and the Allies' motives for launching attacks. This is followed by a short history of the British Expeditionary Force (of which the Canadians were part) and the Canadian Corps in the early years of the War. The rest of Part II includes a brief discussion of the 1916 Battle of the Somme to demonstrate how the inherent problems encountered by the attacker could affect a battle.

It is in Part III "Winter of 1917" that we turn to Vimy Ridge. The Winter of 1917 (the period leading up to the Battle) ties Part I with Parts IV and V. There is discussion of how the weapons of the Great War were used by the Canadians and Germans while they were holding the line at Vimy, culminating in the trench raids both sides launched. Part III is also when Vimy Ridge itself is introduced, including a description of its features and history in the War. Finally, there is a chapter on the Canadian Corps in 1917; both the generals and their men.

Part IV "Plans and Preparations" deals with the lead up to the Battle (March 20 – April 8). It begins with a discussion of the larger picture on the Western Front, including the plans of the Allies and Germans for 1917. The main thrust of Part IV is to demonstrate how the Canadians at Vimy planned to tackle the inherent problems facing any attack on the Western Front. There are chapters on the creeping barrage, infantry assault tactics, training, the artillery preliminary bombardment and other preparations. Emphasis is placed on improvements made in these areas since the Battle of the Somme. There is also a chapter on the Germans, including which units were defending the Ridge and their response to Canadian preparations.

In Part V "The Battle of Vimy Ridge," the Battle is presented as it unfolds through time. Beginning with the opening of the barrage at zero-hour, the first time period is 5:30 a.m. – 7:30 a.m. A chapter is devoted to describing each of the four Canadian Division's experience during this period. Then, after a quick summary of the overall situation at 7:30 a.m., the next time period is 7:30 a.m. – 11:00 a.m., again describing each Division's experience in separate chapters. This process carries on (with necessary modification) until the Battle ends. The intent is that the narrative will flow as the Battle happened.

Part V ends with an analysis of the Battle. There are chapters on the human cost, the German conduct of the Battle and the keys to Canadian success. Particular emphasis is placed on how the Canadians overcame the difficult problems of attacking on a Great War battlefield.

Part VI "Conclusion" begins by taking a step back to look at the wider picture on the Western Front. The Allies' 1917 Spring Offensive, of which the Battle of Vimy Ridge was a part, is briefly examined.

From there, the remainder of the Conclusion is dedicated to discussing the larger significance of the Battle of Vimy Ridge. One chapter is on the importance the Canadians' victory had in developing more effective offensive tactics, not just for the Canadians, but for the whole British Expeditionary Force. Another chapter looks at the impact the Battle had in turning the Canadian Corps into the elite military formation on the Western Front. Finally, a chapter is devoted to discussing how the victory at Vimy, leading as it did to the creation of an elite Corps, in turn affected the development of Canada as a nation.

. . . .

In telling the story of the Battle of Vimy Ridge, first hand accounts and war records are drawn from Canadian sources. Consistent with the idea that the main character of this book is the Battle, soldiers' accounts are used to illustrate points (i.e., how it felt to be bombarded by artillery), rather than focussing on the soldiers' personal histories. As for war records, the War Diaries of the Canadian Corps were particularly helpful and it is hoped that the war diarists followed Lieutenant-General Sir Julian Byng's advice:

> The Corps Commander wishes to impress upon all those whose special duty it may be to keep the War Diary of their respective Units the value and necessity of writing the most careful and painstaking records. The future history of the war will be largely written from these reports and, being official in character, they will be accepted as primary evidence of military events.[2]

Although the Great War was waged by soldiers from many nations on both sides of the conflict, since the Battle of Vimy Ridge was fought on the Allied side largely by Canadian soldiers and the Battle has a particular resonance in Canada, it is the Canadian experience that will be the focus. Having said this, it must be realized that the Canadian Corps served within the larger British Expeditionary Force. Thus, when discussing the larger issues of the War, emphasis is on the British, as the Canadians had little role in such matters and British decisions and actions directly affected the Canadians.

While the Canadians have the central role, it is still hoped that the reader will be able to glean a greater understanding of the nature of the Great War. Too many Great War histories in the past have relied on myths and what this work sets out to achieve is to illustrate how the Battle of Vimy Ridge was actually fought. There were difficult strategic, tactical and technological problems that dictated the manner in which the War was fought and yet, despite these problems and to the credit of the soldiers and generals, they were able to overcome them and achieve victory at Vimy Ridge and, ultimately, in the Great War.

Part I

The Great War Battlefield

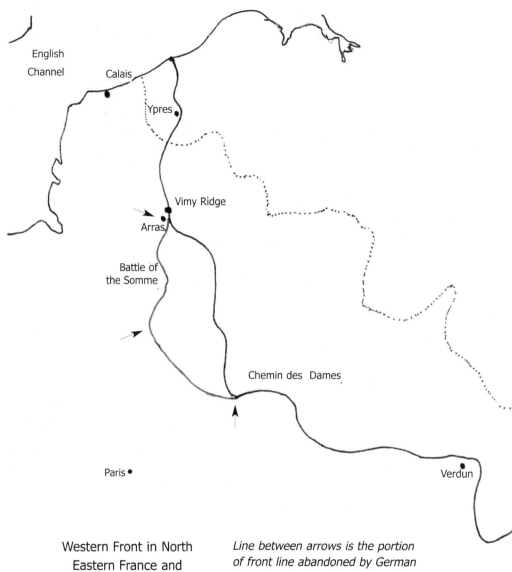

English
Channel

Calais

Ypres

Vimy Ridge

Arras

Battle of
the Somme

Chemin des Dames

Paris •

Verdun

**Western Front in North
Eastern France and
Belgium, 1917**

*Line between arrows is the portion
of front line abandoned by German
Army in retreat to Hindenberg Line*

*The dotted line is the border
between France and Belgium*

The solid line is the front line

One

The Trenches

It is difficult for us today to comprehend a Great War battlefield. People have trouble imagining a modern battlefield with its jet aircraft and fast moving tanks, let alone understanding the chaos and confusion of a shell-torn, heavily barb-wired and corpse strewn Great War battlefield, bisected by a myriad of trenches. As hard as it is for us to imagine, it was the reality for millions of soldiers on the Western Front.

Except for the beginning few months of the War and most of 1918, the Great War was like a long siege, with the opposing armies in entrenched positions staring at each other across No Man's Land that lay between them. From the far western corner of Belgium along the North Sea, through northern-eastern and eastern France to the neutral Swiss frontier, the trench lines cut across Western Europe with no break. There was no way to avoid them, no flanks to turn and no room for manoeuvre. For an Allied soldier looking across No Man's Land at the German lines, as far as he could see in front, to his right and to his left were trenches. Beyond his gaze were even more. Entrenchments on such a vast scale had never been seen before.

In attempting to understand the Great War battlefield, it must be borne in mind that these trench lines were not one long, uniform line cutting across Europe. Rather, the trenches curved and angled as the hills, valleys, rivers and human habitations demanded. They were also constructed to take advantage of natural defensive features, such as the reverse slope of ridges or overlooking ravines.

At some points the opposing front lines were hundreds of yards apart, at others, the trenches were separated by but a few yards. In a letter to his sister, Ernest Mosley Taylor (1st Canadian Mounted Rifles) described the nearness of the enemy at the particular sector of trenches he was holding:

> We had a fairly quiet time during our two days here, then we took our turn in the front line. It was rather different to our previous experiences, the trenches only averaging about 60 yards apart. The part where we bombers held they were about 25 yards apart. It was fatal to even show a hand, and as the trench

was only shoulder high, it meant continual watchfulness. There was a short gap from the German trench from which they could throw bombs into ours. Jack and I and two others were told off to crawl out during the night among the debris of an old stable. We spent our nights lying prone on the wet ground seven yards from the Huns. The idea was to take them by surprise if they came out to throw, but principally to discover what they were up to. They were always at work, we could hear their footsteps on the wooden bath mats and hear them talking and coughing.[3]

Not only did the trenches curve and angle as the locale required, but both sides purposely constructed their trenches so that they would not run in a straight line. To reduce the effect of a shell or grenade explosion, and also to ensure that an attacking enemy could not jump into a trench and blast away at a long line of soldiers manning a straight line, the trenches were built so that every few yards the trench made an angle and its direction changed. This way, an explosion would be contained to some extent and soldiers could barricade a part of their trench if the enemy should happen to break in. From the air the trenches zig-zagged across the countryside.

The trenches did not consist of a single trench either. Instead, multiple trench lines were constructed to defeat an enemy assault. In the British Army (within which the Canadians served), there were generally three lines of trenches: the front line trench, a support line and a reserve line. Linking all of these were communication trenches. On top of this, where attacks were anticipated or had occurred, it was common for the defenders to build successive multiple trench lines.

From the front line saps were constructed; small, relatively shallow trenches reaching into No Man's Land to give the defenders the ability to detect an attack before it reached them. In times of an assault, such as at Vimy, jumping-off trenches were built ahead of the front line to give the attacking soldiers an edge in reaching enemy lines. The effect was that, starting from the Allied rear line and ending at the rear German line, a web of trenches scarred the land between.

Trenches were generally about seven to eight feet deep and six to seven feet wide, with the parapet facing the enemy and the parados facing the rear. As a standing man could not see over the parapet, a fire-step was built for the soldiers to stand on, enabling them to watch over No Man's Land or fend off an enemy attack. Sandbags lined the parapet, providing extra protection. To ensure that the trench walls did not fall in, revetements were placed on the sides of the trench, usually made of sandbags or wood. The bottom of the trench usually was covered with wooden duckboards, so the men could avoid walking on soft or muddy ground.

Built into the sides of trenches and reaching underground were dugouts. Entered from the trench, a gallery with steps lead down to the bunker where the garrison resided.

Officers were often lucky enough to have dugouts that contained beds, tables and sometimes a stove. These few amenities were hardly luxurious though, as the dugouts were often crowded and cramped. For the other ranks, the accommodations were often worse. Sergeant Charles Savage from the 5th Canadian Mounted Rifles remembered the dugouts his unit used in early 1916:

> In each Company area there was generally one fairly large dugout that was used for company headquarters but all the other shelters were small, each holding two to six men. Inside, corrugated iron formed the roof and if you were lucky you had a wooden floor, otherwise it was dirt or mud. The dugout was about three or four feet high and in the center was a post to support the roof and to give you something against which to bang your head when crawling in or out in the dark.[4]

Built to protect the soldiers from shelling, dugouts became increasing complex as the war went on, being dug deep into the ground with multiple entrances, exits, galleries and bunkers.

The defence of the trench system did not rest solely on soldiers manning the parapet. Instead, strong points were constructed, fortified by earth, concrete or steel, and positioned to dominate potential avenues of attack. Difficult to destroy, it was within these strong points that many of the most destructive weapons of war, such as machine guns, were deployed.

Yards ahead of the front line barbed wire obstacles were placed. In some areas multiple belts of sharp, tangled wire, each yards deep, were built in an effort to bog down an assault, making the attackers vulnerable to machine gun, artillery and rifle fire. The wire obstacles were often built on angles (zig-zagging like the trenches), purposely funnelling attackers into pre-planned kill zones.

In between the Allied and German front line trenches lay the infamous No Man's Land. Where battles had not taken place, grass, shrubs and trees still existed, but where fighting had occurred, or was repeatedly occurring such as at Ypres, destruction and desolation reigned. In these parts of the line, the ground was gutted, destroyed by the weight of shell fire thrown by each side at the other. It was a maze of shell holes, disorientating to those who ventured into No Man's Land unprepared. In such a region without discernable land marks, it was all too easy to become confused and lost and end up, accidentally, stumbling into the enemy wire rather than the safety of your own trench.

This hostile strip of land could inspire men's fears and imaginations. Captain George McKean of the 14th Battalion (Royal Montreal Regiment) remembered his first view of No Man's Land:

> I shall not forget the first night when I looked over the parapet into that land of mystery and wonder – No Man's Land. Somewhere out there was the enemy!

Occasionally I saw the flash of a rifle as a German sentry fired, and heard the sing of the bullet. Merely to look out over there seemed to me an act of courage! I tingled with the excitement of my new experience. At last I was in the war, not merely dressed up as a soldier, but actually facing the enemy – not more than a hundred yards away and it was that little strip of land bestrewn with wire and obstacles, that unknown disputed piece of ground called "No Man's Land" – that most readily and quickly appealed to my imagination.[5]

NAC-PA 786 – View from the Canadian front line into No Man's Land. Dead German soldiers unburied (Battle of the Somme, 1916).

In the wake of a battle, equipment, rifles and discarded ammunition littered No Man's Land.

More ghastly human reminders of battle lingered as well. Private Donald Fraser of the 31st (Alberta) Battalion recalled in his journal an experience in the line near Ypres in late 1915:

About 7:00 a.m., when doing sentry, I was surprised to see a couple of fellows in No Man's Land about 50 yds. in, bending over something. It was foggy at the time and extreme vision was about 90 yds. At the moment I thought they were

Germans and was just at the point of covering them when I saw they were our own men.

Being curious and my sentry period just up, I went over the parapet to see what was the matter. It was a dead Gordon Highlander and they were going through his clothes gingerly. A few yards away were some more dead. We found out later there was a fairly even line of dead three or four hundred yards long, principally Gordon Highlanders, though there were a few evidently belonging to an English Battalion. Most of the bodies were skeletons or partly mummified and fell to pieces when moved. Some were half buried. One Highlander was fairly intact. On two of them we found paybooks, a watch and some money. Their names were Robb and Anderson and they belonged to Aberdeen, Scotland. Robb was married and had several letters in his possession. There was one written by himself to his wife. Of course it was never posted. It was last December, namely, December 1914. He was very optimistic regarding the war, went even as far as to say it would be finished in a week or two, and expected to be home for Xmas. His paybook had only one entry, a payment made in October. He was clothed in winter garb and had his equipment over a light coloured goatskin. He was lying facing the German line and his rifle, with bayonet fixed, was laying about a foot to his right.[6]

Near the front line trench, but far enough away to give the soldiers holding them an advantage in detecting enemy movements, were the outposts, usually located at the end of a sap or the lip of a shell crater. Private Fraser recalled his experiences in the outposts near Ypres in his New Year's Eve 1915 journal entry:

One of the most disagreeable duties is "Listening Post." Listening Post is in No Man's Land as far forward as is deemed safe. It is either a shell hole position or the end of a small trench running out from the firing line. The idea is to detect an enemy movement and nip an attack by stealth in the bud. From the post to the firing line there is connection by cord or telephone wire. The sentry at "listening post" pulls the cord; according to the number of pulls one, two or three, the fellow at the other end is made aware of happenings and ready to warn the Company. The signals are few, usually all clear, or small or large hostile parties approaching. The enemy is often aware of these "listening posts" and makes a point of capturing them or bombs the sentry. In consequence, one has to be all alive when he takes on such work.[7]

The armies on the Western Front were not satisfied just digging into the surface of the ground, they also took the war underground. In some ways the underground war mirrored that taking place on the surface. Defensive tunnels were excavated beneath friendly lines, while offensive tunnels were dug under No Man's Land and then below enemy trenches for the purpose of exploding mines beneath important enemy defences. From these tunnels, like saps on the surface, listening galleries fingered out. Men with geophones (sort of like a doctor's stethoscope) listened intently for sounds of enemy mining activity. Meanwhile, on the surface, the soldiers manning the trenches lived with the fear that they could at any moment be blown skyward by a mine from below.

What was created in France and Belgium was a complex system of fortifications, above and below ground, designed to break up any attack that was launched against it. More or less in place from late 1914 to early 1918, it was within this impressive system that the battles on the Western Front were fought.

Two

Life in the Trenches

While the focus of this book is on the Battle of Vimy Ridge, it should be pointed out that battle was the exception, not the rule, in a soldier's experience on the Western Front. It may be more accurate to say that trench life consisted of routine, hard labor and boredom, punctuated by moments of sheer terror.

Contrary to modern public perception, soldiers did not spend all their time in the trenches. In the British Army, within which the Canadians served, it was soon realized that men could not maintain combat effectiveness unless there was a system of trench rotation. Units were rotated between the front line, support line, reserve line and rest. With time spent out of the line training, on average, a British battalion spent ten days out of a month in the trenches.[8]

Moving in and out of the trenches was often a daunting task. Ernest Mosley Taylor (1st Canadian Mounted Rifles) told his sister of his experience going to the front:

These marches into the trenches by night are something never to be forgotten. You go stumbling along in the dark, single file, just like "follow the leader" and "obstacle race" combined. Sometimes scrambling down into a trench when nothing but the quantity of soft mud at the bottom prevents you from damaging yourself. On you go knee deep in mud, and after a while you scramble out again with a supreme effort. Then perhaps there is open ground to cross in full view of the enemy trenches. Each time the star lights go up illuminating everything like a flash of lightening, the procession stands motionless until the light fades away, then onward once more.[9]

Once in the trenches, a front line soldier's day began with "stand to" just before dawn. The soldiers manned the parapet of the trench and peered into No Man's Land, eyes searching for a dawn attack; the time of day that was considered the most likely to experience an enemy assault. As evening was also a dangerous time for attacks, there was a "stand to" at sundown as well. If nothing materialized, the soldiers received the order to "stand down"; usually about an hour after the order was given to "stand to." After standing down, for all except those who acted as sentries, work began.

Work was ever present on the Western Front. Even after the soldiers had completed their tour of the front, support and reserve lines and were on "rest" (a tour in the British trenches generally was four to six days on each line, with four to six days on rest[10]), they were expected to work. In the words of C. Scriven (10th (Canadians) Battalion): "If you weren't fighting you were working."[11]

Referred to by the soldiers as "fatigues," the jobs that the soldiers were asked to do were varied, but routine. There was a constant need to repair trenches that were damaged either by the elements or shell fire. The belts of barbed wire protecting the trenches had to be mended. Duckboards were laid on the bottom of the trenches to make walking easier as, invariably, mud, snow, rain and wear and tear made the trenches impassable without them. There was also the incessant demand for ammunition, equipment, supplies, food and water for the soldiers in the trenches. Many was the soldier who had to struggle, usually in the dark, along zig-zagging communication trenches up to the front line, knee deep in mud, bringing food and ammunition to his comrades in arms.

Private Fraser did not relish being on fatigues. He recorded in his October 29, 1915, diary entry:

> For four months we were continuously wrestling with trenches and dug-outs, shovelling, draining, ditching, digging, revetting, filling sandbags, carrying timber, corrugated iron, etc. When in reserve almost every night, as soon as darkness set in, we had to hike to the Engineer's dump at Kemmel and carry stuff up the line. We were usually too early at the dump and would lay around in the mud and rain for half an hour to an hour waiting for the arrival of the Engineer. Orders called for our presence at a certain time and orders had to be obeyed. Meanwhile we would hang around, too often soaked to the skin and our clothes and equipment as heavy as lead, waiting at the side of the road to load up and move on. These working parties were a regular nightmare.[12]

Most of the work was done at night. It was too dangerous during the day for work parties as they were an easily identifiable target for enemy snipers and gunners. Even at night though, work parties were far from safe. Private Will Bird of the 42nd Battalion (Royal Highlanders of Canada) remembered an experience while on a work party:

> The Germans had blown a mine north and adjoining Durrand Crater, and a party of them had been repulsed by our "A" Company, which was in the line. Thirty yards of front line had been destroyed and it was important that a new trench be made, with saps leading to new posts. This was to be our job. The Germans

shelled the Quarry Line and all back areas as we marched in, and the slippery mud made the going hard.

. . . .

As we entered the communication trench Slim fell in at my heels. Burke was next to him, then Laurie. An officer named Stewart took charge of us, and we filed from the cover of the trench to open ground. Sharp orders hissed at us. A brigade wirer led the way. We had to dig in along tapes and were exposed, in easy range of enemy snipers and machine-guns. The mud was deep and we did not know our location. Each man worked feverishly. All around us in the dark was a deafening clamour of shell fire and rattling of machine-guns. Flares were soaring in quick succession, illuminating the area we dug.

Slim stuck so close to me I had to push him back in his position. We dug and dug. I struck barbed wire in tangles, and the brigade man came with his cutters and helped me clear the lot. He was not twenty feet away when he groaned loudly and sank to the earth, shot through the body. Bullets were snapping all around us. Slim crouched down on his knees and huddled close to earth, yet never slackened his shovelling.

Suddenly there was another call for stretcher bearers. Lieutenant Stewart had been shot through the stomach. He died that night. Finally Slim and I had our portions dug as deeply as required and were out of the rifle fire. We sat there while the others finished, and when we all were done, word came for us to go back. We had not gone a dozen yards when Burke dropped, shot through the head.[13]

Adding to the dangers in No Man's Land at night were the flares each side period-ically fired into the air. Sergeant Charles Henry Savage (5th Canadian Mounted Rifles) described their operation and effect:

These flares, or Verey lights, were really rockets fired from a special kind of gun called a flare pistol. They were used extensively for signaling as well as for light-ing up No Man's Land, so there was sometimes considerable variety in the dis-play. When the rocket burst, the ordinary sort of flare set free a burning tube of magnesium attached to a small parachute. As this floated to the ground it gave a brilliant white light in which anything moving could be distinguished easily. The rule in No Man's Land was for everyone to stand perfectly still while a flare was up; but it was very difficult to impress this on new men, whose first impulse was, of course, to duck into the nearest shell hole. When a flare went up you could be certain that riflemen and machine gunners in the opposite trenches were peering over the parapet eagerly searching for a target, and the smallest move-ment was the signal for bursts of rifle and machine gun fire in the direction of that movement. Of course, if you were with only one or two men it was possible for all to get into a hole quickly and be quite safe, but with wiring and working parties, one nervous or inexperienced man might mean the loss of half the party or more.[14]

Work parties were not only at risk in the front lines. Both sides knew that the other was bringing supplies from the rear areas to the front. These routes to the front were often targets for the artillery. Private Jack O'Brien of the 28th (Northwest) Battalion recalled:

Well, after a few days in the trenches we went back . . . for a rest, or rather we were in reserve. We were now in what was known as the Kemmel Shelters; here we turned night into day – we slept or did nothing in the daytime, but at night we worked like bees – we were busy on fatigue parties carrying up ammunition and provisions to the front lines. Now, don't run off with the idea that this is a bomb-proof job; Fritzie knows all about the supplies that must be brought up, and you can bet your sweet life that he takes a delight in picking off rationing parties, and such-like. Every night our supports were heavily shelled; every road leading to the lines had a battery trained on it and every little while it was swept by shrapnel.[15]

During the day the tasks given to the soldiers were less conspicuous. Most of the daylight work consisted of cleaning rifles, dugouts, clothing and similar jobs that did not require exposing oneself to the enemy. As the nights were full of more intense labor, many soldiers tried to use the day to catch some sleep.

It may have been just as well that the soldiers were occupied with work as it might help take their minds off the wretched conditions that surrounded them. Private Will Bird summarized trench life at Vimy:

We endured much. Dugouts reeked with odours of stale perspiration and the sour, alkaline smell of clothing. There was never enough water to permit frequent washing and when we could get warm the lice tormented us. The vermin were in every dugout, millions of descendants of the originals of 1915. We seared the seams of our shirts with candles, fought them constantly but never conquered them.[16]

In addition to the plague of lice were the rats. Where battles had occurred they grew plump from feeding on the decomposing bodies lying between and within the trenches. In the summer, flies would swarm around the dead and multiply their numbers. However, it was not only the dead who were food for pests. Private Victor Wheeler, 50th (Calgary) Battalion, recalled becoming a rat's "midnight snack":

By nightfall I was very nervous and low in spirit, and my Signal Officer, realizing my condition, told me to get a good night's sleep in the front line Battalion H.Q.

dugout. I bunked down on chicken wire, approximately three feet off the ground, strung between wooden posts that served to support the dugout ceiling. Such luxury!

The following morning, while preparing to shave at our makeshift ablution table, Art Moore exclaimed, "Begad, Vic, how'd you make such a bloody mess of your ear?" I had not yet lathered my face nor unsheathed my straight razor, but a glance in my steel mirror – that would flash like a heliograph in the sun – startled me. I discovered that as I lay asleep a rat had bitten a mouthful of flesh out of the lobe of my left ear.[17]

When circumstances did not permit a proper burial behind the lines, many soldiers were buried near the trenches or even within the trenches themselves. Although this seems inconceivable to modern minds with our need to bring the bodies of our present-day soldiers home for a proper burial before friends and family, such was not the fate for many Great War soldiers, particularly in the early years of the war. Private Fraser recalled a gruesome discovery while in the trenches near Ypres in 1915:

I was watching Steele, of the sanitary police, repairing the side of a trench, when a pair of boots came into view. He stopped and looked curiously when someone came along and pulled one of the boots. It came away and with it the leg bone. Here lay the remains of a dead Frenchman. In a trice there was a terrific odour which just about flattened us. Steele, however, quickly plastered up the place and we moved a few yards away to fresher surroundings. This unfortunate individual was only buried a foot underground. I heard that there used to be a cross but the troops, being short of kindling, thought they could put it to better use and promptly removed it.[18]

Some soldiers received even less of a burial. Private Lockerby recalled the sight that met his gaze after an over-night relief in the Ypres Salient in April 1915:

When day dawned it presented a gruesome sight. Hundreds of dead Germans were lying between our lines with all their equipment on, just as they fell in a charge made several months ago. Many of the French who were killed in these trenches during the winter are buried right here, some have hardly enough earth over them to conceal their clothing.[19]

These decomposing bodies were part of the stench of the Great War. The soil of the trench system was thick with rotting flesh, gunpowder and poison gas.

As if the dirty men, parasites, rats, corpses and stench were not enough, the weather often added to the soldiers' discomforts. Being exposed to and dealing with the elements could wear men down. It was particularly hard when soldiers were on sentry duty keeping a look out over No Man's Land. Private Victor Wheeler remembered holding a cold, wet and muddy outpost (he called it an "Eye Pip"):

The Eye Pip, very close to the enemy line, was nothing more than a mud-lined bomb crater. To occupy this cloaca, under unbelievably wretched conditions for forty-eight hours, while suffering with diarrhea, fighting off *capybara* rats, and straining to hear and interpret the slightest unfriendly noise a few yards away, was a most severe test on one's physical and mental endurance. We talked only when necessary and only in subdued whispers; and we moved about only when our muscles ached from cramp and our bones were stiff from wetness (italics in original).[20]

Poor weather made movement within the trenches difficult and potentially dangerous. Lieutenant Georges Vanier (a future Governor General of Canada) from the 22nd (French Canadian) Battalion recalled a trench relief:

The rain continues: the parapets are caving in. In certain spots, we have water and mud up to our knees. We made the change-over with the 26th this afternoon. In the communication trench there is five feet of water. We are forced to leave the trenches and go out in sight of the enemy. We are receiving a continuous shower of machine-gun fire which luckily has caused no losses.[21]

Even the underground shelter of dugouts could be invaded by the weather. Lieutenant Vanier recorded a particularly unpleasant surprise in his November 10, 1915, diary entry:

A heavy rain continues to fall. The water rises, the tide of mud seems to flood us completely. I returned to my hut at 8 p.m. and found five inches of water and all my personal effects – sox, books, etc. – floating around.[22]

Winters, while not as cold as those felt in most of Canada, were still hard on the soldiers since they had to spend much time outdoors. This could be especially true for those men who served in battalions with Scottish traditions. These units went into the trenches wearing kilts. A.S. Rae of the 16th (Canadian Scottish) Battalion remembered:

You were so cold you would feel almost the marrow frozen in your bones. We were wearing a kilt and at night you would freeze into the ground and when you rose up you would have to pull part of the earth away with you. You had some trouble getting the earth loose from your kilt.[23]

Having conveyed the bleak conditions that were faced by the soldiers in the trenches, it should also be noted that these conditions were not caused by indifference among the High Command towards the soldiers at the front. In the British Army in particular, matters such as soldiers' health and cleanliness, latrine construction and maintenance and trench maintenance were matters of high importance.[24] It may be more accurate to say that, despite the efforts of the British Army, the very nature of trench warfare inevitably lead to harsh conditions at the front.

There was some relief for the men in the trenches from their dreadful situation. Letters from home were always a source of comfort, providing a vital link between life in the trenches and the civilian world which seemed so very distant and almost alien. To the credit of the British Army, postal service was given high priority.[25]

Food, though often welcome in the trenches, was hardly gourmet cuisine and rather monotonous. Meat (often tinned "bully beef"), vegetables (often part of a stew), bread, biscuits, jam, bacon, cheese and tea were all staples. Despite the monotony, the food provided to the soldiers did reach daily caloric requirements for active service and the occasions in which rations did not reach the soldiers at the front were rare. Although the soldiers may have grumbled about the types of food supplied, they rarely went hungry.[26]

Supplementing army rations were packages from home. Families were keen to help their boys at the front and willingly sent candies, cookies and all sorts of canned food. These packages were heartily enjoyed by the recipients, often to be shared with comrades.

Many soldiers took joy in collecting souvenirs from the trenches; either for their own reminiscence or to provide friends and family back home with a glimpse into their lives at the front. Pieces of expended ordinance were common, such as bits of shrapnel. Perhaps most prized of all were items taken from the enemy. Private Leo LeBoutillier, 24th Battalion (Victoria Rifles of Canada), wrote to his father:

> I only wish I could have kept all the souvenirs I picked up, but it's impossible to carry them. I brought out a German greatcoat, rifle and gave them away. I have kept a few buttons and lapels of the coat, which I will enclose and the coat of arms is F.R. that is Friedrich Rex, I think. I also have some German letters and a bit of a diary, which I will give to you. I am using one of their water bottles and a canteen and I have a N.C.O.'s bayonet and a haversack, ammunition, respirators and God Knows what all.[27]

In the British Army leave was granted from time to time, more frequently for officers, but available to the other ranks too. These could involve trips to Paris or London, or, for those Canadians who were recent emigrants from the British Isles, a visit with relatives. However, just being away from the trench system could provide a welcome relief for the men. Perhaps surprisingly, once one was away from the trenches, the countryside had a more normal appearance, as this area was largely untouched by bullets and shells. Farmers still worked their fields and villages remained inhabited, although, with not many young men. Estaminets, located behind the lines, were popular, as they were places where soldiers could purchase food and alcohol.

Alcohol was not restricted to just the rear areas as the British soldier was given a ration of rum. Private Donald Fraser, in addition to spending time as a rifleman and a machine gunner on the Western Front, also saw service with his unit's quarter-master for a while. He recorded the morale raising effect the rum ration could have on soldiers in the trenches:

> The fellow in charge of the party has the two most important things handed to him, namely the mail and the rum. There are always strong enquiries after the rum and it generally takes the form of "Did the rum come up tonight." Smiles of gladness creep over their faces when the answer is affirmative. The features expand still further when they are told there is an extra jar.[28]

Tobacco was another popular distraction for many of the men in the trenches. It was usually consumed in an increasingly common form, the cigarette, which was easier to smoke in the trenches than the more traditional pipe.

These small comforts aside, daily life in the trenches was hardly glamorous and often harsh. The weather, the conditions and the parasites were tests to the men's endurance. Added to this was the constant workload necessary to keep the trenches in a fit state of defence. Home to millions of men, the trenches were like a living organism; ever growing and mending. It was a world in itself, absolutely detached from the civilian world that most of the soldiers came from before the war.

Three

Firepower

The trenches and conditions that developed in the Great War were a direct result of the weapons that were used by the combatants. The lethal power that these weapons possessed was unlike anything seen before. To avoid being killed, the soldiers dug in.

Arching over the trench lines and covering No Man's Land in between, was the grim reality of death. It is misleading though to think that casualties occurred only during major battles; the truth is that death and wounding on a small scale was a common event. What the British High Command referred to as "wastage," took a small, but steady, toll on the soldiers of both sides between battles.

Death in the trenches came by many means; from artillery shell fire, mortar bombs, grenades, bullets and poison gas. Captain Agar Adamson of the Princess Patricia's Canadian Light Infantry commented in a letter to his wife on April 11, 1915, of the dangers to the unwary in the trenches:

> Yesterday at 6:30, one of my best men, William McGregor was shot through the head while standing beside me using my new periscope; he had been constantly warned not to put his head over the parapet, but would insist. The same thing happened to Jennings later on in the morning. They must be using explosive bullets as in each case, half their heads were blown off. We buried them last night behind the trench. Both lives were lost through not taking proper precautions. It is certain death to expose yourself to a man with a fixed rifle from 60 to 40 yards in front of you, with telescopic sights.[29]

Flying metal was often whizzing somewhere about the trenches. Snipers would watch the opposing army's trenches, scanning for a victim who provided a good shot. Machine guns periodically fired into the trench lines, hoping to catch an unlucky soldier out of his dugout.

Dominating all were the big guns; the artillery. These were powerful weapons, with devastating killing power. Artillery shelling was a constant in trench life and all soldiers had to face death from above, delivered by an unseen, distant enemy.

NAC-PA22712 – Crew posed with 18-pounder field gun.

To give a sense of the power of the artillery, take for example the British 18-pounder field gun. This was the most numerous, but one of the smaller British artillery pieces. Still, the 18-pounder weighed about 2 800 pounds and fired a 18.5 pound shell up to 6 500 yards.[30] Six men operated the gun, with a further four men for ammunition supply.

The shells the artillery pieces fired were of two types; shrapnel and high explosive. The shrapnel shell was designed to explode during flight above enemy soldiers' heads. Upon exploding it sent lead balls zipping down, causing devastation to those soldiers caught below. The British Army's main field gun, the 18-pounder, fired a shrapnel shell that contained 375 lead balls, each the size of a marble.[31]

British soldiers had nick-names for the different shells the Germans fired at them. The shrapnel shells fired from the German field guns were called "whiz-bangs." Private Fraser thought they were aptly named:

Several shells came over our redoubt, one bursting quite close sending several pieces of shrapnel into the trench. There was quite a bit of excitement towards the middle of the day over whiz-bangs. It was laughable seeing Major H——- and Asst. Adj. S——- making a bolt for cover on hearing one coming. We were kept busy lying low till the storm subsided. I found my first souvenir, a piece of newly fired whiz-bang. It included the nosecap and aluminium attachment. Whiz-bang is the name given to a light shell of high velocity and trajectory. It is practically on top of you as soon as you hear the report of the gun. It is well termed. First you hear the whiz and almost simultaneously comes the bang, then a metallic singing in the air as the pieces of shrapnel fly through space.[32]

NAC-PA 993 – Shrapnel burst (Battle of the Somme, 1916).

In contrast to the shrapnel shells, which were anti-personnel ammunition, high explosive shells were designed to hit and destroy. They had fuses timed to explode just after contact and blow up what was hit. For this reason, high explosive shells were used to destroy enemy trenches, strong points and artillery positions.

High explosive shells were fired by guns, such as the 18-pounder, but were particularly effective when shot from howitzers. This has to do with the difference between guns and howitzers. Guns shot their shells at a low trajectory, in a sense, like a rifle fires a bullet. The result could be that a shell from a field gun could be blocked by obstructions in front of the target. Howitzers, on the other hand, fired shells at a high trajectory, with the shells going high in the air, enabling them drop into the trench, rather than being blocked by an obstacle, such as the parapet.

Sergeant A.C. Scott (46th Saskatchewan Battalion) described in a letter the effect a high explosive shell had on a German soldier on the opposite side of No Man's Land:

> We see some great sights in the trenches, though, when the artillery opens up. They sure blow the Fritz & Co. trenches into an awful mess. One hears the screaming of the big shells and then the explosion and tons of dirt going up in the air. The last time I was in we saw a Hun blown about thirty feet in the air, together with a few yards of his trench.[33]

While the men on both sides built dugouts deep into the ground, even these were no protection to a direct hit from a howitzer shell. Private Leo LeBoutillier from the 24th Battalion (Victoria Rifles of Canada) wrote to his sister:

> Last week was the liveliest we have had since we are in the trenches, it was one thing after another but I had the best of luck as the dugout I was in fell in on me and I was almost buried alive. It took an hour and some minutes before they could dig me out, but I escaped without a scratch, things will happen you know and I am just about the most lucky animal alive. The same thing happened to two Sigs (signallers) of another Bn. (battalion) and the poor chaps were dead in three minutes. Don't mention this at home they would fuss for a year.[34]

Adding to the effectiveness of the guns and howitzers were pre-war developments in artillery technology. Gone were the days when the artillery had to actually see their target to hit it. No longer would the gunners ride up with their guns to the infantry and blast away at enemy infantry at close range like they did, for example, in the American Civil War. By the Great War the artillery was able to hit targets from great distances that were out of sight of the gunners. While in the American Civil War the artillery could only shoot at targets they could see at distances no greater than 1000 yards, by the Great War even one of the smaller artillery pieces, the British 18-pounder gun, had a maximum range of 6 500 yards.[35]

The range the artillery could shoot increased the depth of the battlefield. Whereas in previous wars only those directly in the line of fire were vulnerable, this had changed by the Great War. Not only were soldiers in rear areas exposed to artillery shells, but those civilians who remained behind the lines sometimes were too. Canon Frederick Scott (1st Division) recalled the plight of some civilians during the Second Battle of Ypres in April 1915:

> On Monday some men had narrow escapes when a house was shelled, and on the following day I went to the centre of town with two officers to see the house which had been hit. They appeared to be in a hurry to get to the Square, so I went up one of the side streets to look at the damaged house. In a cellar near-

by I found an old woman making lace. Her hunchback son was sitting beside her. While I was making a few purchases, we heard the ripping sound of an approaching shell. It grew louder, til at last a terrific crash told us that the monster had fallen not far off. At that moment a number of people crowded into an adjoining cellar, where they fell on their knees and began to say a litany. I stood at the door looking at them. It was a pitiful sight. There were one or two old men and some women, and some little children and a young girl who was in hysterics. They seemed so helpless, so defenceless against the rain of shells.[36]

Great War artillery pieces were recoilless and quick firing. By recoilless, this does not mean that the guns did not "kick" back once fired, rather, it means that the gun's hydraulic recoil system absorbed the recoil, thrusting the barrel back, but not shifting the gun's position. In earlier wars such as the American Civil War, once a cannon was fired, the force of the shell leaving the barrel pushed the whole piece back, knocking the gun backwards out of its firing position. As a result, the gun had to be moved back to where it was before it could fire another shot at its target. With recoilless artillery, the piece did not lose its position and could fire again at its target.[37]

NAC-PA800 – Loading a 15-inch super-heavy howitzer.

Combined with this was the ability to deliver rapid fire. Artillery pieces of the Great War were opened at the breech, allowing the gunners to quickly eject a spent shell case and reload the gun with a fresh shell. Although larger artillery pieces such as the British 9.2-inch howitzer could not fire very rapidly as their large shells, weighing 290 pounds, required several men to load them into the breech, smaller guns like the British 18-pounder could fire many shells in quick succession. The 18-pounder averaged 6 shells in a minute with its maximum rate being 20.[38] Quick firing, recoilless guns added greatly to the ability of the artillery to bring down huge quantities of accurate destructive shells onto the opposing soldiers.

A new generation of powders was also available to propel the artillery shells. For the high velocity shells, this powder allowed the shell to travel a greater distance than was previously possible. We saw above that in the American Civil War shells could only travel about 1000 yards, but by the Great War the field and heavy guns had ranges of 5 900 to 14 200 yards. The new powder also affected the low velocity, howitzer shells as it gave them more hitting power on the target. On human beings, this often caused concussions, sometimes leading to death.[39] Private Donald Fraser recalled the effect a shell explosion had on his body:

> While talking with four of my comrades, the enemy was firing individual shells which angled over our heads, bursting a few hundred yards beyond in the supports on the south. Not much attention was paid to the shelling as the gunners were ranging over us. We heard the gun firing and knew by instinct and experience that although the shells were coming in our direction they were too high to bother us. Suddenly a report that sounded like a premature or a short made us bolt out of the way. Two of the fellows threw themselves into the nearby dugout and stuck in the entrance. Another ran north up the support line, while the fourth rushed up the communication trench towards the firing line. Bordering the trench and behind the dug-out was a little wall of sandbags not more than two feet high. I rounded the end of the wall and threw myself flat behind it on the side nearest the line. At that moment the shell burst with a tremendous explosion on the other side of the sandbag wall where I was standing a second ago and not more than a yard away from where I lay. The report of the explosion dazed me and I was hit with all sorts of debris as they fell on me in their downward course. The concussion or whatever it is called created a terrific strain on the tissues. I felt as if I was being pulled apart, as if some unseen thing was tearing me asunder, particularly the top part of the body, and especially the head. I know I could not have stood a fraction more without bursting, the outward pull on the tissue was so immense. Getting over the daze I quickly pulled myself together and got out of range for the time being. The incident passed off,

although the bursting effect on the body rankled in the mind. It was the greatest body strain I have ever experienced.[40]

In some cases, soldiers would be obliterated by artillery shells, with no bodies recoverable. J.H. Lee (Princess Patricia's Canadian Light Infantry) remembered the fate of a few of his buddies during the Battle of Mount Sorrel:

> . . . word came back to us to move up to reinforce in the front line. We started up the communication trench, such as it was. My first real shock was when there were five of us going forward and this shell exploded. And then there was only one. These four chaps, my pals, that were just in front of me, there was no sign of them at all. That was my first real introduction to the horrors of war. I had seen chaps wounded before that, but not just wiped out.[41]

In addition to physical injuries, the artillery could also psychologically maim a person. Corporal Alfred Andrews of the 10th (Canadians) Battalion described the effects from being buried by shellfire during the Battle of the Somme:

> The Hun started to shell and after four shells it seemed to me he had swung to our left and I told the boys we wouldn't get any more shelling. No sooner had I said this than –bang– and the trench caved in, burying me to my shoulders and the lad altogether. One of our chaps who received a medal for it, climbed up and dug us out. When the 5th Batt. lad had mud cleaned from his mouth, the first thing he said was, "You are a hell of a guesser." I found that a shell had landed just in front of us and blown in the trench. The concussion hurt my ears quite a lot. He asked me how I felt and I said "fine" but as the day wore on my nerves started to go and by the time we were relieved by the 1st C.M.R.'s on the morning of Sept. 28 I could have screamed my nerves were so bad. It was the reaction from being half buried alive I guess.[42]

Danger came not only from the enemy artillery, for sometimes friendly artillery accidentally wreaked havoc on the men in the trenches. Agar Adamson of the Princess Patricia's Canadian Light Infantry related an experience he endured at Ypres in the spring of 1915:

> The artillery were trying to smash up the fort opposite to a trench where it is reported there are 10 to 12 machine guns. An artillery officer was in the trench observing, also the C.O. After each shot he would telephone back giving instructions, the last shot but one landed 50 yards in front of the trench and in perfect line for the fort, he telephoned back to the guns "direction perfect, but a little short add 50 yards." The next shell landed right in our trench. One man was so blown to pieces that they were not able to find enough to bury, one man was wounded by the leg bone of the smashed up man being driven through his body.[43]

Both sides had amassed thousands of artillery pieces on the Western Front. In times of big battles, the guns would be concentrated together behind the infantry, sometimes with individual pieces only a couple dozen yards apart. However, even in the so-called "quiet" periods, the trench systems were still protected by ample artillery. Lieutenant Georges Vanier of the 22nd (French Canadian) Battalion described an artillery fight between the Allies and the Germans near Ypres in a letter to his mother on September 23, 1915:

> This morning I witnessed a most striking scene: some time before dawn artillery duels were opened all around us and the sky was red with the thousand flashes from the cannon. Slowly dawn crept up, the flashes became more intermittent and less distinct and the morning broke on a plain zigzagged by trenches of all kinds. It is the sort of sunrise one does not forget.[44]

A common prelude to an infantry attack was the preliminary artillery bombardment, in which thousands of high explosive rounds were fired at the enemy. The results could be devastating to the men holding the trenches. C.A. MacDonald from the 26th (New Brunswick) Battalion saw what Canadian shelling did to German trenches and soldiers during the Battle of Mount Sorrel:

> You couldn't find a trench. You couldn't find anything of the Jerry line. It was just flattened, and you could find a hand here, a head there, and a leg there, and sometimes you'd find a body with the head on it and some with them off.[45]

Due to the great distances that the artillery could fire, they did not need to be placed close to the front line. Instead, they were generally located in positions behind the support line. The field guns and howitzers, which had ranges between 6 000 to 7 000 yards, were usually in and around the support line. The heavy guns and howitzers, with their longer ranges of up to 12 000 to 14 000 yards, were further back.

Often the artillery pieces were placed so as to be sheltered by some higher ground in front, such as behind a ridge. By having the guns positioned in this manner, the artillery was able to rain fire down upon the opposing army without exposing their guns to easy enemy observation and counter-fire. This left the gunners blind to what they were shooting at, but they had eyes at the front; the forward observation officers ("FOO's"). The FOO's took camouflaged positions in the forward trenches with a good view of enemy lines. So located, the FOO's were well placed to spot targets in enemy lines and communicate this information to the gunners by telephone or other means. Lieutenant C.G. Dowsley (2nd Brigade CFA) described the deployment of the artillery batteries in his Brigade in a letter dated November 3, 1915:

> Depending on the nature of the country, guns are situated two thousand to four thousand yards in rear of the first line trenches. The Forward Observing Station, one to each battery, is manned by a subaltern, a look-out man and telephonists,

and is situated either in the front or support line trenches, or on a vantage point behind the trenches and in front of the guns. It must command a view of all targets likely to be engaged by the battery. We have telephonic communication with the company and battalion commanders in the trenches which we cover, but communication is usually broken as fast as we can repair it during a bombardment. In that case we resort to signals by way of lights of different colors by night, and smoke balls, colored, by day.[46]

Not only were the guns positioned to avoid direct enemy observation, but they were also often protected in gun pits. That way, should the artillery be located and fired on, the gun pits could limit the effect the enemy's shells had on the guns and crew. Sergeant Gordon S. Howard of the 18th Battery CFA described an ideal field gun pit:

Gun pits, . . . were dug about two feet deep, large enough to place the gun inside and give the Gunners room to work, man the gun and store the ammunition. The muzzle of the gun was just high enough above the pit for proper firing position. The dirt taken out of the pit was filled into sandbags and these were used to build walls above ground level on both sides and the back after the gun was run into the pit. The front was built up leaving an opening large enough so as not to interfere with the angles to cover the zone of fire allotted to the gun. The walls were about 2 ft. thick and high enough to permit standing upright. Then whatever material which could be found or salvaged from damaged buildings or timbers to carry a roof of sandbags under which sheet iron, if available, was placed to keep the rain out. Often these gun pits were occupied for weeks or months, and sometimes they were handed over to relieving units, so some pains were taken in their construction for their use and comfort of the gunners as it was usual for them to live and sleep in their gun pit.[47]

By the time of the Great War, the artillery had become a sophisticated weapon, much improved since the days of the smoothbore, muzzle-loading cannon of the American Civil War. Its power, range and technology resulted in it being the most effective and devastating force on the battlefield. Almost 60 percent of all British casualties in the Great War were caused by artillery and mortar fire.[48]

The artillery was not the only armament to benefit from advances in technology. With machine guns the infantry possessed the ability to deliver great volumes of bullets into soldiers struggling across No Man's Land. Sergeant Charles Henry Savage from the 5th Canadian Mounted Rifles recalled the effect British machine gunners had on a group of Germans trying to raid British lines:

One morning I was sitting enjoying the sunshine in the support line, when it occurred to me that if I borrowed a pair of binoculars and climbed a nearby tree I might get a view of the ground around St. Eloi. There was no shelling going on, and as the tree was a very leafy one and there seemed no danger of being seen, I proceeded to carry out my plan. I had been looking over the line for about ten minutes when I got one of the biggest thrills of my life. The Germans suddenly raided the part of the line that I was looking at. It was probably three-quarters of a mile away and the action was exactly like a silent moving-picture. I don't believe that I breathed for the next few minutes; it certainly was a wonder that I didn't fall out of the tree.

The whole thing lasted about three or four minutes, and took place on a front of not more than a hundred or so yards. Four or five salvos of whizz-bangs, followed by a few light trench-mortar shells, started the show. Before the last trench-mortar had landed, about fifty or sixty Germans jumped out of holes in front of their line and rushed towards the British trenches. They were well on their way before the sound of the first exploding shells reached me, so quickly did it all take place. They got almost to the trench before anything happened and then they simply toppled over like rows of lead soldiers: a few seconds later I heard the rat-tat-tat of our machine guns. None got into our trenches, or back to their own.[49]

The British Army used two types of machine guns; one referred to as heavy and the other as light. The heavy machine gun was the .303 Vickers which weighed 28.5 pounds. It had a range of 2 000 yards and fired 500 bullets in a minute.[50] Ammunition was fed by a belt. The Vickers' rapid rate of fire made it liable to over-heating in action, so its barrel was surrounded by a water jacket to cool it down when firing. This water jacket increased the weight of the gun to 38.5 pounds when the jacket was full. This was hefty enough to carry into battle, but added to this was the tripod mount for the gun which added a further 48 pounds. Ammunition for the Vickers also loaded down its crew as a box of 250 .303 rounds weighed 21 pounds.[51] Thirty-two boxes were taken into action.[52] It took three men to carry the Vickers machine gun with tripod and another three to carry its ammunition.[53] All told, the six man crew carried almost 800 pounds into action.[54] Due to its weight and bulk, the Vickers machine gun was used as a defensive weapon, or, following a successful assault, defending the position won.

In defence the Vickers could be a very effective weapon against advancing infantry. This was due, not just to its rapid rate of fire, but also to how its bullets hit the target. There is a tendency to think that when a machine gun fires, all of its bullets follow the exact same path and hit in the exact same spot. In reality, the Vickers' bullets did not all fall in the same spot. Instead, they fell in a cluster, making for a wider and more deadly effect on a group of men. An average cluster for a Vickers was 28 yards wide and 215 yards long. Within this space hundreds of bullets were falling, making anyone in this area liable to be hit by a bullet. These clusters were even more potent where there were multiple Vickers machine guns in separate positions, but all defending a stretch of trench. By having the machine guns fire at angles to each other, rather than directly ahead, each machine gun's line of fire and clusters of bullets would intersect, creating a virtually impassable zone of flying metal.[55]

NAC-PA635 – Soldiers posed with Vickers machine gun.

The light machine gun used by the British Army was the Lewis Gun which weighed between 28 to 30 pounds. Unlike the Vickers, there was no tripod, rather, the Lewis Gun had a small bi-pod attached near the end of the barrel. There was no water-jacket, instead, the Lewis Gun was air cooled. This made the Lewis Gun lighter, but air cooling was not as effective as water, so the Lewis Gun over-heated quicker when firing than the Vickers did. To avoid overheating the Gun, short five to ten round bursts were fired, rather than emptying a full 47 round magazine at one time. The Lewis Guns' maximum range was 1 500 yards, but its usual range was 300 to 600 yards. It fired .303 ammunition like the Vickers.[56]

Although the Lewis was lighter than the Vickers, there were nine soldiers in a Lewis Gun crew. There was a non-commissioned officer, a gunner (also called number one), a number two who assisted the gunner and six others to carry ammunition, act as scouts or replace the gunner or number two if either became casualties. Thirty-two magazines of ammunition were brought into battle.[57]

Due to its lighter weight and lack of a heavy tripod, the Lewis Gun was used as an infantry assault weapon. The Lewis Gunners took part in the attack, providing covering fire and helping to establish an immediate defensive force before the Vickers gunners came up. So effective were the Lewis Guns that the Germans often used captured Lewis Guns themselves. The Germans did not have any mobile machine guns until late 1917 (in fact both the light and medium German machine guns were actually heavier than the "heavy" British Vickers) so they adopted the Lewis Guns in their arsenal whenever possible.[58]

A third type of machine gun, the Colt machine gun, was used by the Canadians in the early years of the war. It was a heavy machine gun like the Vickers. The Colt was not a success though, as its excessive component parts lead to frequent difficulties in action. It was phased out, but a few were still around at the Battle of Vimy Ridge. Eventually the Canadians were armed solely with the Vickers and Lewis Guns like their British comrades.[59] John P. Sudbury from the 9th Canadian Machine Gun Company recalled the problems he had with the Colt machine gun during the Battle of Mount Sorrel in June 1916:

> In early June 1916 the enemy captured some Canadian trenches to the right of our Brigade so a fortnight later we were all set to recapture them, which was eventually accomplished. For this attack I took my Colt gun to a shell hole a little in rear of our support trenches and this was the first time machine guns were used as artillery, that is to say by firing over our forward troops on to map targets such as crossroads behind enemy lines in the hope of preventing reinforcements from coming into the battle. My target was a pathway leading to their trenches. Whether or no (sic) I did any harm to anyone your guess is as good as mine but I fired an awful lot of bullets until the gun jammed. Now when a Colt gun jammed there is nothing for it but to dismantle the whole contraption. This now had to be done in the darkness and rain and the one vital bolt that finally held the gun together on its reassembly slipped from my grasp into the mud at our feet. My companion and I delved after it straining that slime through our fingers for twenty minutes before discovering it and then we were both so covered in mud that it took us even longer time to get it into place. Eventually the gun was again back on its tripod and we again opened fire.[60]

The fire-power of the average infantryman was impressive as well. The standard rifle in the British Army was the .303 calibre Short Magazine Lee-Enfield. It was a bolt action rifle, meaning that a detachable clip holding several bullets was fed into the rifle's magazine and the bolt was manoeuvred forward and down to load the bullet and then up and backwards to eject the spent casing after firing. This process was repeated until the clip was empty. The Lee-Enfield's normal rate of fire was five rounds a minute, but it could fire as many as fifteen aimed shots in that time frame.[61] Its maximum range was 600 yards, but on the battlefield it normally took on targets no further than 300 yards away. Each man carried 150 rounds into action.[62]

Although rifles did not have the extremely rapid rate of fire the machine guns possessed and their bullets did not have the explosive power of the artillery's shells, bolt action rifles could still wreak havoc on the battlefield. H.W. Niven (Princess Patricia's Canadian Light Infantry) recalled the effect Canadian rifle fire had on a German attack during the Second Battle of Ypres:

> Germans could be seen about 300 yards to our front and some could be seen advancing to the left of our position . . . The rifle fire from our trenches during these attacks was devastating and the very rapid fire sounded like machine guns. It seemed to me there were mounds of German dead right up to our front line.[63]

At the Battle of Vimy Ridge the Canadians were armed with the British manufactured Lee-Enfields, but at the beginning of the war they used the Ross Rifle. This was a Canadian designed rifle and, while it was excellent on the target range, it left much to be desired in trench warfare.[64]

To begin with, it was a long rifle, being six inches longer than the Lee-Enfield. Its length made it difficult for movement in the zig-zagging, confined spaces of the trenches. Most troubling though was its propensity to jam in action. Private Donald Fraser recorded the frustrating and life threatening difficulties he faced with the Ross Rifle in his September 19, 1915, journal entry:

> Its chief defects were it was too long and showed above the trenches. It was continually catching in the overhead trench signalling wire. It did not balance on the shoulder well and often tilted to the side, the muzzle catching in the mud. With so much open metal surface and mechanism it was difficult to keep clean and from rusting. But the principal objection was that it jammed. The least thing would jam it – a speck of dust, a shower of rain, even a burst of rapid fire. Very often there was difficulty in loading. The Ross Rifle was a standing joke amongst the Imperial troops. It was a glad day when an exchange was made.[65]

In their early battles, there were many instances when the Canadians' Ross Rifles jammed in action, leaving the soldiers virtually defenceless against the Germans. The Canadians stopped using this unreliable weapon in 1916.

By the time of the Great War the traditional arms, bullet and shell, had developed into incredible killing tools. The artillery, machine guns and rifles all had the ability to fire at longer ranges, with greater accuracy and at much more rapid rates than had previously been possible. This development resulted in a battlefield dominated by firepower.

The dominance of firepower lead to the creation of the formidable trench system on the Western Front. At its most basic, the trenches developed to protect the soldiers from the vast amount of projectiles that could be thrust into the Great War battlefield. However, digging trenches for protection was not a new development, as siege warfare had been practised for centuries in Europe. What made the trench system in the Great War unique from its predecessors was the greater killing power the Great War armies possessed. Thus the need for deeper dugouts, concrete and steel strong points, underground tunnels and multiple trenches lines. It was not enough to fortify the forward trenches, the whole system had to be able to survive the power of Great War rifles, machine guns and artillery.

Having created a trench system that could survive Great War firepower, the balance was in favor of the defence on the Western Front. The defence had the same firepower available as the attacker did. When an attacker did leave the protection of the trenches, he was exposed to defenders utilizing rapid firing rifles, machine guns and artillery from protected positions. No Man's Land could be quickly filled with a deadly hail of lead. Under these circumstances, it is no wonder that so many Great War assaults failed.

Four

Old and New Weapons

Although new technology had increased the killing power of the soldiers and gunners, the combatants were not content to rely on artillery, machine guns and rifles alone. Some of the weapons that were used in the trenches were a throw back to earlier times, while others were of the type never seen before.

One of the weapons that harkened back to an earlier age was the grenade. Used by European grenadiers in the seventeenth and eighteenth centuries, they made a return on the Western Front.[66] At first, since no one was prepared for trench warfare, there were a myriad of primitive grenades employed by the British in the early years of the war. Some were of the "home-made" variety, being little more than a jam tin packed with explosives and metal, and lit with an external wick fuse, sometimes more dangerous to the user than the enemy. By the time of Vimy the Mills Bomb was used, which looked like the now-familiar style of hand grenade.[67] To operate the Mills Bomb, the soldier pulled its pin and threw the bomb towards the enemy. While in flight the safety lever fell off, a plunger within the bomb struck a cap and lit the internal fuse. In about five seconds the detonator went off and with it the Mills Bomb exploded, sending shards of metal through the nearest flesh.[68]

Mills Bombs were an effective weapon because they were easier to use than a rifle in the trenches. At close range it was much easier to lob a bomb in the vicinity of the enemy and (hopefully) kill and wound a few of them, rather than bring one's rifle to the shoulder, aim and fire, which, in addition to taking more time, could in the end be a futile exercise if the shot was off the mark.

The Mills Bomb also had the ability to kill and maim soldiers out of view. Many times during the Great War opposing soldiers were out of sight, separated by a mere bend in a trench, hurling grenades at each other. Similarly, Mills Bombs were effective in clearing enemy hidden in dugouts. If the enemy failed to evacuate a dugout, common practice was to throw a few Mills Bombs down the stairs to kill or trap the garrison within.

The grenade's effectiveness and range was increased when it was attached to a rifle. To load a rifle-grenade, a rod with a grenade at the end was inserted down the rifle barrel. Once the pin for the grenade was pulled, the blank cartridge loaded into the rifle could be fired, expelling the grenade to its target. The grenade could be fired up to 100 yards, well beyond the distance a man could lob a hand grenade.[69] It was particularly useful in the assault, allowing the attackers to destroy defensive positions that would otherwise be out of range.

Another siege weapon of old that made a comeback in the Great War was the mortar. The British Army used several mortars of different sizes, the largest colorfully referred to as the "Flying Pig." Most numerous in British lines was the 3-inch Stokes Mortar which fired an 11 pound bomb to a distance of up to 400 yards.[70]

Stokes Mortars were of simple design, having a smoothbore barrel placed on a base-plate. A bi-pod supported the barrel and a screw-gear lowered and raised the barrel. The mortar was loaded from the end of the barrel by dropping a bomb down it. The bomb slid down the barrel, a charge went off and the bomb was sent out the barrel towards the enemy. This bomb was a high explosive bomb fired at a high trajectory. The advantage of this was that it enabled the bomb to arch high in the air and drop almost straight down into the opposing trench, destroying whatever was hit. Unlike the artillery pieces, the mortars had a short range and, consequently, they were sited in or near the forward lines.[71]

Compared to artillery shells, trench mortar bombs travelled slowly through the air. This sometimes allowed just enough time for the soldiers in the trenches to escape the explosion. Sergeant Charles Henry Savage (5th Canadian Mounted Rifles) remembered his and his comrades' method for avoiding trench mortar bombs:

> At about ten o'clock, I was wakened by a terrific explosion and part of my dugout fell in. Before I could get into the trench there were four or five more explosions, but fortunately for me, not so near. We were being shelled by trench mortars and there would be no further sleep until the shelling let up. We divided into small groups of four or five and took up positions in the trench with as great a distance as possible between groups. Then each group posted a "sky sentry" whose duty it was to watch for trench mortar shells and to tell his group in which direction to run to avoid them. This was fairly easy unless the Germans sent over three or four shells at once and then it required considerable judgment to decide whether to run right or left, or to stand still. It was no unusual thing for a sentry to shout "right" and then almost immediately to change his mind and call "left." The result of such a double command was generally five or six soldiers piled on top of each other at approximately the spot from which they

had started. Although we posted "sky sentries" we all acquired stiff necks from constant watching.[72]

Despite the slow speed of their projectiles, trench mortars were often devastatingly effective. Private Victor Wheeler of the 50th (Calgary) Battalion recalled:

The time of day was nearing noon, and, with a dozen or more Canucks, like hungry dogs eager for a bone, I had gone back to the second line and was standing in front of the cookhouse door – a sheet of galvanized metal roofing, temporarily laid aside to let in the light. We joined the line-up of men with billy cans, knives and spoons at the ready.

As if waiting for a burlesque show to open, our devil-may-care platoon of young infantrymen queued up, clanking our mess tins, cussing the cook for his slowness, and exchanging ribald yarns. The steam from the dixies of boiling rice floated through the crevices in the tin-and-sod roof like incense. Above the general din, we heard the all-too-familiar dull thud of a minenwerfer trench-mortar (T.M.) and saw its catapulted minnie (rum jar) hurtling from the sky end-over-end like a beer barrel suddenly jolted from the back of a brewery lorry.

We scattered in all directions. The minnie struck a 44th Battalion machine-gunner at the cookhouse entrance, and splashed his warm brains against the wall. The rest of him lay brazed against the side of the trench.

"God damn the bastards," we cursed as we stood helplessly around the quivering flesh of our napooed (ne plus) buddy on the red-stained earth, waiting for the twitching to cease.

We carried him a few feet away from the cookhouse, and buried him in a shallow grave, each man throwing a few shovels of earth over the corpse. We made a crude wooden cross from a freshly stained duckboard, drove it affectionately into the now hallowed ground and, with a soldier's brief R.I.P. (rest in peace) prayer by Signal Lance-Corporal Fred W. Daglish, we crowned it with Comrade "44's" tin lizzie.

Our buddy now crudely but tenderly laid to rest with simple battlefield honours, we picked up our mess tins and, though saddened, ate our rice and potato dinner with gusto. *C'est la guerre!* (italics in original)[73]

Being exposed to the destruction wrought by weapons such as trench mortars could push some men "over the edge." Private Wheeler remembered the effect a trench mortar had on a fellow soldier:

We were beginning to feel that "God's in His heaven/All's right with the world," when all hell erupted. From the east came the familiar thud of trench mortars, quickly followed by Heine minenwerfers, exploding with deafening roar and devastating results. From the west our own camouflaged 18-pounders in the Souchez Valley were firing short and dropping their hardware all along our para-doses for a distance of approximately 150 yards, and playing havoc with morale and flesh-and-blood in our own lines.

In the confusion of men cursing and crouching beside or under anything that offered a modicum of protection, one of the Brigade signallers, with uncanny coolness, signalled S.-O.-S. (...–-...) S.-O.-S. (...—...) to his gunners that their range was short.

Within an instant of getting his S.O.S. through to his battery in the pits a minen-werfer exploded very close to our signal station. The terrific blast pinned the artillery operator under what, a moment earlier, had been a supporting roof beam. As Signaller Art C. Moore scrambled to his aid, the operator's buddy, unhurt, became terror-stricken, was seized with a frenzy and his mind suddenly snapped.

Without steel helmet on his head or boots on his feet, the pitifully shell-shocked signaller leaped through an opening that had been blasted in the parados, and raced back from the line like a madman – into oblivion.[74]

NAC-PA1380 – Trench mortar shell exploding in barbed wire.

The Great War also saw the development of new weapons, the likes of which had never been seen before on the battlefield. One of these was poison gas. First used on the Western Front by the Germans during the Second Battle of Ypres in April of 1915, it became a staple of trench warfare for all armies thereafter.

There were two methods used to deliver gas on the battlefield. The first to be used was gas cylinders. These cylinders would be placed in the front line trench and, so long as the wind blew in the right direction, would release a cloud of gas towards the enemy. The obvious drawback of this method was that its use was entirely controlled by the forces of nature. The other method of employment, gas shells fired by the artillery, expelled less gas than a cylinder could when released, but had the advantage of being capable of delivering gas deeper into enemy lines and was less dependant on the weather.

The first type of gas used was chlorine, which affects the respiratory system. Essentially, the unfortunate soldier who inhaled chlorine ended up choking on his own body fluids. Phosgene gas was introduced by the Germans in late 1915. Like chlorine, it too attacked the respiratory system, but phosgene was not as easily detected as chlorine, resulting in soldiers sometimes being gassed before donning protective gas masks. The other major gas used on the Western Front was mustard gas, which did not come into use until July 1917, after the Battle of Vimy Ridge. Mustard gas was toxic if inhaled and also had the ability to blister flesh.[75]

Death by gas was a gruesome end. Private Victor Wheeler recalled the fate of a comrade:

> Just outside the gas curtain we heard groaning and cursing. I stepped out to investigate. Two medics had laid down their stretcher case, threshing about in delirium, to rest for a few minutes. It was a severe test of strength and endurance to navigate the mucky, twisting, narrow trenches with an unco-operative human load of about 185 pounds.
>
> . . . .
>
> Corporal Tom had been badly gassed and horribly wounded – and was already well on his way to meet his Maker – for the gas in his lungs prevented breathing and his bleeding was profuse. Two emergency dressings, floating about in the gaping hole in his right thigh, looked like pieces of red cloth thrown away by a careless tailor. The wheezing and frothing from his mouth like that of a horribly bloated bull-frog, the dilated eyeballs, the pondscum-green discolouration of face and neck, and the gurgling sound issuing from his throat, ironically simulating the hissing of escaping gas cylinders, prompted me to silently beseech Almighty God to hurry His work and take Corporal Tom out of his private hell.
>
> Momentarily propping himself up by only half an arm, old Tom recognized me and sputtered, "Look what a hell of a mess they've made of me!" He writhed

and twisted like a mortally wounded young lion. Green gas suds bubbled up, ran down his chin, and trickled inside his khaki tunic. Gasping always harder for breath, as the poisonous gas kept choking him, he sank back on the bloody stretcher in a moment of quietness before he was seized by another convulsion, his life ebbing fast. We stood cold and helpless as the stretcher bearers carried our buddy along the trench to the nearest emergency field dressing station.[76]

NAC-PA1027 – Posed shot of two soldiers, wearing gas masks, examining a Lee-Enfield rifle.

Although initial counter-measures were primitive, consisting of nothing more than a wet cloth worn over the face (sometimes made wet with urine), gas masks were soon in wide use. By 1917, the British were wearing the box respirator, the most effective gas mask of the War. It consisted of a mask that covered the wearer's face, connected by a rubber tube to the canister worn on the wearer's chest, which held the life saving filters.[77] These hot, stuffy masks, although effective in protecting the wearer, could make the battlefield seem like a horrible dreamland. Canon Frederick Scott (1st Division) recalled an ammunition column behind the front line at night during the Battle of the Somme in 1916:

> Suddenly I heard behind me the sound of a troop of horses. I turned and saw coming towards me one of the strangest sights I have ever seen, and one which fitted in well with the ghostly character of the surroundings. It was a troop of

mounted men carrying ammunition. They wore their gas masks, and as they came nearer, and I could see them more distinctly in the moonlight, the long masks with their two big glass eye-pieces gave the men a horselike appearance. They looked like horses upon horses, and did not seem to be like human beings at all.[78]

Gas masks could be useless if the soldiers did not have early warning of gas coming towards them. Methods were developed during the war to alert soldiers of the need to don their gas masks. Corporal Alfred Andrews (10th Canadians Battalion) recorded the warning system used at Ypres in the spring of 1916:

On the 29th and 30th of April we had gas alarms at intervals. These were given by pounding on a piece of steel rail or a bell hung by a wire. The alarm would start at the line and each post would hear the one in front and pass it back and in a few minutes (like signal fires) gas gongs would be sounding all over the area. The result was you would get an alarm tho there might be no gas in your area but no chances were taken.[79]

Perhaps ironically, although it was the Germans who introduced gas to the Western Front, the Allies used it more frequently because of favorable winds.[80] Nevertheless, due to protective measures, gas never had the capability to be a war winning weapon on its own. Instead, it became one weapon in a vast arsenal of weaponry, to be employed when thought to be of tactical advantage on the battlefield.

The Germans were not the only ones who introduced new weapons on the Western Front. Perhaps the most revolutionary weapon that first saw use during the Great War was the tank. Born from desperation with the stalemate on the Western Front, by 1916 British tanks were ready to be deployed during the Battle of the Somme.

It is misleading to think of these tanks as being anywhere near the equivalent of today's heavily armored, speedy machines, nor even the *panzers* of the German *blitzkrieg* in the Second World War. To begin with, the first tanks looked far different than what we think today a tank should look like. They had a rhomboidal shape, along the outer sides of which were run tracks on the right and left. There was no single gun turret on the top of the tank, instead, the tank's weapons were located on its sides. "Male" tanks were armed with two six-pounder cannons and two machine guns (one of each on each side of the tank), while the "female" version had four machine guns and no cannons. The first tanks were also extremely slow, only managing an average speed of 2 m.p.h.[81]

Lieutenant-Colonel Agar Adamson of the Princess Patricia's Canadian Light Infantry described the tank's attributes in a letter home to his wife. He was much impressed by the tank's debut during the Battle of the Somme:

The great surprise of the attack yesterday was the appearance of Armoured Caterpillars, called "H.M. Land Navy," they can go over any ground, over a 12 foot trench or a 6 foot wall, they knock down anything in front of them, including trees, their great secret is being able to change their centre of gravity. To knock a tree down they rear up and put their weight on it, to knock down a parapet they simply push it. They are very heavy and armed with quick firing guns and manned by the Royal Field Artillery. They carry a search light. Machine-gun fire or a whizz-bang has no effect on them, only a direct hit will put them out and as they are constantly moving, it is difficult to do this. Three of them last night went right through a fortified village and returned. They are the wonder of the war.[82]

Private Fraser (31st Alberta Battalion) remembered the impact one of the first tanks had on his comrades during, until then, a stalled attack in the Battle of the Somme:

Lying low in the shell hole contemplating events with now and then a side glance at my sandy moustached comrade, lying dead beside me, his mess tin shining and scintillating on his back, a strange and curious sight appeared. Away to my left rear, a huge grey object reared itself into view, and slowly, very slowly, it crawled along like a gigantic toad, feeling its way across the shell-stricken field. It was a tank, the "Creme de Menthe," the latest invention of destruction and the first of its kind to be employed in the Great War. I watched it coming towards our direction. How painfully slow it travelled. Down and up the shell holes it clambered, a weird, ungainly monster, moving relentlessly forward. Suddenly men from the ground looked up, rose as if from the dead, and running from the flanks to behind it, followed in the rear as if to be in on the kill. The last I saw of it, it was wending its way to the Sugar Refinery. It crossed Fritz's trenches, a few yards from me, with hardly a jolt.[83]

Despite Agar Adamson's euphoric description and the effect the tanks had during the attack described by Private Fraser, the early tanks were far from perfect. Mechanical breakdowns were frequent and they had difficulty navigating the cratered and muddy battlefield terrain, resulting in many tanks becoming "ditched" in combat. Compared to later wars, the first tanks had relatively thin armor and were vulnerable to direct hits from enemy artillery fire. Problems also came from within the tanks as they had the unfortunate habit of poisoning their crews with the fumes coming from their engines.

Limitations aside, the tanks terrified the Germans when first used and were effective in crushing barbed wire to allow the infantry to enter German defences. They could also supply much needed firepower for the attack with their cannons and machine guns. Although they did not reach their full potential in the Great War, they did contribute to Allied victory and were the way of the future. As for the Germans, they never realized the potential for the tank and thus the tank was a weapon found almost exclusively in the Allied arsenal.

A weapon not invented during the Great War, but which saw rapid development during it, was the airplane. Its development was truly incredible when one remembers that the airplane was only invented in 1903, a scant 11 years before the War started. By the time of Vimy Ridge, both sides had sophisticated flying machines such as speedy fighter planes and long range bombers. It was a remarkable evolution.

Aircraft's main role throughout the Great War was reconnaissance. Aeroplanes provided the opposing armies with the ability to study the opponent's troop dispositions, movements and defences. This intelligence was invaluable either in planning an offensive or making preparations against an attack. Developing from this role was that of artillery spotting. Airplanes proved to be a valuable asset in observing the fall of artillery shells and communicating corrections to the gunners.

At the war's outset the airplanes that wandered across the sky were unarmed, except for occasions when the pilot took the initiative to provide himself with his own small arms such as a pistol or rifle. As the value of aerial reconnaissance became appreciated, so did the need to destroy these inquisitive machines. Thus the fighter aircraft came into being, designed to seek out and destroy enemy aircraft. The development by the Germans (which was later adopted by all combatants) of a mechanism for allowing a machine gun to fire through the propeller increased the accuracy of fighter planes and their killing potential.

What resulted were sophisticated air campaigns designed to dominate the air space above the trench lines. Both sides realized the value of using fighter aircraft to keep this airspace free from opposing aeroplanes, allowing the reconnaissance and spotting aircraft to perform their function and denying the same to the enemy. To clear the skies of enemy aircraft, the "dog fight" was born, and many a pilot met a grizzly end plummeting from the heights above to death below.

Less effective, but a development that was to become increasingly important in future wars, was the bomber aircraft. Compared to modern aircraft, or even to those of the Second World War, the bomb loads that Great War bombers carried were paltry and their accuracy left much to be desired, but the bombers did have the capacity to inflict harm in rear areas of the battlefield that, in previous wars, were immune from damage.[84] Canon Frederick Scott recalled a German bombing raid on the Town of Albert behind the lines during the Battle of the Somme:

> The most unpleasant things at Albert were air raids, which occurred every fine night. One moonlight night I lay on my bed, which was in the top storey of our house, and listened to some German planes dropping bombs upon the town. The machines were flying low and trying to get the roads. Crash would follow crash with great regularity. They came nearer and nearer, and I was just waiting for the house to be struck when, to my great relief, the planes went off in

another direction. Next day a sentry told me that he heard a hundred bombs burst, and, as far as he knew, not one of them had done any damage, all having fallen among the ruined houses and gardens of the town.[85]

There was a remarkable development in weaponry during the Great War. Some weapons, like the grenade, were from an earlier time, but updated to assist the soldiers fighting in the trenches. Others, such as the tank, were new inventions without precedent in history. However derived, many of the weapons that are now commonplace in armies were either re-discovered or used for the first time during the Great War.

Five

Battle

The culminating moment for the soldiers' service on the Western Front was combat. It was in battle that the combatants used their devastating firepower to full effect. Rapid firing artillery, machine guns and a seemingly bewildering terrain of barbed wire, shell holes and trenches made the battles that took place during the Great War like nothing experienced before.

Horrific and intense artillery bombardments usually preceded an attack, sometimes for a week or more. It is not hard to believe that soldiers had mental breakdowns under the strain of the remorseless artillery fire as shell after shell fell nearby, the next shell having the potential to blow one's body into hundreds of pieces. Private Donald Fraser from the 31st (Alberta) Battalion described enduring shelling before a German attack:

> About 7:00 o'clock a bombardment of unprecedented ferocity began and the range was of uncanny accuracy. The shells were bursting in or near the trench and gunfire would run from end to end. It played along the line as if worked by a hose. Gunfire so precise and methodical in its execution strikes terror, even into the bravest hearts. Stuck in a trench, with shells creeping gradually nearer and nearer to you from the right, and through a piece of good fortune you escape, only to go through the same ordeal as the fire sweeps back from the left, is unnerving to the last degree. All the time you hear the noise from the guns and brace yourself for the burst, which you expect every moment on top of you. Such was the situation we had to face until 2:00 p.m. when the assault came. This systematic shellfire, which aims at complete destruction of a helpless foe, has swelled our hospitals and asylums to the brim. No fighting is so tense as at these moments and never has reason hung on so fine a thread. To get up over the parapet and rush to certain death at the hands of machine-gunners or riflemen would be a welcome mental relief to remaining stoically in a

trench with an avalanche of shells smashing and burying everything before it. Standing up to shellfire of such method and accuracy is the hardest part by far of a soldier's trials.[86]

Following the preliminary bombardment and at the appointed time, zero-hour, the attacking soldiers would go "over the top." To the sound of their officers' whistles, the attackers clambered out of their trenches and moved into No Man's Land. Sergeant Charles Henry Savage (5th Canadian Mounted Rifles) remembered a Canadian attack during the Battle of the Somme:

> Two minutes to go! The shelling on both sides was at its maximum. Our barrage had been going for about three minutes and the German counter-barrage for a minute or less. It was impossible to hear anyone speak; the air was full of dust, dirt and smoke; whole sections of our trench, crowded with men, went up into the air as salvos of 5.9s made direct hits on our position. No use to worry where the next one was going to land: they were landing everywhere. Ten seconds to go: thank God we'll soon be out of this! How many of the platoon are left? What luck! Hardly a man has been hit yet. Have I a cartridge in the chamber? Is the safety catch off? Time! Over we go!
>
> As far as one could see along the trench men were climbing up over the parapet and starting across no man's land at a half run, half walk.[87]

NAC-PA648 – Over the top! Well, not quite, as this is a photograph taken during training. Nevertheless, it provides a good impression of the initial seconds of the assault.

At zero-hour thousands of men would rise from their trenches and surge across No Man's Land, hoping to grapple with the enemy in the enemy's trenches before machine-gun, rifle and artillery fire cut the attackers to pieces. Private Donald Fraser (31st Alberta Battalion) took part in an attack during the Battle of the Somme and remembered having to cross the deadly No Man's Land:

> My wits sharpened when it burnt deeply into me that death was in the offing. At this stage an everchanging panorama of events passed quickly before my gaze, and my mind was vividly impressed. The air was seething with shells. Immediately above, the atmosphere was cracking with a myriad of machine-gun bullets, startling and disconcerting in the extreme. Bullets from the enemy rifles were whistling and swishing around my ears in hundreds, that to this day I cannot understand how anyone could have crossed that inferno alive. As I pressed forward with eyes strained, to the extent of being half closed, I expected and almost felt being shot in the stomach. All around our men were falling, their rifles loosening from their grasp. The wounded, writhing in their agonies, struggled and toppled into shell holes for safety from rifle and machine-gun fire, though in my path the latter must have been negligible, for a slow or even quick traverse would have brought us down before we reached many yards into No Man's Land. Rifle fire, however, was taking its toll, and on my front and flanks, soldier after soldier was tumbling to disablement or death, and I expected my turn every moment. The transition from life to death was terribly swift.[88]

If the enemy trenches were reached, brutal close quarters combat often took place, utilizing grenades and sometimes even bayonets, clubs and bare hands. T. Richardson (Princess Patricia's Canadian Light Infantry) recalled an intense struggle during the Second Battle of Ypres:

> One big German loomed up over me, where I was crouched by the only remaining machine gun, at the bottom of the shallow trench, fighting to get a fresh belt of cartridges into it. I looked up as I saw him rise up above me. We looked into each other's eyes. He laughed hysterically and sprang down at me with his bayonet lunging at my stomach. The butt of his rifle was in his shoulder as he literally dived at me, bayonet first, trying to pin me through the body. I gathered my hands and feet under me faster than I can tell it, and tried to throw myself sideways and backwards. I was too weak to get quite clear. He pinned me to the ground through the side of my left thigh. He was laughing hysterically still. I had never carried a rifle that day. My work with the range finder took both hands. But I always carried a .45 colt automatic pistol. Now as I lay there on my back with that German bayonet through my leg, and that German face laughing down at me, I pulled that pistol and shoved it up into his face. A more surprised man there never was. His expression changed as if a hand had wiped that hysterical

laugh off his face. The laugh changed to a scream. His first word was "Kamerad!" But I laughed now. And I pulled the trigger.[89]

When the attackers were not successful in reaching the enemy's trenches, these soldiers could be stranded in No Man's Land for hours, experiencing the strain and panic of being, in the extreme sense of the phrase, stuck "between a rock and a hard place." Further advance meant certain death and retreat was not possible across the projectile swept battlefield. Private Fraser remembered the feeling of being in an attack that seemed to have stalled:

> As the attack subsided and not a soul moved in No Man's Land save the wounded twisting and moaning in their agony, it dawned upon me that the assault was a failure and now we were at the mercy of the enemy. It was suicide to venture back and our only hope lay in waiting until darkness set in and then trying to win our way back. During this period of waiting, I expected we would be deluged by bombs, shrapnel and shell fire, and when darkness set in, ravaged by machine gun fire, altogether a hopeless outlook, especially for our lot, who were lying up against his trench. The situation seemed critical and the chances of withdrawal to safety nigh impossible. So many things had happened, so many lives were snuffed out since I left the comparative safety of our front line, that I lost completely all idea of time.[90]

For the wounded in No Man's Land the ordeal was even worse, suffering from painful wounds that could not be easily or quickly tended to.

Great War battles were often confusing, chaotic events. Many times in the fog of battle it was difficult to understand what was going on. Private Fraser lived through the confusion prevailing during the Canadians' defensive struggle at the Battle of St. Eloi:

> During these days the enemy was raining shells continually; the trenches were a quagmire and unconnected; communications were entirely broken down; there was no such thing as a firing trench; the enemy gave us no peace to consolidate; neither could materials be brought up; our men battered and weary had all their work cut out to shelter themselves from the devastation that was happening around. Casualties were heavy and the men so completely worn out that reliefs were frequent and each change found the situation more obscure; the whereabouts of the enemy unknown, our own bearings in the air.[91]

This confusion could lead to terrible results. Private Fraser recalled an incident during the Battle of St. Eloi:

> About 4:30 a.m., on April 6, after the attack on the 27th, a large body of the enemy, about 150, were seen advancing towards our line in the direction of crater 6. Rifle fire was brought to bear on them and many were killed or wounded, whilst the remainder fled or took refuge in shell holes. Towards evening a

batch of about twenty or so advanced in single file, each man with his hands on his neighbour's shoulders. Fire was opened up on them and only a few regained their lines. There is some division of opinion as to whether they intended to attack or surrender. Some aver they were bombers for they noticed bomber aprons on them. At dawn the next morning a small party, presumably the survivors, came over opposite "D" Company. Firing at them, 7 were killed, 1 wounded and four, including the wounded man, were taken prisoners. They intended surrendering for it was found they had no arms.[92]

Great War battles were protracted events. They did not involve merely a single attack, rather, attacks, counter-attacks and shelling went on for days, weeks and even months. Soldiers who were not present for the opening of a battle would be "fed into it" as the battle raged on. Bob Goddard of the 28th (Northwest) Battalion described going into action at the Battle of Mount Sorrel:

We were marching in single file by this time, and every man carried a sandbag, bomb, rifle and bayonet, rations and a bottle of water . . . Judging from the flares going up all around us, we seemed to be going into a pocket. On our right, the machine guns were going all the time, and they sounded like a thousand riveting machines, only instead of construction their noise meant destruction. Pretty soon we came to a big barrier of sandbags known as "China Wall," and here dead men were lying everywhere, and we couldn't help stumbling over them on our way in. At last we came to the communication trench, and just as we reached it Fritzie sent a salvo of shells across – one or two of the boys caught it – the rest of us kept on our way. We followed the trench, scrambling over parts that were blown in, and stumbling over the dead that were lying everywhere. Finally we came to the trench that we were going to take over, and we relieved what was left of the Royal Canadian Rifles. They were an awful sight, dirty and bloodstained – many were shaking as though with a palsy – their nerves literally torn to pieces by the shell fire.[93]

Some soldiers were awed by the intense experience that they were engulfed in. Others pushed themselves to the limit to get the job done. Corporal Alfred Andrews of the 10th (Canadians) Battalion remembered going into combat during the Battle of Mount Sorrel:

Shortly afterwards Capt. Fisher called a N.C.O. conference and told us we were to follow up the 7th when they reached their objective and consolidate. I never saw a man so obviously frightened as Capt. Fisher was but he never faltered. He was "game." After a few minutes I noticed our men moving. No word had been passed down to me as there should have been because of the gap caused by the shell that "got" Gray. As soon as I saw movement, I called to my men on my right and we filed across the road and joined up with 10 platoon who were going up to the front line. Machine gun bullets hit the earth along our trench and I remember wondering what it would be like to be hit by one of them. I had great difficulty from standing up to find out. Curiously enough, once we started to move I wasn't afraid, I was curious. Here I was in an attack and I wondered what would happen. As I was near 10 platoon I thought we were in our proper place but when we got to the front line I found that Capt. Fisher had taken Sergt. Rayfield, his headquarters, and all of 12 platoon that weren't with me and had "gone over the top" after the 7th Batt. and they had all been killed or wounded. The 7th Batt. attack had not reached its objective owing to intense machine gun fire and Capt. Fisher, according to instructions he gave us, should not have gone forward when he did. My personal opinion was that he was afraid that he would funk and had forced himself to go over in the teeth of a withering machine gun fire. He was almost cut in two by bullets.[94]

Some men found courage in their comrades. R.G. Flemons from the 31st (Alberta) Battalion recalled going "over the top" during the Battle of the Somme:

. . . we were really tied up in knots. And then we got word to go over the top and I remember, well, I don't feel afraid. Directly you got moving you didn't feel afraid, partly because your other boys were there too. And you were taking the same chances they were and they were taking the same chances as you.[95]

Other men were shattered, mentally, by their experience. Captain Harold McGill, the 31st (Alberta) Battalion's medical officer, remembered one man's terrible ordeal at the Battle of St. Eloi:

When he was brought into our dugout we placed him sitting on a bench and facing the entrance. I do not think that he had the slightest idea of where he was or of what he was doing.

We were busy dressing others of the wounded, the shell-shock case in the meantime sitting perfectly still and looking with a fixed gaze towards the door. Suddenly without warning he gave utterance to a high-pitched wailing cry which he kept up without cessation. He was not weeping; he had no tears in his eyes; but his fearful cry denoted terrible mental anguish; and never in my life have I heard other sounds that filled me with such horror and dismay.[96]

The human cost of battle in the Great War was staggering, even in battles little remembered today. Private Fraser described the scene he encountered in the trenches at the Battle of St. Eloi:

When day broke, the sights that met our gaze were so horrible and ghastly that they beggar description. Heads, arms and legs were protruding from the mud at every yard and dear knows how many bodies the earth had swallowed. Thirty corpses were at least showing in the crater and beneath its clayey waters other victims must be lying killed and drowned. A young, tall, slim English lieutenant lay stretched in death with a pleasant, peaceful look on his boyish face. Some mother's son gone to glory. He was wearing a gold signet ring, having an eagle with outstretched wings engraved thereon. It was removed by Munro, who thinking it of no value, handed it to Doull, who has it in his possession today. Another English second lieutenant was lying at the edge of the crater, huddled up, with his legs uppermost. One of the most saddening cases was a stretcher bearer near half a dozen dead Tommies, a little to the right of the trench – leading to crater 7. He was sitting with a bandage between his hands in the very act of bandaging his leg, when his life gave out, and his head fell back, his mouth open, and his eyes gazing up to heaven, as if in piteous appeal. There he sat in a natural posture as if in life, the bandage in his hands, and the Red Cross bag by his side. Lovett was his name, and he belonged to the King's Liverpool. Another strange, appalling spectacle was a couple of Tommies sitting on the firing step; the head of one had fallen forward on his chest, and between his fingers he still held a cigarette. There he was as if asleep, yes, but in a sleep that knows no awakening. His comrade beside him was in a sitting position but inclining sideways. Both were unmarked and must have met their doom by concussion.[97]

NAC-PA128 – German dugout entrance after capture by the Canadians. Dead German soldier in foreground (Battle of the Somme, 1916).

Sometimes the fate of an attack could be learned by following the trail of bodies across No Man's Land. Sergeant Charles Savage was able to do so after one of the many assaults made during the Battle of the Somme:

It was possible to read the story of attack and defence by the grouping of the dead. Here was the assault trench, broken by shell holes, each one with its circle of mangled and half-buried bodies: the German counter-barrage had been accurate. Immediately in front of the assault trench the ground was clear – it had been crossed before the enemy had had time to bring his machine guns and rifles into action. Then for fifty yards the rich harvest reaped by machine guns playing on massed men lay thick on the ground. But at one spot there were few dead: our artillery had made at least a dozen direct hits on about fifty yards of German trench. There had been no one left to resist: our men were in. But what of that circle of huddled bodies on the left? About what deadly centre had this line been drawn? A machine gun superbly handled stopped everything there. It was never reached from in front: the gunners were shot or bayoneted by our men coming in from the flanks. They died on their gun. And those men half kneeling, half lying in grotesque attitudes? The wire had not been cut in front of them: that is what is holding them up. They died on the wire, the worst fate a soldier could suffer.[98]

What struck W.F. Graham (2nd Eastern Ontario Battalion) was the sound of battle:

One thing that I noticed more than anything else in the front lines was the noise of a big battle. The screaming of wounded men was something you'd never thought of before. You never realized that things like that would happen.[99]

Battle temporarily hardened some men's souls. Private Victor Wheeler from the 50th (Calgary) Battalion described his and his comrades' feelings towards killing during the Battle of the Somme:

There was no escape from the maelstrom of man's inhumanity to man. As we faced our Westphalian cousins from beyond the Rhine, we found ourselves shooting them down without hesitation or remorse. We slaughtered them in hot blood and cold blood and found a diabolical delight, along with our hidden snipers, in counting the notches on the stocks of our rifles. To kill or be killed, to maim or to be maimed, we were left with no choice. In the white heat of battle, this was our justification for the abandonment of elemental brotherhood.[100]

Lieutenant R. Lewis of the 25th Battalion (Nova Scotia Rifles) "turned off" his feelings in battle:

People talk about Fear; I must confess there is such a thing before you start over, but once you get started you are callous to everything. You see your own best friend killed alongside of you, but that does not stop you for you keep right on, never thinking that you may be next . . .[101]

The inevitable consequence of battle was casualties. Men were blown apart by shellfire, bodies were riddled with machine gun bullets, while others were killed by the concussion of an exploding shell. Many soldiers suffered grievous wounds from the metal projectiles fired into the battlefield by both sides. A.L. Potenteir (Princess Patricia's Canadian Light Infantry) remembered receiving his wound during the Battle of the Somme:

> We had just started to capture the 2nd trench and I got mine through the hip. It felt as if someone had hit me with a hammer. I went spinning around about four times and fell in a big shell hole. I tore my field dressing out and clapped it on the wound. I lay in the shell hole until it was dark. God, it was awful! Dead and dying were lying everywhere.[102]

When it was safe to do so, the injured men went to the rear area for medical treatment. Those that could usually had to walk. W. Stirling (Princess Patricia's Canadian Light Infantry) recalled making his way to the rear with a group of wounded men during the Battle of Mount Sorrel:

> With my left arm useless it was rather difficult getting across the open spaces in the trench with the machine guns and rifles doing their best to finish the job. However, a young fellow, one of the company runners I think. He was bandaged over the eyes, helped me and I guided him, and by helping each other we made it although many did not and during that journey the bravery of many was in evidence by the piles of bodies we had to crawl over.[103]

Those soldiers who could not walk were taken to the rear by the stretcher bearers. In Great War battles the number of wounded was tremendous. W.E. Bastedo (Princess Patricia's Canadian Light Infantry) remembered the hard work that a stretcher bearer, Private Harry Tretheway, had to endure during the Battle of Mount Sorrel:

> This was a big day for Treff as a stretcher-bearer. During the afternoon the heat became intense and he removed his tunic. There was no room for stretchers in the trench, so he carried the wounded on his back. His shirt became soaked with blood, so it too was removed.[104]

The stretcher bearers often become casualties themselves. Sometimes their efforts came to naught, when the wounded man died on the way. The 31st (Alberta) Battalion's medical officer, Captain Harold McGill, remembered from the Battle of Mount Sorrel:

> . . . many of the poor fellows that were brought in were beyond any hope of resuscitation because of the severity of their wounds. In a number of cases it seemed too bad that other men should have been placed in danger in order to

carry them to the dressing station. In one instance three out of four of the carrying party were wounded in bringing a man a long distance through the rain and mud. The casualty on the stretcher was stone dead when the party reached the aid post.[105]

In times of battle the amount of work performed by the medical staff was tremendous. Captain McGill recalled the constant, hard exertions required during the Battle of Mount Sorrel:

> Now began the hardest and longest tour of sustained duty that I experienced during the war. We began work at dusk, June 12, worked without break or rest throughout the night, all the following day and through the second night until the early hours of June 14, when the stream of casualties began to slacken and diminish in volume. We were never without wounded. As fast as a man could be dressed and the stretcher removed, another took his place.[106]

Canon Frederick Scott (1st Division) described a visit to a medical dressing station in the rear area during the Battle of the Somme:

> In the largest room, there were the tables neatly prepared, white and clean, for the hours of active work which began towards midnight when the ambulances brought back the wounded from the front. The orderlies would be lying about taking a rest until their services were needed, and the doctors with their white aprons on would be sitting in the room or in their mess near by. The windows were entirely darkened, but in the building was the bright light and the persistent smell of acetylene gas. Innumerable bandages and various instruments were piled neatly on the white-covered table; and in the outer room, which was used as the office, were the record books and tags which the wounded were labelled as they were sent off to the Base. Far off we could hear the noise of shells, and occasionally one would fall in the town. When the ambulances arrived every one would be on the alert. I used to go out and stand in the darkness, and see the stretchers carried in gently and tenderly by the bearers, who laid them on the floor of the outer room. Torn and broken forms, racked with suffering, cold and wet with rain and mud, hidden under muddy blankets, lay there in rows upon the brick floor. Sometimes the heads were entirely covered; sometimes the eyes were bandaged; sometimes the pale faces, crowned with matted, muddy hair, turned restlessly from side to side, and parched lips asked for a sip of water. Then one by one the stretchers with their human burden would be carried to the tables in the dressing room. Long before these cases could be disposed of, other ambulances had arrived, and the floor of the outer room once more became covered with stretchers. Now and then the sufferers could not repress their groans. One night a man was brought in who looked very pale and asked me piteously

to get him some water. I told him I could not do so until the doctor had seen his wound. I got him taken into the dressing room, and turned away for a moment to look after some fresh arrivals. Then I went back towards the table whereon the poor fellow was lying. They had uncovered him and, from the look on the faces of the attendants round about, I saw that some specially ghastly wound was disclosed. I went over to the table, and there I saw a sight too horrible to be described. A shell had burst at his feet, and his body from the waist down was shattered. Beyond this awful sight I saw the white face turning from side to side, and the parched lips asking for water. The man, thank God, did not suffer acutely, as the shock had been so great, but he was perfectly conscious. The case was hopeless, so they kindly and tenderly covered him up, and he was carried out into the room set apart for the dying. When he was left alone, I knelt down beside him and talked to him. He was a French-Canadian, and a Roman Catholic, and, as there happened to be no Roman Catholic chaplain present at the moment, I got him to repeat the "Lord's Prayer" and the "Hail Mary," and gave him the benediction. He died about a half an hour afterwards.[107]

This was what the tremendous firepower on the Western Front caused; death, maiming and destruction. Used in battle on a mass scale, the fate of the unfortunate French-Canadian soldier remembered by Canon Scott occurred on a mass scale.

Six

The Great War Battlefield

From late 1914 until early 1918, stretching northward from France's border with Switzerland all the way to the coast of north-western Belgium, was a continuous, stalemated, battlefront. In the relatively small area of land where the opposing armies met was the trench system that millions of men met their end. On first glance it seems impossible that so many soldiers would die in such a confined space over so many years. However, a closer look at the trench system itself and the armies that held them helps explain why the trenches were such a formidable obstacle.

The trenches each side constructed were extremely complex. Pains were taken to use natural features for defensive advantage. Trenches were dug on the reverse slopes of ridges, on dominating hills and to command valleys and ravines. Added to this, strong points were built to dominate potential avenues of attack. All defensive positions were protected by belts of sharp, tangled barbed wire. Compounding an attackers' problems, there was not just one trench line, instead, there were multiple lines of trenches all connected by communication trenches.

While the trench system itself was formidable enough, what made the trenches so difficult to attack was the enormous firepower each side could bring to the battlefield. Manning the trenches were millions of men armed with bolt-action rifles, hand-grenades, rifle grenades and trench mortars. Even more devastating were the machine guns with their ability to fire hundreds of rounds a minute at advancing infantry. King of all was the artillery. Placed behind the front lines, the artillery's quick firing guns and howitzers could pulverize the battlefield. To this dangerous mix were added new weapons, such as poison gas, tanks and aircraft. The amount of firepower the armies of the Great War could unleash was like nothing the world had seen before.

In battle, barbed wire and extensive trenches with strong points bogged down attacks, allowing time and opportunity for the artillery and machine guns to cause mass casualties to the infantry as they tried to cut their way through. Even if successful in making it past the wire and the first few trenches, the attackers were often drained by exhaustion and casualties and were ripe for destruction by an enemy artillery bombardment and counter-attacking infantry. The combination of fortification and modern firepower created a terribly lethal battlefield, brutally efficient at accomplishing its purpose; the death or maiming of anyone who tried to cross No Man's Land.

Part II

The Offensive in the Great War

One

Factors in Play

The Battle of Vimy Ridge that took place in April of 1917 was one part of a larger Franco-British offensive on the Western Front. Offensives were not new by the time of Vimy Ridge, as both the Allies and the Germans had launched large scale assaults in the preceding years (although the Allies were more aggressive in this regard). Despite the intensity of these earlier attacks, the trench lines had not moved materially.

The Great War was in some ways a unique war, with commanders being faced with issues that were either not present in past conflicts or which were to be addressed in subsequent wars through advances in technology. Looking at some of the factors that have influenced conflicts throughout history (firepower, mobility, manpower and communications), these came into play in such a manner to make any decisive, "war winning" offensive on the Western Front a near impossible operation.

Turning first to firepower, the most powerful and effective form of firepower available during the Great War was the artillery. From their gun positions in the rear lines, the artillery had the capability to deliver huge volumes of destructive shells onto the opposing forces. These shells had the ability to destroy defensive positions and attacking infantry with a thoroughness not seen before in any conflict.

However, what the artillery lacked was mobility. If the infantry was successful in their attack and advanced beyond the range of their guns, it was very difficult to bring forward the artillery through the devastation of No Man's Land to continue supporting the attacking infantry. Unlike subsequent conflicts, such as the Second World War, there was no mobile firepower to support the infantry during the attack.

For example, in the Second World War, tanks were mechanically reliable, relatively fast moving, had thick armour and carried considerable firepower. Because of this, Second World War tanks could advance ahead of or with the infantry, blowing up enemy defences and advancing deep into enemy lines. The tank's effectiveness was not limited to the range of the artillery. While there were tanks in the Great War, these tanks were mechanically unreliable, slow, had thin armour and less firepower than a Second World War tank. That there was such a difference has to do with technological advances between the wars, however, the fact is that Great War tanks were not the mobile firepower vehicles that they became in the Second World War.

NAC-PA1323 – Moving a 8-inch heavy howitzer.

A similar situation presents itself with respect to aircraft. In the Second World War, aircraft could be used as a form of flying artillery with dive bombers and medium and heavy bomber aircraft being able to hit and destroy enemy defences virtually anywhere on the battlefield and even beyond the battlefield itself (i.e., railways, transport columns behind enemy lines, reinforcements, etc.). This type of mobile, flying firepower was not available during the Great War. While fighter aircraft sometimes did strafe ground troops and there were rudimentary bomber aircraft, these airplanes could not deliver near the same amount of firepower onto the battlefield as their descendants would in the Second World War.

The only mobile weapon available to Great War generals was the cavalry. This was not a satisfactory alternative to the tanks and aircraft of the Second World War though. Not only did the cavalry lack firepower, the cavalryman and his horse were extremely vulnerable to all forms of enemy weapons and could not easily navigate the shell-torn ground of No Man's Land.

Thus, in terms of mobile firepower in the Great War, there really was none. This left the infantry alone to press forward the attack. While this could be done under the protection of the artillery, once the infantry had advanced beyond the range of friendly artillery, they were extremely vulnerable. In past wars, such as the American Civil War, it had been possible for infantry to overcome enemy defences with rifles alone. However, during the Great War, the vast array of highly efficient and destructive weapons available to defenders, such as machine guns and quick firing artillery (both not present in the U.S.

Civil War), made such a feat virtually impossible. The result of this lack of mobile firepower is that any attack on the Western Front was effectively limited to the range of the artillery.

Compared with the Second World War, fighting within the range of the artillery created a constricted battlefield. However, looking at past wars like the American Civil War, this was a much more expanded battlefield, with Great War defenders able to deliver much greater killing power from much greater distances than was previously possible.

However, just because Great War armies had greater long range fire power than their predecessors did not create a more fluid battlefield. The reason for this seems to be manpower. The armies fielded by the combatants on the Western Front were massive, on a scale previously unheard of. Millions of men were mobilized for war on each side and were deployed for battle in the relatively small area of western Belgium and north-eastern and eastern France.

On the other hand, in the American Civil War a comparable area of land was occupied by combatant armies numbering, at the very most, one hundred thousand men each. Thus, when armies in the American Civil War gave battle and an advantage was gained by one or the other combatant, there was room to manoeuvre to grasp the opportunity. Flanks were open and it was possible to send infantry to attack the enemy's flank or rear.

In the Great War, should an attacker break through enemy defences, the huge numbers of soldiers available to the defender allowed the defender to shift reinforcements to seal any breach in the defences. That Great War armies also had the benefit of extensive railroads and a good road system safely behind the trench lines allowed such a move to be made relatively quickly. Further, the long range weaponry Great War armies possessed assisted in closing gaps made in defences by an attacker. Once an attack had made a breach and was at the limit of the artillery support, the attackers were met by more defenders. Compounding the attackers' problems, it was very difficult to bring forward reinforcements for the attack from friendly lines, across No Man's Land and through the enemy trench system.

It should be noted that Second World War armies were mass armies like those fielded in the Great War, however, the mobile firepower that Second World War armies possessed could offset the difficulties presented by mass warfare. Should a breach in the enemy's defences be made, Second World War tanks could support the infantry's advance or make one of their own, while aircraft could be used to strafe and bomb enemy reinforcements coming up to seal the breach. The fluid battle that was possible in the American Civil War re-emerged in the Second World War.

Complicating matters in the Great War was the lack of effective communications. Communications technology had advanced since the American Civil War, most notably with the invention of the telephone, but telephone lines were not reliable during a battle.

Phone lines, unless buried deep within the ground (which was impossible to do in No Man's Land), were vulnerable to artillery fire. It was common for generals in the rear area to be out of communication with units in combat on account of cut lines. There were other less complex forms of communication such as runners, carrier pigeons or visual signals like flags, but whether a message could get through had much to do with whether the message bearer could survive the battle. In a battle involving mass armies, it was likely that many message bearers would not survive, leading to a general in the rear area having incomplete information from many of his units in battle. Often, the situation was a communications chaos. It is quite true to say that, no matter how detailed the pre-battle plan, once zero-hour arrived the battle was no longer within the control of the generals who planned it. The soldiers who went over the parapet into No Man's Land were on their own to execute the plan and the generals were unaware of, or able to control, what was going on; good or bad.

The lack of adequate communications was an issue for the defence too, but the defence was not as affected as the attacker was. To begin with, a soldier facing an attack knows what his job is even if he cannot communicate to those in the rear; stop the attack! Since the defender usually had at his immediate disposal the means to deal with the attack (i.e., weapons and ammunition) there were less occasions for the defender to require contact with the rear. When those situations did arise, the defender's knowledge of the terrain and defences he was holding assisted in communicating.

It should also be borne in mind that the deeper an attacker went into a defender's position, the more unbalanced the communications situation became. For the attacker, he was advancing across a shattered, foreign landscape, trying to maintain communication by unreliable means (phone lines running overland, visual signals, runners, etc.). On the other hand, the defender was being forced back into his trench system. Communications within a trench system were more secure, relying largely on buried telephone lines. Thus, as the attacker advanced, his communication system became worse, while the defender's could remain operational.

Compared with the Great War, communications during battle in the American Civil War were technologically primitive (using mounted dispatch carriers with messages). However, the lack of high-tech communications did not really matter. A Civil War battle was no where near as large as a Great War battle. A general in the Civil War often could observe a battle in progress, something impossible in the Great War. A Civil War general was usually aware of what was going on during the battle. Being aware of what was happening, he could communicate orders as the need arose.

As for the Second World War general, communications had advanced by then, particularly in the availability of portable radios. This allowed for reliable instantaneous communication, something unavailable to a Great War general. Although Second World War communications were never 100 percent reliable (nothing ever is, particularly in battle), the communications technology available in the Second World War was a significant improvement on that used in the Great War. Like the U.S. Civil War general, the Second World War general had the means to control the battle while it was in progress.

What resulted from the interplay of firepower, mobility, manpower and communications was that Great War battles were static and fought within the range of the artillery. Once beyond this range, the infantry were vulnerable and further advances without friendly artillery support were near impossible. Enemy artillery could pound the attackers from afar and infantry reinforcements could be relatively quickly brought up from other parts of the enemy line to close the breach in the defences.

It would also take time to bring forward friendly artillery to support the advancing infantry. Not only was the artillery heavy and the ground it had to cross in poor shape from battle, but there often would be a communications gap between the advancing infantry and the generals controlling the artillery. It would take precious time for any support for the infantry to come forward into action. In the meantime, the infantry advance would have to halt and dig in lest the infantry be wiped out by the enemy reinforcements.

Being limited to fighting large, static battles had important strategic effects. Breaking through the trench system was not possible. No army on the Western Front found itself in the situation of being through the enemy defences and in his rear, able to push deeper unopposed, or turn to the left or right to outflank and destroy his opponent. We may appreciate then that it was extremely difficult, if not impossible, for any Great War general to turn any particular attack into a decisive "war winning battle" that comprehensively defeated the defender.

Two

Problems in the Early Years

While there were factors in play that prevented any "war winning battle" throughout the Great War, the attacks in the early years of the War, 1914 and 1915, stand out as being particularly ineffective and costly. The assaults launched in these years consistently failed, usually with very little to show for the hundreds of thousands of casualties suffered. Not only was there no "war winning battle," but it was rare for the attackers to even reach the limit of their artillery's range. In many cases, the attackers failed to capture any ground of significance, being pushed back into their own trenches. Why was this so?

The starting point is the artillery. While artillery was the most important weapon of the Great War, there were deficiencies with it at war's outset, particularly with the French and British. Both lacked sufficient numbers of heavy artillery pieces. The French Army was dependant on the 75 mm field gun and the British relied on their 18-pounder. Although these small field guns were useful for tearing gaps into advancing enemy infantry with their shrapnel bursts, they were not adequate for supporting infantry attacks on fortified defensive positions. Devastating to human beings, the shrapnel bursts were useless against defences made of earth, concrete and steel. Essentially, the French and British artillery was prepared for a mobile war of manoeuvre, not static trench warfare.

Soon after the dawn of trench warfare the Allies took a first step to rectifying the problem, using high explosive shells for their field guns. This was only a partial solution, for while the field guns could now destroy German forward defences, they still lacked the range to destroy German defences, troop concentrations and artillery pieces in the rear areas. Only heavy artillery pieces firing high explosive shells had the power and the range to destroy these. With few of these available at the beginning of the war, it would take time for the Allies to produce the required amount. In the event, this would not occur for the British until late 1916.

Compounding Allied problems was the lack of sufficient ammunition for those guns they had. Prior to the War no one had imagined the vast amount of shells that were to be expended and pre-war arrangements were unable to keep up with demand. In 1915 it was common for British gunners to be rationed only a few shells for firing each day. This lack of artillery ammunition caused such a scandal in Britain that it brought down the government of Prime Minister Herbert Henry Asquith. Similar to the heavy artillery situation, it took time for British industry to make good the deficiency and it was not until 1916 that British gunners could fire their weapons without fear of exhausting their ammunition.

The scarcity of heavy artillery and lack of ammunition for any guns created difficult problems on the battlefield. The German defensive system often remained operational following an artillery bombardment. Trenches, strong points and dugouts were undamaged, while barbed wire remained an obstacle. To the rear, German artillery pieces were free to pound the battlefield. From their defences, the German soldiers and gunners were able to deliver withering rifle, machine gun and artillery fire onto the Allied soldiers trying to cross No Man's Land. Often, the attackers were stopped at the German barbed wire, where they were easy targets for the German defenders and the attack would bog down in bloody failure. Reinforcements sent in to salvage the situation usually only added to the casualty roll.

Even when an attack was successful in seizing the German forward defences, the Allied artillery lacked the capability to break up German troop concentrations readying for a counter-attack. The attacking infantry often were placed in the unenviable position of having to prepare for and defend themselves against the inevitable German counter-attack alone. In many cases these counter-attacks were supported by German artillery that had survived the Allied bombardment. Depleted in numbers after having gone through the gauntlet of No Man's Land, the attackers were often overwhelmed by these counter-attacks.

The lack of sufficient artillery was not the only problem facing the attacker in the early years of the War. Most of the weapons of war discussed in Part One had not yet appeared on the battlefield. Trench mortars and grenades had not been produced in great numbers yet. The Lewis Gun had not made its appearance on the battlefield and, as has been discussed earlier, the heavier machine guns were too difficult to bring forward in the initial assault. The tank was but a dream. The infantry attacked with only their rifles and bayonets.

We can only try to imagine the difficulties attacking soldiers faced trying to neutralize, for example, a protected machine gun emplacement with rifle fire alone. Not only was it difficult to shoulder the rifle, aim and hit the machine gunners, but it was also difficult to create an accurate, intense barrage from multiple rifles to try to keep the machine gunners' heads down so the attackers could advance. Soldiers caught in this not uncommon situation were, in a real sense, powerless. Their rifles were no match for the hundreds of bullets being fired by the machine gun.

While the defence was powerful throughout the Great War, the imbalance between the attacker and the defender was greatest in 1914 and 1915. This imbalance was even greater for the Allies since, although none of the combatants were prepared for trench warfare, the Allies were worse off with their lack of heavy artillery and ammunition for their guns. Without sufficient artillery support, grenades or portable machine guns, the Allied infantry assaulted with only their rifles and bayonets. Under these circumstances, it is perhaps not surprising that many Allied assaults failed in the face of an enemy dug in and protected by machine guns and defensive artillery barrages.

We can appreciate then that there were deficiencies in the weapons available in the early years of the War that seriously hindered the attacker. These deficiencies created real tactical problems on the battlefield that could turn an attack into a bloody defeat. However, as we will see, the soldiers and generals did not sit idly by indifferently allowing these problems to destroy attack after attack. Instead, tactical and technological innovations were developed to deal with the problems of the Great War battlefield. Nevertheless, it was not an easy or bloodless journey.

Three

Why Attack?

The discussion from the previous Chapters begs the question; why did the Allies even attack at all? As we have seen, launching an attack in the early years of the Great War was an extremely costly and ineffective undertaking. Why did the Allies not just remain on the defensive?

On a tactical level, at the beginning of the War a breakthrough into the open land beyond the trench lines appeared a more likely possibility than it did later in the War. While at the time of the Battle of Vimy Ridge there were successive multiple trench lines, this was often not the case early in the war. For example, at the March 1915 Battle of Neuve Chapelle, the German defence line consisted of only a front line trench with a weak support line and some concrete strong points behind this.[108] Facing such a relatively thin line, one can see how the British thought they could break through it.

However, the main motivation behind the Allied attacks was political. To remain on the defensive was not an acceptable option for the Allies. It must be remembered that Belgium and France had been invaded by the Germans in August 1914.

In the years leading up to the Great War, many in influential circles within Germany became increasingly paranoid over what they saw as a threatening formal alliance between Russia and France. In particular, there was concern over Russia's recent economic resurgence, coupled with its enormous population. While France and Russia's alliance was largely defensive in purpose, to protect them from Germany, it was still viewed as a threat by Germany's leaders.

Contrary to myth, the population of Europe was not seething for war in 1914. However, when a crisis erupted in the Balkans involving Germany's ally, the Austro-Hungarian Empire, Germany turned this local event into a world war. In June 1914, the heir to the Austro-Hungarian throne was assassinated in Sarajevo. Believing that the Serbian government was involved, and fearing the nationalist ambitions that the new

Serbian state had and its potential effect on the multi-ethnic Austro-Hungarian Empire, the decision was made to launch a punitive strike against Serbia. The German government supported this decision, despite the realization by both the Germans and the Austro-Hungarians that an attack on Serbia would likely lead to a larger war.

The risk was taken because German leaders believed that the time was right for taking on Russia and France, before Russia's economic resurgence made it more militarily powerful. When Russia sided with little Serbia, the decision was made in Germany to launch an unprovoked attack against Russia's ally, France, via Belgium.

Because France was an industrialized nation while Russia was not, it was believed that France could mobilize its forces quicker than Russia. The Germans thought that they could defeat France before Russia was ready. Then they could turn all their might against Russia. However, by attacking France through neutral Belgium, Germany provoked Britain into joining the war.

The result of this invasion in August of 1914 and subsequent battles was that by November that year Belgium was almost completely occupied by the Germans except for a small piece in its west, while the north-east and east of France had been captured, with both areas' resources open to the invaders. It is noteworthy that the part of France occupied by the Germans contained much of France's industry and its natural iron and coal reserves, important losses to an industrialized nation.[109]

More troubling were the rumors of German atrocities committed against Belgian and French civilians in the occupied areas. Although the more outlandish claims were unfounded (such as German troops bayoneting babies), others were not (such as the sack of Louvain). It is estimated that in their invasion in August of 1914, the Germans killed 6 500 innocent civilians, often by rounding them up and summarily executing them for no proven cause.[110]

The hardship did not end with the invasion, for the Germans embarked on a premeditated policy in Belgium geared towards crippling the country with a view to making it a nation subservient to Germany's interests. Requisitions of industrial equipment, levies of money, *flamenpolitik* (a policy of officially favoring the Germanic Flemish Belgians over the French Walloons with the ultimate goal of creating a state allied with Germany) and forced deportations of civilians were carried on throughout the war for the benefit of Germany, not just during the War, but beyond should Germany win.[111]

Similar events were occurring within the occupied portion of France. Requisitions, forced labor and deportations, all done to support the German war effort, were the experience of many French civilians behind the German lines. Indeed, due to occupied France being closer to the front lines than much of occupied Belgium, the oppression of French civilians by the German Army was even harsher than that imposed on Belgian civilians.[112]

There were compelling motives for the French to take the offensive against the entrenched Germans. A significant portion of their country was occupied, including economically important areas, with the civilians in the occupied territory living under German military rule. Added to this, German atrocities (both rumored and true) added a further level of urgency in French peoples' minds for the need to take back occupied France.

For the British, their motives for taking the offensive are not as obvious. Not formally allied with France before the War, Britain still had vital issues at stake. Ostensibly entering the war in defence of Belgium, it was not in Britain's interests to have Germany defeat the French and dominate continental Europe. Not only would a German dominated Europe impair Britain's commercial and colonial interests, but it would pose a threat to Britain itself. With the rest of Europe under German control, Britain would be an enticing "next target" for Germany. Having entered the War, it had to be seen, both to the people at home and to their Allies, that the British were doing their "fair share" to assist France and Belgium.

As for the Germans, while they did launch some offensives prior to the Battle of Vimy Ridge, they were less aggressive than the Allies in this regard. Politically, the Germans could remain on the defensive. They had captured and were occupying most of Belgium and economically important parts of France. Germany was in an advantageous position as it could, and did, use these occupied territories as "bargaining chips" to try to obtain a peace settlement on terms favorable to Germany. In a sense, the Germans were holding the occupied territories "hostage" and they did not have as compelling a motive to assume the offensive as the Allies did.

Although it may seem incomprehensible to us today that the Allies launched assaults across the deadly No Man's Land against formidable German trenches, there really was no other option. The Germans were occupiers and there was tremendous pressure to push them out. For the Allies to sit passively in their trenches was not politically acceptable.

Four

The Junior Partner

The offensives launched by the Allies on the Western Front in the early years of the War were directed by the French. Britain was the junior partner in the Allied war effort at this time and largely followed French strategic initiatives. While this arrangement had something to do with the fact that France had been invaded, it was based more on the military realities of the situation. The British Army was much smaller than the French, so British politicians and generals did not have much influence on Allied strategic planning.

The disparity in size between the British and French Armies in 1914 was due to their respective methods of recruitment. The French Army, like its German opponent, was based on conscription. That is, both countries had compulsory military service before the War. In France, young men were conscripted to serve for three years, then were placed on reserve.[113] Once on reserve, they were liable to be called upon for active service in time of war. A similar system existed in Germany. Therefore, when war broke out in August of 1914, both the French and Germans had large standing armies and the ability to quickly reinforce them by calling their reserves to active service. These large armies were further reinforced throughout the war as young men became eligible for conscription.

The British Army at War's outset had a completely different composition. It was made of professionals who had volunteered for long-term service prior to the War. Unlike the French and German Armies which were created for national defence, the British Army was largely viewed as an overseas force for "policing" the colonies. This had the effect of making the British Army a highly trained and professional force in the summer of 1914, but it was dwarfed by the conscript Armies that the French and Germans fielded. The British Expeditionary Force (the "BEF") (that part of the British Army intended to fight in Belgium and France) totalled about 120 000 men at the outbreak of war and the whole British Army (including Regulars, Reserves and Territorials) came to approximately

773 000. On the other hand, the Germans were able to mobilize over 4 000 000 men and the French about 3 680 000 in August of 1914.[114]

The state of Britain's Army, along with the armament and ammunition supply problems discussed in Chapter Two, had its roots in pre-war politics. With total war on no one's mind, there was little emphasis on preparation before 1914. Understandably, the British government was more interested in spending money on social programs and the historically vital Navy than preparing the Army for a long war. Tied to this, Britain traditionally in European wars relied on allies to engage the main enemy in the main theatre of war. The British would concentrate on peripheral operations utilizing their economic strength and their Navy. The Great War was a departure from this and Britain lacked experience in major operations in the main theatre of a war, which the Western Front was. It also should be remembered that there had not been a major, international war in Europe since the wars of Napoleon in the late 18th/early 19th century. Thus, when war came in 1914, the British were unprepared for the demands of a modern, international, total war against the main enemy in the main theatre of war.[115]

Despite the original BEF being a highly competent force, the battles of 1914 took their toll so that, by the end of the year, the original BEF was in practical terms no more. Regulars serving overseas in the colonies were brought to the Western Front, but this only temporarily filled the ranks. For further reinforcement, the British turned to their Territorial battalions. Territorial soldiers were not professionals, rather, they were part-time soldiers with civilian occupations. At the outbreak of war the British were reluctant to use these citizen soldiers in battle, but the heavy casualties suffered by the BEF forced otherwise. Deployed in small numbers at the First Battle of Ypres in the autumn of 1914, the battles of 1915 were to be increasingly fought by non-professional British soldiers like the Territorials.

These Territorials were not the bottom of Britain's manpower resources. While most leaders (and most people for that matter) believed at the beginning of the War that it would be a short conflict, one man in power, Britain's pre-eminent soldier in 1914, the larger than life, Field Marshal Lord Horatio Kitchener (War Minister), was not so optimistic. He authorized the raising of a huge volunteer army drawn from civilians without prior military training. Thousands of men enthusiastically enlisted in 1914, swelling the ranks of what would become known as the "New Army." Although eager for the fight, these factory workers, shop clerks, accountants and teachers needed to be trained and equipped for war and it would not be until mid-1915 that the first of these volunteer soldiers made their appearance on the Western Front. Even then, the impact of the New Army would not be fully felt until 1916.

Due to the casualties suffered by the British Regulars and Territorials and despite reinforcement from some of the New Army divisions, the BEF still remained a small force compared to the French Army in 1915. Although the BEF had expanded to contain two

Armies by this point in the War, the French, in contrast, had eight Armies readied for action on the Western Front.[116] Until the New Army (which contained several Armies) arrived in force the British would remain the junior partner in the alliance with France.

Britain's ally was an aggressive one as the French Army was not inclined to stay on the defensive. Rather, with its officers schooled on a pre-war doctrine of offensive *a la outrance* (attack at all costs), the French willingly rose to the assault. It was believed in the French Army that their soldiers' *élan* (spirit or morale) would carry the day regardless of the metal projectiles fired at them. The French soldiers' moral strength and belief in success would allow them to storm a position and give the Germans the bayonet. At the bayonet point, *cran* (guts) would ensure that German defenders would be vanquished. This almost mystical doctrine of offensive action at all costs guided French officers and was to prove costly to the French Army in the early years of the War.[117] (It should be noted though, that all armies of the time were influenced by the "cult" of the offensive, but it appears that the French took it one step further and made it central to their strategy and tactics).[118]

Motivated by the desire to expel the invader from their homeland and believing in the superiority of the offensive, the French launched failed offensives in 1914 and 1915. The cost to the French was staggering. In their 1914 offensive on the frontier with Germany at the outset of the War, some 200 000 casualties were suffered by the French in a few weeks for no advantage.[119] A further 240 000 French casualties were incurred in a failed offensive in late 1914/early 1915. During their 1915 spring Artois offensive (centred against Vimy Ridge) about 300 000 French soldiers became casualties in return for small gains.[120] The autumn Artois/Champagne offensive (with Vimy Ridge again as an objective) added another 200 000 casualties.[121] Despite this effort and blood, the Germans still held virtually all of their occupied territories.

The British, keen to do "their bit" to help their ally, added a further 275 000 casualties in 1915 to the grim French totals.[122] With the exception of the March 1915 Battle of Neuve Chapelle, these British attacks were at the prompting of the French and were small parts of the larger French Offensives mentioned before. However, even Neuve Chapelle was influenced by French desires as it was launched by the British to rebut a feeling within the French Army that the BEF was not doing all it could on the Western Front.

The battles of 1914 and 1915 were largely French battles on the Allies' side. Before the War the French had maintained a large standing army with reserves, ready to mobilize for war in anticipation of a German attack. When this threat materialized in August 1914, the French had the trained manpower to defend their nation and attempt to force the Germans out.

The British were not so prepared. Traditionally, Britain was not a land power in wars on the European Continent. When the British took on the commitment to assist their ally on the Western Front, they lacked the immediate means to do so on the scale that the French and Germans were fighting. It would take time for the British Army and industry to adjust. In the event, this would not occur until 1916. Until then, the British were the junior partner in the alliance with France.

Five

The Canadians

An important part of Britain making the transition from peace-time to total war involved mobilizing the British Empire. In addition to the colonies that stretched across the world, Britain had Dominions that were loyal. These Dominions were sovereign in their domestic affairs, but on the international stage had no voice separate from Britain's. Thus Canada, one of these Dominions, automatically was drawn into the War when it began in the summer of 1914.

Any help from Canada would not be immediate though. Canada had virtually no pre-war preparations. There was a permanent military force, but it was very small and inadequate for a major overseas operation in Europe. Like Britain, Canada needed volunteers. There was no shortage in 1914 as thousands of Canadians rushed to enlist motivated by a mixture of patriotism, duty, excitement, boredom in civilian life and poverty. Most of these initial volunteers were men who had immigrated to Canada before the War from the British Isles. Nevertheless, since most had immigrated years prior, they still considered themselves "Canadian."

It is interesting to note that many of these men did have some prior military experience. For some it was through membership in a pre-war militia unit. These militia units were popular in Canadian society before the War, as many men enjoyed the experience of being a "week-end warrior." While such military service hardly prepared the men for the rigors and horrors of the Western Front, it had, at least, exposed them to the military. There were other volunteers with more relevant experience as quite a few men had served in Britain's Army before the War, including active service, such as during the Boer War (1899-1902).

Following cursory training in Canada, the first Canadian contingent left for England on October 2, 1914. They were placed under the command of the British Lieutenant-General Sir Edwin Alderson and continued their training in England until February of 1915.

At that point the Canadian contingent, now re-named the Canadian Division, finally arrived in France.

The Canadian Division's first battle was the Second Battle of Ypres, which was fought in late April/early May 1915 in Belgian Flanders. It was a horrific introduction to Western Front warfare as the Canadians' endured German gas attacks (the first on the Western Front) without the protection of gas masks. A defensive battle, the Canadians, some of whom wore urine soaked cloths over their mouths and noses to fend off the gas, blunted the German assault. While some ground was given up, no breakthrough occurred and the Canadians earned themselves a reputation as formidable troops. The cost of their stout defence was high though, for out of a pre-battle strength of about 18 000, approximately 6 000 became casualties.[123]

Shortly after Ypres, the Canadian Division became involved in the Allied spring offensive in 1915. Attacking at Festubert and Givenchy in late May and June, the Canadian assaults, like those launched by the British at the same time, were made over wet and muddy ground and with totally inadequate artillery support. British and Canadian bravery met with failure and heavy casualties. The same fate befell the main Allied offensive, launched by the French against Vimy Ridge. About 3 000 Canadians were killed, wounded or missing.

While the Canadian Division had suffered many casualties in its first battles, reinforcements were on the way. Like the BEF of which they were a part of, the Canadian armed forces in France expanded in late 1915. The 2nd Division had been formed in Canada from men who volunteered in the autumn of 1914 and it arrived in France in September of 1915. With two Divisions now on the Western Front, the Canadian Corps was created to command both, headed by General Alderson. Another division, the 3rd Division, was also added to the Canadian Corps in December of 1915, but would not begin holding the line until 1916. It was composed of a mixture of pre-war permanent force soldiers, men who initially volunteered for mounted units and further volunteers from Canada. Of particular note is that among the volunteers, an increasing number were Canadian born.[124]

The 2nd Division's baptism of fire occurred at St. Eloi in the beginning of April, 1916. Like the 1st Division's (the re-named Canadian Division) introduction to combat on the Western Front, the Battle of St. Eloi was a defensive struggle for the Canadian troops.

The British had detonated several underground mines beneath German lines and seized the large craters created by the explosions. For the 2nd Division, the battle was one of holding these crater positions in the face of German shell-fire and counter-attacks. Due to the devastation wrought on the landscape by the detonation of the mines and artillery shell-fire, maps were useless, direction was lost and communication was near impossible. In the confusion, it turned out that the Canadians were actually holding the wrong portion of the line. To the surprise of the commanders, it was learned that four of the largest craters were actually held by the Germans, rather than the Canadians. It was a painful start to the 2nd Division's service on the Western Front. Casualties came to about 1 300 men.[125]

After St. Eloi there was a change in command of the Canadian Corps. Possibly due to his conduct of the Battle, or maybe because of the conflict he had with Canada's controversial Minister of Militia, Sam Hughes, over the unreliable Ross Rifle, General Alderson was removed and Lieutenant-General Sir Julian Byng took over.[126] Although Alderson was a competent general, this was a fortunate turn of events for the Canadians as Byng was an excellent, experienced commander.

Armament for the Canadian front line infantryman was about to change too as the Ross Rifle was on its way out in 1916. Despite Sir Charles Ross' pleas that the difficulties experienced with the Ross Rifle were due to poor packaging prior to shipment, poor ammunition and a lack of familiarity with the rifle amongst the troops, the experiences of the Canadian Corps in battle had showed that the Ross Rifle was a deficient weapon.[127]

Front-line troops detested the weapon due to its propensity to jam. General Sir Arthur Currie, commander of the 1st Division, stated that the Ross Rifle caused more unnecessary casualties than any other factor in the War. The British High Command launched an investigation and it was found that the Canadian soldiers lacked confidence in the Ross Rifle. The fact that many soldiers discarded their Ross Rifles for the more favored and reliable British Lee-Enfield spoke volumes on the Canadian soldiers' opinion of the Ross. The end result was that in June of 1916 the Canadian Corps made the transition to the Lee-Enfield.[128]

The transitions within the Canadian Corps in early 1916 were not limited to the high command and the soldiers' rifles. Canadians of all ranks were also going through an intense learning process on Western Front warfare. When the Canadians arrived in France they were all inexperienced in trench warfare; from general to private. Men who had no pre-war military experience other than as "week-end" militia officers were now placed in command of thousands of men in combat. Front line soldiers, perhaps store clerks or laborers before the war, were now being asked to charge across No Man's Land and capture modern, fortified, defensive positions.

It took time for these "citizen soldiers" to learn their trade. None of the Great War armies had predicted before the War how it would actually be fought. There was no knowledge, accumulated by experience, for how to conduct trench warfare. This was even more true for the Canadians, and the BEF as a whole, bearing in mind how unprepared they were at the War's outset compared to their French allies and German opponents. In this context, pre-war training methods could only go so far and much had to be learned by experience.

Through the grind of the Western Front the Canadians were learning how to become "professional soldiers." Some of this knowledge was accumulated by their own hard experience, some from lessons learned by British units and circulated throughout the BEF. Unfortunately in war, this type of a learning process takes time, all the while costing lives.

It was this evolving force that would meet the Germans at the Canadians' next fight – the Battle of Mount Sorrel near Ypres in Belgium. Mount Sorrel would be the 3rd Division's first experience in battle. Like the other Canadian Divisions' initiation to Western Front combat, it would be a defensive encounter and would prove to be a grisly affair.

On June 2, 1916, following a brutal, punishing artillery bombardment and the detonation of underground mines below the Canadians, the Germans attacked the 3rd Division's position. The 3rd Division's commander was killed in the opening moments and a brigadier-general seriously wounded and captured. The Canadians suffered crippling casualties and the Germans seized the Canadians' forward trenches, including the high ground of Mount Sorrel. However, rather than pushing deeper into Canadian lines, the Germans stopped, adhering to their pre-battle plans. It is fortunate they did so for the Canadians were in disarray. They had suffered terribly from the German artillery bombardment and, of those who survived it, many were over-run in the German infantry advance. Not much was left of 3rd Division to stop any further German advance.

The unexpected respite allowed the Canadian Corps to re-organize and seal off the area that had been attacked. Reinforcements in the form of machine guns were brought forth and a new defensive line was created in front of the ground that the Germans had captured. On the following day the 3rd Division, reinforced by units from the 1st Division, made a hastily organized attempt to re-capture the lost ground, resulting only in chaos, confusion and casualties. The losses from this counter-attack, combined with those from the initial German attack, forced the depleted 3rd Division from the battle. The brunt of the fighting would now be borne by the men of the 1st Division. The Canadians were still intent on reclaiming their lost positions.

Unlike the first counter-attack, the Canadians' next effort would not be a haphazard affair. An important component in the Canadians' plan was the artillery support. A high concentration of guns allowed the Canadians to smother the Germans with a lengthy and intense artillery bombardment prior to the counter-attack. When the infantry made their assault in the early hours of June 13, 1916, the soldiers from the 1st Division swept into German lines meeting little resistance. Although the Canadians did have to overcome some machine gun positions and isolated pockets of defenders, the victory was complete in about an hour. All the ground lost on June 2 had been re-gained and the Germans were back in their original trench lines. The Canadians quickly consolidated the re-captured ground, putting it into a fit state to repel any German counter-attacks. In the event, two German counter-attacks on June 14 were beaten back by the artillery. Key to Canadian success was the sound planning and preparation for the counter-attack. While much was still to be learned by the Canadians in the ways of Great War warfare and mistakes would be made, the foundation for future success was laid during the counter-attack at the Battle of Mount Sorrel. From June 2 to 14, Canadian casualties came to about 8 000.[129]

By June of 1916 the Canadian Corps was developing into an experienced combat formation. The Canadian armed forces had started the Great War as an inexperienced collection of citizens, but this was beginning to change. Its three active Divisions had all seen combat, while a fourth Division was coming to the Western Front. The Canadians' experience in the war to this point had been largely in defensive actions, but the future would be different. The Allies were planning another large scale offensive; this time near the River Somme.

Six

Background to the Battle of the Somme

Despite the ferocity of the Battle of Mount Sorrel, it was really a sideshow for the "big push" planned by the Allies along the River Somme in the summer of 1916. One part of a larger co-ordinated Allied offensive (the Russians and the Italians were to simultaneously attack in their theatres of war), the Somme was designed as a joint Franco-British effort. Since the River Somme was near the junction of the French and British Armies on the Western Front, it was a convenient place from which to launch an attack, even though there were no strategic targets of value nearby. It was hoped that by putting pressure on the Germans and their allies in all theatres of war, somewhere they would crack.

For purposes of this book, the Battle of the Somme provides a good illustration of an offensive operation prior to the Battle of Vimy Ridge. The Somme was the first large scale British offensive of the War. It also involved the Canadian Corps; representing the Canadian Divisions' introduction to large scale assaults on the Western Front. Relevant too is that by mid-1916 the British had accumulated many of the weapons necessary for combat in the Great War; large amounts of artillery and ammunition, Lewis Guns, trench mortars, rifle grenades and Mills Bombs.

The Somme would be the first offensive for many of the untried, citizen soldiers of Britain's New Army. Formed by close-knit volunteer battalions of men from the same area and often friends and family, these citizen soldiers were, man for man, of the highest quality, but were low on combat experience. Their officers and senior non-commissioned officers (NCOs) were not in a much better position. The pre-war trained officers and NCOs were in France and Belgium fighting the Germans during 1914 and 1915, with many becoming casualties. Because of this, the men leading the New Army were often officers and soldiers promoted to positions they would not otherwise have held before the War, or civilians just as inexperienced as the men they were commanding. Even with the generals, the expansion of the BEF and demands of war resulted in men who commanded a battalion in peacetime (about 1 000 men) being in charge of a division (about 20 000 men). Just like their men, these generals were having to learn "on the job." Because of this lack of battlefield experience, the training of the New Army also suffered. In hindsight it is easy to criticize the development of the New Army to this point in the War, but the realities of having to quickly raise a mass army lead to the result.[130]

This burgeoning force of inexperienced soldiery was under the command of the stoic General Sir Douglas Haig, who took charge of the BEF from the personable, but too emotional, Field Marshal Sir John French on December 19, 1915. Haig, a devoutly religious Scottish gentleman, had served in the cavalry and held various important command positions before the war. During the Great War, prior to assuming command of the BEF, he had lead a corps and then an army. He was 55 years old at the time of the Somme campaign.

Haig was a shy man, his aloofness distancing him from others. Not the most articulate of individuals, his inability to clearly express his thoughts verbally compounded his difficulties in interacting with people. Haig was also an intimidating figure and this, coupled with his difficulty expressing himself, sometimes lead to misunderstandings with fellow officers, particularly subordinates. However, Haig's ability to express himself in writing was not affected by his shyness and his written orders were invariably clear. It is important to also note that Haig retained the loyalty and respect of his subordinates throughout the War.

Haig had an optimistic streak, which sometimes lead him to pushing too hard in the hope of breaking the strength of his adversary; often to the cost of Haig's soldiers. On the other hand, he was a strong willed man whose determination to win the War remained intact throughout the conflict. This determination, along with an open mind for new weaponry and tactics that would assist his soldiers to win the War, were important to Britain's ultimate success.

Haig understood that his officers and men of the New Army were inexperienced in Western Front warfare. It was his preference to have the Somme offensive start as late as possible to provide more time for his troops to gain experience. However, events would not allow him this opportunity. The Germans pre-empted Allied plans by attacking the French at Verdun on the River Meuse.

The German offensive, launched on February 21, 1916, was aimed at knocking the French out of the War. It was planned as an attritional slugging match to "bleed the French Army white." The German commander, Colonel-General Erich von Falkenhayn, selected Verdun as his target due to its historic significance to France. However, he was not that concerned with capturing the Town of Verdun itself. Instead, he wanted to threaten Verdun with his attack, which would lure the French into sending more and more men into the battle, only to be destroyed by the German machine guns and artillery.

Matters did not turn out as Falkenhayen intended. The Battle of Verdun ground on into the summer with both sides being "bled white." German attacks over land churned and cratered by vast quantities of shell-fire were followed by French counter-attacks over the same shattered ground. By July the Germans were exhausted and their goal had not been achieved; the French Army, while badly battered, still existed. Even more disturbing to the Germans was that in the autumn of 1916 the French found the strength to launch massive counter-attacks that re-captured much of the territory they had lost in the first half of the Battle. By the end of it, about 350 000 Frenchmen and 330 000 Germans became casualties in the "meat grinder on the Meuse."

The Battle of Verdun lead to a change in Allied planning for the upcoming offensive on the River Somme. With the French heavily engaged at Verdun, they lacked the capacity to defend Verdun and at the same time lead a massive offensive on the Somme. The result was that the French would have a reduced role during the campaign, but still pressured the British to attack earlier than the British wanted to in an effort to relieve the strain on the French Army at Verdun. The burden of fighting on the Somme would now fall largely on the inexperienced soldiers of the New Army.

Seven

Plans and Preparations for the Somme

The Allied plan was for three Armies to attack German lines in the early summer of 1916. It was to be a massive assault, with 13 British and 5 French Divisions earmarked to attack on the opening day. While the French Army had experienced large offensives like this in 1914 and 1915, the Battle of the Somme would be the first for the BEF.

The main assault was to be made by the 11 Divisions of the British Fourth Army under General Sir Henry Rawlinson. An infantryman, Rawlinson was an experienced commander by this point in the War, having held division and corps command before being promoted to lead Fourth Army. While his performance in the upcoming Somme campaign was "spotty," Rawlinson remained in High Command throughout the War and became one of Britain's best Army commanders by 1918.

To the north of Rawlinson's Fourth Army, two Divisions from General Sir Edmund Allenby's British Third Army were to make a diversionary attack at Gommecourt. The French contribution was the five Divisions in General Fayolle's 6th Army attacking along the River Somme itself, to the south of Fourth Army. As mentioned earlier, the original Allied plan called for a larger French involvement on the Somme, but the demands for French manpower at Verdun resulted in them having a reduced role. Should there be a breakthrough, the British Reserve Army under General Sir Hubert Gough was ready to join the fray and pursue the Germans.

A massive artillery bombardment preceded the Allied assault. From their experiences in previous battles, the British had concluded that a great artillery bombardment was necessary, not just to neutralize the German defences, but to destroy them. For the British Fourth Army alone, 1 010 field guns and howitzers, 180 heavy guns and 233 heavy howitzers were deployed on a frontage of about 20 000 yards. They were to pound the German defences for five days (later extended to seven) before the infantry went over the top.[131] During this week long bombardment the British artillery fired about 1.5 million shells; more than were fired by the BEF in the first 12 months of the war.[132]

Three objectives were to be achieved by the preliminary bombardment. First, the German barbed wire protecting their trenches was to be cut. This would provide the attacking infantry with pathways through the German wire to the German trenches. The artillery was also tasked with destroying the German trenches and strong points. Finally, counter-battery work was to be done. If enough German artillery batteries could be destroyed during the bombardment, the German guns would not be able to fire on the British infantry during their attack and following capture of the German trenches.[133] The first objective was to be achieved by the 18-pounder field guns, the latter two by the howitzers and heavy guns.[134]

Turning now to the infantry who had to actually carry out the attack, British assault tactics on the Somme, much maligned after the fact by historians and commentators, were much more varied than is usually recorded in the history books. There were some general directives passed down from the BEF's High Command, such as the replacement of rushing tactics with a more slow, steady infantry advance, but, by in large, it was left to the corps and division commanders to actually plan how the infantry would make the assault.[135]

This "hands off" role the British High Command showed had much to do with the High Command's view of its own role in battle. Sir Douglas Haig saw his role as that of strategic decision maker, with tactics to be left to those lower down in the command structure.[136] Rawlinson, the main Army commander, had a closer grip on tactics, but he also distanced himself from the planning of the actual assault, leaving this aspect of the planning to his corps and division commanders. For Rawlinson, based on his experience in earlier battles, the real dilemma was, not the initial attack, but how to ensure that the soldiers were able to consolidate their gains once captured and then to exploit them.[137]

Generally, the assault tactic used was the "wave system." This involved the infantry advancing in a series of waves, each wave separated by about 100 yards, with an interval of a few yards between each man. These waves would all advance at the same time. It was intended that the first waves would break into the German defences and the successive waves would be used to mop up any German defences left, consolidate the ground seized, push the attack forward and bring up ammunition and equipment.[138]

Within this basic model there were tactical variances within corps, divisions and brigades, depending on the commander of the unit and the ground the attackers had to cover.[139] For example, it was realized that there was a need for the troops to be already in No Man's Land before zero-hour, to give them a "head start" in their assault. How this was to be done was left to the local commander. In some places, where No Man's Land was hundreds of yards wide, jumping-off trenches were dug halfway across No Man's

Land.[140] Other commanders were reluctant to dig jumping-off trenches for fear that this would alert the Germans to the impending attack as it had sometimes done in earlier battles. Instead, they ordered their troops to advance into No Man's Land prior to zero-hour under cover of darkness and lie there until the signal was given to attack.[141]

Once the infantry started their attack, the artillery's protective barrage would support them. This involved the artillery firing on targets (usually German trench lines) in front of the advancing infantry. As the infantry advanced deeper into German territory, the artillery fire would move forward on a series of predetermined "lifts." Each "lift" was the next infantry objective and were timed to coincide with the infantry timetable for attacking and seizing their objectives.[142] In essence, once the artillery had "lifted" from bombarding a German trench and moved to the next one, the British infantry would attack the trench and overcome what defenders were left alive. This process would then be repeated as the British infantry made their way through the successive German defensive positions.

To ensure that their infantry would take the German front line, the British had dug tunnels under No Man's Land. At the end of these tunnels, below German strong points, mines were planted and packed with explosives, timed to explode just before zero-hour. By timing the explosion of the mines this way, it was hoped that the British infantry would be upon the disoriented German defenders before they had a chance to recover from the shock of the blow.

By the end of June 1916, all appeared to be in place for a great Allied victory. Over a thousand artillery pieces had bombarded the Germans for seven days. Mines, packed with thousands of pounds of explosives, were ready to be blown beneath German positions. Zero-hour for the great assault, the first "big show" for the soldiers of the New Army, was 7:30 a.m. July 1, 1916. The British generals were confident in their plans and this confidence filtered down to the other ranks. No previous British battle in history had been planned to the extent of the Battle of the Somme. Would the Germans react according to plan?

Eight

The First Day

July 1, 1916, dawned a beautiful summer morning. Unlike many past Allied offensives, it appeared that the weather would finally cooperate with Allied designs. To many, impressed already by the massive Allied preparations, this may have seemed a good omen for the great attack. At 7:30 a.m., confident in imminent victory, thousands of British soldiers rose from their jumping-off positions and made across No Man's Land towards the German trenches. To their surprise and horror, the Germans were ready to meet them.

In some places the Germans started firing at the British as soon as they began moving forward. The waves of men, expecting to advance into the German trenches relatively unopposed, instead met a storm of steel from the German lines, quickly thinning the ranks of the British. Where moments before to the right and left were "pals" or "chums," now there were few, the rest having been forced to ground by grievous wounds. In other places the British advance was blocked by uncut German barbed wire. Here the men collected, making excellent targets for German machine gunners and riflemen. Many was the British soldier who tried vainly to find a way through the German barbed wire, only to become hung up on the wire and riddled with German bullets.

The defending German infantry had escaped the British artillery bombardment. In the week prior to the assault they had "hunkered down" in deep underground dug-outs that had protected them from the British shell-fire. Well trained for the task of defence, they immediately emerged from their dug-outs and manned the fire-steps of their trenches once the British artillery barrage "lifted." Even where the British had exploded underground mines, the Germans were quick to react, usually capturing the craters before the British reached them. Now with the bombardment over and the British barrage having "lifted," the Germans were unmolested by British shells, and were able to pour rifle fire, machine-gun fire and lob grenades into the British attackers.

Adding to the maelstrom, the German artillery pounded No Man's Land as the attackers made their way across. In effect, the British infantry were trapped. They were unable to advance through the barbed wire and strong front line defences. Nor could they retreat for fear of being hit by shells and bullets. Many soldiers were forced to spend the whole day stranded in No Man's Land, their nerves strained to exhaustion. For some, refuge from the carnage came only by ducking into a shell-hole, often masked from German observation by the bodies of comrades lying nearby.

The experience was even worse for the many wounded British soldiers as German bullets and shells seriously interfered with the ability of the stretcher bearers to collect the wounded. Those men who were wounded were largely left to their own devices. Some of those with minor wounds waited until darkness to make their way to the safety of British lines on their own, but for those with more serious wounds, this option was not available. For them, they had the agonizing ordeal of waiting in No Man's Land for medical relief. Many would be dead before it reached them.

In some places the British were able to enter the German front line. However, by the time they had overcome the German defenders and organized themselves to move further forward, their protective artillery barrage had moved on. The barrage had kept to its strict timetable that did not allow for delays and was now too far forward to protect the troops in any further advance. For these soldiers, no further objectives could be achieved and they remained where they were, soon to endure German counter-attacks. No reinforcements were forthcoming as the German barrage in No Man's Land blocked any such attempt. In many cases, by the end of the day, the survivors of these forward pockets of British soldiers were pushed back to where they had started in the morning.

It was not just the first waves of attackers that suffered from German defensive fire. Many supporting units, moving either through communication trenches or overland from behind the British front line to support the attack, were cut down making their way forward. One estimate has it that about 30 percent of British casualties suffered this day were incurred by support troops before they even reached their own front line.[143] The result was that, not only was No Man's Land littered with casualties, but the whole British forward trench system became choked with dead and wounded soldiers.

One of the units that met with disaster on July 1 was the 1st Newfoundland Battalion (since Newfoundland was a British colony separate from Canada at the time, the Newfoundland Battalion was not part of the Canadian Corps, rather, it served in a British unit). Before the Battle, the Newfoundlanders were earmarked for a supporting role. They were to move up to German lines after the initial assault had breached the German forward system in their sector and were to push the attack deeper. However, plans had to be changed as the first British assault had failed and the results from the second assault were uncertain. To ensure the capture of the German front line the Newfoundlanders were ordered to attack.

As support troops, the Newfoundlanders were positioned 300 yards behind the British front line. To reach the German front-line they had to pass this distance, along with No Man's Land. The Newfoundlanders crossed the first 300 yards over open ground to quicken their pace rather than utilizing the slower but safer route through the communication trenches. This decision proved disastrous as the Newfoundlanders were easy targets for the alert German machine gunners. Since the 1st Newfoundland Battalion attacked alone in this sector of the battlefield, all the German defenders in the area were able to deliver fire into their attack.

Not only did the Newfoundlanders have to cross open ground, but once they reached the British front line they had to navigate their way through gaps in the barbed wire protecting the British line. This caused the Newfoundlanders to bunch where the gaps were located, providing perfect targets for the German machine gunners who poured bullets into the advancing men.[144]

Despite the bodies of Newfoundlanders clogging the gaps in the British wire, a resolute few managed to make their way through the wire and into No Man's Land towards German lines. These few were not enough to reach German lines, let alone tackle the German defenders, and the attack of the 1st Newfoundland Battalion was beaten before the Newfoundlanders had a chance to come to grips with the enemy. Those who survived spent the day stranded in No Man's Land.

The cost to the Newfoundlanders was devastating. Of the 752 all ranks who went into the attack, 684 became casualties; a shocking casualty rate of 91 percent. Even more disturbing is the fact that it took only about forty minutes to destroy the 1st Newfoundland Battalion.[145] Unfortunately, the Newfoundlanders' fate was not unique on this day. Thirty-one other battalions suffered more than 500 casualties each.[146] For many of the "pals" battalions, they were two years in the making, but only ten minutes in the destroying.[147]

Why did the British attack fail so spectacularly? As discussed in the previous Chapter, the British had taken pains to plan their offensive in great detail. Yet, despite all the thought given to the attack before the Battle, everything seemed to go wrong.

The main reason for the British failure lay with their artillery program. Much faith was placed in the idea that the artillery would wipe out the German defences and defenders, allowing the infantry to easily seize their objectives. In essence, the Somme was planned as an artillery battle, with the artillery doing the killing and the infantry occupying the trenches full of enemy dead.

As we have seen, this was not what ended up happening and this was due to problems with the preliminary bombardment that were not appreciated before the Battle. A key failing of the bombardment was the type of artillery used. Most of the artillery deployed were 18-pounder field guns. These were, relatively speaking, small guns that fired shrapnel rounds or small high explosive shells, neither of which were effective in destroying German defences.

Due to this limitation, the field gun's main role during the preliminary bombardment was to destroy the German wire, however, the 18-pounders were also ineffective at this. Their shrapnel rounds often merely rattled the wire, without any destructive effect. As for their high explosive rounds, they had a slow acting fuse designed to explode after impact with the ground rather than on contact with the wire. For this reason, the explosion took place below the wire, shifting the wire, but not breaking it. Therefore, on July 1, much of the barbed wire remained uncut and a serious obstacle for the British infantry.

Another key problem with the preliminary bombardment was the lack of howitzers, especially the heavy howitzers, the trench destroyers. The howitzers made up a minority of the artillery used, but were given the important task of destroying German trenches and defences. With most of the guns being devoted to wire cutting (and not doing an effective job at that) only a minority of the artillery was devoted to trench destruction.

British problems were compounded by disagreements within the High Command before the Battle. General Rawlinson, commander of Fourth Army, favored a limited assault with limited objectives. He wanted to seize the German forward lines only, consolidate, bring the artillery up to support the infantry and then move on with another limited attack. However, Haig, possibly enticed by the thought of the always seductive and elusive breakthrough, overruled Rawlinson and increased the first days' objectives to include deeper German positions. Haig wanted a more ambitious offensive. In this, Haig did not play a "hands off" role with his Army commander.

To further Haig's wish for deeper advances on the first day of the assault, British artillery during the preliminary bombardment fired on the Germans' first line positions and those behind. This deeper bombardment may have been possible with increased artillery support, particularly howitzers, however, the necessary increase did not occur. In essence, the same number of artillery pieces were firing on an increased number of targets. This change in plan only spread artillery resources thin which negatively affected the bombardment's impact on German trenches and defences.[148] As a result, many of the German soldiers were able to survive the bombardment and man operational defensive positions.

High Command planning mistakes were compounded by tactical problems on the ground. British artillery tactics were not in tune with the requirements of a modern war. Part of this is due to the fact that in the early years of the War the artillery was viewed by many in the High Command as being merely an auxiliary to the infantry, thus not requiring close attention by them to its tactics. However, it also seems that the artillery itself did not give much thought to ensuring that their shells would actually hit their targets. Matters such as weather conditions and wear and tear on the guns, both of which can effect the accuracy of shots, appear not to have been taken into account often. Further, while techniques for aircraft/artillery cooperation for the spotting of targets were developing, they were in their infancy.[149]

It must be borne in mind though, that many of the gunners, like the infantrymen, were from the New Army. This was the first experience at preliminary bombardment for many and, understandably, the gunners' accuracy and efficiency was not as great as it would become in later battles.[150] For example, earlier we discussed the failure of shrapnel as a wire cutter. This is true only to an extent, for shrapnel could be an effective wire cutter, but it required precise shooting so that the shell exploded just above and in front of the wire. Many of the gunners of the New Army could not achieve this level of accuracy, leading to the wire remaining uncut on July 1.[151]

Even when British shells did hit a German position, sometimes the shells would not explode. There were latent defects in the artillery ammunition. Although British industry had made great strides in supplying the BEF so that the ammunition shortages of 1914-15 would not happen again, this increased output resulted in some quality control problems. One estimate has it that one-third of the shells fired by the British were duds.[152] Whatever the true number is, defective ammunition was a factor in diluting the effectiveness of the preliminary bombardment.

Therefore, despite the massive amount of shells hurled at the Germans prior to the infantry assault, much of the German defences, barbed wire and artillery batteries remained intact and the German soldiers unscathed when the British infantry went "over the top." The defects in the preliminary bombardment were fatal for much of the British attack plan depended on the artillery destroying the German defences and clearing the way for the infantry advance. When the artillery failed, the infantry attack failed.

While the preliminary bombardment was the main cause of failure, it was not the only one. The artillery's protective barrage was often ineffective during the attack. Its "lifts" were often too far spaced. This, along with an inflexible time-table for the "lifts," lead to the barrage out-pacing the infantry that were following. Without a protective barrage in front, it was impossible for the British to successfully assault the well-manned German trenches.

The Germans had a hand in defeating the British too. They held the high ground on the Somme and were able to observe the build up of British forces in the area. The seven day preliminary bombardment put the Germans on notice that an attack was in the offing. They had also tapped British telephone lines, enabling them to obtain details of the coming attack.[153] Further information was obtained from the interrogation of British prisoners captured during raids before July 1.[154]

Also relevant is the effectiveness of the German Army at this point in the war, particularly when fighting on the defensive. As was touched on earlier, with conscription before the War Germany was able to field a huge, well-trained army at War's outset. Although the German Army had sustained heavy casualties in 1914 and 1915, the core of this force still remained in the summer of 1916. Being largely on the defensive in 1915 and following a practice of keeping units in the same sector of front for long periods (contrary to the British practice of rotating troops to different sectors), the German defenders on the Somme were very familiar with the terrain and their defences and were well trained to man them. Pitted against these experienced defenders were the "green" citizen-soldiers of the New Army.[155]

As gloomy as many parts of the front were, it is important to note that disaster did not strike everywhere on the first day of the Somme. In the southern sector of Fourth Army's attack, near the French, four British Divisions experienced success. Here the terrain was more suitable for the attack than in the north, better observation of German defences could be obtained by the British and these defences were not as well developed. Although not all objectives were seized, many were, while one, the Village of Fricourt, fell to the British the following day.

More striking was the success of the French to the south of the British. Using a larger number of heavy howitzers in their preliminary bombardment than the British and employing more sophisticated infantry tactics (advancing in small groups that took advantage of available cover), the French captured virtually all of their objectives for the first day.[156] It is not a coincidence that the only permanent British successes of the day were in the south. Bordering the French, the British here were able to take advantage of the thoroughness of French planning and execution.

These successes aside, the first day of battle on the Somme was a startling defeat for the British. In most places that were attacked, only failure was experienced. Of the approximately 100 000 British soldiers who took part in the attack, about 60 000 were casualties at the end of the day, of which a staggering 20 000 were dead. It became, and still is, the bloodiest day in British military history.

Nine

Summer on the Somme

Despite the massive amount of blood spilled on July 1, British resolve did not crack. Following the disastrous first day, the British High Command changed its strategy. The immediate breakthrough concept was temporarily abandoned in favor of a strategy of attrition. The Battle of the Somme now turned into a wearing out contest, a grisly competition to see who could kill more of the other side.

That the Battle of the Somme turned into a battle of attrition has much to do with Haig's understanding of battle itself. He viewed battle as a structured affair consisting of preparation, attack and exploitation. The attack on the first day of the Somme was seen as a decisive assault, preceded by the Battle of Verdun and the preliminary artillery bombardment as acts of preparation. Haig's concept of battle remained unchanged after the bloody first day of fighting and he viewed the summer fighting as being a renewed act of preparation, wearing down the Germans for a later decisive attack that would lead to a breakthrough.[157]

All through the summer the British attacked. These attacks were based in the south where success had been achieved on the first day of the Battle and were directed in two general directions. From German positions captured on the first day the British attacked to the east, trying to push the Germans back. At the same time, another effort was made to the north and northeast in an effort to capture the Thiepval Ridge that dominated British positions in the south and which had eluded capture on the first day of fighting. The sector in the north that had witnessed such carnage on the first day would remain "quiet."

Compared to July 1st, the British attacks in the summer were on a smaller scale and involved fewer troops. Some of these attacks, such as the one undertaken by XIII and XV Corps on July 14 were successful. In contrast to the attack on the 1st of July, the British employed a short preliminary bombardment, but with a greater concentration of guns. Meanwhile the infantry, under cover of darkness, were able to creep most of the way across No Man's Land before the attack commenced at 3:25 a.m. Shielded by the dark and benefiting from a well conducted artillery program, the initial assault was a complete success and resulted in the capture of the forward German lines. The British attempted to exploit this success by pushing beyond the Germans' forward system, but the infantry were unable to advance further due to strong German defences behind the forward lines. Nevertheless, the capture of the German forward system stands in stark contrast with the failed first day of operations on the Somme.

Other assaults, such as the one which took place on July 22-23 between Guillemont and Pozieres met with no success. On a larger scale than the July 14 attack, but still smaller than July 1, this assault involved III, XIII, XV and Anzac Corps. Unlike the July 14 assault, this attack was poorly coordinated, with soldiers from different divisions attacking at different times. This, compounded by hasty preparations and an inadequate artillery program, allowed the Germans to defeat each separate assault in turn.

It would be a mistake, though, to imagine the Battle of the Somme during this period to involve only large attacks such as those launched on July 14 and July 22-23. Instead, most of the fighting over the summer was on a much smaller scale, consisting of attacks by a mere division, brigade or even just a battalion. These attacks, launched against small sections of the German defences, were often bloodily repulsed by German artillery and machine guns as the defenders on the front and flanks of the attacks could concentrate their firepower on the small and isolated British units struggling across No Man's Land. The net result of these piece-meal attacks was very small gains in return for heavy casualties.[158]

Although the British suffered severe casualties during the summer, the same was true for the Germans. Part of the reason for the Germans' high casualties was due to their defensive strategy. Falkenhayen made it German policy to hold all ground to the last man and, if lost, to immediately counter-attack the British to re-capture it. The consequence of this was that, not only did the Germans lose men in defending their trenches from their British adversaries, but the Germans then went one further and lost more men in counter-attacks. According to one historian, at least 330 counter-attacks were launched by the Germans during the Battle of the Somme.[159]

During this phase of the Battle the composition of the British Armies engaged was transforming. Whereas on July 1 the attackers were almost exclusively from the British Isles (the Newfoundlanders being a notable exception), in the summer of 1916 units from other nations became involved in the fighting. For example, the South African Brigade took part in the battle for Delville Wood in July and the Australians arrived to fight for Pozieres during July and August.

There was also a change in the British command structure. General Sir Hubert Gough and his Reserve Army took charge of the northern sector of the Somme, leaving Rawlinson and his Fourth Army to fight in the south. While most of Gough's area of command was "quiet" he was to direct operations to capture the Thiepval Ridge.

Gough was a cavalryman and a protégé of Haig's. He rose rapidly during the early years of the Great War, starting with leading a cavalry division, but becoming Britain's youngest Army commander in 1916. Gough was thought of by some in the BEF as a "thruster"; being always willing to push forward. A difficult man to work with, he was insistent on his generals having the "offensive spirit" and was quick to remove those from command who were not eager to attack, even when their reasons for hesitating were sound.[160] He was a man who, when a subordinate general, did not mind overstepping his superiors' instructions when he saw fit, became an Army commander who constantly looked over his subordinates' shoulders.

Gough's career in High Command was, on balance, not successful, despite his being an Army commander in all major British actions starting with the Somme and ending with the German 1918 Spring Offensive, following which he was relieved of command. Ironically, while his performance up to the 1918 German Spring Offensive was "spotty," he displayed skill in countering the German Offensive, but was relieved of his command at this point, it seems, for political reasons. All this was in the future though as the Somme was Gough's first battle in High Command.[161]

The summer on the Somme, therefore, was characterized by small scale, fierce British attacks on narrow fronts over increasingly shell-torn and desolate terrain, usually with bloody results, often immediately responded to by the Germans with equally fierce and bloody counter-attacks. As the bodies piled up during the summer on both sides, the strategy of attrition was being carried out in its grimmest sense.

Ten

The Tank Arrives

September 1916 found the Canadians on the Somme to take part in a renewed major offensive. As the summer months drew to a close, Haig believed his forces were ready for another major push and that the Germans were on the verge of cracking. He thought that his wearing down strategy was damaging German morale and that the time was ripe for a decisive blow. In his view, he had to take advantage of the opportunity he thought was presented.[162]

Haig's offensive would involve Rawlinson's Fourth Army delivering the main blow with Gough's Reserve Army and the French 6th Army attacking, respectively, to the north and south of Fourth Army. The plan was for the infantry to attack and break the German line between Flers and Courcelette and for the Cavalry Corps to follow up and exploit the breach he believed the Fourth Army would create. In all, the British deployed 11 infantry divisions. Two of these divisions were Canadian which, as part of the Reserve Army, were given the task of capturing Courcelette on the left flank of the offensive.

Not only did the British have better artillery support for their attack at Flers-Courcelette than they had on July 1, a new weapon that was to change warfare forever, the tank, would make its debut in battle. Despite being few in number (there were only 49) and untested on the battlefield, Haig had high hopes for the new weapon and was keen to use tanks in the upcoming assault. To his mind, anything that could help in the attack should be used in the attack.

The offensive was set for September 15, 1916 with a 6:20 a.m. zero-hour. Focussing on the Canadians, it was 2nd Division that had Courcelette itself as an objective. Jumping-off on time, the Canadians secured the first German line after stiff fighting and taking advantage of the support provided by the single tank that got through. A two-phase battle, the Canadians moved on and captured Courcelette itself later in the day. As usual, the Germans retaliated with shelling and counter-attacks, the 22nd (French

Canadian) Battalion fending off seven counter-attacks that night, but the Canadians could not be dislodged from their newly won territory.[163] Even then the battle for Courcellete was not over, for there were still Germans hiding in cellars and dug-outs and it took two days to completely clear the German defenders.[164]

On the 2nd Division's left, the 3rd Division also met with success, despite not being allowed the time to do a reconnaissance before the attack and the men having to endure heavy German machine gun and artillery fire as they struggled across No Man's Land.[165] They captured most of the German trench system called the Fabeck Graben, finishing off the rest of the task on the 16th. Like their comrades in the 2nd Division, they too were forced to repulse German counter-attacks aimed at re-taking the trench system lost to the Canadians.[166]

As for the larger Flers-Courcelette Offensive, overall it was a limited success. Although most objectives had been achieved and twice the ground had been captured than on July 1 for half the casualties, the German defences were not decisively broken and there was no breakthrough as had been hoped for by Haig.[167] The cavalry did not get the chance to pursue any fleeing Germans.

As for the tanks, they were impressive in terrifying the Germans and assisted in capturing some objectives. However, there were problems associated with their use. The tanks were susceptible to mechanical breakdowns and became bogged down in the shell-torn battlefield environment. Of the 49 tanks available for the offensive, only 30 crossed the start line into battle and of these, only 21 actually did any fighting.[168] As for the 6 tanks that supported the Canadians' attack, 5 went into action, but all were disabled by shell-fire, mechanical breakdowns or became bogged during the fight, with only one reaching its objective.[169] Many "bugs" had to be worked out before the tank could become a truly efficient and effective weapon of war.

Haig has been criticized by some for using tanks on the Somme at a time when they were not available in large numbers. The argument goes that had he waited until larger numbers were available, he could have unleashed a furious, massive tank assault that would have taken the Germans by surprise, terrified them, crushed their defences and swept to victory.

This criticism seems a bit misguided for a number of reasons. First, the tank was an experimental weapon and there were real practical difficulties in deploying tanks in battle. These difficulties could only be overcome by experience on the battlefield, not on the training ground. This early use of tanks was, in actuality, a prudent decision from which the commanders could learn lessons from for future deployments.

The criticism also assumes that the tank was a war winning weapon in itself, which it was not. The tank, slow, mechanically unreliable and vulnerable to battlefield conditions and German artillery, was unsuited for any sort of breakout role once the first German lines were breached. Tanks could only be successful if part of an overall integrated assault including infantry, artillery and aircraft. In the Great War there could be no "tank victory."

Finally, it is easy to imagine that, had Haig decided not to use tanks on the Somme, these very critics would have found fault in Haig for not using tanks and making his attacks with flesh and blood alone.

Criticisms aside, the Flers-Courcelette offensive ushered in a new era in warfare. Armored warfare was born. This important development still has impact and application on the battlefield to this day.

Eleven

Regina Trench

Ever since the disastrous 1st of July, British attention on the Somme was mainly directed in the south, the area in which the most success had been experienced that day. As a result of British attacks since the opening of the Battle, the British had slowly and bloodily pushed forward (east) in the southern sector of the battlefield, while the trench lines in the north remained unmoved. As such, the British (with the French to their south) were steadily creating a large salient pushing into German lines. In an effort to deal with this situation, for the next major offensive on the Somme, not only would Rawlinson's Fourth Army continue to push further east beyond the line gained during the Battle of Flers-Courcelette, but Gough's Reserve Army would launch a major attack northwards.

On the northern flank of this salient lay the Thiepval Ridge which contained strong defensive positions in and around the Village of Thiepval and along the Ridge itself. The Village, on the western edge of the Ridge, was an objective on the first day of Battle, and remained in German hands that day and thereafter, despite subsequent attempts by the British and Australians to dislodge them from their strong position. It was this Ridge, with its formidable trench system and dominating position, that the British and Canadians were now tasked with capturing. Two British divisions attacked on the left with the Village of Thiepval among their objectives, while the Canadians were to attack the right of the Ridge. It was to be a difficult task for the Canadian 1st and 2nd Divisions, as the Thiepval Ridge was criss-crossed with German trenches, seemingly running in all directions.[170]

The British and Canadian attack was set for 12:35 p.m. on September 26 and was preceded by a three day preliminary bombardment, including the use of tear-gas shells. At zero-hour 800 guns erupted, blasting the German trenches with shrapnel and high explosive shells. As the artillery boomed, the British and Canadian infantry, advancing in four waves spaced about 70 to 100 yards apart, went "over the top" and advanced on the German positions.

Looking at the Canadians' attack, despite the intense shelling by the artillery, German resistance was fierce as shells and bullets tore into the attacking soldiers. The Germans had become wise to British artillery tactics, which focussed their bombardment on German trenches. To counter this the defending Germans had moved out of their trenches prior to the attack, manning instead shell holes and ditches ahead of their front line. They were largely able to escape the mass of shells hurled at them and remained in position to mow down their Canadian adversaries.

In the face of such intense opposition, Canadian success was "spotty." Some battalions were stopped in No Man's Land, unable to surmount the storm of steel lashing at them. Those battalions that were able to penetrate the German defences found themselves cut off behind German lines and were pounded by German artillery and counterattacked by German infantry. Despite the enemy onslaught, the Canadians were able to hold onto their gains in some places by day's end, but overall their success had been less than intended.[171]

The Canadians' gains looked especially meagre when compared to the British who, on their left, had taken most of Thiepval Village and were able to complete their conquest in the following days. In addition, to the south, Rawlinson's Fourth Army had made further advances.

On September 27, the Germans made a partial withdrawal on the Canadians' front to Regina Trench, but the depressing fighting continued for another day. Repeatedly the Canadians attacked the German defences, sometimes capturing trenches and positions, but always incurring heavy casualties. By month's end, although most of the Thiepval Ridge had been captured by the British and Canadians, Regina Trench, and thus the northeastern edge of the Ridge, remained under German control.[172]

Regina Trench was a formidable obstacle. Dug on the reverse slope of the Thiepval Ridge, the trench and its wire were difficult for the artillery to hit. Located as it was, protection was given to German reinforcements moving up to the front and they took advantage of this feature, bringing in more troops to repulse the next attack they were sure the Canadians would launch.

It was the 2nd and 3rd Divisions that would make the next attack, already badly depleted by the earlier bitter fighting. Waiting in their jumping off positions in a drizzling rain, many of the Canadian soldiers were hit by "shorts"; friendly shells falling short of their targets. It was a bad omen for things to come. At 3:15 p.m. on October 1 the men attacked and were immediately deluged by enemy artillery, machine guns and rifles. Despite the Canadians' artillery having fired on Regina Trench since late September, the difficulty in hitting the Trench and its wire left the defenders and their defences largely undamaged.

Most of the Canadians' assault broke down in No Man's Land. The German wire, uncut by the bombardment, proved an impossible obstacle to surmount and many of the attackers were blown or shot to pieces in front of the wire. The survivors sought shelter from the fusillade in any spot they could; in a shell hole or behind dead comrades. As in past battles on the Thiepval Ridge, some attackers were able to penetrate into German lines but these men, isolated from their comrades, were overcome by the German defenders, some of these pockets of Canadians fighting to the last man. By day's end, those that could retreated to their original positions, leaving No Man's Land carpeted with Canadian bodies.

A reprieve of sorts was granted to the worn out Canadians as the weather took a turn for the worse inhibiting the generals from any idea of quickly resuming another attack on Regina Trench. It was just temporary though, as the High Command still intended for Regina Trench to be taken and it was still the job of the Canadians to do it.

Between October 2 and October 7 the familiar pattern of activity prior to an assault took place. The artillery shelled Regina Trench and its protective barbed wire, while the infantry busied themselves digging jumping-off trenches; as close as possible to the enemy to leave the Canadians as little time as possible in the dreaded No Man's Land.

This next attack on Regina Trench was made by the 1st and 3rd Divisions on October 8. Like the earlier effort on October 1, this assault was made in the rain. Also like the prior attack, it was a failure.

"Going over the top" at 4:50 a.m., the Canadians were largely able to make their way across No Man's Land with light casualties, but, as before, the German barbed wire was mostly uncut. Even where there were sufficient gaps in the wire, the fact that the artillery could not effectively hit Regina Trench and defences meant that there were ample Germans to wreak havoc amongst the attacking Canadians. Again, parties of Canadians were able to make their way into Regina Trench in places, but with No Man's Land being shelled by German artillery and thick with bullets, it was impossible to reinforce these parties. As on the 1st of October, these small bands of gritty attackers were thrown back to the Canadian trenches by German counter-attacks. The attack on Regina Trench had been another failure, with casualties amounting to over 1 300 (double those suffered in the October 1 assault).[173]

The repetitiveness of this summary of Canadian attacks between September 26 and October 8, while not fully capturing the human suffering of those making the assaults in a meaningful way, does in a sense convey the remorseless, unrelenting nature of much of the fighting during the Battle of the Somme. It should also be noted that the Canadians' experience was not unique during this period. While Rawlinson's Fourth Army assault on September 25 and Gough's Reserve Army assault on September 26 had been, on the whole, successful, the fighting on the Somme thereafter again bogged down into a slug-fest, much as it had during the summer.

There are several reasons why the Canadian attacks on Regina Trench ground down in No Man's Land and before the German wire. As was so often the case with prior assaults, part of the failure lay with the artillery. The British were still relying on 18-pounders to perform wire cutting; not an efficient wire cutter. This, together with the difficulty in actually hitting the German wire and the German practice of repairing any gaps in the wire at night, resulted in the barbed wire still presenting a deadly obstacle for the attackers.

The heavy artillery was similarly ineffective. Tasked with destroying Regina Trench and German strong points, insufficient heavy shells were fired at the German defences. Added to this the heavy artillery, like the 18-pounders, had difficulty hitting Regina Trench, located as it was on a reverse slope.[174]

It was also apparent that the artillery's counter-battery work was ineffective. Time and again during these Canadian attacks, the assault troops and their support were heavily shelled by the Germans after an attack had started. With Canadian attacks being stalled in No Man's Land or at the German front lines, the German artillery was able to pound the infantry as they tried to make some headway.

The result of these deficiencies was, as we have seen, that attack after attack was stopped by uncut German wire, plentiful defenders still manning their defences and German artillery barrages. Infantry alone could not overcome this. It seems as though the Canadian Corps had forgotten the lessons learned from the Battle of Mount Sorrel; that infantry could not capture enemy positions without effective artillery support. However, there were factors at play on the Somme that were absent from the Battle of Mount Sorrel.

While at Mount Sorrel the Canadian Corps was, in a sense, on its own to carry out the battle, the Battle of the Somme was being directed by Haig, the Army commanders and their Headquarters. Pressure from above was placed on subordinate generals to keep on the Germans and wear them down by successive attacks. The assaults launched on Regina Trench were not geared toward any breakthrough, as was the Battle of Flers-Courcelette, rather, they were aimed at capturing tactical points and furthering Haig's concept of wearing out the German Army. Haig was still of the belief that the Germans were on the breaking point and he felt that, if pressure was constantly maintained on the Germans, they would have to crack at some point. His belief was misplaced for, despite the ceaseless British pressure, the Germans never did break under these assaults.[175]

Under this pressure from above to continually launch assaults, attacks were made under unfavorable conditions.[176] With less pressure and more time, attacks like the ones made on Regina Trench may have been avoided or prepared in a more thorough manner.

The Canadian assaults in late September and early October were flawed, tactically at Corps level and strategically by the British High Command. For the men of 1st, 2nd and 3rd Divisions, the depressing attacks on Regina Trench marked the end of their time on the Somme. They were taken out of the line and placed below Vimy Ridge. Here they would remain over the winter and would begin preparations for the great assault on Vimy Ridge in the spring.

Twelve

4th Division

The departure of the 1st, 2nd and 3rd Divisions, along with the Canadian Corps Headquarters, did not sound the end for Canadian involvement on the Somme. The Corps' Divisional artillery remained on the Somme and the newest division, 4th Division, arrived. Having come to the Western Front in the summer, the 4th Division moved to the Somme in the fall to take part in the closing acts of the Battle. Fighting as part of the British II Corps, their initial role on the Somme was to complete the task that their comrades had been unable to finish; the capture of Regina Trench.

The 4th Division's attack went in on October 21, aimed at capturing a portion of Regina Trench. Unlike previous efforts to take the Trench, the artillery bombardment was very effective, breaking up the German barbed wire and the infantry experienced little problem in entering the enemy's trench. Once there, they witnessed the effect the improved artillery performance had on the German defenders as many Germans were found dead, while those who had survived were quick to surrender. Casualties amongst the Canadians were light, most being incurred after the portion of the Trench attacked had been captured when the Germans shelled the victorious Canadians. Unwilling to leave the Canadians alone, the Germans also counter-attacked, but the artillery was effective again and repulsed the German efforts.

There still remained a portion of the formidable Regina Trench in German hands; the far eastern portion. Originally scheduled for the morning of October 24, the 4th Division's attack to secure the rest of the Trench was delayed until the next morning due to wet weather. This postponement did not benefit the assault troops any, as they were forced to remain in their jumping-off positions all day and over-night in a pouring rain.

Attacking with half the strength of the assault on the 21st and much reduced artillery support, the attack became another in a growing list of Canadian failures before Regina Trench. German riflemen shot at the Canadians from the front, machine guns from the flanks and artillery shells fell from above. None of the attackers made it to Regina Trench. Those who survived the metal storm went to ground in shell holes, waiting for darkness to slip away to the safety of friendly lines.

The inevitable next effort at Regina Trench was delayed as rain and mud had turned the battlefield into a quagmire. However, by November 8 the weather became cold and the ground more suitable for offensive operations. No date was set for the Canadians to renew the fighting, rather, the attack was to go in once the heavy howitzers had the opportunity to effectively bombard the remainder of Regina Trench for two straight days. This they had the chance to do and the 4th Division's assault was scheduled for 12:00 a.m. on November 11.

This operation, made with greater infantry strength than previous attacks by 4th Division and with strong and effective artillery support, was entirely successful. The infantry moved quickly across No Man's Land, avoiding the German artillery barrage, and stormed Regina Trench. German resistance was light, as were Canadian casualties, and within two and a half hours the objective was captured and consolidated. As usual, the Germans launched counter-attacks, but they were repulsed. Finally, after great effort, over a month of battle and many lost lives, the whole of the now battered and broken Regina Trench was in Canadian hands.[177]

But the Battle of the Somme was unrelenting and there would be no let up in the fighting. The 4th Division's success at Regina Trench was only a preliminary move for the next part in Haig's plan. Now, to further Haig's aim of wearing down the Germans, but also to put him in a better position vis-à-vis Britain's allies at the upcoming Allied conference at Chantilly, another major offensive was going to be launched on the Somme.[178] (In Haig's defence though, it should be noted that the French High Command was pressuring the British to continue offensive operations and on a much more ambitious scale than Haig would allow.)[179]

Like the effort of the Canadian Corps in the capture of Courcelette, the 4th Division's forthcoming attack was one part of a larger offensive; the Battle of the Ancre. As was touched on earlier, the northern front of the Somme battlefield had not moved since the horror experienced there on July 1. From that date on the British had been steadily pushing east (albeit slowly and at much cost) into German held territory on the southern sector of the battlefield. This southern advance left a bulge of German held territory to the north of the ground captured by the British since July 1.

Under General Gough, the British Fifth Army (the re-named Reserve Army) was to attack this bulge from the west and south using 11 infantry divisions. Particular importance was placed on the capture of Beaumont Hamel, the German defensive position that had devastated the Newfoundland Battalion on July 1. However, unlike the earlier major offensives of July 1 and Flers-Courcelette, the Battle of the Ancre was not planned as a breakthrough offensive. Instead, its goals were limited; to secure some of the original objectives that were not captured on July 1 and to extend the gains achieved by the British in the south since then. If all went well, the German bulge would be, to some extent, flattened.[180]

Taking place between November 13 to 19 in cold weather and muddy terrain, the Battle of the Ancre, like Flers-Courcelette before it, was only partially successful. Many objectives were achieved by the British attackers, but others remained beyond their reach. Strong points like Beaumont Hamel were taken, but the German bulge was not flattened as much as had been intended.[181]

As for the Canadian 4th Division, its objective was symbolic of the Battle of the Ancre itself. It was to attack and capture Desire Trench, the next trench to the north after Regina Trench. The assault was not geared at any breakthrough, rather, it was meant simply to improve the Fifth Army's tactical position.

Following the first snow of the year that fell the night before, 4th Division's attack commenced on November 18. In the centre of the assault things went well. Artillery support was effective and the Canadians secured Desire Trench and pushed a ways beyond. Over 600 Germans were captured and two counter-attacks were beaten back. However, on the left (attacked by a British unit) and the right (attacked by the Canadians), success was elusive, with most of the attackers being forced back by the Germans to their start line.[182]

After the grim battle for Desire Trench, the Canadians' time on the Somme was over. The soldiers of the 4th Division made their way to Vimy Ridge to join their comrades in the Canadian Corps. The fighting on the Ancre was also to be the end of the Battle of the Somme. While it is questionable whether the British could, or should, have continued pushing on, the weather once again intruded and heavy rains made any further offensive operations impossible. After almost five months of brutal combat, what did the Battle achieve?

Thirteen

The Somme

The Battle of the Somme is truly one of the most important battles in the history of the English speaking world. It, more than any other battle, changed peoples' views towards warfare. War was no longer a glorious adventure, rather, it was a dreadful, bloody business.

The human cost of the Battle was tremendous. British casualties amounted to about 420 000 with the French adding another 200 000 to the grisly total. German losses were between 500 000 to 600 000. The Canadians' share of the British casualty roll came to just over 24 000 killed, wounded and missing.[183]

These massive losses came as a huge shock to the people of the British Empire. Most disturbing to the people at home was that it was the volunteers that bore the brunt of the "butcher's bill." While a human life is a human life, prior to the Somme most casualties in the BEF were suffered by Regulars or Territorials, individuals who had prior military experience. On the Somme, the losses were suffered by clerks, accountants, lawyers and grocers. In this context, the casualties sustained had a different, more personal effect, on the people back home. Most people knew someone who was killed, wounded or missing. Added to this was the fact that the Somme was the first battle in which the British had suffered such mass casualties.

Bearing in mind the huge losses, it is difficult to assess whether the Battle of the Somme was a victory or a defeat. On one side is the clear fact that the Somme did not result in any breakthrough of the German lines as had been anticipated on both July 1 and at Flers-Courcelette. The Battle of the Somme did not result in the decisive defeat of the German Army. Although an advance twenty miles wide and six miles deep had been made into German held territory and the German defences were being continually pushed back, the German line never broke. Despite incessant and determined attacks, the Germans were always able to form new defensive positions behind the one that the British had just captured. Under these circumstances, it is difficult to equate mere territorial gains, bought in blood, as a victory.

Strategically, the performance of Haig and his Army commanders was not very good. Haig seemed to be consistently operating under the illusion that a great break-through and a decisive battle that would comprehensively defeat the German Army was possible on the Somme. This was illusory as it is arguable that a breakthrough was never possible on the Western Front. Great War armies could never move faster than the pace of the infantry or beyond the range of their slow moving artillery. As such, even when trench lines were captured, the German defenders were always able to build a new line out of reach of the British infantry and artillery and move reinforcements from other sectors to man them.

This emphasis on the breakthrough had a negative impact on the battlefield. In times of major offensives, the artillery resources often could not adequately deal with the large number of objectives given. The result was that assaults often broke down either before the front line or when trying to push on following the capture of the forward lines. Too many German defences, defenders and artillery pieces were able to survive the artillery bombardments and the attacks, or the attempts at pressing on beyond the first defences, were beaten back.

Even when there was success in capturing objectives, the infantry could not turn this into a breakthrough. By this point the infantry were spent by casualties and exhaustion and it was impossible for them to attack further German positions. Being at the limit of British artillery range, the Germans at these points could then amass counter-attacks and artillery to pound the British infantry in relative safety. A breakthrough was impossible.

Major offensives are only part of the story of the Somme. As we have seen, Haig believed that a period of preparation, or wearing out, was necessary before launching a "breakthrough" offensive. It was during these "wearing out" phases of the Battle of the Somme that incessant small scale attacks were made to inflict casualties on the German defenders and damage German morale. However, at no point during the Battle of the Somme did these wearing out attacks succeed in breaking German morale to a point that a breakthrough could be made. Rather, the effect of these wearing out battles was to commit British soldiers to hurried, piece-meal attacks, without adequate preparation or artillery support. The majority of these attacks were unsuccessful, inflicting heavy casualties on the British and, even when there was success, made no impact on the larger Battle.

Looking further down the chain of command, the performance of British and Canadian corps and division commanders on the Somme appears to be "spotty." While there were some notable successes, such as the Canadian Corps' capture of Courcelette, there almost seems to have been one unsuccessful assault for each successful one. When there was a successful attack, the methods employed were not necessarily used in subsequent attacks.

An example may be the 4th Division's attacks on Regina Trench. Their first effort on October 21 was a well conducted affair, both with regards to infantry and artillery. However, the next attack on October 24 was made with half the infantry and reduced artillery support and met with failure. The Canadians then seem to have reverted to their earlier methods and the attack on November 11 met with success similar to that experienced on the 21st.

In defence of the corps and division commanders, that many of their attacks met with no success may have had less to do with the methods that they employed than with the directions they were receiving from above. It was the High Command that set the objectives, pushed for incessant attacks and controlled most of the artillery resources. In essence, there was only so much that the subordinate generals could do within the parameters the High Command set for them.

However, on the positive side, in any discussion of the Somme it must be remembered that it involved a relatively "green" citizen army matched against a German Army filled with soldiers who had prior military experience. In this context, it is to the credit of the New Army and the Dominion volunteers that they "gave it as good as they got it." It is often overlooked that the Battle of the Somme did cause the Germans huge casualties. Their accounts of the Battle match those of the British with respect to blood, mud and suffering. Between the Battles of the Somme and Verdun, the German Army suffered about one million casualties and their strong core of experienced junior officers and NCOs had been gutted.[184] These heavy losses would be felt keenly by the Germans as the War dragged on.

Relevant too is that British power and prowess on the battlefield was just emerging in 1916. The Battle of the Somme was the first battle in which the British were the major player, rather than the French, and employed multiple British Armies. The BEF's performance at all ranks, including the Canadians, would improve as the war went on and the Battle of the Somme was really the starting point for this development.

Seen in this light, there were advantages gained by the British in terms of damage to the enemy (both human and material) and experience in major operations. Nevertheless, the heavy losses suffered made these gains seem deeply tainted, especially in popular opinion, then and since.

Fourteen

The Offensive

With Germany invading Belgium and France in 1914, occupying portions of these countries and exploiting their occupied territories, the Allies were motivated to drive the Germans out. While the Germans launched offensives too, they were more inclined to stay on the defensive and use their occupied territories as "bargaining chips" to force a peace on terms favorable to them. The Allies were in a difficult strategic position.

Taking the offensive in the Great War was no easy task. The lack of mobile firepower, the inadequate communications and the vast reserves of manpower created a situation in which any offensive would run out of steam once the attackers reached the limit of their artillery. Technology had advanced to give the defence great firepower, but without corresponding developments to assist the attackers in overcoming these defences.

In the early years of the War the balance was even more tilted towards the defence. The key to any successful Great War attack, adequate artillery support, was not present. The Allies' lacked the necessary guns, howitzers and ammunition at the War's outset. It would take many months to correct this situation. Compounding the attackers' difficulties, weapons that would become common place in trench warfare, such as trench mortars, grenades and light mobile machine guns, were not available as the Allies had not expected a war in the trenches. Attacks relying on the infantry armed with rifles alone failed with heavy casualties.

By the time of the Battle of the Somme, the first large British offensive in the Great War, steps had been taken to address these problems. Artillery and its ammunition were in abundance and the infantry were armed with suitable weapons for trench warfare. The New Army had arrived on the Western Front and the Dominions, such as Canada, had expanded their forces. It would appear that the time was right to launch a grand offensive and win the War.

It did not turn out this way as British inexperience in modern offensive warfare became apparent. Overly ambitious objectives were often set for the artillery and infantry, leading to failed attacks with very heavy casualties. Effective cooperation between the artillery and infantry was often lacking as was cooperation between attacking infantry units. At times the battle bogged down into small, hastily prepared, piecemeal attacks that were relatively easily repulsed by the Germans. Adding to British problems was that the BEF, including the Canadians, was a "green" army, compared to their veteran German opponents. In general, the quality of British preparations and execution was "spotty."

Nevertheless, the British were learning the ways of modern warfare during the Battle of the Somme and some successful operations were undertaken, involving effective coordination between the artillery and infantry. The unveiling of the tank at Flers-Courcelette ushered in a new dynamic; armored warfare. Arguably the most important development arising from the Battle was that the BEF changed from a "citizen's army" to a professional fighting force.

Following the Somme the BEF, including the Canadians, digested its experience in the Battle and tried to formulate more effective methods for overcoming the power of the defence. As we shall see in the upcoming discussion on the Battle of Vimy Ridge, these lessons were taken to heart and successfully applied there.

Part III

Winter 1917

One

Vimy Ridge

Located in north-eastern France, Vimy Ridge was an important military objective on the Western Front because it is the commanding feature in the surrounding landscape. Being higher than any nearby hill or ridge, whoever held Vimy Ridge could dominate their foe holding the lower ground. However, perhaps surprisingly, it is not an insurmountable ridge from the Canadian (western) side. Instead, the Ridge rises gently, with its highest point being in the north at Hill 145, the location of the modern day Vimy Memorial. From this high point, the crest of the Ridge gently slopes to the south-east, with another high point (Hill 135) around the Village of Thelus before the Ridge tails off. From Hill 145 to the Ridge's southern end is about 7 000 yards. To the north-west of Hill 145 and separated from Vimy Ridge is a small hill named the Pimple (also known as Hill 120). Once on the crest, the importance of Vimy Ridge becomes clear. Dropping steeply off on the eastern side, Vimy Ridge provides a dominating view of the Douai plain stretching out to the east.

Although Vimy Ridge was new to the Canadians, Vimy was not new to combat. The Germans took possession of the Ridge early in the War and two massive French offensives in 1915 were aimed at the capture of it. The scars of these battles were still clearly visible in early 1917. Signaller Donald MacPherson (9th Battery CFA) wrote in his diary on February 20, 1917:

> The whole countryside is a desolate ruin, showing unmistakable evidence of very severe fighting earlier in the war. The fields and hillsides are pocked with shell-holes and lined with the networks of old trenches. Where once stood happy villages now only battered walls and ruined streets remain. Here and there by the wayside a rude cross marks the lonely grave of some departed hero. The civilian population has long since gone to places more remote from the frontline.[185]

Echoing these comments, G.T. Hancox (Princess Patricia's Canadian Light Infantry) recalled that: "For months we had been on the lower slopes of Vimy Ridge looking up at the Germans. All we could see was a barren waste of mine craters and shell holes; no buildings, no trees, nothing but churned up earth and chalk."[186]

At night No Man's Land could appear even more grotesque. Private Will Bird of the 42nd Battalion (Royal Highlanders of Canada) remembered the strange and illuminating effect a Verey Light flare had over No Man's Land on one of his early tours in the line at Vimy:

> Over the tangle of wire in front lay the no man's land about which we had heard. Not two hundred yards away were the Germans in their trenches. A thin stalk of silver shot up as we looked, curved over in a graceful parabola and flowered into a luminous glow, pulsating and wavering, flooding the earth below with a weird, whiteness. It was a Verey light. We craned our necks and stared. Jumbled earth and debris, jagged wreckage; it looked as if a gigantic upheaval had destroyed all the surface and left only a festering wound. Everything was shapeless, ugly and distorted.[187]

The shattered human remains from the earlier fighting between the French and the Germans were still strewn around Vimy. Corporal Donald Fraser (now promoted and in the 6th Machine Gun Company) recorded:

> As soon as we were settled down in our new home, my failing exerted itself and when I noticed the sky was downcast and the lighting poor, I set out on the prowl to reconnoitre the ground for evidence of fighting. We were at the tail end of a dark ravine and a series of old fallen down trenches crisscrossed from one side to the other. Bending low I had only gone a few yards when I came across a couple of graves, one containing the remains of an unknown Frenchman, and the other that of a Foot Chasseur. As the light further waned and I could expose myself more, evidence of terrific fighting revealed itself. French and German dead lay around in strange confusion. I was kept busy cutting buttons off their tunics for souvenirs.
>
> . . .
>
> I made a cursory exploration of several hundred yards, carefully picking my way along the trenches. There were several crosses here and there, but most of the dead were unburied and though there were many Germans, the French predominated. Seventy yards away was a German cemetery. Most of the crosses were broken. The inscriptions showed that the deaths occurred in August of 1915.
>
> . . .

Proceeding up the ravine along a broken-down trench, I observed a row of dug-outs built against the side of the ridge. The first dug-out had a corrugated iron roof pretty well smashed in by a shell. Peering through the entrance I was astonished to see, almost in the skeleton stage, a man in underclothes reclining on a bed. Below on the floor lay the remains of two other Germans. They must have met death suddenly. I cut three buttons off the tunic of one of them. Several of the other dug-outs that were smashed in contained more bodies, or rather skeletons. The dug-outs were lavishly furnished with beds, dressing tables, chairs and rugs, obviously stolen from neighbouring French houses. The Germans must have been caught in a surprise attack for most of them were half dressed, and apparently those that escaped destruction, ran away for good when their comrades were left where they fell. Even to one nerved to the sight of dead, it was a peculiar experience peeping into dug-outs in this quiet and dark ravine and witnessing the result of tragedies enacted over a year ago. I am perfectly sure I was about the first to explore this ravine since the attack swept forward and left it a second No Man's Land. A little distance away a cross was seen stating that underneath were buried seven Frenchmen and eight Bosches.[188]

For the Canadians, having to live amongst the uncollected dead from these earlier battles was difficult, and the rats that feasted on the corpses were not a welcome addition. Lieutenant-Colonel Agar Adamson of the Princess Patricia's Canadian Light Infantry related in a letter to his wife:

We are suffering a good deal of irritation from rats. At the bottom door of this cellar we have to screen it off two feet high with chicken wire to keep them out, but they still get in. When the French took this part of the line, they found many large caves, one large enough to hold 2000 men, but the air soon became so bad and only 100 are allowed to occupy it. In one cave leading into the trench, the Germans refused to come out and shot a French officer who went down, shouting out you will not be killed if you give yourselves up. They then put smoke bombs down the shaft and suffocated them all. 280 of them. They are still huddled together as they died. It is a dreadful and unsavoury sight with thousands of rats. I am having the shaft closed and sealed up with cement. Next tour I think I will have a cross put up.[189]

In the spring of 1916 it was the turn of the British to hold the line around Vimy Ridge, relieving the French forces who were needed as reinforcements for the desperate battle being waged at Verdun. While Vimy was a quiet sector compared to what was happening at Verdun and what would take place on the Somme, there were nevertheless some bitter encounters. The spring of 1916 would see an intense period of mining and counter-mining by the combatants at Vimy, and the detonation of these underground mines created a battlefield dotted with large craters. Captain D.E. Macintyre (Brigade-Major 4th Brigade) remembered how they shaped No Man's Land:

> After months of this kind of underground warfare, the front lines disintegrated and were replaced by dozens of enormous craters, some of them 120 feet across by 60 feet deep, large enough to hold a fair-sized building. These gradually were filled two-thirds with water . . . In an air photograph, it looked exactly like a picture of the moon. We had forty of these mine craters on our Divisional front, so thick that they sometimes touched each other.[190]

There were small shifts in the line as a result of the small, but sharp, engagements that followed the explosion of mines, but none of these changed the overall situation; the Germans held the high ground and the British below wanted to take it.

Having been in German hands for years, they took pains to try to ensure that the key position of Vimy Ridge would not fall to the Allies. Beneath its clay topsoil, Vimy Ridge consists of chalky earth. Within this chalky earth the Germans discovered medieval tunnels and caves which they supplemented with deep dugouts and tunnels of their own. These dugouts and tunnels, both ancient and modern, provided the Germans with excellent refuge from Allied artillery bombardments.

In addition to the dugouts and tunnels, the Germans had constructed a formidable trench system to defend the Ridge. From the front line facing the Canadians all the way up the Ridge and behind the crest, the Germans had made extensive defensive preparations. The area was cut by firing trenches running north to south and communication trenches going west to east. Machine gun emplacements, trench mortar emplacements and other strong points were built into the trench system to command potential avenues of attack. Deep dugouts were made into the trench walls, reaching down into the earth to protect the German garrisons from Canadian shelling.

No Man's Land was not very wide at any point on Vimy Ridge, but this was particularly true at the centre of the Ridge. In many places here No Man's Land was only as wide as old mine craters. Even a veteran officer such as Lieutenant-Colonel Agar Adamson (Princess Patricia's Canadian Light Infantry) found this to be a unique situation. Referred to at the time as the Crater Line, he described it to his wife:

> Our front line is most curious, consisting of craters with the Boche on one lip and we on the other, less than thirty feet apart. The craters are about 20 feet deep, filled by barbed wire thrown in by both sides.[191]

At spots like this the Canadians and Germans were uncomfortably close. Private Will Bird of the 42nd Battalion (Royal Highlanders of Canada) recalled an experience on sentry duty:

We could hear the Germans walking in their trenches, hear them coughing, hear them turning a creaking windlass that would be hauling up chalk from a dugout under construction. At daylight we put up small periscopes on slivers stuck in the sandbagged parapet and watched them until dark.[192]

The Germans ensured that their artillery was positioned to take advantage of Vimy Ridge's dominance. Much of the German artillery was placed behind the steep eastern slope to utilize the protection it offered from Canadian observation and artillery shells. Complimenting this was the advantage the Ridge gave the Germans in observing Canadian lines. So situated, the Germans were in a good position to shell the Canadian soldiers in the lower ground below.

Due to the natural and man-made defences of Vimy Ridge, it was considered by the Germans to be impregnable; their most powerful position on the Western Front. Indeed, one cocky German officer captured by the Canadians in a trench raid brashly remarked to his captors that, while the Canadians may try to reach the crest of Vimy Ridge, those who make it will be so few that they could be brought back to Canada in a rowboat.[193]

It was a difficult task facing the men of the Canadian Corps. The strong defences of Vimy Ridge had withstood attacks before. From the Ridge the Germans had the advantage of observation and shelter for their artillery. The Canadians would have to be extremely careful in their preparations for the offensive, lest their activity be spotted, triggering a German artillery response. Their foe was up to the challenge, realizing the importance of the position they held and buttressed by their confidence in having defeated earlier Allied attempts to capture Vimy Ridge.

Two

Winter Weather

The Winter of 1917 was not a pleasant one for the Canadians or their German counterparts. While the weather during this period may not be of great concern for historians, it was for the troops. They were the ones who had to work, do sentry duty and conduct patrols each and every day.

January 1917 started dull and wet. The Royal Canadian Regiment's January 2 War Diary entry captured the muddy conditions:

> Cloudy with scattered showers. All dugouts excepting large one on "C" Co. front are leaking badly. B.H.Q. (Battalion Headquarters) dugout has half an inch of mud and water on the floor. The trenches are in as bad condition as they have been up to the present. Some of the Crater Posts cannot be reached in day time, as the only route is overland. Overland routes are generally in use on the whole front. The German trenches seem to be quite as bad, for they are also going overland. (parenthesis added)[194]

Not only did wet weather such as this make movement difficult, it also made movement dangerous. Exposing oneself to enemy eyes by moving overland rather than through the trenches was tempting fate. The snipers of 3rd Division took advantage of their German adversaries' difficulties, claiming 25 hits on January 1 alone.[195]

The wet weather was soon replaced by a cold spell. Starting with a heavy snow in mid-January and ending in late February, the weather at Vimy Ridge became quite cold. In the words of the War Diarist for the 7th Brigade CFA (perhaps with a tinge of homesickness), the weather was "not unlike Canadian weather."[196] Private Will Bird recalled the conditions at their coldest:

The weather turned the coldest France had known in thirty years. All the ground was frozen like iron. We wore leather jerkins over our greatcoats, had Balaclavas under our steel helmets and socks on our hands. The supply of gloves was only enough for oldtimers.[197]

While cold weather such as this may make a sentry's finger tips freeze, it was not altogether a bad development. Cold weather hardened the ground, allowing the soldiers to repair their trenches and dugouts that were crumbling from the recent episode of wet weather.

The weather became milder in late February and it remained quite variable for the rest of the Winter. Clear and bright spells, dull and grey days or cold and snowy periods were the soldiers' experience. Whatever the weather, it impacted the men on the ground and military operations.

Ground mist (which was common during the Winter) impeded the artillery observers from finding targets and watching the fall of the shells. Clear and bright weather, while good for the artillery observers in the day, was not so good for patrols in No Man's Land at night. A bright moon at night provided just enough light for enemy sentries to see patrols creeping about in No Man's Land. Snow added to the patrollers' difficulties as the crunch of footsteps on snow could give away a patrol's presence. Wind direction and strength were important too, for they affected the feasibility of releasing poison gas from cylinders and smoke barrages to cover raids.

Of all the kinds of weather experienced during the Winter at Vimy, it was the periodic thaws that were likely the least welcome. While thaws did bring with them warmer weather, they caused much damage to the trench systems. Trench walls would fall in, mud would stick to boots and anyone moving through the trenches became bogged down. The mud benefited no one. Lieutenant W.T. Alexander described the mud in a letter:

> The worst feature of the war in the winter time especially, is the mud. I don't think I could describe it for you and do it justice. However, you will have some idea of it when I tell you that I walked in one place for half-a-mile and each step I took landed me away over the knees. Of course we have rubber boots which come up to our thighs, but, although they save us to some extent from being troubled with wet feet, they are very slippery, and often one finds oneself sitting in a sort of miniature lake of mud admiring the scenery and making the air blue with cuss words.[198]

As can be imagined, the weather was an important factor in daily life at Vimy. Overall cold, there was variation, from snowy winter storms to clear and crisp days, with muddy thaws in between. Having to hold the trenches at Vimy, the soldiers were exposed to them all.

Three

Generals and Their Men

By January 1, 1917, the Canadian Corps was an experienced military formation, all Divisions having endured intense combat during the Battle of the Somme. While the soldiers were originally drawn from civilian ranks, it was not really a "citizen's army" anymore. Many of the men and officers were combat veterans and those who were "green" reinforcements were absorbed into experienced Canadian units and learned from their seasoned comrades. Through its combat experience, the Canadian Corps was turning from a "citizen's army" into a professional fighting force.

For the first time in the Great War, all four of the Canadian Divisions were united in one place. A division was a powerful fighting force, consisting of about 20 000 men at full strength.[199] Commanded by a major-general, within each division there were units of infantry, field artillery, Vickers machine gunners, trench mortars, engineers and field ambulances.[200] On the march a division took up approximately fifteen miles of road and it took about seven hours for the whole division to pass any given point.[201]

Each division contained three infantry brigades. Consisting of about 4 000 soldiers (at full strength) and commanded by a brigadier-general, a brigade had four infantry battalions. Each battalion had about 1 000 men when up to full strength (a rarity). Command of an infantry battalion was entrusted to a lieutenant-colonel. It was with his battalion that the soldier most identified with. When asked what unit he served with, the infantry soldier would invariably reply with his battalion's name or number. The battalion was also the unit the soldier felt the most pride in, taking satisfaction in the battalion's accomplishments and, to an extent, competition with other battalions.

The battalion was not the smallest unit in the infantry, though, as it was divided into four companies, each company being commanded by a major or a captain. Within a company there were four platoons, each under a lieutenant. The smallest unit was the section, of which there were four in a platoon, each lead by a NCO. It was within the platoon and section that the closest personal ties and friendships were often made. These were the men that a soldier lived with, marched with, held the trenches with and went into battle with.

Turning to the divisional artillery, it was also organized into brigades, with three artillery brigades in each division. While the infantry was further sub-divided into battalions, the artillery's organizational equivalent was the battery. Like the infantryman and his battalion, it was with his battery that the gunner most identified with. There were four batteries in an artillery brigade with each battery having four field guns or howitzers (the number of guns or howitzers per battery was increased to six for the offensive).

Looking now at the men who lead the Canadians at Vimy, the Canadian Corps was part of the BEF's First Army, commanded by the 56-year-old General Sir Henry Horne, an artillerist. Horne rose rapidly up the ranks in the Great War. Starting as a brigadier-general, he lead a Corps on the Somme and rose to command First Army in September of 1916. Always conscious of the casualties his men faced in battle, Horne was an efficient and capable general whose consultative command style allowed him (and his Army) to benefit from suggestions provided by subordinates. Leading First Army for the rest of the War, Horne was a reliable Army commander. He was also to have a long association with the Canadian Corps, since the Canadians were part of his Army for most of the War's remainder, with a couple of notable exceptions (the Battles of Passchendaele in 1917 and Amiens in 1918).

In terms of battle planning, the ideal in the British Army was for the "man on the spot" to do it, leaving the High Command to oversee the plan (although, as we have seen from Haig's interference with Rawlinson on the Somme, the ideal was not always achieved). At Vimy Ridge the "man on the spot" in charge of the Canadian Corps and planning the upcoming Battle was Lieutenant-General Sir Julian Byng. A 55-year-old British aristocrat who served in the cavalry before the War, Byng was on familiar terms with the British royal family. The King referred to him by nickname, "Bungo" (this was a nickname from Byng's school days, his older brothers being nicknamed "Byngo" and "Bango").[202] Byng had a distinguished record in the War to date, having served on the Western Front and at Gallipoli, but he was initially puzzled over his appointment to command the Canadian Corps, a people he admitted he knew nothing about.

Nevertheless, the aristocratic Byng and the "rough and ready" Canadians made a good match. Byng's earnest interest in the welfare of his troops, his casual manner and sense of humor, his frequent tours of the line and emphasis on pre-battle preparation for all ranks, won him the respect of the Canadians who served under him.[203] Lieutenant-Colonel Agar Adamson (Princess Patricia's Canadian Light Infantry) described a visit from General Byng to his Battalion in a letter to his wife:

I have had the Corps Commander with me all morning. He is very intense and wants to know and see everything. He is very thorough. I wish we had more men like him.[204]

NAC-PA1356 – General Officer Commanding the Canadian Corps at the Battle of Vimy Ridge, Lieutenant-General Sir Julian Byng.

Byng would be the Canadian Corps' commander until just after the Battle of Vimy Ridge when he was promoted to command the British Third Army; a position he held until the end of the War. Later in life, he would become Canada's Governor-General. Like Horne, Byng was open to suggestions from those who served below him and this commendable characteristic allowed Canada's greatest general to rise to prominence.[205]

This general was Major-General Sir Arthur Currie who commanded the 1st Division. Prior to the War he had been a British Columbian teacher, real estate and insurance broker and member of Canada's militia. Despite this inauspicious background in military affairs, Currie rose during the conflict to become one of the most accomplished generals of the War, on either side, and the greatest general in Canada's history. Not only did General Currie lack a distinguished military pedigree before the war, he did not look like the stereotypical commander. A rather large man with a pear shaped figure and soft face, he was nick-named "Guts and Gaiters" by his troops.[206] At the time of Vimy Currie was 41 years old.

Beneath this unmilitary appearance resided a mind that quickly grasped the fundamentals of trench warfare. Currie realized the value of reconnaissance, pre-battle training and preparation for all ranks and the requirement for cooperation between the artillery and infantry. His orders were clear and invariably based on a sound understanding of his soldiers' strengths and lessons learned from past battles, as well as an appreciation of the strengths and weaknesses of his adversary.

NAC-PA1370 – Canada's most successful general, Major-General Sir Arthur Currie. He commanded 1st Division at the Battle of Vimy Ridge and later the Canadian

Currie adhered to the "bite and hold" offensive philosophy. This placed emphasis on limited advances, with objectives within the range of friendly artillery support, followed up by consolidation of the objectives once captured. In the years of trench warfare, the "bite and hold" offensive philosophy became the most effective method of attack.[207]

Arthur Currie's rise in the Canadian Corps was rapid. Starting the War leading a brigade, he was elevated to command the 1st Division in the autumn of 1915. Following the Battle of Vimy Ridge and the promotion of General Byng to Britain's Third Army, Currie was promoted to command the Canadian Corps in June 1917. He was the first Canadian to hold this position, which he held for the rest of the War.[208]

Currie was shy and reserved, which gave him the appearance of aloofness. Thus, while those who served closely with him came to love the man, this feeling did not filter down to the other ranks. For them there was not love, but respect, based on General Currie's genuine concern for their welfare, along with his ability to lead them to victories.[209]

This was the man who lead the 1st Division at Vimy and later the Canadian Corps. Currie's contribution to the Allied war effort was impressive. Although he did not look the type, he was one of the best generals that the Great War produced.[210]

Commanding the 2nd Division was Major-General Henry Burstall. An English speaking Quebecker, General Burstall was unlike Currie in that he was a regular army officer before the War. He also had prior military experience having served in the Boer War at the turn of the century. During the Great War, Burstall had been in charge of the Canadian Corps' artillery before taking command of the 2nd Division.[211]

Following the death of General Mercer at the Battle of Mount Sorrel, command of the 3rd Division passed to Major-General Louis Lipsett. From Ireland rather than Canada, Lipsett, like Burstall, was a professional soldier. He began the War as a Lieutenant-Colonel heading the historic 8th Battalion (90th Winnipeg Rifles) and his rise followed in Currie's wake. The 8th Battalion was part of Currie's 2nd Brigade at the beginning of the War and when Currie was promoted to command the 1st Division, Lipsitt took over the 2nd Brigade. Perhaps surprisingly, it was Lipsett who taught Currie tactics when Currie was in the militia before the War.[212]

Lipsett, like most commanders in the BEF, was concerned for the welfare of those who served under him. The officers in his Division were well aware of his instruction that the soldiers' needs had to be placed before those of the officers.[213] Tied to this was Lipsett's habit of prowling the front lines so that he could understand the situation his soldiers faced. Both of these qualities made Lipsett popular with his troops.

Leading the 4th Division was Major-General David Watson. An English speaking Quebecker like General Burstall, Watson came from humble origins. An orphan child with little formal education, he nevertheless overcame these obstacles and became owner of the Quebec Chronicle newspaper. Like Currie, Watson was a member of Canada's militia before the War and he went from commanding the 2nd (Eastern Ontario) Battalion, to the 5th Brigade and finally the 4th Division. He was the oldest of Canada's divisional generals, being 48.[214]

These generals were members of a group much maligned by historians. No myth surrounding the Great War is more pervasive than that of the "chateau generals." According to it, while the soldiers suffered in the trenches, the generals sat in their comfortable, extravagant chateaus, far from the line, sipping champagne and eating caviar, oblivious to the discomforts of the other ranks and safe from all dangers. This was not quite the truth.

Being a Great War general was not a safe occupation. In the years 1914 to 1918, 78 British generals were killed and a further 146 were wounded or captured, the vast majority in action.[215] One battle, the Battle of Loos in 1915, was particularly hard on the generals as eight became casualties, including three major-generals who were killed in action.[216]

As for generals in the Canadian Corps, Major-General Malcolm Mercer, commanding the 3rd Division at the time, was killed in action at the outset of the Battle of Mount Sorrel in June 1916.[217] In the entire War, eight brigadier-generals from the Canadian Corps were wounded in action. One of these was Brigadier-General Williams who was wounded at Mount Sorrel when General Mercer was killed. Unable to escape from the attacking Germans, he was captured and became a prisoner of war.[218] Added to these casualties was the death of Major-General Lipsett, commander of the 3rd Division at Vimy Ridge. Near the end of the War, when he was in charge of the 4th (British) Division, General Lipsett was killed while doing one of his famous reconnaissance's of German lines.[219]

These numbers are striking, particularly when one remembers that it is not the place of a modern general to be in the front lines. Modern battles depend much on communication with and the coordination of large bodies of troops to be successful, neither of which can be effectively achieved by a general in the front line. Rather, the place for a modern general is in the rear, where he can more effectively organize the movements of all the troops under his command. It is interesting that while many historians praise General Ulysses Grant of the American Civil War for being the first "modern" general through his practice of commanding from the rear, Great War generals are castigated for the same practice in a truly modern war.

It also should be remembered that the generals of the Great War were not inclined to shrink from battle. Virtually all of them had combat experience in wars prior to the Great War, many being decorated for bravery in action.[220] As a response to the high general officer casualties suffered by the British during the Battle of Loos, the High Command felt it was necessary to circulate an order directing generals to avoid their inclination to go to the front lines during a battle. The BEF could ill afford such casualties being suffered by their most experienced officers.[221] In a war in which the majority of soldiers and junior officers were civilians, it was not prudent to expose the experienced general officers to the risk of becoming a casualty during the course of a battle.

Even staying back from the front lines during a battle did not exempt the generals from becoming casualties. Some generals, like Major-Generals Mercer and Lipsett, were killed while doing inspections or reconnaissance's of the front lines prior to or between battles. In addition to these risks, the powerful range of Great War artillery pieces made generals vulnerable even in the areas behind the front line as headquarters were often targets for heavy artillery.

The point of this aside is not to argue that the generals were more "hard done" than the soldiers they commanded, for they were not. Life as a Great War general was clearly safer and more comfortable than that of a private. However, it is a mistake to assume that Great War generals were immune from the dangers of battle. It may be more accurate to say that, although the experiences of front line soldiers were worse, the generals did bear risks too and were not afraid to do so.

NAC-PA1033 – Canadian soldiers waiting prior to moving into the line (March 1917).

Looking now at the soldiers these generals commanded, all of the Canadians at Vimy Ridge were volunteer soldiers. Few had a military background, with most leaving their civilian occupation to join the army. While the initial Canadian Contingent that went overseas in October of 1914 consisted largely of Canadians who were born in Britain but immigrated to Canada prior to the Great War, battle casualties incurred in the years following took its toll on the originals. By Vimy, the proportion of Canadian born recruits in the ranks was rising, however, looking at the total Canadian enlistments over the entire War, only a bare majority of the troops were Canadian born.[222] Nevertheless, this statistic should not detract from the Canadian Corps being considered "Canadian," for Canada is a country composed largely of immigrants and there was a boom in immigration to Canada around the turn of the 19th century. Even though many of the soldiers in the Canadian Corps were immigrants from the British Isles, many of these men had lived in Canada for years before the War and considered themselves "Canadian."

The vast majority of the soldiers in the Canadian Corps were Anglo-Saxon or English speaking. Of the 49 Battalions in the Corps, only one was French speaking; the 22nd (French Canadian) Battalion. However, within the western Battalions in particular, it was not uncommon to find some soldiers of Japanese and First Nations heritage.

In terms of the soldiers' age, it varied. The Great War was a societal effort and this was reflected in the ranks. While most of the men were in their twenties and early thirties, it was not uncommon to find under-age soldiers in the ranks, or men in their late thirties and early forties. Similarly, the men of the Canadian Corps were drawn from all socio-economic classes. While the officers were usually drawn from the educated and "well to do," the Great War was not a "poor man's war."

The motivation for Canadian civilians to "join up" were varied. For some, the British Empire was in danger and it was their duty to protect it. This motivation was likely stronger for those who had recently emigrated from the British Isles, however, it must also be remembered that many Canadian-born people took pride in being part of the British Empire and believed that it was their duty to defend the Empire in its time of need.

Some men enlisted out of a desire to right the wrong of the German invasion of France. Lieutenant Georges Vanier of the 22nd (French Canadian) Battalion wrote to his mother soon after arriving in France in the autumn of 1915:

> Never in my wildest flights of imagination could I have foretold that one day I would march through the country I love so much in order to fight in its defence. Perhaps I should not say in <u>its</u> defence because it is really in defence of human rights, not of French rights solely. (emphasis in original)[223]

For others, there was the desire to "do one's bit," particularly for those who had friends and family already overseas. Adventure motivated some. With historic events occurring in Europe, the lure to be part of this took precedence over remaining a farm hand or shop clerk back in Canada. Less glamorous, but practical considerations, prompted others to enlist, such as steady wages and meals.

What strikes the writer, however, is not so much the soldiers' motives for joining up, but that their motivation to carry on with the fight remained throughout the War. While it is no doubt true that some soldiers were "broken" by their experience in war, the majority were not and Canadian morale remained intact for the duration of the War. Despite the experiences of Ypres and the Somme, the soldiers were not down-hearted. They had lost their naiveté and were still willing to take the fight to the Germans. This may be due to the comradery between soldiers and the fear of letting fellow soldiers down rather than patriotic ideals, but this should not detract from the admiration that is their due, especially bearing in mind the ordeal that was warfare in the Great War.

Four

The Artillery

For the first few months of 1917, the Divisions of the Canadian Corps were holding the line at Vimy Ridge. The frontage they held during this period was longer than that which they would attack from in the upcoming offensive. This longer frontage was also held by only three Divisions. One Division was stationed in front of the bulk of the Ridge, another Division was holding the line from Hill 145 to the Pimple and one Division was placed to the north in the area of Souchez. This northern Division was separated from the two other Divisions by the River Souchez, which ran in a general east-west direction north of the Pimple. In March, when it came time for the Canadians to prepare for the big offensive, they would turn over the Souchez sector to a British division. While three Divisions were holding the trenches during the Winter, the remaining Division was in Corps reserve training. As might have been gleaned from the discussion in Part I, holding the line during the Great War was not a safe and uneventful occupation. The Canadians' experience prior to the Battle of Vimy Ridge was no different.

Turning first to the king of the Great War battlefield, the artillery, it is no exaggeration to say that each day the Canadians were holding the line at Vimy, somewhere on the front artillery shells were exploding. Generally speaking, the Canadians were the aggressors.

This was not mindless, erratic shooting. The days of blasting away at the enemy hoping to hit something or someone were over. Instead, much attention was paid to trying to ensure that the artillery rounds actually hit an identifiable target. Before we discuss in the next Chapter what military activities the artillery was doing during the Winter at Vimy, we should first turn our attention to how the artillery actually engaged its targets.

It is trite to say that, in order to hit a target, the artillery had to locate it first. To do this, the Canadians were continually observing activity within German lines from the air and the ground. In the air, observation balloons and aircraft had the ability to locate targets deep within enemy lines. On the ground, the observers were artillery officers, referred to as forward observation officers ("FOO's"). These FOO's would take up concealed positions throughout the Canadian trench system, for example, on the lip of a shell hole or crater. From here, with a periscope, binoculars or the naked eye, the FOO's would identify German defences and locate them on their maps.

NAC-PA1183 – Canadian forward artillery observers. Probably a posed shot as no signaling equipment is apparent (May 1917).

These maps were in incredible detail. Soon after the onset of trench warfare, the British had undertaken extensive mapping of the Western Front through aerial and ground observation and continued to update these maps as the war went on. Thus, when the Canadians came to Vimy, they inherited extensive knowledge of the Germans' trench system from these maps.

Once a German defensive position was located on a map, this information was communicated to the gunners by telephone. Knowing the whereabouts of German defences, the artillery would fire on the locations given, despite the gunners having never seen what they were shooting at. However, this is a rather "neat and tidy" summary of target location and its complexities and difficulties become apparent with closer examination.

Before the gunners fired on a target to destroy it, they had to register their guns on it. Registration was the process by which the artillery ensured accuracy on the target. Take for example a machine gun emplacement. It has been located within enemy lines and the artillery are going to take it out.

For the smaller field pieces, firing on targets closer to Canadian lines, observation could be obtained from a FOO positioned in friendly lines. He could observe the fall of the rounds and communicate corrections to the gunners by phone. Once the shells fell on target the guns would be registered on it and could fire with the object of destroying it.

This process of ground observation relied heavily on telephone communication. If the lines were cut by enemy shelling, the artillery would be blind. It was imperative that, if telephone lines were wrecked, they were immediately repaired. This was the job of the linesman. Signaller Wilfred Kerr (11th Battery CFA) remembered the process of repairing the phone lines:

> I may say that the Battery telephonist called the Brigade Headquarters and the O.P. (observation post) every fifteen or twenty minutes; if he could not get an answer, he assumed that the line was broken, and called out the linesmen. Two of these would then start out to seek the break; a lone man was never sent under ordinary circumstances, since he might easily become a casualty and be left helpless. In daylight, it was usually not difficult to see the break; in the dark, we would take the lines in our hands and walk along, feeling for the telltale end. We usually carried a phone with us, decorated with two short wires ending in safety pins; these pins we would thrust through the insulation to the strands, and thus established a circuit, we would call the Battery at intervals as we progressed to make sure we had not missed the crucial point. . . . When we found the break, we would strip the insulation from about two inches of each broken end, wind the bare ends around each other and cover with adhesive tape.[224] (parentheses added)

For targets deeper in enemy lines, usually fired on by the heavy artillery, ground observation of the fall of shots was often not possible. For these targets, aerial observation would be used. Sometimes this was done from an observation balloon, other times by artillery spotter aircraft.

Observation balloons were a common feature on the Western Front and Vimy Ridge was no different. Both sides had balloons situated behind the lines, floating high in the air so observers could locate targets for the artillery and report on the gunners' accuracy. Private Victor Wheeler (50th Calgary Battalion) remembered the balloons' appearance and their vulnerability:

> Richthofen's (the "Red Baron") favourite target was our vulnerable Observation Balloons (O.B.s) that, a short distance behind, paralleled the lines for miles, in echelon formation, like scores of huge, shiny sausages, 150 feet in length.
>
> These, our best Caquot "captive" balloons, filled with highly inflammable hydrogen gas, could rise to six thousand feet, and were held aloft, like great kites (and were called "Kites" as frequently as "Sausages") at the end of steel cable windlasses anchored to heavy reel trucks. Each balloon was manned by one Observer and one Signaller who occupied the basket or cage and had direct telephonic

contact with the artillery unit they served. These two men, however, were veritable sitting ducks for skilled airmen.[225] (parentheses added)

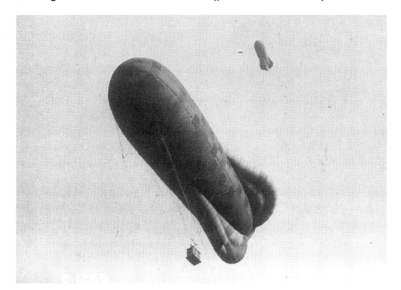

NAC-PA1194 – Observation balloons.

Turning to the spotter aircraft, telephone connection, as one would assume, was not possible over enemy lines. However, wireless radio connection was, and although wireless was too bulky to bring with the infantry in the attack, it could be fitted within an airplane. The wireless connection was only one-way, so only the observer in the aircraft could communicate to the artillery, but not vice-versa. Further, communication was made through Morse Code, not by voice.

To simplify this one-way process, the airmen and gunners used a Clock Code system. Under this system, one must imagine the target as being the centre of the clock. North is 12:00 and south 6:00. Around the centre are a series of successive rings, each ring named by a letter (i.e., A, B, C, etc.) and representing a distance from the target (i.e., 50 yards, 100 yards, etc.).

For the sake of this example, A is the first ring and represents 50 yards away from the target. If the artillery's shells fell just to the north-east of the target, the observer would communicate by wireless to the gunners; A1. This process would be repeated until the target was hit. At that point the artillery would be registered on the target and the artillery would then shoot to destroy.[226]

Billy Bishop, later a renown Canadian fighter ace, spent time as an artillery observer before becoming a fighter pilot. He recalled spotting for the artillery:

Leaving the border-guarding "Archies" (anti-aircraft fire) far behind, you fly on until you pick up the four mounds that indicate the German battery position. You fly low to get a good look at it. The Huns generally know what your coming means and they prepare to take cover. You return a little way toward your own lines and signal to your battery to fire. In a moment you see the flash of a big gun. Then nothing seems to happen for an eternity. As a matter of fact twenty to thirty seconds elapse and then fifty yards beyond the German battery you see a spurt of grey-black earth spring from the ground. You signal a correction of the range. The next shot goes fifty yards short. In artillery language you have "bracketed" your target. You again signal a correction, giving a range just in between the first two shots. The next shell that goes over explodes in a gun pit.

"Good shooting," you signal to the battery, "carry on." This particular battery is silenced for good and all. (parentheses added)[227]

As important as registering on a target was calibration of the guns. This involved, essentially, measuring how accurate a particular gun shot. Over time an artillery piece's barrel wears down from use. This wear decreases a gun's muzzle velocity, resulting in the shell falling short or wide of its target. To find out the muzzle velocity, gunners would select an easily observable target for which the range was known and shoot at it. As long as other factors that could inhibit accuracy were not present (such as high winds), the distance that the rounds fell from the target could tell the gunners how accurate (or inaccurate) their gun was shooting. Thus, if the gun was consistently firing just short of the target, the gunners would know to factor this into their calculations when asked later by the observers to engage German defensive positions.[228]

The complexities of gunnery in the Great War do not end here though. Even once a target was located, it was also not an easy task to actually hit a defensive position with an artillery shell. To begin with, no two shells would fall in the exact same place, even if they were fired at the same target. Added to this, factors such as the weather and faulty shells ("duds") made actually hitting a defensive position rather difficult. For example, a shell fired on a windy day could be blown off target.

By this time in the war though, gunnery had become more of a science. The gunners at Vimy did take into account the weather and factored this into their calculations for hitting the target. Further, industrial output had improved such that, while there would always be some duds, they never again occurred in the numbers they had at the Somme. Nevertheless, despite improvements in artillery methods since the Battle of the Somme, there always was the possibility of human error.

It was not just the inherent difficulties of gunnery that made the artillery's ability to hit their targets a demanding job. The Germans' activities also have to be kept in mind. They did not sit idly in their trenches, helplessly hoping that Canadian shells would not hit them. Rather, they took counter-measures such as, for example, moving their trench mortar emplacements from position to position. The Germans also took care in constructing and siting their defensive emplacements. Their defences were often fortified with concrete or steel so that they were not easily destroyed and were placed in locations that were not easily spotted. Thus, even if a target was hit, it was not always destroyed or, if hit and destroyed, the Germans would often install a new one, sometimes in a different location.

Like their enemy, the Germans observed Canadian lines too. They had concealed forward observation officers looking for targets for their gunners and some of the Germans' methods of concealment were rather creative. For example, when the 3rd Division was holding the line during January and February, they were confronted by German observation posts hidden within fortified phony haystacks. These phony haystacks, along with other German observation posts located in the trenches, damaged houses or tree stumps, were much sought after targets for the Canadian gunners.

While gunnery had evolved since the Battle of the Somme, it was still a difficult process to hit and destroy a target. Observation of targets was not easy, communication with the gunners had to be continually maintained and scientific calculations were necessary for the shells to fall accurately. Complicating matters further, the targets, the Germans, were constantly taking steps to prevent destruction of their defences. It was no simple matter to reduce the defensive strength of Vimy Ridge.

Five

Making Life Difficult

Much of the shooting done by the Canadian Corps' artillery during the Winter of 1917 was referred to at the time as being part of a "general trench destruction policy."[229] Essentially, the Canadians were continually making life difficult for the Germans through sporadic, and sometimes intense, shelling of the German lines. Trenches, dugouts, machine gun and trench mortar positions, headquarters, field kitchens, trench railways, roads and overland tracks were common targets for the Canadian gunners.

The Canadian artillery fire was at times opportunistic, at others deliberate. Probably the most common target of opportunity was the work party. Work was a constant in trench life, and the Germans were continually repairing their trench lines and defences, be they damaged by Canadian artillery or the weather. When a work party was observed, it was common for this information to be communicated by an observer to the gunners. Soon after, shells would rain down on the German work party, dispersing it, often with casualties. For the Canadians, not only did this tactic have the benefit of causing casualties to the Germans, but it also inhibited the Germans from repairing their damaged defences. Sometimes, if the work was important enough or the work party determined enough, the party would return and the Canadian artillery would fire on it, dispersing it again.

A target that was sometimes one of opportunity, at other times deliberately planned, was an enemy relief. It was during a relief that the infantry were at their most vulnerable as one unit was leaving the front and being replaced by another from the rear. Troops would be moving either up or down a communication trench and were away from the protection offered by their dugouts. It was a chance for the artillery to cause casualties to the usually well hidden enemy infantry. Sometimes, through prisoner interrogations, consistent observation or intercepted telephone messages, the Canadians would know when a German relief was likely to occur. The Canadians would then draw up plans so that the artillery would smother the German relief route with shells at the time when the enemy relief was expected. Other times, a relief would be spotted in progress by a forward observation officer and quick communication to the gunners would allow the relief to be intercepted.

The Canadians also harassed German communications. In February, a program of systematic night firing on roads, communication trenches, overland tracks and billets in the rear was put into effect. This was done for the express purpose of harassing the Germans; preventing the delivery of rations, ammunition and supplies and to wear down German morale. The artillery fire, performed by both the field and heavy artillery, was to be irregular, but with occasional bursts. This irregularity avoided the potential problem of the Germans predicting when and where night firing would be done and making plans to avoid it. Hundreds of rounds were fired at German communications each night.[230]

The most intense form of artillery activity during the Winter were the organized shoots. These shoots were carefully planned, often days in advance. Based on information obtained from observation, detailed fire plans were created by artillery commanders and provided to all concerned in operation orders. As such, matters such as zero-hour, the length of the bombardment, rates of fire and the types and number of guns to be used were decided well in advance.

The organized shoots could involve complicated fire plans. It was not uncommon for a shoot to be designed such that the artillery would fire on, for example, the German front line for a set number of minutes, lift to fire on the support line for a fixed number of minutes and then lift to shoot at a further trench line for a set amount of time. Even this example is rather simple for organized shoots could also involve lifts forward and back, increases and decreases in rates of fire, cease fires to lure the enemy out of their dugouts before the firing resumed and different calibres of guns shooting on different trench lines or targets at the same time.

Generally, the organized shoots involved both field and heavy artillery batteries with the heavy artillery often being tasked with firing on distant targets and fortified defensive positions. It was also common for the organized shoots to involve the cooperation of other weapons. Trench mortars would assist in bombarding forward defences, machine guns would spray bullets into German lines and rifle grenades would be fired by the infantry into enemy saps and posts near the front line trench.

If the artillery planned to bombard the German front line and its protective barbed wire and the opposing front line trenches were close, it was necessary for the artillery to warn the infantry holding the Canadian front line. This advance warning allowed the infantry to withdraw from their forward positions and avoid becoming caught by friendly fire. True to their name, these organized shoots involved a great deal of organization, not just within the artillery, but also with other arms in the Canadian Corps.

While the destruction of enemy defences was usually the purpose of an organized shoot, there could be subsidiary goals as well. A shoot might be designed to draw enemy artillery retaliation so that the Canadians could gain an idea of the strength of German defensive fire. The Canadians might also go one step further and draw German retaliation for the purpose of locating the German guns so that the Canadian heavy artillery could attempt to destroy them. Shoots were sometimes done to simulate a pending infantry raid. If the Germans took the bait and manned their trenches when the barrage lifted, the Canadian artillery would then roll back their barrage onto the enemy front line and deluge the deceived defenders with shells.

A good example of one of these "dummy" operations is that conducted with the cooperation of the 19th (Central Ontario) Battalion and the 4th Canadian Machine Gun Company on January 17, 1917. In order to lure the Germans into manning their defences, the Canadians blew an underground mine, fired rifle grenades across No Man's Land and pulled dummy figures toward German lines by means of running wires. All this was done to simulate an infantry raid. Then, after a pause to allow the Germans to man their positions, the artillery fired on the German front line, lifted to the support line and returned back onto the front trench. This program was repeated following another pause. Meanwhile, the Vickers machine gunners and Lewis gunners fired on German trenches in the area, coordinating their actions with the artillery program.[231]

Turning to the intensity of these organized shoots, it would vary, but they were always concentrated and were clearly more intense than the usual harassing fire. An organized shoot could last for as little as 7 minutes, but also for several hours. Depending on the length of the shoot, target, planned rates of fire and types of artillery used, the amount of shells fired varied. Bearing these factors in mind, some shoots involved the firing of a few hundred rounds, while others used thousands of rounds.

For example, on January 24, 1917, the artillery on 4th Division's front held an organized shoot against a section of German trenches opposite. Preceded by an hour of artillery registration on the targets, the shoot itself lasted 40 minutes. The field artillery (18-pounders and 4.5-inch howitzers) fired 700 rounds during the registration and shoot. As for the heavy artillery, 324 rounds were fired by the 6-inch howitzers, 152 rounds by the 8-inch howitzers and 179 rounds by the 9.2-inch howitzers. According to the 4th Division's War Diary, the shoot went well, with lumber and material being thrown into the air within German lines and smoke was seen issuing from a hit by a heavy shell.[232]

While the Canadians were generally more aggressive with their artillery, the German artillery was not silent. They too fired on work parties, trenches and performed organized shoots. January on the 4th Division's front around Hill 145 and the Pimple was notable for the prominence of the German artillery.

On January 3, 5 and 11, the Germans conducted what appear to be organized shoots on sections of the trenches held by 4th Division. All three shoots were extremely intense, lasted for several hours and engaged large portions of the 4th Division's front. Parts of trenches were obliterated, defensive emplacements destroyed, dugouts caved in and communications cut. Similar to Canadian shoots, it was not just artillery that was involved, as machine guns chattered away and trench mortars played a large role in destroying forward Canadian defences. As a result of the destruction wrought, the routine work parties were cancelled as the men were needed to rescue comrades from collapsed dugouts and repair damaged trenches. The 46th (Saskatchewan) Battalion's War Diarist described the German shoot on the 3rd as being comparable to the artillery fire the unit experienced during the Battle of the Somme. He also noted that the shoot on January 5 was even more intense.[233]

It is possible that the Germans intended to intercept a Canadian relief. During the shoot on the 5th, the 73rd Battalion (Royal Highlanders of Canada) was caught mid-way through their relief of the 78th Battalion (Winnipeg Grenadiers). Half of the 73rd Battalion was forced to hunker down in the communication trenches, delaying completion of the relief until the shoot had ceased. Then, on January 11, the 73rd Battalion (Royal Highlanders of Canada) was again caught in the communication trenches, this time on their way out of the front line.[234]

Canadian casualties, while nowhere near as heavy as those incurred during a Great War battle, were nevertheless significant. For example, in the German shoot on the 3rd, the 46th (Saskatchewan) Battalion suffered 8 men killed, one man missing and 27 wounded (including a shell shock case). From the January 5 shoot the 46th Battalion incurred a further 4 men killed (one of whom was buried alive) and 15 wounded (including another shell shock case).[235]

If the intensity of these German shoots was not disturbing enough, there were problems with the Canadians' retaliatory fire. While no doubt damage to the Canadians' telephone lines contributed to the problem, the Battalions holding the front were not impressed with their artillery's response to the Germans' aggression; describing it in War Diary entries as "weak." In some cases the British reply was negligible. In others it was temporarily successful in making the German fire slacken, only to have the German guns renew their intensity once the British retaliation died down (the artillery is described as "British" because it was British, not Canadian, artillery backing the 4th Division on this sector at this time).

Retaliation was an important role for the artillery on both sides. Whenever one side's artillery opened up in significant strength, the other side was usually quick to reply, bringing fire down on the enemy's trenches and gun positions. As with other aspects of the artillery activity during the Winter (and contrary to the January German shoots described before), the Canadians were generally more effective in bringing prompt and heavy retaliatory fire than the Germans were. However, while success in silencing German artillery is often claimed in the War Diaries, it is difficult to determine if any particular silencing of German shelling was due to effective Canadian retaliation, or simply the German guns falling quiet at a pre-determined time according to their operation orders. Nevertheless, the result of the organized shoot and the inevitable retaliatory fire were, in essence, mini artillery duels, with sections of each sides' trenches being battered for a number of minutes, or even hours.

Between general trench destruction, shooting at targets of opportunity, harassing communications, organized shoots and retaliation, the Canadian gunners were busy during the Winter of 1917. Although not on the same scale, the Germans responded in kind. The net result of this repeated artillery activity was that holding the trenches at Vimy, particularly for the Germans, was a difficult and dangerous occupation.

Six

Weapons in the Mix

The artillery were not alone in making life difficult for the Germans at Vimy Ridge. As we have already seen, by early 1917 a variety of different weapons for trench warfare were available and in abundance. Assisting the artillery in harassing the Germans were the trench mortars, soldiers armed with machine guns or rifle grenades and the snipers.

Rifle grenades were used for close range fire. That is, while the rifle grenade could lob a grenade further than a man could throw one, it did not have the range to fire at targets beyond the German front line. However, they proved effective in causing damage to saps, posts in advance of the front line trench and the German front line trench itself. If work parties were spotted, rifle grenades provided a fast and effective means of dispersing them. Private Will Bird of the 42nd Battalion (Royal Highlanders of Canada) recalled bombing German work parties one night at Vimy:

> Twice in one night Sammy and I had a bomb target. A sentry stopped us and whispered as he pointed to dark blurs working at the German wire. We sent two rifle grenades among them and a Lewis gun helped to complete the job. Later another sentry said the Germans were working at something opposite his post; he could hear thumping sounds, as if they were driving posts. We listened and heard the noise, set our rifles carefully and fired. There was the red flash of explosion and then a long-drawn yell that ended in a screaming heard all along the line. The enemy sent over "darts" in reply, but none fell near us.[236]

Trench mortars were very common on both sides at Vimy Ridge. Their low velocity and high trajectory were well suited for trench warfare as they lobbed projectiles high in the air which plunged down into opposing trenches. Different calibres of trench mortars were used by the Canadians at Vimy Ridge (light, medium and heavy trench mortars), with the heavy trench mortars being the least numerous, but firing the largest shell. All calibres of trench mortars had a longer range than rifle grenades, but shorter than that of the artillery. As such, the trench mortars, which also took part in trench destruction and organized shoots, were usually tasked with shelling defensive positions in the German forward trench system.

Turning to the machine guns, two types of machine guns, the heavy Vickers and the light Lewis Gun, were active harassing the Germans, each and every day (the Canadians still used heavy Colt Guns, but they were less numerous). Nightly, the Vickers machine guns, set in gun emplacements all along the Canadian line, carried out what was described as "indirect fire." Basically, this involved the machine gunners firing thousands of rounds at German communications (roads, paths, approaches to the trench system, trench junctions and communication trenches) and other points in the German line where overland movement was common, such as at ammunition dumps. The firing was indirect in that the machine gunners did not fire at targets they could see. Instead, the machine gunners were given pre-arranged targets to shoot on, set their guns on these targets and, essentially, blindly fired at them. The bullets would arch over friendly lines, No Man's Land and the German front trenches to fall deeper into enemy lines. The Vickers machine guns were being used like artillery.

While sometimes the Canadian machine gunners knew that their rounds were likely causing casualties, such as when the target was a suspected German relief, this was not usually the case. By and large, the purpose of indirect fire during this period was to harass the enemy by firing thousands of rounds at places in German lines where movement was likely. In doing so, movement within German lines would be impeded by the threat of their infantry being hit by the machine gunners' bullets and, hopefully, cause some disruption and casualties.

Despite its utility, indirect firing was usually rather dull work for the machine gunners. Corporal Donald Fraser of the 6th Machine Gun Company recorded his thoughts on this aspect of his job in his February 23, 1917, journal entry:

> Tonight I shot away a couple of thousand rounds of indirect fire. Indirect firing is not very satisfactory – you cannot see your target and, of course, do not know what damage, if any, is done. Besides, the belts have to be refilled and it is a blistery job forcing the shells in with the palm of the hand without a protective covering.[237]

As for the Lewis Guns, their harassing fire was usually not deliberate like that undertaken by the Vickers machine gunners. Unlike the Vickers gunners who were usually positioned behind the front line, the Lewis Gunners were deployed in posts just forward of the trench line or within the front line itself. The Lewis Gunners' role was largely opportunistic, seeking out targets in No Man's Land such as German work parties. They did some indirect firing, shooting sporadic bursts of automatic fire at night on places where work parties were likely to appear, such as gaps in the German wire where repair work was necessary, but usually the Lewis Gunners fired on groups of enemy visible to the gunners.

While the shooting done by the Vickers gunners was not very exciting, that of the Lewis Gunners could be intense. They were often directly engaging the enemy in short, but sharp encounters, that frequently caused casualties. A good example of this is an engagement in No Man's Land that occurred on the 3rd Division's front at the Crater Line on January 17, 1917.

An early morning Canadian patrol from the 2nd Canadian Mounted Rifles in No Man's Land noticed a German work party outside the German front line. Having made this discovery, the patrol returned to Canadian lines and informed a lieutenant. This lieutenant organized a small party of eight men with a Lewis Gun who proceeded into No Man's Land to within about 75 yards of the still unsuspecting German work party. At that point, the small Canadian party deployed, with the Lewis Gun resting on one soldier's back as a firing support. The Lewis Gun, along with six riflemen, opened fire on the Germans, inflicting casualties and forcing the remainder of the work party to rush back to the safety of their front line. The Canadians did not have it all their way though as, on their return to Canadian lines, German snipers opened fire on them, causing two Canadian casualties.[238]

As for the German machine gunners, they were less aggressive than their Canadian counterparts. The Germans carried out less indirect firing than the Canadians did. Instead, much of the German shooting consisted of intermittent sweeps of fire along the parapet of the Canadian front line; no doubt hoping to catch an unlucky Canadian poking his head above the trenches. Nevertheless, the combined activity of the Canadian and German machine gunners ensured that a steady flow of bullets was sent across No Man's Land into the trench lines throughout the Winter of 1917.

Making a small, but often deadly, contribution to the bullets whizzing across No Man's Land were the snipers. Each day snipers on both sides scanned the opposing lines looking for targets. Sometimes hidden in No Man's Land, other times firing from a protected position in the front line, the snipers made day-to-day life difficult for front line soldiers.

The snipers were stealthy hunters, taking up a concealed position and, with their observer, waiting for a target to come along. Areas where damage was done to German trenches were good places for snipers to focus on. If there was a breach in the German parapet, the Canadian snipers would watch and wait until movement was seen at the breach, firing at whoever was passing by the opening. German work parties were also drawn to these spots and the snipers were keen to interrupt their repair work.

It took a certain type of individual to do a sniper's work. Unlike much of the killing done during the confusion of battle, sniping was cold and calculated. A sniper would essentially wait in ambush, see his prey and, when the time was right, pull the trigger and kill his unsuspecting enemy. This type of work did not appeal to everyone. Private Will Bird spent time as a sniper prior to the Battle of Vimy Ridge. He recalled the experience:

Pearce led the way out the next day. We watched all the morning and much of the afternoon and saw nothing. There was no need to be impatient, he said. He had eighteen kills to his credit and had taken months to get such a bag. It was dull and chilly but the next morning there was sunshine and we were out early. I was no more than in position than a German in full pack rose almost waist-high at a place in their trench. The sight was so amazing it took me a moment to discover that during the night our guns had knocked down some of the German parapet. The German was evidently a new man in the sector and unaware of the nearness of our lines. He was looking around as I scored my first hit. It was not a great shot, the distance was not more than one hundred yards and I had cross-hair sights - but I had really killed a Hun.

"Good stuff," praised Pearce. He rubbed his hands gleefully and noted down the facts in his record book, but had not finished when a second German, also in pack, rose in the same place. I shot him as soon as he appeared, as my finger was taut on the trigger. Hardly had he fallen than a soldier without any pack and a rifle in his hands stepped up on the piled earth. I could count the tunic buttons through the telescopic sights and shot him through the left breast. As he pitched down from view two more Germans suddenly appeared at a spot to the left. They did not have packs and neither wore a helmet. One had an immense head, almost round, and he glared and pointed a finger. His mate was dark and his hair close cropped. He had binoculars in his hand. I shot him and as he went down the binoculars were flung in a high loop over his head.

The fellow with him was aiming a rifle in our general direction. Pearce gripped my shoulder. He had been watching with the glasses outside the plate. "Shoot!" he rasped. "You won't get a chance like this all day."

I drew back and handed him the rifle. A queer sensation had spread over me like nausea. "Go ahead yourself," I said. "I've had enough."

He seized the rifle and took quick aim. I saw the dark flush that spurted over the face of the big-headed man as he sank from view, one hand clawing at the sandbags. Then, over on the left, a German got up and walked overland carrying a big dixie. He was clearly a cook and his actions indicated that a new battalion was in the line. Pearce shot him and the dixie was flung away, spilling some liquid. Then an officer stepped into view at a blown-in part and waved to someone. He sank down as Pearce shot him, and pitched forward. No other Germans appeared but we could see their shovels as they cleared the damage our shelling had done. Pearce shot at a helmet twice and twice a spade waved a miss. Then we went back to the dugout and Pearce said I would have to explain myself to Sergeant Cave.

Cave looked at me oddly as I told him I had all I wanted of sniping. He said I had too big a kill for the first time, that if I had only shot one German I would have been all right.[239]

Despite what some might see as unpalatable work, the snipers did valuable service during the Winter of 1917. One Canadian sniper of note whose name continually appears in the War Diaries associated with hits on the enemy is Henry "Ducky" Norwest; a man of Métis ancestry from the 50th (Calgary) Battalion. He had 115 confirmed kills during the War, including 29 in the Winter of 1917. According to Private Victor Wheeler, a comrade in the 50th Battalion, "Ducky" Norwest had the skills and temperament necessary for a sniper:

Ducky (his surname was seldom used) fought at a suitable (to him) distance, always controlled, steady, unperturbed, motionless, unseen and quite alone except for his dead-silent and immovable Official Observer, who was always at his side to authenticate his every "kill" for the record. Private Oliver F. Payne, a Sniper of his own right, served for a considerable period as Ducky's Official Observer.

This Cree Indian never, if preventable, wounded a German, nor did he give him a second chance. Whenever Norwest pulled the trigger of his telescopic rifle, it spelled *Death*. "Fire from the furnace of his eyes/Blazed a red trail through the snow."

While Ducky's comrades were in the Souchez Valley rehearsing tactical stratagems, he was somewhere in the front line, unknown even to the men who, at the time, may have been within arm's length of him. He was often so expertly camouflaged or hidden that a point-blank view did not reveal his presence. It was only when one heard the sharp click of a trigger and the simultaneous whizz of a .303 bullet, as it left the barrel of his rifle, that one became aware of the Sniper's nearness. I once saw something as motionless and camouflaged as a white bunny in the snow, but I did not realize it was Ducky until he noiselessly hopped into the trench beside me (italics in the original).[240]

Perhaps fittingly, "Ducky" Norwest met his end at the hands of a German sniper in the summer of 1918.[241]

The Germans sniped too, but, consistent with all other harassing activity during this period, they were less active and successful than the Canadians. To keep down the threat from opposing snipers, snipers on both sides were keen to strike down their counterparts on the other side of No Man's Land. For this reason, it was not uncommon for snipers to seek protection behind a metal sniper's plate which could stop a regular bullet. Snipers, however, were not prepared to allow their counterparts any security. They would fire armor piercing ammunition at the sniper's plate, breaking through the plate and hopefully scoring a "hit" on the enemy sniper.

Less deadly, but quite useful, were the snipers' attempts to prevent enemy observation. As discussed previously, observation of enemy lines was vital, particularly for directing artillery fire. Forward observation officers were continually scanning the opposing trench system for potential targets and reporting back on the effects of shooting. Due to the dangerous nature of this work, it was not uncommon for these officers to observe enemy lines through a periscope, allowing the officer to remain protected in the trench. While a periscope is a rather small target, it is clear that Canadian snipers made a point of seeking out and destroying them. The Canadian War Diaries consistently report hits on periscopes, almost as often as hits on enemy soldiers.

With artillery, trench mortars, rifle grenades, machine guns and snipers, the Canadians were well armed for carrying out harassing fire throughout the German trench system. Rifle grenades would fire on forward posts. Light trench mortars shelled front line wire, posts, saps and the front line trench, while the medium and heavy mortars would bombard targets all over the German forward defensive system. The field artillery added to the destruction wrought on the forward defences and defenders, but was also capable of hitting more distant targets. While the field artillery did shoot on distant targets at times, these targets were generally the domain of the heavy artillery. Meanwhile, the Vickers machine guns fired bullets into the German trench system hoping to hit Germans on the move, as the Lewis Gunners shot automatic bursts at any work parties discovered in No Man's Land. Keeping a close eye on all activity at the front were the snipers, scanning the German trenches for unlucky prey.

Seven

Patrolling Vimy

Despite the Canadians' harassing fire and the Germans' reply, No Man's Land was a place of much activity during the Winter of 1917. Both sides were curious to obtain information about the enemy's intentions, his strengths and his weaknesses. One of the ways to collect this valuable intelligence was through patrols.

Patrolling No Man's Land was a feature of holding the line on the Western Front and the Canadians' experience at Vimy was no different. Almost every night during the Winter of 1917 the front line battalions would send patrols consisting of a few soldiers into No Man's Land. Some of these were defensive patrols, designed, as the name implies, to keep a look out for any threatening enemy movement in No Man's Land. Listening posts were set up, for example, in a shell hole. The patrol members would remain silent and camouflaged for a period of time in the hope of detecting some German activity. These listening posts were like the "eyes and ears" of the Corps, intended to pick up any aggressive action by the enemy before they could reach the Canadian front line.

Also defensive, in a sense, were covering patrols. These were employed when work needed to be done outside the Canadian front line, such as repairs to wire. The concealed covering patrols would guard the work party by keeping their eyes open for any German patrols that might want to fire rifle grenades or throw bombs at the work party.

Just as common as the defensive patrols were the reconnaissance patrols. Designed to obtain information about German defences, these patrols were quite dangerous for the soldiers involved. Generally, a single soldier or a small group would slip out from Canadian lines, usually after dark, crawl on their stomachs or on hands and knees towards German lines, all the while trying to minimize conspicuous movements and sounds that could unleash a terrible response from the enemy. Once at the desired point in No Man's Land (or sometimes even within German lines), the patrol would begin intelligence gathering. Captain George McKean, a scout officer with the 14th Battalion (Royal Montreal Regiment), recalled a patrol:

> We carefully wriggled our way into the German wire and lay there listening. In the trench, not many yards to our right, we could plainly hear a German working party. We could hear a succession of dull thuds as they knocked some timbers into the ground, apparently repairing a trench. We carefully noted the location, so that, as soon as we returned to our trench, we could notify the trench mortar men, and they would lob a few rounds over, to the discomfiture of the working party.[242]

The reasons behind the need for information varied. Sometimes it was to locate a defensive position, such as a machine gun post, so that it could later be fired on by the artillery. Other times it was to check on the condition of the German wire for purposes of an upcoming raid. German trenches, saps, wire, craters and posts were commonly subjected to thorough investigations by patrol members. If the soldiers actually entered German lines, once their objective had been scouted patrols sometimes would stay in German territory for a period of time, even up to an hour, in the hope of obtaining further information on the enemy or to capture a prisoner.

No Man's Land at Vimy Ridge, heavily cratered throughout and not just at the Crater Line, presented unique difficulties for patrols. Captain George McKean remembered patrolling during the Winter of 1917:

> We were now out in the land of mine craters; huge holes, some of them forty and fifty feet deep in the centre and from fifty to a hundred yards across, with probably a post of ours on the lip and, immediately opposite, a post of the Germans. The possession of these mine craters was often fiercely disputed, and every night at the slightest suspicion of a noise bombs would be dropped into these yawning holes. No Man's Land on Vimy Ridge was pitted with them – large and small; and our patrols consisted chiefly in crawling into and around them, trying to establish definitely the location of the German posts. At day-time the mine craters were lightly held; but at night-time, as soon as men could move around unseen, they came crawling out to different points of vantage on the lip – bombs and machine gunners all determined to hang on grimly to their particular piece of crater![243]

A good example of Canadian patrolling activity is the 11th Brigade's patrol system. For each Battalion in the Brigade, upon starting their tour in the front line, the first three days (more likely nights) were for conducting defensive patrols to allow the soldiers to become familiar with the area. Once acquainted with the terrain, the fourth day was spent reconnoitring German defences, making note of posts, emplacements, etc. On the fifth day no patrols were sent out as the artillery, trench mortars and machine guns fired at the defences that the patrols discovered. The sixth day was used for reconnoitring the German defences again.[244]

As with all other trench activities, the Germans patrolled No Man's Land too. It appears from a review of the Canadian War Diaries that the Germans were less active in patrolling than the Canadians. This is speculative though because, understandably, the Canadians did not notice every German patrol and the Germans took care to avoid detection (on the other hand, Canadian dominance in patrolling would be consistent with the Canadians' overall dominance over the Germans during the Winter of 1917).

Useful in deflecting German patrols from Canadian lines were the Lewis Gunners and rifle grenadiers. If a patrol was spotted, the Lewis Gunners would immediately respond with sharp bursts of automatic fire at the patrol while the rifle grenadiers would deposit grenades within the group of Germans. More often than not, this defensive fire would deter the inquisitive enemy from approaching any further.

While rare, there were occasions when Canadian patrols encountered the enemy in No Man's Land. If it was a German patrol, shots and bombs would often be exchanged before one side withdrew from the scene of action. More commonly the Canadians would encounter a German work party. Upon spotting the enemy party, the patrol would then make their way back to Canadian lines and report their finding. Having been informed as to the location of the Germans, the Lewis Gunners or rifle grenadiers would fire on the work party from a post in the Canadian front line, usually dispersing the work party and sometimes causing casualties.

No Man's Land at Vimy Ridge during the Winter of 1917 was not a desolate space, barren of human activity. Patrols on each side were making continual sorties into No Man's Land, often coming very close, or even into, the opposing forward trench system. While dangerous, these forays into No Man's Land were useful for the Canadians. Patrols protected defensive positions, allowed repair work to be done, obtained intelligence on German defences and sometimes caused casualties to the enemy. It was not glamorous work, but it was a necessary part of trench life at Vimy.

Eight

The Air War at Vimy

There was one aspect of trench warfare during the Winter of 1917 in which the Germans dominated their enemy; in the air. Aerial activity was a common sight above Vimy Ridge. Almost as common were British planes plunging down to earth in flames.

The term "British" is used to describe the airmen over Vimy Ridge as the Royal Flying Corps ("RFC") was not organized on national lines. Therefore, while there was a Canadian Corps within the BEF, there was no unit within the RFC that was exclusively Canadian. Instead, the pilots over Vimy Ridge were "British," being supplied from all over Britain and the Dominions, including Canada.

By the Winter of 1917 aerial warfare was integral to the fighting on the Western Front. When most people today think of the Great War in the air, the image that comes to mind is the dog-fight between fighter aircraft. While this was indeed part of aerial warfare, and a deadly part at that, the dog-fight was actually an incidental aspect to the main role for aircraft in the Great War. The *raison d'être* of the air forces was to support the armies on the ground. To provide this support the aircraft performed two vital functions; aerial reconnaissance and artillery spotting.

As was touched on previously, early in the War the British had mapped out the entire portion of the Western Front that they held. This was accomplished by photographing German lines from aircraft. However, as can be imagined, the Germans' trenches and defences did not remain exactly the same as they were at the beginning of trench warfare, rather, defences were improved and modified as the War dragged on. Thus, there was a continual need for the aircraft to perform photo reconnaissance to update the British as to what was going on within German lines.

Photo reconnaissance was a dangerous job. In order to obtain accurate photographs, the pilot had to position himself either over the stretch of German trenches he was to reconnoitre or at an angle to them (if what was wanted were oblique photos capturing features of the terrain) and fly slowly in a straight line at a low height. The camera was placed outside the cockpit and a series of photographs was taken to ensure that the whole area to be reconnoitred was visually recorded. From these photos detailed trench maps would be created and distributed to the infantry and artillery.[245] However, these valuable photographs came at a price, as the low, slow and straight flying made the aircraft vulnerable to ground fire and enemy fighter planes.

Just as dangerous was artillery spotting. The Clock Code system used for communication between aircraft and the artillery has already been discussed, but the risks this task entailed has not. As with photo reconnaissance, the artillery spotter had to remain over enemy lines for some time, always keeping the target in view and observing the fall of artillery shells. While he was circling above watching the shells below, the pilot was just as vulnerable to ground fire and enemy fighters as was the photo reconnaissance airman.

Despite the danger, both reconnaissance and artillery spotting were vital. Without them, the infantry would go into the attack largely "blind" to what they would face and the defences would be sure to be in operation as the artillery would not have had the means to destroy them. Thus, it was imperative that the pilots make the dangerous sortie over enemy lines regardless of personal risk.

It was to protect and to destroy these valuable reconnaissance and artillery spotter airplanes that the fighter aircraft was born. Both sides' fighters zipped across the sky, aiming either to shoot down the enemy's reconnaissance and spotter aircraft, or to intercept the enemy's fighters from doing so to friendly planes. It was in fighter aircraft that the Germans had the advantage at Vimy Ridge.

While the air war between the fighters ebbed and flowed to each combatants' advantage throughout the War, during the Winter of 1917 the Germans had the edge. Their Albatros fighters were state of the art for the time, outclassing any planes the British had. The effects of this technological advance in fighter aircraft was felt by the British all across the Western Front, but the British airmen at Vimy Ridge had something more to contend with, the Red Baron.

Baron Manfred von Richthofen (or the Red Baron) lead the *Jasta* (hunter squadron) 11, based at La Brayelles near Vimy Ridge.[246] Although he would not survive the War, by the end of it he remained the most successful fighter pilot on either side. With his gifted flying skills and superior airplane (painted brightly red), Richthofen wreaked havoc on British planes in the Winter of 1917, downing the slow reconnaissance and spotter aircraft and any inferior British fighters who tried to get in his way. It was not uncommon for the Canadian War Diarists to note in their daily intelligence reports that a British aircraft was downed by the "red plane."

However, we should not be quick to conclude that all British airmen downed by the "red plane" were actually shot by the Red Baron. His red plane was auspicious and the members of his *Jasta* sought to reduce the risk of him being the target for all British airplanes in the area. Thus, each pilot of *Jasta* 11 adopted a red plane, with each member other than Manfred von Richthofen adding a dash of distinguishing color.[247] Bearing this in mind, while the Red Baron may not have accounted for all the downed aircraft he was credited with by the Canadians, the unfortunate British airmen were definitely victims of his *Jasta* 11.

It is clear that the German fighter aircraft dominated the aerial combat at Vimy during the Winter of 1917. While it is not uncommon to find reference in the Canadian War Diaries to British planes being shot, it is rare to find an entry noting the downing of a German plane. Despite this imbalance, the British persisted with their photographic reconnaissance's and artillery spotting, incurring much heavier casualties than the German airmen did, but also supplying the Canadian Corps with valuable information for their upcoming offensive against Vimy Ridge.

Nine

Trench Raids

The most complex and bloody events that occurred during the Winter at Vimy Ridge were the trench raids. Raiding was a common feature of trench warfare for all combatants, however, the Canadians had developed a reputation during the War as skilled raiders, second to none. They lived up to their reputation in the Winter of 1917.

Raids were a controversial aspect of trench warfare on the Western Front. Some generals in the BEF had it in their minds that trench raids were necessary to keep up the offensive spirit and morale of their troops, while also damaging the morale of the enemy. Although this could be true of a successful raid, it does not recognize the loss in morale should a raid go terribly wrong. General Sir Arthur Currie (commander of the 1st Division at Vimy and later the Canadian Corps) refused to sanction any raid that was aimed at such an intangible objective as morale alone.[248]

Another, more serious drawback of raids was that, although damage would often be done to enemy positions and casualties inflicted on enemy soldiers, raiders became casualties too. A large amount of the "wastage" suffered by the BEF on the Western Front between major battles was no doubt due to the aggressive stance the British took on raiding.

On the other hand, there were real tangible benefits to the practice. One advantage was in intelligence gathering. If an enemy prisoner was captured (which was often the goal of a raid) he would be brought back for interrogation. At the very least, the raiders would be able to learn what German unit was opposite them in the trenches. If the interrogators were adept or the prisoner was a willing captive, much useful information could be obtained such as the strength of the enemy unit, its intentions (i.e., was an attack imminent), the location of other units and the strength and location of German defences. This type of intelligence was invaluable and sometimes could only be obtained through raiding.

Another benefit of raiding was that it was good training. Units that had never been in battle before could practice tactics and become familiar with their weapons under battle conditions, but on a smaller, less disorienting scale than in an actual battle. The training benefits of raiding did not end with green troops though. For veteran and new soldier alike, raiding provided an opportunity to develop new tactics and familiarize soldiers with new weapons.

Turning to the Canadians at Vimy, between January 1 and March 16, 1917, the Canadian Corps launched 29 trench raids, compared with 17 undertaken by the Germans during the same period. Of particular note is that the majority of Canadian raids were successful, while German raids were usually repulsed with no apparent objective being achieved. Most German raids were on a small scale with the largest involving around 50 to 75 raiders. On the other hand, the Canadians launched many raids using hundreds of soldiers, the largest of which saw over 1 600 Canadians attempt to penetrate the German trench lines.

To the modern reader, trench raids employing hundreds of soldiers might seem more like battles than raids, but it is the purpose behind the raid that distinguishes it from a battle. Unlike a battle, which is designed to capture and hold a particular piece of terrain or to annihilate enemy forces, a raid is a temporary attack with no intention to hold the ground attacked or to bring on a major engagement with the enemy. The raids undertaken by the Canadians during the Winter of 1917 had various objectives in mind, with the most common being to capture prisoners, inflict casualties on the enemy, perform reconnaissance of German defences and to damage those defences.

The simplest, but arguably the most daring type of raid, was the stealth raid. These raids were small, usually involving about a dozen raiders, and designed for a specific objective, such as to capture a prisoner or to destroy a post jutting out from the German front line. In addition to their small size, what made this type of raid a "stealth" raid was that the raiders were usually not supported by any artillery or machine gun fire to suppress the German defenders. Instead, the raiders would essentially "sneak" into enemy lines and seek to avoid being discovered by an alert sentry before completing their mission. Once they had performed their task, the raiders would then slip out of enemy lines and cross No Man's Land to the safety of friendly trenches.

A good example of a stealth raid is the one undertaken by the 42nd Battalion (Royal Highlanders of Canada) in the early hours of January 1, 1917. The raid party consisted of two lieutenants, two sergeants, one corporal and four privates. Their plan was to leave a sap, cross No Man's Land and enter enemy lines with the objective of capturing a prisoner. The raid took place at the Crater Line, so the portion of No Man's Land they intended to cross consisted only of that space of ground between the lips of two large craters formed earlier in the War by the explosion of underground mines.

Before the raiders tried to enter enemy lines, the corporal and three of the privates were placed by a lieutenant just in front of the enemy wire with the task of covering the raiders as they carried out their mission. Shortly after, the other lieutenant with the rest of the raiders joined the men near the enemy wire. From here, the raid party proper (two lieutenants, two sergeants and one private) slipped into one of the craters, moved along the inside lip and cut through two rows of German barbed wire. Having avoided detection, they entered the German trench.

Once in the enemy trench the raiders found it to be full of mud. The raiders did not spend much time slopping about in the mud, however. Instead, the raid party split, with a lieutenant and sergeant moving along the parados and a lieutenant, sergeant and private working along the parapet. They proceeded in this manner until they reached a point where a communication trench made a junction with the German front line. The raiders suspected that an enemy post was located at this trench junction, making it a good place to capture a prisoner.

For twenty minutes this small band of Canadians waited in the dark, until two enemy sentries were noticed. One appeared to be in a makeshift shelter, while the other was moving down the German front line trench. Not suspecting the danger he was in, the roving sentry carried on towards the silent, hidden Canadian raiders. Then, as the roving sentry came near, one of the sergeants jumped into the German trench, pointed his revolver at the sentry and demanded his surrender. Caught unaware, the sentry did as he was told. As for the remaining sentry, he was called out of his makeshift shelter (the War Diaries are unclear as to whether he was called out by his now captured comrade or by one of the Canadians impersonating a German sergeant-major). Realizing he was surrounded by the Canadians, the man surrendered too. With their mission accomplished, the raiders slipped out of enemy lines to the safety of the Canadian trenches with their prisoners in tow.[249]

This raid received the praise of the Canadian Corps commander, General Byng, who referred to it as "most successful and enterprising."[250] In a summary of Canadian raids dated January 4, 1917, he went further stating:

> "Stealth" raids, such as that by the 42nd Battalion, seem to be especially adapted for the purpose of getting identifications, while the enemy is holding his front line so lightly as at present. With skilful scouting and resourceful officers and men, they should produce excellent results with very few casualties.[251]

The most common type of raid launched by the Canadian Corps at Vimy was the bombing raid. These raids were larger than stealth raids, comprising between a couple dozen to a few hundred raiders. They usually involved multiple objectives such as the capture of prisoners, destruction of defences and the reconnaissance of enemy lines.

Bombing raids were also more complicated affairs, often involving the cooperation of the infantry, artillery, trench mortars and Vickers machine guns.

Another trench raid undertaken by the 42nd Battalion (Royal Highlanders of Canada), this time on February 13, 1917, provides an example of a typical bombing raid on the Vimy Ridge front. This raid involved two lieutenants and 48 other ranks, all from the same Company. Their objectives were cause to casualties to the enemy, destroy his dugouts and obtain the identification of the German unit opposite the 42nd Battalion.

Following reconnaissance of enemy lines, an area of 275 yards was selected for attack. Nine-fifteen a.m. was chosen as the time for the raid as prior observation of German movements indicated that the Germans were not particularly vigilant at this hour. Like the January 1 stealth raid, this bombing raid occurred at the Crater Line, so No Man's Land was narrow and filled with craters from old mines.

Prior to the raid three pairs of snipers were positioned to cover the raiders. The raid opened at 9:13 a.m. with soldiers occupying posts on the Canadian side of the crater lips firing rifle grenades into German lines on the opposite side of the craters. The effect of these exploding rifle grenades was meant to force the Germans to go for cover within their dugouts. Then, two minutes later the artillery, assisted by Stokes trench mortars and Vickers machine guns, opened a box barrage on enemy lines.

A box barrage was a common type of barrage used in support of raids. Essentially, the artillery, trench mortars and machine guns fired on the flanks and rear of the area raided to prevent the Germans within the "box" from escaping and to isolate them from outside reinforcements. This box barrage was fired at full intensity throughout the 42nd Battalion's raid and a forward artillery observation officer with a telephone was stationed in No Man's Land to report back on the barrage to artillery headquarters.

At the same time that the artillery opened, the raiders, divided into four parties, left Canadian lines. They passed through the Canadian barbed wire which had been cut the previous night, but left in position to be pulled away at the last minute. While the ground in No Man's Land was difficult to cross due to the large amount of shell-holes, the German barbed wire proved to be no obstacle for the raiders as it had been broken by trench mortar shells in the days prior to the raid. All four raid parties entered German lines, which were in a poor condition, having been damaged by Canadian artillery and trench mortar fire.

In the south, Party A, consisting of a lieutenant and 12 other ranks, divided on entering the German trench. Five men went to the right until they met a fork in the trench. Here they found two dugout entrances which they bombed with hand-held Stokes trench mortar Bombs and P-Bombs (phosphorous bombs that burned when they exploded, much like napalm). Then, as pre-arranged, they halted and acted as a covering party for the rest of the raiders in case a German counter-attack took place.

The rest of Party A went left until they met a loop in the enemy trench. This was unexpected as the loop did not appear on the aerial photographs studied before the raid. For the raiders of Party A, this could have upset their strict time-table since their training for the raid on "practice trenches" modelled on the aerial photos emphasized speed within German lines.

Without hesitating, three soldiers went down the right side of this unexpected loop. The lead man came upon two Germans standing in a small shelter. He immediately opened fire on these surprised Germans, wounding one, which resulted in both of them surrendering. The three Canadians then proceeded to bomb a nearby German dugout with Mills Bombs and hand-held Stokes Bombs before reaching the end of the loop.

Meanwhile, the lieutenant and four soldiers took the left side of the loop and came upon a German sheltering in the entrance to a dugout. His surrender was demanded, but it appeared to the Canadians that he was reaching for a bomb, so the lieutenant shot him. The raiders bombed the dugout entrance, along with two other entrances to the same dugout, with P-Bombs, Mills Bombs and hand-held Stokes Bombs. Moving on, the lieutenant and the four soldiers exited the left side of the loop and re-united with the raiders who had taken the right side. Soon after this re-union, these men met up with the raiders of Party B.

The 12 men of Party B had a less eventful time than Party A. Upon entering enemy lines, they turned left making for their pre-arranged junction with Party C to the north. On their way they bombed three dugout entrances with P-Bombs and hand-held Stokes Bombs. No Germans were seen and the raiders were not sure whether the dugouts were occupied.

Party C, consisting of 9 soldiers, entered the German line and turned right. They encountered a dugout with three entrances and from one entrance emerged a German soldier. His surrender was demanded and when it was not forthcoming he was shot and killed by the sergeant leading Party C. The raiders then bombed each dugout entrance with P-Bombs, Mills Bombs and hand-held Stokes Bombs, following which they linked up with the raiders from Party B to the south and Party D to the north.

Party D, the northernmost of the raid parties, met with the most difficulties. This Party, numbering 14 other ranks under the command of a lieutenant, encountered enemy resistance even before they had entered the German trench as the lieutenant was wounded in his side by a grenade while crossing No Man's Land. Nevertheless, he carried on, leading his men into enemy lines.

Upon entry, the raiders divided into two groups. Seven men went right, skirting the outside of one of the craters that was incorporated into the German line. They aimed for a known crater post, which was found to be unoccupied. However, the raiders did notice smoke coming from a chimney to a nearby dugout. Mills Bombs were dropped down the chimney while hand-held Stokes Bombs were thrown into the dugout's entrance. This done, the raiders met up with the men from Party C and then returned to the point where they had entered enemy lines to re-join the remainder of Party D, whose story we will turn to next.

The remaining seven soldiers and the now wounded lieutenant from Party D turned left on entering the German trench. Soon after entry they encountered a group of German soldiers who fired rifles and threw "potato masher" stick grenades at the raiders. The lieutenant, pushing himself to the front of his raiders, fired his revolver at the Germans, killing two of them. His bravery had a price though for the Germans responded by throwing a grenade that severely wounded the lieutenant. Nevertheless, the Canadians got the best of their adversaries as three more Germans were hit with the remainder fleeing from the sharp little engagement.

At this point the raiders turned back and moved towards the point where they had entered the German trench to meet up with the other half of Party D. One soldier carried the wounded lieutenant on his back while the others acted as a covering party. Moving back the raiders were attacked again, this time from a group of Germans who had emerged from a dugout in a nearby trench. "Potato masher" grenades were thrown at the raiders and they were in trouble.

Fortunately for the beleaguered raiders, they received some very timely intervention. The artillery's forward observation officer, who had been reporting back to the artillery on their fire, had moved forward from his position in No Man's Land to obtain a better viewpoint (this officer was Lieutenant Conn Smythe, future owner of the Toronto Maple Leafs professional hockey team and namesake of the most valuable player trophy for the National Hockey League's Stanley Cup Playoffs). The artillery officer noticed that the raiders were in trouble so he made his way into the German trench and lead the raiders in an attack on the enemy, killing two and wounding another with his revolver. The raiders helped, causing at least three more casualties to the Germans, who were forced to retreat. The dugout from which the Germans emerged was discovered and the raiders bombed all five of its entrances with Mills Bombs and hand-held Stokes Bombs. It is likely that the dugout was occupied by the enemy when it was bombed as rifles were seen stacked outside the entrances and movement was heard from within the dugout. Having bombed the troublesome dugout, the raiders returned to the point where they had entered enemy lines to re-unite with the remainder of Party D.

By this time, the pre-arranged moment to vacate German lines had arrived. Wisely, the raiders had two signals for withdrawal. One was bugle blasts blown by soldiers stationed in the craters in No Man's Land, which was heard by only two of the raid Parties. The other signal was time. Thus, when the raid leaders glanced at their watches and noted that it was 9:25 a.m. (the pre-arranged withdrawal time), the raiders slipped out of enemy territory with all but one Party using the point from which they had originally entered German lines. They brought their wounded and prisoners with them.

Upon their return to Canadian lines, the raiders immediately took cover in Grange Tunnel to escape the expected German artillery retaliation. In addition to safety from artillery, of great benefit to the raiders was that there was an Advanced Dressing Station in Grange Tunnel where the wounded raiders could get their injuries immediately tended to. In the event, the Germans were slow to respond to the raid. Their signal flares to their artillery to open up were not fired until the raiders had began their withdrawal and what German artillery fire there was turned out to be not heavy.

The 42nd Battalion raid was judged a success (and rightly so). The raiders' casualties were light with no dead, a lieutenant severely wounded, four other ranks wounded and a lieutenant and four other ranks slightly wounded and still on duty. In return, the raiders killed at least 10 Germans, with further Germans wounded (Canadian snipers also claimed three hits during the raid, two of which were on Germans fleeing overland from the raid).

The raiders believed that additional casualties were inflicted when they bombed the German dugouts as most of the dugouts were thought to have been occupied. However, these casualties were speculative. Not only did most dugouts have multiple entrances (making it difficult to entomb the garrison), but it was also common for the dugout shafts to be angled, allowing the bomb to burst at and be absorbed by the angle, rather than down in the dugout. In all, the raiders claimed to have bombed 10 enemy dugouts.

Finally, identification of the enemy opposite the 42nd Battalion was obtained as the raiders captured two prisoners from the 23rd Reserve Infantry Regiment. All objectives had been achieved. Thorough reconnaissance and observation prior to the raid, excellent training on "practice trenches," well executed artillery, trench mortar and machine gun support and individual bravery and initiative by the raiders, their leaders and the forward artillery observation officer all contributed to the success of this raid.[252]

As mentioned earlier, the Germans at Vimy Ridge undertook raids too, but were not as aggressive nor appear to have been as skilled as the Canadians were. German raids were generally of the stealth pattern, with a few attempts at what appear to have been bombing raids. One of the more interesting raids launched by the Germans was that conducted by *Sturm* Battalion Stark on February 9, 1917.

Before discussing the raid, however, a moment should be taken to mention the significance of the *Sturm* Battalion Stark. This was an elite assault unit within the German Army. As both sides in the Great War tried to develop tactics and technology to break the trench stalemate, one of the results of this effort was the creation of elite *Sturmtrupps* (Storm-troops) by the Germans. These storm-troops were composed of young, fit, highly motivated soldiers (preferably bachelors), specially trained in assault tactics. They were usually employed in small, lightly equipped, but heavily armed assault units. First developed in small numbers in 1915, they were deployed successfully at the Battle of Verdun in 1916. Impressed by their performance, the German High Command authorized an expansion of the storm-troops in October of 1916.[253] One of the new storm-troop units was *Sturm* Battalion Stark, formed around the end of December, 1916.

Sturm Battalion Stark did not come to Vimy Ridge as a whole battalion to hold a section of trench line. Instead, true to their nature as specialist assault troops, only two parties of 25 men each were attached to the 38th Reserve Infantry Regiment. While the 38th Reserve Infantry Regiment held the trenches, the 50 storm-troopers were tasked with special patrol and reconnaissance work in No Man's Land and into Canadian lines.

Turning to the raid on February 9, it was conducted by a sergeant-major leading 29 other ranks. The defensive position the storm-troopers sought to enter was known as the "Paris Redoubt," located in the southern end of the line held by the Canadians. The Paris Redoubt was held by men from the 60th Battalion (Victoria Rifles of Canada). The storm-troopers did not know this at the time, for their objectives were to obtain a prisoner and learn the method by which the Canadians defended their trenches.

During the afternoon of the 9th, German trench mortars fired on the Canadian trenches and barbed wire, doing damage to them in preparation for the storm-troopers' raid. At 6:30 p.m., the trench mortar fire ceased and, under the cover of rifle grenades fired from German lines, the storm-troopers advanced on the Canadian positions.

One party of storm-troopers tried to enter Canadian lines in front of the Paris Redoubt. It appears that they intended to enter via an advanced post that was connected to the main Canadian position. Whatever this party's intentions were, they were not fulfilled. The storm-troopers could not pass through the Canadian barbed wire and were detected by the defending Canadians. Acting promptly, the Canadians opened up with Lewis Gun and rifle fire on the storm-troopers bogged down in the barbed wire. The raid leader, the sergeant-major, was killed and the rest of this raiding party withdrew, leaving behind the body of their leader, some weapons, a couple of explosive charges and a pair of blood stained gloves.

The other party of storm-troopers advanced through No Man's Land along the outside of a group of craters. They intended to enter Canadian lines south of the sergeant-major's party. The storm-troopers were spotted when they reached the Canadian barbed wire and Canadian soldiers manning advanced posts threw Mills Bombs at the Germans, wounding one of the storm-troopers.

The German raiders abandoned their attempt to enter at this spot and, noticing a gap in the Canadian barbed wire and trench to the north, advanced through it and entered Canadian lines. Upon entry the storm-troopers divided, some moving north and the others south. Neither group was able to spend much time in Canadian lines as the Canadians reacted quickly and drove both groups out of the trench with rifle fire and Mills Bombs. The storm-troopers withdrew, leaving another wounded man behind.

Sturm Battalion Stark's raid must be counted as being unsuccessful. Due to the fact that one party did not enter and the other spent a very short time in Canadian lines, it is doubtful that a satisfactory reconnaissance was done. As for their objective to capture a prisoner, the storm-troopers failed and, worse, the two wounded storm-troopers were captured by the Canadians and interrogated afterwards. In addition to killing the German sergeant-major and taking two prisoners, the Canadians suspected that further casualties were inflicted on the storm-troopers as men were seen limping and helping others as they retreated from Canadian lines.

As for Canadian casualties, one corporal was killed and an officer and a private were wounded. Only the wounded private was caused by the Germans though. The wounded officer and the corporal who was killed were hit by friendly fire during the raid. It appears that in their rush to reach the sector threatened by the Germans they proceeded overland rather than through a communication trench and were hit by machine gun fire, likely coming from Canadian positions to the rear (no fault was attributed to the machine gunners).[254]

The third and final type of raid that was undertaken at Vimy Ridge were the largest in size and the most complex in planning and execution. While no name for this type of raid appears in the War Diaries, for our purposes they can be named "penetration raids." Not only does this distinguish these raids from the smaller bombing raids, but also reflects the fact that these raids were designed to penetrate German trenches beyond the front line.

During the Winter of 1917 at Vimy Ridge, penetration raids were the sole domain of the Canadian Corps. Like bombing raids, penetration raids were conducted for multiple objectives, such as damaging German defences, performing reconnaissance of enemy trenches and capturing prisoners. However, they were larger operations than the bombing raids and always involved soldiers from more than one battalion. In addition, the penetration raids were always supported by artillery, trench mortars and Vickers machine guns.

Three penetration raids were launched by the Canadians in the Winter of 1917. In a January 17 raid, 830 all ranks from the 20th (Central Ontario) and 21st (Eastern Ontario) Battalions took part. It was quite a success, capturing an officer and 99 other ranks.[255] The largest of the penetration raids was put on by 1 679 all ranks from four Battalions of the 4th Division on March 1. This raid was not a success and about 700 Canadians became casualties. The other penetration raid was conducted by 870 all ranks from the 44th (Manitoba), 46th (Saskatchewan), 47th (British Columbia) and 50th (Calgary) Battalions on February 13. It is the latter raid, performed by the four western Battalions from the 10th Brigade, that we will examine further.

The area selected for the raid was near the small hill to the north-west of Vimy Ridge proper, the Pimple. On the north end of the area raided was a trench complex known as the "Triangle," while on the south end was a group of craters with a maze of trenches behind the German side of the crater lips. In between these two points and about 700 yards beyond the German front line was a position known as the "Quarry." It was suspected that German trench mortar emplacements were near the Quarry. The objectives of the Canadians were to destroy the German defences in the area raided (including any trench mortars found), capture prisoners for intelligence purposes and inflict casualties on the enemy.

Preparations for the raid were intense. On February 9, practice trenches were taped out behind the lines by the engineers from the 10th Field Company CRE. These practice trenches were based on aerial photographs and included all known strong points that the raiders would encounter. Other features in the raid area, such as the craters, the Quarry and a trench railway near the Quarry, were marked out with black slag (Vimy Ridge being near a mining area of France). Repeated practice runs of the raid were done on these taped trenches between February 10 to 12, observed by officers from Corps down to Battalion.

The artillery support for this raid was quite complex, involving a series of lifts, a standing box barrage and then a returning barrage. The complexity of the artillery barrage has much to do with the distance to the final objective of the raid (the Quarry and nearby trenches) and the series of German trench lines between No Man's Land and the final objective. Thus, an artillery barrage was developed to closely support the raiders as they advanced through enemy lines.

At the designated zero-hour, the artillery would barrage the German front line. This barrage would last for four minutes and then lift to fire on the German trench behind the front line. After four minutes of shelling this trench, the barrage would lift to fire on the next trench behind. This trench would be subjected to a four minute barrage, following which the artillery would lift to form a box barrage. The box barrage would last for a half an hour and then the barrage would return. The returning barrage would move in the exact opposite direction as the lifts, but the time spent barraging each trench line was longer and no barrage would fall on the German front line.

The rationale behind this type of artillery fire-plan was to protect the infantry. Essentially, the artillery shells would always be just ahead of the raiders as they moved deeper into enemy lines, killing the enemy in front of the raiders or forcing the Germans to take shelter until the raiders were upon them. The box barrage would keep German reinforcements from interfering with the raiders as they completed their objectives, while the returning barrage would follow the raiders as they withdrew, protecting them from enemy counter-attacks.

As can be imagined, the success of this raid depended on excellent cooperation and execution by the artillery and infantry. The artillery would have to ensure accuracy and keep to their time-table. Failure to do so could kill the raiders. As for the raiders, they would have to keep to the time-table as well lest they lose the close support of the barrage as they moved deeper into enemy lines. The raiders would also have to complete their objectives in a timely and efficient manner since delay could lead to the returning barrage causing serious casualties to them.

Zero-hour for the raid was set for 4:00 a.m. Just prior to zero, the raiders assembled in the Canadian front line and immediately behind the parados of the front line, massing opposite gaps specially cut in the Canadian barbed wire. At zero, the artillery barrage opened on the German front line. The trench mortars, which had already cut gaps in the German barbed wire, assisted the artillery in barraging the German front trench. Meanwhile, Vickers machine guns began spreading bullets along the flanks and rear of the area to be raided. To the right, units from the 11th Brigade made a demonstration with artillery, trench mortars, machine guns and rifle grenades to distract German attention away from the raid. Under the cover of this intense opening barrage and the darkness of early morning, the raiders left Canadian lines, passed through the Canadian wire and waited tensely in front of the German barbed wire for the barrage to lift from the German front line.

Right on time the barrage lifted from the German front line. The artillery lifted to barrage the next German trench behind, the trench mortars switched to firing on the flanks of the raid and the raiders rushed the German front line. The German barbed wire proved to be no obstacle.

The lead raiders were the 5 officers and 200 men from the 50th (Calgary) Battalion. They advanced on the German front line and immediately engaged the German defenders. The Germans were overcome after stiff resistance and the raiders exited the front line trench and moved to attack the next trench. There was some confusion on the left as three lieutenants and several non-commissioned officers became casualties. However, a quick thinking officer from the 46th (Saskatchewan) Battalion moved forward and organized the leaderless soldiers for their attack. When the artillery barrage lifted from this trench the raiders were quickly upon its defenders. Strong resistance was met at this trench as well and the Canadians had to bomb and bayonet the German defenders.

Meanwhile, the 205 all ranks from the 44th (Manitoba) Battalion followed behind the 50th (Calgary) Battalion, passed over the German front line and met up with the men of the 50th Battalion in the trench they had just captured. Both Battalions prepared to move forward and capture the next enemy trench.

Behind the 44th (Manitoba) Battalion were the 5 officers and 200 soldiers from the 46th (Saskatchewan) Battalion on the left and the 205 all ranks from the 47th (British Columbia) Battalion on the right. They were tasked with following the 50th (Calgary) and 44th (Manitoba) Battalions as they advanced and garrisoning the first two trenches that the 50th and 44th Battalions captured. Flank guards were also established on the left and right flanks of the raid. However, the most severe combat experienced by the 46th (Saskatchewan) and 47th (British Columbia) Battalions occurred when they attacked their own respective objectives.

The 46th (Saskatchewan) Battalion's objective was the Triangle strong point, a collection of enemy trenches and defences roughly resembling a triangle shape. It was a difficult task, but the men of the 46th Battalion were up to it. This Battalion was a particularly aggressive one, launching four raids in the Winter of 1917, with all but one being a success. To assist them in tackling the Triangle, engineers with mobile explosive charges were attached to the Battalion for the purpose of blowing up the strongest enemy defences.

NAC-PA971 – German dugout bombed with phosphorous bombs, still burning days after.

Despite the area being damaged by the artillery, the 46th (Saskatchewan) Battalion met strong enemy resistance at the Triangle. The defence seems to have centred around a series of deep dugouts dug into a trench that was 12 feet deep. Using the fearsome P-Bombs, the raiders forced the German defenders out of their dugouts. These Germans, blinded by the phosphorous from the P-Bombs, began to collect in the bottom of the 12 foot trench, unable to make their way out. Chaos reigned as the raiders tried to bring the blinded Germans out of this deep trench, all the while being mindful of the returning artillery barrage. With the time for withdrawal and the return of the artillery barrage nearing, the raiders made the difficult decision to kill the Germans that were blinded and trapped at the bottom of the deep trench.

As for the 47th (British Columbia) Battalion, its objective was to clear out the maze of German trenches behind the group of craters on the right of the raided area. Attached to the 47th Battalion were engineers, as well as men from the British 176th Tunnelling Company, who were both tasked with destroying any mine shafts found with mobile explosive charges. Rather than advancing through the craters, the raiders entered German lines to the north and south of the crater group. Two platoons entered to the north and two to the south. Unlike most of the trenches encountered during the raid, the men from the 47th Battalion found the enemy trenches to be in excellent condition. Trench blocks were established on entry to deter any German infiltration into the area being cleared out. Both groups worked towards each other, bombing dugouts and capturing prisoners. Many of these dugouts were bombed with P-Bombs, setting fire to their wooden entrances. It appears that the artillery barrage had been particularly effective in this region as the raiders were often forced to walk over dead German bodies. The mobile explosive charges were also put to good use, destroying three mine shafts located by the raiders.

While the 46th (Saskatchewan) and 47th (British Columbia) Battalions were engaged in combat at their objectives, the 44th (Manitoba) and 50th (Calgary) Battalions moved forward to attack the last German trench before their final objective. The raiders followed the artillery barrage and captured this trench once the barrage lifted. Flank guards were established to the left and right and the raiders prepared to assault their final objective; the Quarry. The artillery lifted and formed a standing box barrage around the entire area raided, isolating it from any enemy intervention from the outside.

On the left, the 50th (Calgary) Battalion, accompanied by engineers with explosive charges, attacked the Quarry itself. Unlike their experience earlier in the raid, the raiders from the 50th Battalion found the Quarry weakly defended. This may have been due to the extensive damage the Quarry had endured from the artillery as the trenches and nearby trench railway were in a shattered condition. The raiders also noticed some enemy fleeing as they advanced. Nevertheless, the raiders methodically bombed the dugouts found in the Quarry and nearby with the engineers' mobile charges.

To the right, the raiders from the 44th (Manitoba) Battalion, with attached engineers, attacked the trenches to the right of the Quarry. Just as they were to go forward the lieutenant in command of the raiders was severely wounded. This was only a momentary set back, as another lieutenant promptly stepped forward and lead the raiders in their attack. Once on their final objective the raiders searched the area for dugouts, located many and set about bombing them.

Behind the forward elements of the raid force, preparations were being made for the withdrawal. Engineers placed four bangalore torpedoes (long, metal tubes packed with explosives) in the remaining German barbed wire in No Man's Land. The torpedoes were exploded and 40 yards of barbed wire were cleared away, making the raiders' return to Canadian lines easier when they were withdrawing.

Telephone communication had been established by the raiders just beyond the German front line. From here, a non-commissioned officer was able to relay information on the progress of the raid back to headquarters. He continued to do so until withdrawal, despite being wounded. For all raiders, but particularly those behind the forward elements, they were assisted by the fact that German artillery retaliation was weak and scattered and did not interfere with the conduct of the raid.

At the pre-arranged time (4:38 a.m.) the raiders began to withdraw. Flares were fired from within Canadian lines to help guide the raiders in the proper direction. The units deepest in enemy lines (50th (Calgary) and 44th (Manitoba) Battalions) withdrew through those behind (46th (Saskatchewan) and 47th (British Columbia) Battalions). By withdrawing in this manner, in addition to the protection of the artillery's returning barrage, the raiders at the far end of the raid were covered by the men of the 46th and 47th Battalions. Once the soldiers from the 50th and 44th Battalions passed through, the last remaining raiders vacated German lines and assembled at their pre-arranged rallying points in Canadian lines. It was all over by 5:10 a.m.

The damage done by the Canadians was extensive. An officer and 47 other ranks from the 11th Bavarian Infantry Regiment were captured, along with a soldier from the 2nd Company, *Minenwerfer* (trench mortar) Battalion 5. All prisoners were interrogated in the days following the raid with much intelligence being obtained.

In the opinion of the officer commanding the raid, Lieutenant-Colonel R.D. Davies (44th Battalion), the number of prisoners captured was low bearing in mind the large number of enemy engaged. It was noted though that the Germans put up stiff resistance, often preferring to fight to the death than becoming prisoners. Further, in addition to the potential prisoners killed by the 46th (Saskatchewan) Battalion at the Triangle, the raiders at the furthest end of the raid (the Quarry and nearby trenches) had to kill potential prisoners rather than take them captive, due to time constraints and the fear of the raiders being hit by the returning artillery barrage.

There is a harsh practicality about the Canadians killing potential prisoners rather than taking them captive, particularly with respect to the blinded Germans killed in the Triangle. While the Canadians did earn a reputation during the Great War of being "rough" with their prisoners at the point of capture, the moment of surrender is always a tense and uncertain moment in any conflict. This is especially true in situations such as the 10th Brigade's raid. Time was of the essence, German resistance was stiff and the artillery barrage was returning. Rather than running the risk of being hit by "friendly fire," the raiders killed potential prisoners. Unfortunately, such is the nature of war.

Aside from the prisoners, the Canadians estimated that they caused 160 casualties to the Germans, including several officers. Most of the casualties claimed were men killed and did not include those Germans found who had already been killed by the artillery before the raiders entered enemy lines. Added to this the raiders bombed 41 dugouts, 5 mine shafts, a sniper's post and a machine gun emplacement. It was also learned that the Triangle contained inter-connected dugouts and a medical dressing station. No trench mortar emplacements were found, but the presence of trench mortar ammunition and the capture of the *Minenwerfer* soldier suggests that they had recently been in the area.

Keeping in mind the casualties and damage the Canadians did to the Germans, Canadian casualties were light, but still significant. Two officers and 9 soldiers were killed, with a further 18 soldiers missing (due to the destructive power of Great War weapons and the confused nature of combat in the trenches, most of the "missing" were likely dead rather than captured by the Germans). Seven officers and 126 other ranks were wounded. In total, out of a raid force of 870 all ranks (including engineers and tunnellers), 162 became casualties.

That Canadian casualties were significant speaks to the tenacity of the German resistance. In spite of this opposition, through detailed planning and training, excellent execution by the artillery, close cooperation between the infantry and artillery and tough fighting in enemy lines, the Canadians were able to overcome the German defenders and accomplish their objectives.[256]

Raiding was an integral part of holding the trenches at Vimy during the Winter of 1917. Both sides were continually planning these minor operations, digesting the information gained from them and keeping alert for enemy raids. Out of 49 Battalions in the Canadian Corps, 26 Battalions performed at least one raid in the Winter of 1917 (9 additional Battalions conducted at least one raid between October and December 1916 at Vimy).

At least for the Canadians, the benefits from raiding appear to have outweighed the negatives. The most obvious negative impact of raiding was the casualties caused to the raiders. However, with the exception of the failed March 1, 4th Division penetration raid, the Canadians generally inflicted more casualties than they incurred on raids. In a war between such large and powerful combatants, attrition was an important factor.

The benefits of raiding did not rest solely on grim body counts. Arguably the most important result of raiding was the practice it gave the Canadians in military operations.

This is particularly true with respect to the important matter of co-ordinating the activities of the infantry and the artillery. Such co-ordination was planned and executed in most bombing raids and all penetration raids. In the majority of cases it worked extremely well. This was a good omen for the big offensive in April.

Reconnaissance and intelligence were also important benefits. While air-planes were useful for reconnaissance and intelligence gathering, raiding assisted as well. Not only could the raiders actually explore enemy positions on the ground, but captured prisoners could provide information that aerial photographs could not.

The Canadians learned from their prisoners tactical information such as the Germans' order of battle, the identification of enemy units, their method of holding their trenches, the manner in which machine guns were deployed and their rotation of unit reliefs. Information of a more strategic nature could also be obtained such as the age of the prisoners (and the average age of the soldiers in their unit), the prisoners' personal histories (i.e., when they joined the army, where they have been deployed, etc.), the strength of enemy formations, the number and nature of recent reinforcements and the prisoners' thoughts on the war. Finally, prisoner statements on the location of defences could supplement or be used to cross reference ground observations and aerial photographs. The Canadians wanted to be as informed as possible about their enemy before undertaking their major assault in April.

While a controversial aspect of trench warfare during the Great War, aggressive raiding by the Canadians at Vimy Ridge appears to have paid dividends. Through raiding casualties were inflicted on the Germans and their defences were damaged. Of particular relevance for the upcoming offensive, cooperation between the artillery and infantry was practised and valuable intelligence on the enemy was gained.

Ten

Winter's Value

The Winter of 1917 was a period of continual, small scale activity. Both sides, but the Canadians in particular, were active conducting small military operations. While these small operations did not materially affect the War's outcome, they were important for the assault on Vimy Ridge. Indeed, this was the view of Lieutenant-General Byng after the Battle. The Canadian Corps' Report on the Battle stated that: "The actual attack (on Vimy Ridge) was only the culminating phase of a long and insistent offensive which the Corps maintained during the winter and which included a large number of successful raids and a most destructive artillery preparation."[257]

During the Winter the attrition of German defences and soldiers was performed by a variety of different weapons; the artillery, trench mortars, machine guns, rifle grenades and snipers. Each weapon played a different attritional role, but all added to the daily harassment of the enemy. The Canadians clearly dominated No Man's Land and this was important for the upcoming assault. So long as the Canadians were dominating the Germans, the Germans would be wary of undertaking activity in No Man's Land, except that which was absolutely necessary. This dominance allowed the Canadians to use No Man's Land for the offensive, such as through aggressive patrolling and reconnaissance in the days leading up to the assault.

Necessary for carrying out effective small scale operations to damage the German defenders and defences was the gathering of intelligence. During the Winter the Canadian Corps was continually observing German defences from the ground and the air. Supplementing this was intelligence gained from patrolling and raiding. Not only did this continual intelligence gathering assist the Canadians in their general "trench destruction policy," but the information gained was valuable for the upcoming offensive. The Canadians had a comprehensive knowledge of the Germans and their defences before "going over the top" on April 9. We will soon see how important this was.

The Canadians also practised multi-arms operations during the Winter of 1917, such as through raiding. The coordination of the artillery, machine guns and infantry in these raids would be repeated, on a much larger scale, during the attack on Vimy Ridge. The success obtained by the Canadians in their raids showed that, not only were Canadian soldiers formidable fighters, but also that they were skilled in the use of the weapons at their disposal. Success such as this breeds confidence and the Canadian Corps was a confident formation leading up to the great Battle.

Part IV

Plans and Preparations for Battle

N

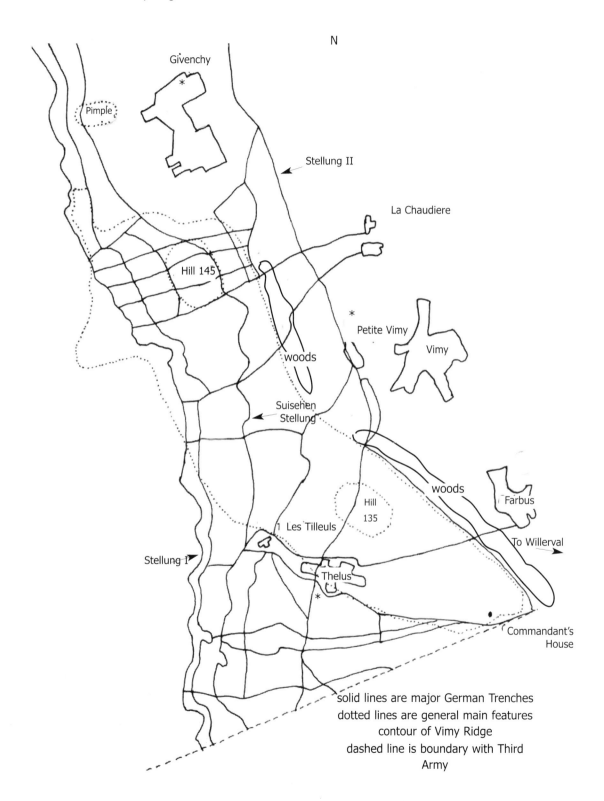

Givenchy

Pimple

Stellung II

La Chaudiere

Hill 145

Petite Vimy

Vimy

woods

Suisehen
Stellung

woods

Farbus

Hill
135

Les Tilleuls

To Willerval

Stellung I

Thelus

Commandant's
House

solid lines are major German Trenches
dotted lines are general main features
contour of Vimy Ridge
dashed line is boundary with Third
Army

One

A Spring Offensive

The Battle of Vimy Ridge, as a historical topic in Canada, has often been viewed as an isolated battle on the Western Front. This is a distortion for Vimy Ridge, like almost all other Canadian engagements in the Great War, was one part of a larger military action. To properly place Vimy Ridge in its true historical context, an understanding of the wider military picture in early 1917 should be reached.

Despite their inability to dislodge the Germans from France and Belgium to date, the Allies were intent on a renewed attempt in the spring of 1917. As was the case with almost all military campaigns on the Western Front up to this point in the War, the French were the major player. The strategy for the Spring Offensive was, by and large, dominated by French plans and the British, along with the Canadians, followed the French lead.

The French, who had survived the crisis at Verdun in 1916, had suffered terribly in the War to date. By the spring of 1917 France had already suffered about 1 000 000 fatalities.[258] It was the French Army that had, in the main, carried the Allies' prosecution of the War on the Western Front to this point. Nevertheless, despite their setbacks, heavy casualties and the first signs of failing morale amongst their soldiers at Verdun, the French were not willing to allow the Germans to remain on French soil. They remained determined to evict the invaders.

That the French were keen to take the offensive in 1917 has much to do with the Army's new commander, General Robert Nivelle, who replaced General Joffre in December of 1916. A colonel in charge of an artillery regiment at the outbreak of the War, Nivelle's star rose rapidly. By October of 1914 he commanded a brigade and became a general. At the beginning of 1915 he was promoted to lead a division and, by the end of the year, was in charge of a corps. During the Battle of Verdun he was an army commander and successfully orchestrated the French counter-attacks in the closing stages of that Battle.[259] Such was the confidence the French government had in Nivelle that he was promoted to the head of the French Army over Generals Foch (future Allied Commander-in-Chief) and Petain (the hero of the defence of Verdun), both of whom outranked him.[260]

Part of the reason for Nivelle's rapid rise was his personality. Energetic, self-confident, personable and articulate, he had the ability to win people over to his ideas. As his mother was English, Nivelle was fluent in English, an advantage in dealing with British politicians and generals.

Personality was only part of the equation. Nivelle believed that he held the key to victory and boasted that he could breakthrough the German trench lines within 48 hours anywhere he chose on the Western Front. While his predecessor, Joffre, thought it was necessary to wear the Germans down in attritional battles before their lines could be broken, Nivelle's approach was to sweep through their defences in one powerful stroke. His grasp of artillery tactics, as well as his belief in the power of the offensive, lead him to the conclusion that an overwhelming artillery bombardment, coupled with the French infantry's *élan*, would sweep the French Armies to victory. That Nivelle succeeded as he did at Verdun gave his ideas credibility.[261]

Neville's plan was simple. Overwhelming force, surprise and speed were his keys. A massive preliminary artillery bombardment would destroy the German defences. Then, at a time of Neville's choosing, the infantry would attack and rapidly push through any remaining German defences under the cover of a creeping barrage. If all went to plan, the German trench system would be ruptured and a war of manoeuvre would develop behind the German lines, resulting in the defeat of the German forces in France. This was a grand scheme, but Nivelle was confident in success. To a war weary Army and nation, his ideas were seductive.[262]

One politician, amongst many, won over by General Nivelle was the new British Prime Minister, the fiery David Lloyd George. A Welshman who made his name prior to the War as a radical liberal politician, Lloyd George's steady rise in politics lead to his being Prime Minister of Britain following successful tenures as the Minister of Munitions and then Minister of War.

Like Haig, Lloyd George is a controversial figure. A man made for politics, he was out of his depth in military matters. Appalled by the casualties suffered by the British on the Somme, he was in constant search for an "easy" path to victory, exploring options in all other theatres of war to avoid battle on the Western Front. Lloyd George was of the belief that if Germany's allies (the Austro-Hungarian and Ottoman Empires) were knocked out of the War, Germany would follow. In this he was directly opposed by the British High Command, particularly Douglas Haig and the Chief of the Imperial General Staff, Sir William Robertson. Both of these men were of the firm view that Germany was the main enemy and must be engaged and beaten on the Western Front before the War could be won.[263] As Germany had to "prop" its allies throughout the War and was only defeated when its Army was defeated on the Western Front, hindsight favors the generals.

Nevertheless, Lloyd George's contribution to the War was impressive. As Minister of Munitions he was instrumental in ensuring that the production of artillery shells and other munitions achieved wartime demands. Under his leadership as Prime Minister, Britain was on a total war footing (that is, an all-out societal effort involving civilians, industry, government and the military all geared towards prosecuting the war); a necessary development for Britain to effectively fight the Great War. Further, despite his disagreements with Britain's military leaders on how the War should be waged, it is clear that Lloyd George was committed to victory, a requirement for a wartime leader.[264]

Lloyd George was impressed with General Nivelle's optimistic plan for a quick breakthrough on the Western Front. Even more to Lloyd George's liking was that the plan had the French in the lead role with the British providing support. To ensure that the BEF followed Nivelle, and, at least in Lloyd George's mind, to prevent Haig from committing the BEF to another Somme, Lloyd George reached an arrangement with the French that undercut Haig's authority.

At a conference between the French and British held at Calais on February 26 and 27, 1917, ostensibly to discuss railway communications, Lloyd George announced his controversial plan to place the BEF wholly under Nivelle's command. Unity of command is not an undesirable development in coalition warfare, but what Lloyd George envisioned was something even more. Rather than having an Allied Commander-in-Chief leading two separate and independent armies, Lloyd George wanted the BEF to be under Nivelle's command as if it were just another French Army to be employed at Nivelle's discretion. Haig would be nothing more than a figure head. Not only was this an unprecedented move, Haig was not aware of Lloyd George's plans until he announced them at the conference.[265]

Lloyd George's proposal was, not surprisingly, disapproved of by Haig and Robertson and the manner Lloyd George went about trying to implement it created resentment between the British military and civil leaders. In the end, Lloyd George relented to an extent. The BEF would be under Nivelle's lead, but it remained an independent military body from the French Army under Haig's command. It would also only be under Nivelle for the Spring Offensive, rather than the duration of the War as Lloyd George had initially planned.[266] Nevertheless, the BEF was now committed to taking part in Nivelle's Spring Offensive.

As for the Germans, their Army was now commanded by the stoic, nationally revered, Field Marshal Paul von Hindenburg and the intelligent and energetic, but emotional, First Quartermaster General Erich Ludendorff. Both men had experienced substantial success on the Eastern Front before replacing Falkenhayen in the summer of 1916. Falkenhayen was relieved of command, in part, due to the failure of the German offensive at Verdun and the high casualties inflicted on German soldiers during the defensive Battle of the Somme. Although military commanders rather than political leaders, as their tenure in command continued, they both, but Ludendorff in particular, exercised greater control over the whole German war effort. Germany became, to an extent, a military dictatorship. Both men were committed to total victory for the German people and ensured that the German nation was mobilized for total war.

For the Germans, their strategy in 1917 would be part defence/part offence. On the Western Front the German Army would stand on the defensive, waiting to break the next Allied offensive. To this end, the Germans made a strategic retreat on the Western Front.

While the German Army was taking punishment on the Somme, a new, incredibly strong defensive position was being built to the rear. Dubbed the Hindenburg Line by the British (the *Siegfried Stellung* by the Germans), the position was completed in early 1917. In mid-March the Germans made their move, withdrawing on a front about 100 miles wide and averaging twenty miles deep between Arras in the north and Soissons in the south. The Germans protected their retreat by completely devastating the ground they abandoned. Anything that could be of use to the Allies was destroyed. This "scorched earth" policy included the destruction of all habitations, the forced removal of about 125 000 French civilians that were fit to be used for the German war effort (the "unfit" were left for the Allies to take care of), the demolition of communications and the poisoning of wells, to name a few. The speed with which the retreat was done and the "scorched earth" policy prevented the Allies from any effective pursuit. The net effect of this withdrawal was to considerably shorten the line the Germans had to hold on the Western Front, freeing reserves to counter a future Allied offensive.[267]

While the Army was on the defensive on the Western Front, the German submarine force would take the offensive against the British at sea. The Germans sought to strangle Britain into submission by sinking merchant ships of any nationality off the British Isles, thus cutting the British people off from vital outside supplies and foodstuffs. Such a move was not without precedent in the Great War. Britain's Royal Navy had been blockading Germany since 1914, isolating its population from the rest of the world. The "Turnip Winter" of 1916/1917 (referred to as such in Germany as turnips became a staple out of necessity) had demonstrated the effectiveness of a naval blockade. The Germans were keen to do to the British people what the Royal Navy was doing to the German nation.

In the event, the submarine offensive, launched on February 1, 1917, would back fire against Germany. That this happened had much to do with the tactics used by the German submarine fleet. While in its blockade the Royal Navy intercepted, boarded and inspected ships heading for Germany, the German submarines were not so discriminating and sunk any ships around the British Isles without warning, regard to what the ships were actually carrying or nationality. This, not surprisingly, angered nations not already in the War, particularly the United States. In response to the submarine threat, the United States declared war on Germany on April 6, 1917.

Aside from raising the Allies' morale, the American declaration would not have an immediate impact on the Western Front though. We have already seen how unprepared for war the British were in 1914. The American forces were in an even worse state in 1917 and it would not be until the spring of 1918 that the Americans were able to make a significant contribution to the fighting on the Western Front. Even by the end of the War in November of 1918 the American forces engaged were relatively small and inexperienced compared to their Allies. Nevertheless, with its economic and manpower resources, the mere fact that the United States entered the War spelled doom for Germany.

The American entry into the War and their distant arrival in France aside, the scene was set for renewed hostilities on the Western Front in the spring of 1917. General Nivelle was to command a major offensive, lead by the French, but with significant British contribution. He believed he possessed the key to victory; it was now a matter of opening the door.

Two

Arras

General Nivelle envisioned a three pronged assault on the Germans, with the main French attack being delivered at the Chemin des Dames, while diversionary attacks were to be launched by the French north of the Oise River and by the British at Arras.[268] The plan was for the British and French diversions to draw German attention and reserves away from the main assault on the Chemin des Dames. If all went well, as Nivelle was sure it would, a breakthrough of the German line would result at the Chemin des Dames, leading to the ultimate defeat of the German forces on the Western Front.

Sir Douglas Haig, recently promoted to the rank of Field Marshal, had the British Third Army bear the main burden of the British assault at Arras. Third Army was commanded by General Sir Edmund "the Bull" Allenby, whose nickname reflected his size and temperament. A cavalryman, he had lead the British diversion at Gommecourt on the first day of the Battle of the Somme, but now he would command the main British effort. After Arras Allenby would be transferred to the Middle East where he would gain distinction fighting the Ottoman Turks.

Allenby's task was to drive the Germans from the series of low ridges that dominated the City of Arras from the east. Though hardly soaring heights, these ridges gave the Germans an advantage in observation over the British and provided protection for the German artillery. General Allenby's Third Army was to deploy ten infantry divisions in the attack, with a further two in reserve; all divisions having seen action on the Somme. The infantry were to be supported by 1 720 artillery pieces and forty tanks. The 3rd Cavalry Division was readied to exploit any breakthrough.[269]

Like the Battle of the Somme, the British effort at Arras would involve multiple Armies. To the north of Arras lay Vimy Ridge and any advance from Arras would be threatened by this dominating feature. Nivelle was against any attack on Vimy Ridge, believing it to be impregnable (likely influenced by past French failures to take the Ridge). Haig, recognizing the threat Vimy Ridge posed to Third Army and the advantages to be gained from capturing it, persisted.[270] Nivelle relented and Haig gave the task of attacking Vimy Ridge to General Horne's First Army. The Canadian Corps would be First Army's assault formation.

Placed in the context of the 1917 Spring Offensive, the upcoming Battle of Vimy Ridge was a supporting attack for Third Army's Arras operation which was, in turn, a diversion for Nivelle's "war winning" offensive on the Chemin des Dames. Thus, the Battle of Vimy Ridge was planned from the outset as a limited "bite and hold" operation designed to seize the tactically important Ridge. There was never any intention to turn the Battle for Vimy into a decisive breakthrough.

Three

The Terrain and Defences of Vimy Ridge

In trying to understand the Battle of Vimy Ridge, it is important to have a grasp on the terrain and the defences that the Canadians would face as both influenced the battle plan. Generally, the opposing front lines ran in a north to south direction with a slight bulge to the west north of Vimy Ridge. However, the front lines did not mirror the Ridge itself as, from north to south, Vimy Ridge ran in a south-eastern direction. Thus, on the northern half of the Ridge, the Canadian front line was quite close to the crest of the Ridge, while in the south the crest was much further away.

Vimy Ridge is not a soaring height of land. From Canadian lines to the crest of the Ridge the land rises gently. The highest point is Hill 145, located at the Ridge's north end, with a secondary height, Hill 135, just south of the Ridge's mid-point. Near the Ridge's south end was a building known as the Commandant's House. North-west of Vimy Ridge where the opposing lines bulged to the west is a small hill; the Pimple (Hill 120). The entire Ridge and the Pimple were Canadian objectives.

There were a number of small villages around Vimy Ridge, uninhabited and damaged on account of the War. Most of the villages, including Vimy itself, were located to the east of the Ridge, but two, the villages of Les Tilleuls and Thelus, were on the western slope in front of Hill 135. Both would have to be captured in the upcoming offensive.

While the western slope is gentle, the eastern slope of the Ridge is steep. On and below the steep eastern slope were a series of wooded areas named the *Bois de la Folie, Bois du Goulot, Bois de la Ville* and Farbus Wood. Damaged by shellfire and barren of foliage in the cool early spring weather, the woods did little to beautify the locale. However, the combination of a steep slope with woods did provide good cover for the Germans. They took advantage of this by constructing deep dugouts into the eastern slope and placing many artillery pieces and further dugouts in and around the wooded areas.

The German defence of Vimy Ridge rested largely on their strong forward trench system; the *Stellung I.* This was a series of trench lines with strong points, connected by communication trenches and underground tunnels, garrisoned by soldiers in deep dugouts. In terms of location, the *Stellung I* mirrored No Man's Land, rather than the Ridge. In the north, the *Stellung I* was on the western slope of Hill 145, but as it moved south, the *Stellung* I kept a north-south direction, resulting in it being well forward of the Ridge's crest in the south.

Just to the east of Vimy Ridge was the *Stellung II.* Located for the most part in the plain below the Ridge, this was the Germans' second main defence line (the third defence line, the *Stellung III*, was about 3 miles to the east). While the *Stellung II* was close to the *Stellung I* in the north around Hill 145, the gap between the two defence lines widened the further south one went along the Ridge. To defend this gap between the main *Stellungs*, the Germans constructed the *Swischen Stellung*; an intermediate defence line. Like the *Stellung I*, the *Swischen Stellung* was a series of inter-connected trench lines with strong points and underground tunnels, defended by garrisons in deep dugouts. Emerging from the *Stellung I* on the northern part of the Ridge around Hill 145, the *Swischen Stellung* followed the crest until about the middle of the Ridge. There it left the crest and zig-zagged south on the western slope behind the *Stellung I* and in front of the Villages of Les Tilleuls and Thelus and Hill 135.

Even with the *Swischen Stellung* there still was a gap in the south between it and the crest of the Ridge. To defend this area, the Villages of Les Tilleuls and Thelus were fortified and a series of trenches were dug between the *Swischen Stellung* and the crest. Excepting those around Les Tilleuls, Thelus and Hill 135, these trenches were not as thick-ly placed as those comprising the *Stellung I* and *Swischen Stellung*, but were nevertheless serious obstacles to the Canadians' upcoming advance.

While the crest of the Ridge, including Hill 145, was strongly held in the north, the same was not true in the south. Trenches were few on the southern crest. Instead, the Germans had placed two thick rows of barbed wire on the crest, hoping that the Canadian and British artillery would not be able to cut gaps in it, allowing the Germans to destroy the attackers on the wire.

This then was Vimy Ridge, the Canadians' objective for their upcoming offensive. With its gentle western slope it was not an insurmountable natural obstacle. However, the Germans had held Vimy Ridge since 1914 and put this time to good use. In the words of the Canadian Corps' Report, the Germans had built:

> . . . an extensive and intricate system of defences, of fire trenches, communica-
> tion trenches, deep and elaborate dug-outs, caves and tunnels, concrete
> machine gun and trench mortar emplacements and cunningly constructed

redoubts upon all of which the enemy had expended great labour and skill during more than 2 years of occupation.[271]

It was not the Ridge itself, but the defences the Germans constructed that lead many to believe that Vimy Ridge was impossible to capture.

Four

Division Objectives

Each Division in the Canadian Corps was assigned a sector of Vimy Ridge to capture. The 1st Division was the southernmost Division and was tasked with attacking the south end of the Ridge. From here, south to north, were the 2nd, 3rd and 4th Divisions; the 4th Division given the objective of Hill 145.

The attack on Vimy Ridge was to be done in successive steps, rather than in one rush. Thus, a series of objectives were set, culminating in the capture of the whole Ridge. Each objective was named by color. The first objective was the Black Line, the second the Red Line, the third the Blue Line and the final objective was called the Brown Line.

The Black Line was the German forward trench system, the *Stellung I,* and that portion of the *Swischen Stellung* that ran along the Ridge's crest in the north. What constituted the Red Line differed from Division to Division. Illustrating the differing depths that each Division had to penetrate into German lines, the Red Line was the final objective for 3rd and 4th Divisions in the north. For 4th Division, the capture of their Red Line would place Hill 145 well within Canadian lines, while the Red Line for 3rd Division was on the eastern slope of the Ridge, including part of the *Bois de la Folie*. If all went well, the capture of the Red Line would end the assault for 4th and 3rd Divisions.

The situation was quite different for 1st and 2nd Divisions in the south. Their Red Line included that part of the *Swischen Stellung* which ran well in front of the crest on the southern half of the Ridge. For these Divisions, the capture of the Red Line only put them about halfway to their ultimate objective. In the case of 2nd Division, they would be just in front of the fortified Village of Thelus and Hill 135 to its north-east.

For 1st and 2nd Divisions, their next task was to take the Blue Line. The capture of this Line would involve 2nd Division attacking Thelus and Hill 135, and would place both Divisions in front of the double row of barbed wire on the Ridge's southern crest. In 1st Division's sector, Commandant's House was located within this double row of wire. It was only after these Divisions pushed on and captured the Brown Line that they would they be on eastern slope of the Ridge. By that point, 1st and 2nd Divisions would be about 4 000 yards into German territory.

As long as the attack on Vimy Ridge itself went according to plan, the 4th Division would follow up this success with an assault on the Pimple the following day.

This all sounds quite simple, but the reality was very different. Vimy Ridge had withstood Allied assaults in the past and the Germans were confident that the next attempt would lead to the same result. Having broadly explained the Canadians' objectives, we will now examine how they planned to achieve them.

Five

The Creeping Barrage

Compared to battles in other military conflicts, Great War battles on the Western Front are often ignored when it comes to discussing matters such as "great commanders" or "brilliant battles." The frontal assaults on the Western Front are dismissed as "simple" and "unimaginative," especially when contrasted with what appear to be more "sophisticated" battles, such as Robert E. Lee's victory against the odds at Chancellorsville in the American Civil War, or the Germans' quick defeat of France in 1940. This is a dis-service to both the Great War generals and their men.

As we have already seen, factors such as the lack of mobile firepower and adequate communications, together with enormous static firepower and manpower resources, created a massive trench system that was very difficult to decisively breach. Within these parameters, the only attack that could be mounted was a frontal assault, the depth of penetration being limited to the range of the supporting artillery. On the surface this does appear to be "simple" and "unimaginative," but a closer look at how a Great War battle such as Vimy Ridge was actually fought suggests the contrary. Indeed, how the Battle of Vimy Ridge was planned and executed could be described as "sophisticated simplicity." That is, the concept for the Battle of Vimy Ridge was simple, a frontal assault, but how the soldiers actually performed the attack was sophisticated. So complex was the assault at Vimy that soldiers from the American Civil War, or even from 1914, could not have even imagined it.

Looking first at the artillery support for the infantry attack, much had been learned from the Battle of the Somme. As we saw earlier, a problem on July 1, 1916, was that the artillery and infantry were not coordinated. When the artillery barrage lifted from the German front line, the British infantry often still had much of No Man's Land to cross, providing the Germans with ample opportunity to pour machine gun and rifle fire into the attackers. The Germans, freed from having to take cover from the barrage, were able to emerge from their dugouts, man their defences and cut down the vulnerable British infantry. Meanwhile, the supporting barrage drifted away from the infantry. In essence, the artillery left the battlefield, forcing the infantry to fight their way forward alone. However, during the course of the Battle of the Somme the British developed a technique called the creeping barrage. While not consistently applied on the Somme, by 1917 the creeping barrage became "standard operating procedure" within the BEF.

As its name implies, the creeping barrage was an artillery barrage that crept forward just in front of the advancing infantry. The shells would explode just far enough ahead of the attackers so that friendly casualties were avoided. However, they burst close enough to the advance that the Canadian infantry would be upon the German defenders as soon as the barrage lifted from the German trench and before the defenders could man their parapets. In this sense, the creeping barrage was a neutralizing barrage. It was not intended to kill the defending Germans (although that was, of course, welcomed), but instead was meant to hold the Germans in their dugouts until the Canadian infantry were close enough to kill them.

This is a simple explanation of the creeping barrage and its complexity becomes apparent with closer analysis. To begin with, for the creeping barrage to be effective, it had to be accurate. This involved, not only accurate shooting by the artillery (difficult in itself as we saw in Part III), but also close coordination with the infantry. The creeping barrage would be of no value if it moved too fast and left the infantry vulnerable and lethal if it moved too slow and shelled friendly troops.

To deal with this potential problem, the creeping barrage was timed to creep forward at a pace complimenting the infantry advance. Thus, at Vimy Ridge, the creeping barrage would advance at a pace of 100 yards every three or five minutes (depending on the difficulty of the terrain and defences the infantry had to tackle). The barrage paused where obstacles to the advance were anticipated or follow up infantry formations had to form up to re-new the attack. Behind the creeping barrage the infantry would advance as close as safely possible, which was generally about 75 yards.

As may be imagined, timing was essential. The whole plan depended on the artillery and infantry closely following the barrage time-table. Any delays could be fatal. At Vimy the necessary split second timing between the artillery and infantry was achieved by watches being synchronized.

The creeping barrage was not a single barrage either. Instead, there were several separate barrages that worked together to form the creeping barrage. That which exploded immediately in front of the attacking infantry was referred to as the rolling barrage. This was fired by the 18-pounder field guns and consisted of shrapnel rounds exploding over-head and raining shrapnel down below onto the German trenches.

The artillery batteries firing the rolling barrage were super-imposed on each other. That way, if an emergency occurred during the course of the barrage, a battery could be switched from firing the barrage to shooting at the trouble spot. The remaining battery would continue firing the rolling barrage and the creeping barrage as a whole would not be affected. This system allowed for some flexibility in case of emergencies, without hampering the barrage plan.

Firing deeper into the German defences was a standing barrage. This fell on a trench system ahead of the rolling barrage and was fired by 18-pounder field guns and 4.5-inch howitzers. The shells used were a mixture of shrapnel and high explosive so that not only would the shrapnel neutralize defenders, but the high explosive rounds would also damage German trenches. The standing barrage would "jump forward" to a further German trench system when the rolling barrage crept close to it.

Even deeper than the standing barrage, 4.5-inch field howitzers and heavy howitzers (6-inch, 8-inch and 9.2-inch) fired on German trench systems and defences. For the 4.5-inch howitzers, this included dropping shells into communication trenches, or, in the phrase used in operation orders "walking up communication trenches." As all these howitzers fired high explosive shells, the barrages they put on were designed to destroy the trenches that were being hit.[272]

Added to the artillery's creeping barrage was a machine gun barrage fired by the soldiers manning the Vickers heavy machine guns. Shooting from positions behind Canadian front lines, the machine guns' barrage was synchronized with the rolling barrage fired by the artillery, creeping forward deeper into German lines at timed phases as the infantry advanced behind it.[273] This was, in essence, using machine guns as a form of artillery as the machine gunners fired over the heads of the advancing infantry at targets the machine gunners could not see. The desired effect was to kill any Germans above ground, or to force them to take cover until the Canadian infantry closed on them.

Using machine guns in this manner (referred to as indirect firing) was a Canadian tactical innovation. Pioneered by Lieutenant-Colonel Raymond Brutinel of the Canadian Machine Gun Corps in 1916, it was standard practice in the Canadian Corps by the time of Vimy Ridge. Its usefulness was realized within the larger BEF so that later in the War indirect firing by Vickers machine guns became a facet of all British attacks.[274]

What was devised for the Battle of Vimy Ridge was a sophisticated artillery barrage, supplemented by machine guns, that was hundreds of yards deep and slowly crept its way through the German defensive system. Within the creeping barrage the howitzers at the far end ploughed through and destroyed trenches and defenders as it worked its way forward. This howitzer barrage, coupled with the standing barrage that fell in the middle of the creeping barrage, ensured that German reinforcements could not assist their comrades in forward trenches and made escape for any Germans within the barrage virtually impossible. Near the infantry, the rolling barrage and machine gun barrage crept forward, keeping the Germans' in their dugouts until the Canadian infantry were close enough to finish them off on their own. The creeping barrage would protect the whole advance from north of Hill 145 to the Commandant's House at the Ridge's southern end. Not only was the creeping barrage complicated, it was massive.

Six

The Powerful Platoon

The artillery was not the only arm that had absorbed lessons from the fighting on the Somme. The infantry, too, gained from post-battle reflection. The result was a new platoon organization designed to deal with the formidable German defences that were an ever present feature on the Western Front.

The importance of this development is not obvious, so a bit of background is appropriate. In prior wars such as the American Civil War, the smallest tactical unit on the battlefield was the battalion (or its equivalent in that war, the regiment), numbering about 300 to 500 men in combat. The battalion would move as one and all soldiers within the battalion were armed with the same weapon; the rifle (in that war the rifled musket).

In battle, the infantry soldier would move in synchronization with his comrades, close together and in long lines, advancing or retreating under the direction of the officers. When the line of soldiers came close to the line of enemy infantry, both lines blasted away at each other with their rifles until one line or the other broke. As can be imagined, this system was totally inadequate for the Great War with its powerful artillery, machine guns and grenades.

By the Battle of the Somme, the infantry weapons of trench warfare (grenade, rifle grenade and Lewis Gun) had appeared in the battalions of the BEF. However, the main armament of the infantry battalion in the attack was still the rifle, supplemented by specialists armed with weapons such as the Lewis Gun or rifle grenades. While the infantry no longer advanced in closely packed lines like in the American Civil War, the individual soldier still was often unaware of his battalion's objective and relied on his battalion or company officers for guidance. The battalion (usually 700-800 all ranks going into action) or company (of which there were four companies in a battalion) remained the main tactical unit.[275]

We can try to imagine the difficulties this arrangement could produce on the battlefield. Imagine a situation where a German machine gun position holds up an infantry advance. The soldiers facing the machine gun are armed with rifles and cannot bring sufficient firepower to bear on the Germans. To tackle this enemy position, weapons such as rifle grenades or a Lewis Gun are needed, but the soldiers carrying these weapons are some distance away. Bearing in mind the communication problems on the Great War battlefield and the high casualties suffered in any Great War attack, it might be impossible to bring a rifle grenade or Lewis Gun to assist. The German machine gun fire could be preventing any attempt to cross the projectile swept battlefield to communicate with the specialists. Worse for the attackers, those in command may have become casualties and no one is available to even make the decision to bring the specialists' firepower to bear on the German machine gun. The attack has been stopped.

Prior to the Battle of Vimy Ridge there was an overhaul in infantry tactics. Rather than the battalion or the company being the main tactical unit, it would now be the platoon. The infantry platoon was a small unit, consisting of about 40 men, with four platoons making up a company. The platoon was commanded by a junior officer (a lieutenant) and was divided into four sections, each under a NCO. Most important was that each section would be based around a different weapon for trench warfare. One section was still composed of riflemen, but now there would be one each armed with a Lewis Gun, hand grenades (the Mills Bomb) and rifle grenades (all men, except the No. 1 on the Lewis Gun, did bring a rifle and a couple of Mills bombs into combat too).[276]

This change in platoon tactics may seem technical, but it was of fundamental importance. Returning to the hypothetical German machine gun example above, those infantrymen facing the enemy position could now deal with the problem on their own as all the weapons they needed were accessible. The Lewis Gun could provide automatic covering fire on the enemy machine gun while the rifle grenadiers tried to take it out from a distance with long range bombing. Using this covering fire, the riflemen or bombers could close in on the enemy position and kill any remaining defenders. The new platoon organization was a much more efficient and flexible system as each platoon was now self-sufficient and could operate on its own without the need to communicate with company or battalion commanders.

On the day of the Battle, the Canadians would attack with their new platoon organization in a wave formation. That is, for the actual assault on any given trench or defensive position, the Canadians would attack in a series of waves. The distance between each wave varied according to local circumstances and tasks (from fifteen yards to 100 yards), with about five yards between each man in a wave (this was the ideal, of course, and bunching and spreading out would invariably occur in combat). Each wave had a particular objective, such as a trench, so that once a wave had taken its objective, follow up waves would pass through and carry the attack forward to their own objectives.

While this may appear to be a somewhat inflexible assault formation, should a unit within a wave be held up, for example, by a German machine gun, the units on the flank were not to stop their advance because part of the wave was held up. Instead, the flank units were to push on despite the hold up, make for their objective and then envelop the machine gun from the flanks and rear, using their new platoon organization to full advantage.

As we saw previously, some of the objectives, particularly those on the Blue and Brown Lines, were deep in German territory. To capture these objectives troops would "leap frog" through each other. For example, in 1st Division, the 2nd and 3rd Brigades were to attack and capture the Black and Red Lines. Once the Red Line was captured, the 1st Brigade would pass through, or "leap frog," the 2nd and 3rd Brigades and carry the assault on to capture the Blue and Brown Lines. This leap frogging was designed to ensure that fresh troops could maintain the momentum of the attack. It was deemed that by the Red Line the 2nd and 3rd Brigades would become weakened by casualties and exhaustion and the fresh 1st Brigade would be needed to carry the attack to the eastern slope of Vimy Ridge. Once having "leap-frogged" through the 2nd and 3rd Brigades, the 1st Brigade would deploy into wave formation for their attack.

Tying the new platoon organization and leap frogging tactics with the artillery's creeping barrage, the Canadian Corps had an efficient method for dealing with German defences that was not seen during the Battle of the Somme. The creeping barrage would pass over the German trenches, the howitzers smashing defences followed by the exploding shrapnel rounds keeping the German infantry men's heads down. Once the barrage had passed over, the Canadian infantry would be immediately upon the Germans, using the firepower of their platoons to deal with any Germans who survived the artillery barrage. These advances in artillery and infantry tactics, while not glamorous, were intelligent and effective.

Seven

The Intelligent Soldier

These tactical developments would be wasted unless the soldiers understood them. Thus, training was essential. This emphasis on training, in itself, distinguishes the Great War soldier from his predecessors. Other than parade ground manoeuvres, actual battle training was foreign to a soldier from the U.S. Civil War. Once in battle, the Civil War soldier often had no idea what his unit's objective was and attacked or retreated under the direction of his officers. On the other hand, for those in the Canadian Corps, training for combat was an integral part of being a soldier.

During the Winter of 1917, all Battalions in the Canadian Corps spent time training when they were out of the line. Under the direction of their officers, training in the Winter of 1917 focussed on matters of a more general nature such as physical exercises, musketry, bomb throwing and bayonet fighting. However, some training was geared towards the future offensive as men practised platoon and company attacks and also learned the new platoon organization.

The intense training during the Winter of 1917 lead the more astute men in the Canadian Corps to suspect that something big was in the making. The War Diarist for the 13th Battalion (Royal Highlanders of Canada) noted as early as January 4:

> Hard training is now the order of the day, and if there is any truth in the old saying that "Coming events cast their shadows before" there is a stormy time in store for someone in the near future.[277]

As the offensive neared, training took on a different character. While general matters such as physical training were still part of the training syllabus, battle practice became standard. Behind Canadian lines the engineers taped out practice trenches. Based on aerial and ground observation and intelligence, they replicated the actual German trenches the soldiers would face. Each practice trench was custom designed for the defences each unit would assault. Not only would a Battalion do practice runs on taped trenches, but whole Brigades would rehearse the attack with officers from Corps on down observing and making corrections.

Captain D.E. Macintyre (Brigade-Major 4th Brigade) remembered the battle practices:

> A large open field with a gentle slope had been requisitioned for use as a training ground. On this had been staked out with broad tape, a replica of the trenches we were to capture. Over these tapes we put the men again and again, first by platoons and then by increasing numbers, until the day came when the entire brigade carried out the exercise together, one battalion following another in line, everyone walking, the officers timing the advance by their watches and the men with their rifles at the high port, bayonets fixed, ready to shoot or lunge. At each taped barrage line, all would halt and wait a few minutes until the barrage lifted to the next line. Mounted officers carrying flags represented the rolling barrage. Any delay at a given point meant that, if our men were not in a position to pounce as soon as the barrage lifted, the enemy would come out of his dugouts and open fire, so perfect timing was essential.
>
> To reassure myself that all ranks understood the scheme, I would occasionally question a man picked at random.[278]

Private Victor Wheeler of the 50th (Calgary) Battalion recalled how detailed the practice trenches were:

> There were "White Tape" rehearsals in which literally miles of white and coloured tape were strategically laid out over the ground representing our proposed jump-off positions and those of the enemy which would be our objectives during the various stages of the advance. The tapes also represented trenches, communication trenches, strongholds, redoubts, pill-boxes, barbed wire snares (entanglements), suspected mine positions, machine-gun emplacements, buildings and topographical features that would pose special difficulties.
>
> The tapes comprised the blueprints that had to be studied carefully and understood thoroughly before the "builders" (in this case the "wreckers") took up their tools to go to work. The tape rehearsals simulated the obstacles we could expect to encounter the moment we jumped over the top and advanced on the enemy. We rehearsed for the coming battle, over these sham trenches and obstacles, with earnestness and, in fact, with such realism that it was to spell immortal victory when the real Zero Hour struck.[279] (parentheses in original)

Not only were the practice attacks detailed, but they were repeated again and again so that the troops fully understood what was expected of them. Years later, W.S.

Wilson's (38th Ottawa Battalion) view was that "Every time the battalion was out of the line and in support or reserve we were practising on the tapes . . ."[280]

Corporal Fraser (6th Machine Gun Company) reflected after the Battle on the value of his prior training:

> When at Servins a month ago, we marched to fields where a plan of our front was laid out to match as near as possible the terrain we had to cover. The principal features that we would meet on the actual battlefield were marked out. This rehearsal gave us a very good idea of the distance we had to travel, and when the actual test came I had absolutely no difficulty in making for my objective without the least deviation. Everything loomed up as clear as crystal – the wire, the roads, the village, the cemetery, the separate woods and the railway embankment beyond.[281]

The effort to make the training as realistic as possible was not limited to reproducing the defensive obstacles that would be faced during the attack. Some practice attacks, particularly those performed close to the date of the offensive, were done in full fighting equipment. Mounted men with flags represented the creeping barrage so the infantry would be familiar with how the barrage operated and the need to stay close to it. The soldiers also practised sending flare signals to contact airplanes; those planes tasked with following, noting and communicating to the generals in the rear the extent of the infantry's advance on the day of the attack.

The soldiers did not only practice "best case" scenarios. Some rehearsals were undertaken to teach the officers and men to meet and overcome potential difficulties on the battlefield. There were practice attacks designed, for example, to train the soldiers to deal with the situation where a unit is held up by a strong point and neighboring units outflank the strong point. Another scenario practised was to remove senior officers from the rehearsal. That way, junior officers and NCOs could practice leading the attack should casualties be severe amongst officers on the day of the attack. W.J. Home of the Royal Canadian Regiment remembered:

> It even got so that if every officer was knocked out the non-commissioned officers would know what to do. For instance, we'd go out today and we'd practice the attack and the Colonel would say, "Now so many officers have been knocked out," and you'd find perhaps a sergeant taking command of a company, and it got so that every man knew exactly what he had to do.[282]

In all cases, emphasis was placed on using the firepower and flexibility of the new platoon organization to deal with potential obstacles to the advance.[283]

To increase the flexibility of the new platoon formation, the soldiers were trained, not just in the use of their own personal weapons, but also in the use of the other weapons in the platoon.[284] That way, should casualties be severe in any section within a platoon, the soldiers in the other sections could take over and use the weapons of their fallen comrades. In addition to this, Lewis Gunners and Vickers machine gunners were trained in the use of German machine guns.[285] If enemy machine guns were captured in the attack, the Canadians would be able to turn them against their former owners.

Complimenting the training were informational lectures given by officers to the other ranks. The 13th Battalion (Royal Highlanders of Canada) April 3, 1917, War Diary entry records:

> Units paraded at 9 am for practice of Battalion in attack: and in the afternoon a little variety was introduced into the work, by way of a lecture, held in the YMCA Hut, dealing with the various features of the attack, which was being rehearsed. The lecture was illustrated by means of large sized maps, showing clearly the different objectives, trenches, positions to be occupied by the different Companies, etc., and, the men were also given as much information as possible, concerning the nature of the Country over which they had to advance, and a general idea of what Artillery support etc., would be available, also instruction in the various methods of light signals.[286]

There were also plaster models of Vimy Ridge and its defences at Divisional Headquarters for officers and senior NCOs to view.[287]

In Sergeant E.S. Russenholt's (44th Manitoba Battalion) opinion, the training for the Battle of Vimy Ridge was superior to that done on the Somme. He recalled:

> We were an entirely different army than at the Somme. I suppose that some of the terrible things that happened at the Somme were of some benefit in turning out the type of army that we had at Vimy. We had mastered our job. I think that's the basis of the whole show. Training, training, training![288]

What was intended was to provide the men with the knowledge and skills to get the job done and the confidence to do it. It was successful, as can be gleaned from A.A. Bonar's (Princess Patricia's Canadian Light Infantry) description of the tactics he practised during the pre-Battle training:

> The infantry advance in long waves, the first wave keeping forty yards behind the barrage or as near it as comfortable. When the barrage lifts the waves jump forward a given distance, keeping close to the barrage until it lifts again, when the same tactic is repeated.

> The great advantage of this style of attack is apparent. The concentrated drum-fire from artillery and machine guns keeps the enemy in his dugouts. When the barrage lifts he hasn't time to come out of his subterranean galleries to work his machine guns before our infantry are on top of him. This plan of attack is based

on the theory of modern trench warfare that the artillery takes the trench. The infantry hold them after they are taken.

The infantry formation is modelled, so that should an enemy machine gun or strong point not having been put out of action by the artillery, offer resistance and threaten to hold up the main attack, the platoon being a self-contained unit can handle the problem itself.

Each platoon has a complement of 50 men made up of a Lewis gun, rifle grenadier, bombing and bayonet sections, and a couple of runners and stretcher bearers. A platoon advances in two waves. Working as a unit it is most formidable in attack and able to overcome local opposition.

During our rehearsals work developed in each platoon, and in every company. The officers gave lectures to the men, and took them into their confidence in a manner that would have surprised old warriors.

The men saw maps of the actual frontage assigned to each battalion and brigade. The officers showed them maps taken from aeroplanes with the topographical features clearly outlined. An espirit de corps was developed. Everyone was on his toes, enthusiastic, keen and confident.[289]

The intense and detailed training designed to familiarize the men with their role on the battlefield created a new type of soldier; the "intelligent soldier." Whereas soldiers in prior conflicts such as the American Civil War were, in a tactical sense, merely platforms for their rifles following their officers wherever they lead, such was not the case for the Canadian soldiers at Vimy Ridge. Each soldier knew what his objective was before the Battle, had practised the attack, was familiar with the artillery tactics to be employed, knew how to use his weapon as part of the new and powerful platoon organization and could carry out the attack even with the loss of his officers. The development of the "intelligent soldier" was a complete departure from the past and leads directly to the modern, 21st Century fighting man or woman.

The "intelligent soldier" added a further level of sophistication to the well thought out creeping barrage and new platoon tactics. While none of these tactical improvements were of the kind noted in books on "brilliant battles," the superficially simple frontal attack on Vimy Ridge would be the most complex frontal assault to that point in history.

Eight

The Artillery Support

Before the day of the attack on Vimy Ridge, the artillery would first reduce the Germans' defensive capacity. To accomplish this, an impressive amount of artillery was amassed to bombard the Ridge prior to the infantry attack. A total of 1 106 artillery pieces were used in the operation at Vimy.

Underlining the fact that the assault was a First Army assignment, 238 of the 1 106 guns were not on the Canadian Corps' front at all. These guns were located to the north of Vimy Ridge on the front held by the British I Corps. The I Corps artillery was to assist the Canadian Corps' artillery by firing at the German defences on Vimy Ridge in enfilade (at an angle). They would also create a diversion for the Canadians' assault by cutting the German wire and destroying German trenches to the north of the Ridge to give the Germans the impression that there would be an attack in that area as well.[290]

Below Vimy Ridge, the Canadian Corps had 854 artillery pieces. Under the command of the Canadian, Brigadier-General Edward Morrison (GOC Canadian Corps Artillery), most of these pieces had not been with the Canadian Corps during the Winter of 1917. Instead, once again demonstrating that the attack on Vimy Ridge was a First Army operation, the Canadian Corps artillery was substantially reinforced for the assault.

During the Winter of 1917, the Divisions in the Canadian Corps were supported by their divisional field artillery. However, for the attack on Vimy Ridge First Army provided field artillery reinforcements from its own reserve; 72nd, 26th, 28th, 93rd, 18th, 242nd and 76th Brigades Army Field Artillery. A brigade of artillery was also supplied from the 5th Brigade Royal Horse Artillery (a cavalry unit). Further field artillery came from other Divisions not Canadian, the British 31st, 5th and 63rd Divisional Artillery.[291]

A moment should be taken to mention the unique history of the 63rd Divisional Artillery. The 63rd Division was actually not an army unit, rather, it came from the Royal

Navy and was designated the 63rd (Royal Naval) Division. Composed of Royal Marines and naval reserves that were not needed to man the ships, the Royal Naval Division saw action throughout the War at Gallipoli and on the Western Front.[292] The soldiers and officers of the Division retained their naval ranks and served in battalions named after great naval heroes from Britain's history such as the "Drake" and "Nelson" Battalions. While it was only the Royal Naval Division's artillery that served at Vimy Ridge, the infantry would see action soon after during the Battle of Arras.

It was not just the field artillery that was reinforced by First Army, as the important heavy pieces were also increased in numbers for the offensive. Eleven Heavy Artillery Groups were supplied, two of which were Canadian.[293] Of the 854 artillery pieces in the Canadian Corps, 238 were heavy calibres. To this must be added 14 super-heavy pieces provided by First Army for use against Vimy Ridge. Finally, out of the 238 guns and how-itzers from I Corps that were helping the Canadians, 136 of these were heavy pieces.[294]

To give these numbers meaning a comparison is appropriate. The Canadian Corps had 1 106 artillery pieces supporting its attack, of which 374 were heavy calibres and 14 were super-heavies. The Canadian Corps' assault was to be made by four infantry divisions on a frontage of just under 7 000 yards. In contrast, at the Battle of the Somme, Fourth Army attacked on July 1, 1916, with eleven infantry divisions on a frontage of about 20 000 yards metres). This assault was supported by 1 423 artillery pieces of which 413 were heavy calibres.[295] As can be seen, there was a much greater concentration of artillery for the Battle of Vimy Ridge than there had been for the Battle of the Somme, particularly with respect to the powerful heavy artillery pieces. While these numbers are impressive, what really matters is how the artillery was used and it is to this that we will turn to next.

Nine

The Preliminary Bombardment

History records that the Battle of Vimy Ridge was fought between April 9 to 13, 1917. Although true with respect to the infantry assault, the artillery had already been in action for several weeks. The preliminary bombardment in preparation for the attack began on March 20 and continued right up until the infantry left their jumping-off trenches in the early morning of April 9. During this period the artillery performed a number of important tasks; trench destruction, wire cutting, harassment, concentrated bombardments of villages, feint barrages and counter-battery work. Each will be briefly examined in turn.

Trench destruction was the domain of the howitzers. Their high explosive shells, fired at a high trajectory, were perfect for plunging into trenches and blasting gaps in the German trench system. The amount of destruction wrought by a particular shell depended on what size of howitzer was used and the Canadian Corps had several calibres available. The most numerous were the quick firing 4.5-inch howitzers of the field artillery, of which there were 138 in the Canadian Corps. Less in number, but firing a larger and more devastating shell, were the 6-inch howitzers (104 in the Canadian Corps) and the 8-inch and 9.2-inch howitzers (36 of each).[296] By way of comparison, the 4.5-inch howitzer fired a shell weighing 35 pounds, while the 9.2-inch howitzer's shell weighed 290 pounds.[297]

The howitzers' task was no less than the systematic destruction of the German trench system at Vimy Ridge. This included, not just the trenches of course, but also defensive positions that formed part of the trench system, such as machine gun emplacements and other strong points. German dugouts and tunnels were also targeted. As these were built underground, they were particularly difficult to destroy. However, the dugouts and tunnels did have entrances into the trenches and these were what the artillery mainly fired at. Entrances were collapsed, entombing the German garrison or rendering the dugout or tunnel useless. To complete their destruction of the German trench system, the howitzers were active each day, with accuracy being obtained through both ground and aerial observation on the drop of shells.[298]

NAC-PA1058 – The bombardment of German defences on Vimy Ridge.

Wire cutting was necessary prior to the infantry assault to avoid the potentially lethal problem of an attack being stopped and then destroyed on the German barbed wire. However, this problem was not limited to just the German front line, for each successive trench that the Germans dug on Vimy Ridge was wired. All the German wire at Vimy Ridge would have to be comprehensively destroyed.

We saw earlier during the Battle of the Somme that wire cutting was a major problem in that engagement. Many attacks had failed due to the barbed wire remaining an obstacle despite prior bombardment by the artillery. This was largely due to an over-reliance on the 18-pounder field guns, usually firing shrapnel shells. The shrapnel rounds often exploded harmlessly, rattling the wire, but not breaking it.

While 18-pounders were used for wire cutting at Vimy Ridge, they were not used exclusively. Instead, the task for cutting the German wire protecting their forward trench system was given to the medium (2-inch) and heavy (9.45-inch) trench mortars which fired high explosive bombs. For wire protecting trench systems deeper in German lines, the heavy artillery was used.[299] Only the barbed wire located between that being dealt with by the heavy artillery and the trench mortars was fired on by the 18-pounders.[300] For this wire the 18-pounders still used shrapnel, but by early 1917 the gunners were more experienced and accurate than they were at the Somme. They were able to place their shots so that the shells exploded just in front of and above the wire, where shrapnel had the most effect.

Assisting the heavy artillery in wire cutting on the deeper enemy lines was an improvement in shell design. Recently developed was a shell with what was called the 106 fuze. What made the 106 fuze so important was that, unlike the high explosive delay fuze rounds used on the Somme which burst ineffectually below ground under the wire, the 106 burst on contact. Thus, as soon as the shell touched the wire or the ground it burst, which made for a much more devastating impact on the German wire. Being more effective, it resulted in less shells having to be fired to destroy any given stretch of wire.[301]

The 106 fuze also played a "clean up" role at Vimy. Should the 18-pounders or trench mortars have difficulty with any particular stretch of wire, the 106 fuze was used to smash the obstacle.[302] The unwelcome spectre of uncut wire faced the soldiers of the 1st and 2nd Divisions in front of the southern half of Vimy Ridge. Here, the trench mortars were experiencing difficulty in breaking up the German wire. In some places the failure was due to terrain, as the craters from old mine explosions made the German wire a hard target to hit.[303]

German artillery retaliation was a factor too, particularly at the south end of Vimy Ridge. The trench mortar crews in 1st Division were having a very trying time as poor weather, faulty rifle mechanisms and German shell fire conspired to seriously hinder their wire cutting. In a summary after the Battle, the 1st Divisional Trench Mortar Group's War Diarist recorded that each day there were 5 to 6 hits on their medium trench mortar positions from enemy shell fire. By April 9 only one heavy trench mortar (out of 6) was still in action.[304] To avert the potential disaster of having the infantry attack trenches still protected by barbed wire, the 18-pounders, assisted by the 4.5-inch howitzers firing the 106 fuze, were able to break the wire facing 1st and 2nd Divisions in time for the assault.[305]

All this trench destruction and wire cutting would come to naught if the Germans were able to repair their defences. To deal with this, the artillery placed great emphasis on nightly harassment. Similar to that done during the Winter of 1917, but at an increased rate, the artillery fired at night on communication trenches, overland tracks, light railways, etc. in an effort to catch German soldiers exposed and on the move. This harassment would, it was hoped, impede the delivery of supplies and intercept unit reliefs.

What was added for the offensive was nightly firing, mainly by 18-pounders and 4.5-inch howitzers, on parts of the German trench system or barbed wire damaged by Canadian and British shelling during the day. By doing this it was hoped that casualties would be inflicted on German work parties or, at least, that the Germans would be dissuaded from repairing their defences. While this night shooting was unobserved and, thus, the artillery did not know if their rounds were actually hitting the enemy, it was noted in the days leading up to the infantry assault that the Germans were not repairing their damaged defensive system.[306] The danger this night firing posed to the Germans was increased by the Vickers machine gunners firing on the same targets.

During daylight, as in the Winter, the artillery was always keen to take on a target of opportunity, such as a work party moving overland between trenches. However, with the artillery engaged in a multitude of tasks for the preliminary artillery bombardment, it was not always easy to find a gun available to shoot at such fleeting targets. To deal with this situation, a few artillery pieces were designated sniper guns to shell any targets of opportunity the forward observation officers discovered.

Part of the Germans' defence of Vimy Ridge were a number of French villages. Most of these villages, such as Vimy itself, were located on the east side of the Ridge and were outside the infantry's assault objectives. However, two of them, Les Tilleuls and Thelus, were on the western slope and would have to be captured. Of these, Thelus caused the commanders in the Canadian Corps considerable concern.

Thelus was strongly defended. Not only did the Germans protect it with trenches and dugouts, but the Village's buildings and cellars provided additional defences. Thelus was also located just to the south-west of Hill 135; the second highest feature on Vimy Ridge. Being a high point, the Hill provided an observation advantage for the Germans and it dominated the ground to the west, south and east. Bearing in mind that the Battle of Vimy Ridge was a supporting operation for Third Army's larger attack further south, the capture of Hill 135 was the Canadian Corps' primary objective for the Battle.[307] If Hill 135 did not fall, this could place Third Army's offensive in jeopardy. Thus, the capture of Hill 135 was crucial, and to take the Hill and hold it, Thelus would have to be captured as well.

The artillery placed a series of concentrated bombardments on each village, with particular attention paid to Thelus. These concentrated bombardments involved 10 to 15 minutes of intense shooting by the super-heavy howitzers (12-inch and 15-inch), heavy artillery and field artillery on each village. Following a pause after the intense bombardment, the 18-pounders (field gun) and 60-pounders (heavy gun) would fire bursts on the village hoping, no doubt, to catch Germans emerging from their dugouts or soldiers rushing to the village to assist wounded comrades.[308] So that the Germans were kept off-balance, the time of the concentrated bombardments varied from day to day.

While the other villages were shelled for the purpose of causing casualties to and demoralizing the German defenders within, Thelus was bombarded with the aim of destroying it. To achieve this level of destruction, not only was Thelus subjected to intermittent concentrated bombardments like the other villages, but the super-heavy and heavy howitzers undertook a program of systematically destroying it. The super-heavy howitzers were particularly useful in turning Thelus into a pile of rubble as their shells were of considerable weight. Earlier in this Chapter it was noted that the heavy 9.2-inch howitzers fired a shell weighing 290 pounds. Those fired by the 12-inch howitzers weighed 750 pounds, while the 15-inch howitzer's shell was 1 400 pounds![309] Not only were the trenches and wire on Vimy Ridge being systematically and comprehensively destroyed, so too was the Village of Thelus.[310]

The artillery fired a number of feint barrages during the preliminary bombardment. These were essentially rehearsals of the creeping barrage to be fired on the day of the attack, but did have some key differences. To begin with, the feint barrages were not a full rehearsal. While the actual rolling barrage would lead the infantry across the entire Ridge, the feint barrages only went as far as the Black Line. Once on the Black Line, instead of continuing to advance, the barrage would drop back onto one of the trenches that made up the front line system. Feint barrages were conducted on the entire Canadian Corps front and on individual Division fronts, and involved both field and heavy artillery.

These feint barrages were useful in providing the opportunity to observe the barrage and make any necessary adjustments prior to the attack. There was also an element of deception to the feints. With all the artillery activity that was going on, it was impossible to disguise the fact that an offensive was upcoming. By firing feint barrages, the Canadians could at least deceive the Germans on its timing. When the actual barrage came, they might be fooled into thinking that it was just another feint. Further, by having the feint barrages drop back after reaching the Black Line, the commanders of the Canadian Corps hoped to induce the Germans to delay manning their trenches when the actual barrage came. Having manned their trenches in response to feint barrages only to have the barrage come crashing down on them again, it was hoped that on the day of the attack the Germans would have become wary from past experience. This delay could give the infantry valuable extra time to reach the German trenches.[311]

While the feint barrages were being performed, observers were tasked with noting the German artillery's retaliation.[312] As we saw earlier, British counter-battery work (the locating and neutralizing of enemy artillery pieces) during the Battle of the Somme was poor. Because of this, when it came time for the infantry to assault, it was not uncommon for them to be subjected to heavy German artillery fire as they crossed No Man's Land. Often, this caused severe casualties to the attacker and could stop an assault. Even if there was success in capturing German trenches, reinforcements and supplies for the attack would be blocked by the shelling in No Man's Land. The attackers would then be cut off in German lines and vulnerable to counter-attack. Therefore, for the Canadian offensive to succeed, the German artillery had to be dealt with.

For the Canadians, advances in technology and tactics since the Battle of the Somme would greatly assist counter-battery work at Vimy. One such advance was a technique known as sound ranging. At its most basic, this involved the placing of microphones at different points behind the Canadian Corps' front lines. These microphones would pick up the sound of a German artillery piece firing and by noting the differences between when each microphone picked up the sound, the position of the German gun could be calculated.

Also now developed was flash spotting. With flash spotting, an observer would note the bearings where he saw the flash from a German artillery piece firing. As there were many observers at different points of the line, each observer would make his own notation. By collecting these bearings and plotting them on a map, the Canadians could tell where the German artillery pieces were located by the intersection of the observers' bearings.[313]

Gunnery in the Great War was a science by 1917, and the counter-battery techniques of sound ranging and flash spotting are examples of this scientific approach. The Canadians also had the right type of man in charge of the counter-battery work at Vimy; the Canadian, Lieutenant-Colonel Andrew McNaughton. Educated in the sciences, he had received a Bachelors of Science with Honors in Electrical Engineering and a Masters of Science from McGill University before the War. He also had a pre-war interest in gunnery, having served in a militia battery. A young man at 30 years of age, with a thoughtful, scientific mind, McNaughton was naturally receptive to these counter-battery techniques (some of which he had experience with in civilian use before the War) and was committed to their proper application in battle.[314]

Taking advantage of these new techniques, Lt-Col. McNaughten and his counter-battery staff were able to effectively locate their adversary's artillery positions. While most of the actual counter-battery work would take place on the day of the attack, the British and Canadians still kept the Germans busy before then by firing on some of their artillery batteries.[315] Unlike on the Somme, the German artillery would feel the full effects of an offensive at Vimy Ridge.

The preliminary artillery bombardment for the assault on Vimy Ridge was, in a word, thorough. An enormous number of artillery pieces, ranging from 18-pounder field guns to the 15-inch super-heavy howitzers, were amassed to bombard German defences from March 20 to April 9. The British and Canadian gunners systematically destroyed German defensive positions, barbed wire and fortified villages, harassed work and supply parties at night, practised their barrages and maintained surveillance and harassing fire on German artillery batteries. Life was made more difficult and dangerous for the German soldiers as each day passed, all in the hope of breaking the Germans' will and ability to resist the upcoming infantry onslaught.

Ten

Phasing in the Bombardment

Having reached an understanding of what the artillery did during the preliminary bombardment, it should be realized that the bombardment did not commence at full force on March 20. Not only would this have involved a stupendous expenditure of ammunition, but it would also have clearly indicated to the Germans at too early a stage that an offensive was coming. Instead, the artillery had a plan to gradually increase their preparations for the attack.

The artillery's plan was divided into phases. Phase I ran from March 20 to April 2, Phase II from April 2 to zero-hour on April 9 and Phase III being the barrage supporting the infantry assault on the 9th. Phase IV involved the forward movement of the guns after the infantry had captured their objectives. For our present purposes, we are concerned with Phases I and II.

Phase I could be described as transitional with a gradual increase in artillery activity on the Canadians' front. To begin with, the 854 artillery pieces that the Canadian Corps would have for their attack were not all present on March 20. Many of the artillery reinforcements from First Army arrived during the period March 20 to April 2.

To accommodate this increase, Phase I involved much labor. New gun positions were constructed and artillery pieces moved into them. Telephone communication with observation posts had to be established and ammunition dumps built to supply the guns. The War Diarist for the 3rd Canadian Siege Battery recorded the situation at the guns:

> It is a busy scene, new troops and new Batteries are moving in and taking up their positions. Registrations are being carried out, roads being built and preparations going on at a brisk rate for the big advance, which it is rumored will come off shortly.[316]

To disguise this increase in guns, not all available artillery fired during Phase I. Instead, only a proportion of the field guns and not more than 50 percent of the heavy artillery were active. New gun positions were concealed and the registration of undisclosed artillery pieces on their Phase II targets was done under the cover of artillery bombardments. By such actions, it was hoped that the Germans would not discover that the Canadian Corps artillery was reinforced.

In terms of the tasks the artillery performed during the preliminary bombardment, full scale preparations were not yet undertaken. With respect to trench destruction and wire cutting, the artillery were only to fire on targets within the Red Line. Night firing and counter-battery work was done, but not at the levels that would occur closer to the date for the assault. By limiting the bombardment in this manner, the Canadians sought to confuse the Germans as to their ultimate intentions; the capture of the whole Ridge.

Phase I involved a methodical intensification of the British and Canadian artillery program, with the artillery gradually increasing their shooting. The intensification would reach a point such that the end of Phase I and the beginning of Phase II would not be noticed by the Germans.[317]

Although Phase I was a transitional stage from routine artillery activity to full scale bombardment, it still caused great hardship to the Germans. Prisoners captured by the Canadians during this Phase admitted to their captors that "life is being made unbearable" by the artillery fire.[318] It was only going to get worse.

Phase II was the full preliminary artillery bombardment and commenced on April 2. Many Canadian War Diaries describe this period as being one of "continuous bombardment." The Germans called it their "week of suffering."[319] Comparing Phase I to Phase II, the field artillery in the Canadian Corps fired 190 787 rounds and the heavy artillery 85 181 rounds during Phase I. In Phase II, the field artillery fired 537 836 and the heavy artillery 152 501 rounds. To the Phase II totals 1 392 rounds from the super-heavies should also be added.[320]

Initially, Phase II was expected to last until April 8, but the British and Canadian offensive was postponed by Third Army so the infantry assault would take place on April 9 instead. The extra day was put to good use as the gunners took the opportunity to ensure all their tasks were completed before the attack.[321]

By April 2, all of the 854 artillery pieces in the Canadian Corps were present and all guns became active, with one notable exception. The exception was the "forward batteries" (mainly 18-pounder batteries). Other than the forward batteries, the artillery in the Canadian Corps was placed behind the Canadian support line. This was close enough to shell the entire Ridge and east of it in the north, but in the south the 18-pounders firing the creeping barrage could only reach the Blue Line. To ensure that on the day of the attack the infantry would have the support of the creeping barrage beyond that, forward batteries were positioned in and around the Canadian support line. So placed, they had the range to carry the creeping barrage beyond the Blue Line all the way to just east of the Ridge once the 18-pounder batteries behind them lost the range. However, being so close to the front lines, the forward batteries remained silent so as not to "tip off" the Germans to their location or the Canadians' ultimate intentions (they did, however, register their guns under the cover of artillery bombardments).[322]

As the super-heavies had arrived by April 2, it was during Phase II that the concentrated bombardment of all villages and the systematic destruction of Thelus began in earnest. Trenches and defences along the whole of Vimy Ridge were comprehensively shelled, all wire that could present an obstacle was destroyed and night firing made any German movement and attempts at repairs a deadly undertaking. The trench mortars joined the artillery in this Phase by assisting in the destruction of the Germans' forward trenches.[323]

Captain Harold McGill from the 31st (Alberta) Battalion had an opportunity to watch, from well behind Canadian lines, the artillery in action during Phase II. He recalled:

> . . . my path crossed high ground from where I had a good view of a wide stretch of our objective two days thence. All around me in the valleys and folds of ground our heavy batteries, mostly 12-inch and 15-inch howitzers, were in full action, Vimy Ridge was boiling like a kettle under the storm of shells.[324]

During Phase II close liaison between the infantry and artillery was particularly important. At the front the infantry were well placed to note any wire or defences that remained undestroyed and could potentially hold up the advance. Where trouble spots were noticed by the infantry, this information was passed on to the artillery to finish the job.

On the 12th Brigade's front at the far north of Vimy Ridge, the commanding general of the Brigade, Brigadier-General McBrian, personally made requests for artillery fire on troublesome trenches and wire. Rather than waiting to be informed by his men as to the effect of the artillery's shooting, General McBrian accompanied the artillery's forward observation officer to an observation post in a sap in front of Canadian lines. From this forward position General McBrian was able to observe the effect of the artillery fire and also took the opportunity to snipe at Germans as they scrambled through their damaged trenches.[325]

Despite the obvious increase in shelling, there still was an element of deception to the artillery plan. While the artillery had been gradually increasing the intensity of their shooting from March 20 on, there was a conscious effort to halt this increase in the days immediately prior to the infantry attack. By stabilizing their fire, the Canadians wanted the Germans to become accustomed to the intense level of artillery activity and sought to confuse the Germans as to the actual date and time of the assault.[326]

NAC-PA 1070 Another photograph of the preliminary bombardment of Vimy Ridge.

The phasing in of the preliminary bombardment was an important element to the artillery plan at Vimy. Done partly to avoid expending too much ammunition, it also played a deception role. New guns were carefully brought into position and registered on their targets to avoid alerting the Germans to their presence. The British and Canadians also gradually increased, and then stabilized, the intensity of their shooting over the course of this period, hoping to confuse the Germans as to the date and timing of the attack. By the end of Phase II, with virtually all guns having been active for a week, Vimy Ridge had become a shattered wreck.

Eleven

Up in the Air

In common with their comrades on the ground, the pilots and observers of the RFC were busy preparing for the upcoming offensive against Vimy Ridge. Like the artillery, the RFC's offensive began before the infantry attack, commencing on April 4. Just as much of the artillery preparation for the attack consisted of an intensification of the work done in the Winter of 1917, so too was it for the airmen above Vimy Ridge.

In command of the RFC was Major-General Hugh Trenchard. To him, the RFC's role was clear. It was to support the army in the upcoming offensive. He realized that his pilots were flying inferior machines compared to the Germans (a situation he and Haig tried to redress without success) and that this would result in high casualties for his pilots and observers.[327] Despite these casualties, Trenchard felt that only aggressive flying would ensure air supremacy which would, in turn, allow the RFC to effectively support the army.[328]

The RFC's offensive was geared toward clearing the sky above Vimy Ridge of German aircraft. This would allow the artillery spotter aircraft to assist the artillery in their preliminary bombardment and the reconnaissance air-planes to take their photographs of German defences. Although the RFC's aircraft were inferior to the Germans', they did have the advantage in numbers of planes. Using this numerical advantage, the British fighters pushed offensive patrols deep behind German lines to engage the German fighters there, rather than allowing the fight to occur at Vimy Ridge where the vulnerable spotter and reconnaissance aircraft were performing their vital functions.[329]

In this the RFC was largely successful in that the artillery was able to effectively bombard German defensive positions and the required aerial photographs were taken. However, the British could not, of course, clear the air above Vimy Ridge entirely of German aircraft and the toll on RFC aircraft and men was heavy. Bob Goddard (6th Trench

Mortar Battery) remembered that: "It was heart-breaking to see our air men being shot down. I have seen six or seven of our planes come down in one day."[330]

For the British airmen, April 1917 was "Bloody April." Out of the 365 aircraft amassed for the offensives against Vimy Ridge and Arras, 75 machines were downed between April 4 to 8 alone with a loss of 105 pilots and observers.[331] While these casualties may seem light compared to those suffered by the infantry, they were heavy for the small and closely knit RFC. Nevertheless, despite their casualties, the RFC fulfilled its mission in the lead up to the attack on Vimy Ridge.

Twelve

Underground

As with other areas on the Western Front, the combatants took the war beneath the ground at Vimy. We have already seen that before the Canadians took over the line at Vimy Ridge the area had gone through an intensive period of underground warfare. The ground beneath the front lines of both sides and No Man's Land was already penetrated by mining shafts and tunnels, while the surface was pock-marked with enormous craters from the explosion of underground charges.

The existing shafts and tunnels provided the Canadians with the opportunity to plant further underground charges, set to blow German trenches into the sky at zero-hour. However, General Byng decided not to rely to any great extent on underground mines for the big attack. With the front lines and No Man's Land already a cratered wasteland, Byng was concerned that the detonation of mines would make the infantry's initial rush even more difficult and disorienting. For this reason, only two small mines were charged to explode at zero-hour. Both were to be detonated just to the north of Vimy Ridge, on the northern edge of the Canadians' assault, with the infantry in this area tasked only to seize the crater lips and advance no further.

While underground mines were a minor feature of the Canadian Corps' offensive, the Canadians did not ignore other advantages that tunnels and shafts could provide. A problem in previous attacks on the Western Front was protecting the soldiers as they moved from the rear into their assembly positions in and around the front line. A related problem was the protection of reserves in Canadian lines and headquarters once the battle had started. In these cases, German shelling could have a devastating effect. Heavy casualties could be caused to the infantry as they moved forward to their jumping-off trenches or to reserve troops as they waited for their time to advance. A direct hit on headquarters could also disrupt a unit's command and control capabilities.

To alleviate these potential problems, thirteen underground tunnels (also referred to as subways) were built under Canadian lines. Starting from behind Canadian lines, some exited in No Man's Land where the Canadians were digging their jumping-off trenches. Each Tunnel had several entrances throughout its length. This ensured that no Tunnel could be rendered useless by a German shell hit on an entrance and allowed the Canadians the ability to enter and leave a Tunnel from various points in the Canadian trench system. The longest, Goodman Tunnel, was over 1 800 yards long while the shortest, Gobron Tunnel, was just under 300 yards. All were impervious to shelling, having twenty feet of ground above the Tunnels' ceiling.

Built into the sides of the Tunnels were dugouts where unit headquarters were located, reserves could be stationed and medical dressing stations were set up. Since the soldiers would have to stay in the Tunnels for a significant length of time prior to the attack, cookhouses were placed in some dugouts, while others became latrines. Water supply was also available. Some of the Tunnels were wide enough to allow for two-way traffic and most had electric lighting. Phone lines were run through the Tunnels, and in some, signal stations were set up from which phone lines could be run forward during the attack to maintain communication with the infantry.

In the south the Tunnels were mainly used for headquarters, dressing stations, communications and garrisoning reserves. The Tunnels were used for these purposes in the north too, however, in this area the Tunnels also held assault troops. In Tunnels such as Grange Tunnel (located in 3rd Division's area on the Crater Line), the assault troops would move up to the front in the complete safety of the Tunnel. Once at the front they would wait in Grange Tunnel until just before zero-hour, then would leave the Tunnel which exited at their jumping off trenches. By using the Tunnels in this manner, the Canadian infantry could move to their jumping off trenches in safety and without exposing themselves to German observation.[332]

The work on these Tunnels had been going on for months prior to the offensive, done by British Tunnelling Companies with assistance from Canadian infantry. Through their effort, a complex underground tunnel system was created beneath the Canadian trenches. Immune from German shells, the Tunnels would provide security for command and control, comfort for the wounded and safety for the infantry as they assembled for the great attack.

Thirteen

Probing German Lines

While aerial observers were busy performing reconnaissance above German trench lines, further information gathering was taking place on the ground. As we have seen, reconnaissance through patrols and raids was an important feature of trench life in the Winter of 1917. These "intelligence forays" in No Man's Land and into German lines only increased in importance as the day of the great offensive neared.

Day and night Canadian patrols probed around and into German defences. Barbed wire was examined to determine whether or not it still presented an obstacle for the infantry's upcoming advance. The large craters in No Man's Land were explored for passages through or around them. When the opportunity arose, patrols would slip into the German front line and gather as much information as possible while at the same time keeping an eye open for an alert German sentry.

In the back of the soldiers' minds was the thought of capturing a prisoner. During the period of preparation prior to the attack, the Canadian Corps' High Command emphasised an urgent need for the capture of German soldiers.[333] Thus, risks were taken by patrols to secure this valuable human intelligence.

For example, in a period of less than 12 hours the 2nd (Eastern Ontario) Battalion had two separate patrols vigorously pursuing Germans within German lines. The first patrol of 8 men had entered enemy lines at 4:00 a.m. on April 5. There they waited for over three hours before a group of five enemy soldiers appeared coming to the German front line from a communication trench. At this point the Canadians tried to take them prisoner, but the Germans fled. The Canadians took up the pursuit, followed the enemy and managed to badly wound a German officer. While his men continued their hasty retreat, the Canadians began carrying their badly wounded prisoner back to Canadian lines. The German officer did not make it, succumbing to his wounds before the patrol returned to their trenches. In death he did provide the Canadians with some information as the patrol noted that the officer came from the 3rd Bavarian Reserve Infantry Regiment.[334]

Not 8 hours later another patrol from the 2nd Battalion, numbering 21 all ranks, entered the German front line trench for the same purpose; obtaining identification of the defending German soldiers and further reconnaissance of German defences. The patrol was discovered and, like what happened with their comrades in the early morning, the Germans fled. The Canadians followed their enemy deeper into German lines, all the way to the next trench, bombing dugouts along the way. On reaching this trench the Germans were reinforced and they counter-attacked. A vicious fire-fight then took place all the way back to the German front line with casualties being incurred on both sides. At this point Canadian machine gunners and artillery joined in, covering the Canadian patrol as they crossed No Man's Land back into friendly territory. As with the early morning patrol, no prisoners were taken, but identification of the German unit was secured.[335]

The Corps' need for prisoners meant that, not only were aggressive patrols sent out, but there was also an increase in Canadian raiding activity. Between March 20 and April 8, the Canadian Corps launched 19 raids. These included stealth, bombing and penetration raids, and were done all along the Corps' frontage. Compared with the raids undertaken in the Winter of 1917, the Canadians encountered more difficulties. No one factor accounts for this, however, German resistance (or the complete absence of defenders) and poor weather were prominent. Nevertheless, by April 8, all Divisions in the Canadian Corps had captured prisoners for intelligence purposes.

There were drawbacks to aggressive patrolling and raiding. While the Canadians were sensitive to the need to bring back their own casualties suffered during a raid or patrol, this could not always be done. With an offensive drawing near, leaving behind a wounded man in enemy lines opened the possibility of the Germans capturing and interrogating him, with the potential for details of the upcoming attack being disclosed.

Indeed, on a two man patrol conducted by the 1st (Western Ontario) Battalion on April 4, a fire-fight occurred in the German front line. The captain leading the patrol was badly wounded and the NCO, who was wounded as well, managed to escape but without the captain.[336] For the Germans, to capture a prisoner of such relatively high rank was an intelligence coup. Fortunately for the Canadians though, there appears to have been no negative consequences resulting from this incident. That no damage was done leads to the possibility that the badly wounded captain died of his wounds before he could be interrogated.

One man who had a "close call" during a raid was Private W. Painter from the 31st (Alberta) Battalion. Originally reported as "missing" following a March 29 raid, he made his way back to Canadian lines and gave this account:

In the retirement (<u>from the raid</u>) we passed another dug-out from which two bombs were thrown killing Sgt. ELLIOT and Pte. CULLEN. Prior to reaching this dug-out we had expended all our bombs. Pte. Bruce and myself then made a run for it, he (Bruce) taking to the right. (this was the last I saw of him). I jumped over the C.T. (<u>communication trench</u>) and lay behind what I presumed to be Bosche front line, all night. At sunrise the following morning and at stand-down I worked my way through the enemy's line, lay out in No Man's Land all day, and when darkness set in crawled back to our lines and reported to Company Headquarters. (underlined added)[337]

Canadian dominance of No Man's Land came at a price. In the two weeks prior to the big assault about 1 400 Canadians became casualties, a large number of these through patrols and raids.[338] Despite the risks, the Canadians pursued a policy of aggressive patrolling and raiding during the period leading up to the attack on Vimy Ridge. While the weather and German resistance made these forays difficult, the Canadians were rewarded by obtaining valuable intelligence from the reconnaissances they were able to perform and the prisoners they captured.

Fourteen

Tanks and Poison Gas

As we have already seen, the onset of trench warfare in the Great War provided fertile ground for the development of new weapons to overcome the deadlock. Two of these new weapons, tanks and poison gas, had roles to play in the upcoming assault on Vimy Ridge.

Turning first to the tanks, eight tanks from the British No. 12 Company, "D" Battalion, Heavy Branch, Machine Gun Corps were attached to the 2nd Division. Four tanks were to assist with the 6th Brigade's attack on the Village of Thelus, as the remainder advanced with the 13th (British) Brigade.[339] While a new Mark IV tank was soon to arrive on the Western Front, the tanks to be used at Vimy were the out-dated, Somme-era Mark II version.[340]

We have seen how, in planning for their offensive, the Canadians placed great emphasis on close cooperation between the infantry, artillery, aircraft and machine gunners. However, noticeably excluded from this group were the tanks. It was made clear in the Canadians' operation orders that the infantry and tanks were to attack independently. Instead of cooperating, the infantry were to advance as if the tanks were not even there and any hold up of the tanks was not to affect the infantry attack.[341] The extent of the cooperation between the tanks and other arms was that on the night of April 7/8 the machine guns and artillery would provide covering fire to drown out the noise of the tanks as they moved into their assembly positions.[342]

To the extent of their tank plans, the Canadians were not "forward-thinking." As the War progressed beyond the Battle of Vimy Ridge, integrating tanks into an all-arms battle would become an important and successful feature of British offensives, including those involving the Canadian Corps. However, even though ignoring the tanks in planning for the Battle was not "the way of the future," it would not actually matter when the Battle was fought, as we shall see.

As for gas, its use would be limited, but important. To begin with, there would be no large scale release of gas from cylinders prior to zero-hour to poison the German defenders on the day of the attack. The Canadians had learned a hard lesson on poison gas during the Winter of 1917.

On March 1, the 4th Division launched the Canadian Corps' largest raid of the Winter involving 1 679 all ranks. Two discharges of poison gas were planned, to be released from cylinders placed in the Canadian front lines. The raid took place below Hill 145 and shortly after the first gas discharge the wind changed direction and some of the gas floated back into Canadian lines. This caused some confusion and chaos, and with the wind having changed direction, the second discharge of gas was cancelled. Since the first discharge was almost three hours before the raiders advanced, all the gas achieved was to place the Germans on alert. In the event, the raid was unsuccessful, causing the Canadians about 700 casualties. In some places the raiders did not even enter German lines and were stopped in No Man's Land. Adding "insult to injury," those raiders that were able to enter German lines did not see any casualties caused by poison gas. As a result of this experience, the Canadians concluded that gas was an unreliable weapon in assisting the infantry entering German lines.[343]

There were other methods for using poison gas though, one of which was for the artillery to fire gas shells. On the day of the attack, the heavy artillery was going to fire gas shells at German artillery batteries commencing at zero-hour as part of their counter-battery program. The gas shells, in combination with high explosive rounds, were expected to neutralize the German gunners.[344] That is, if the gas and high explosives did not kill the German gunners or damage their pieces, at the very least it would force them to stay under cover, take gas precautions and delay manning their guns. This delay was important as it would provide the attacking infantry the opportunity to cross No Man's Land and enter enemy lines before the German artillery started firing.

Thus, while gas would not play a central role in the Battle of Vimy Ridge, it did have an important role. Whether or not it succeeded in neutralizing the German artillery would have an effect on the infantry's assault. As for the tanks, the most that can be said is the Canadians hoped they would help, but also hoped they would not hinder.

Fifteen

Impact of the Weather

If the Canadians hoped that the weather would cooperate with their offensive, these hopes were soundly dashed. By and large, the weather between March 20 and April 8 was miserable. This cool and wet weather made the Canadians' preparatory work that much more difficult than it already was. Nevertheless, to the Canadians' credit, they persevered.

Even though the start date for the Canadians' offensive preparations coincided with the beginning of spring, the weather was decidedly un-spring like. Instead, it was almost as if winter intensified. Signaller Wilfred Kerr (11th Battery CFA) remembered:

> The weather continued with rain, snow, slush, sleet and cold as had as December (sic); the trenches were knee deep in mud. Around the Battery the mud was like gruel; it flowed about one's puttees, soaked them, filled one's boots and penetrated one's socks until he was obliged to scrape it out between his toes with a knife.[345]

Movement in parts of Canadian lines was extremely difficult. Lieutenant Cyril Jones from the 16th Battalion (Canadian Scottish) recalled the effort getting to the front line:

> The next night we received orders to go and relieve a company in the front-line trenches, and in a downpour of rain and snow, we moved up. The trenches were the worst I had been in; water up to the knees, and none of us had waders. Even the dugouts were flooded, and, when I was relieved for my "hour off" duty, I went sound asleep sitting on a box beside a brazier.[346]

We saw that in the Winter, wet weather, particularly the mud, interfered with normal trench routine, such as repair work or bringing up supplies. In the context of preparing for a large offensive, these problems were magnified.

A massive amount of work was needed for the attack. Ammunition of all types, but particularly for the artillery, had to be brought from bases in the rear to dumps near the guns. Gun pits had to be dug for the artillery and trench mortars, a huge task bearing in mind the large number of artillery pieces that First Army reinforced the Canadian Corps with. Robert Gordon Brown (6th Battery CFA) remembered supplying the guns:

> As we approached the gun pits many star shells could be seen along horizon and flashes of light from different parts as guns were fired (sic). We could as yet hear no sound from these except occasionally a report from a larger gun or an exploding shrapnel shell. It reminded one of fireworks. About midnight, we turned off the road and drove up to the gun pits and dugouts. Here we unloaded our ammunition. It was 4.5 howitzer we had this time. There was a row of how-itzers about 100 yds in rear of another row of 18 pdrs. The howitzers, of course, were silent as we drove up in front of them, but the 18 pdrs were hammering away. The guns here seemed to be only 10 or 15 yds apart.[347]

The Vickers machine gunners too had to find positions, from which they would bar-rage German lines with bullets during the assault. Communications had to be established between units and the men were busy burying telephone lines so that the lines would be protected from German shelling. The infantry were digging jumping-off trenches in front of friendly lines and within the Canadians' forward trench system to give them a "head start" in crossing No Man's Land on the day of the attack.

All of these jobs, difficult as they were in any event, were even more taxing when the weather was cold and wet. Corporal Donald Fraser of the 6th Machine Gun Company described in his March 27 diary entry an aptly named "fatigue":

> Tonight a number of us were detailed to carry ammunition (rifle shells) from a dump beside a road leading out from the north side of Neuville St. Vaast to a point several hundred yards further up Vimy Ridge. As the roads and terrain were in a sodden, muddy condition, we were directed to a spot in a trench where several pairs of long rubber boots lay and were told that we better make use of them when packing up the boxes of shells. We looked them over careful-ly and found that they were for most, partially filled with mud and water and decided against their use. However, a few hardy souls struggled into them. We started together on the job, but it was not very long before we separated and got strung out. Up and down the trail we went, sliding and slipping and emitting curses in the darkness until we found Moodie, one of the rubber boot fanatics, was in dire distress. Then our misery turned to levity. We razzed him every time we passed. He was all in due to trying to keep upright on his slippery rubber boots, but he was determined that he would not discard them. Wearily he strug-gled on. Bud Willox particularly took great pleasure in taunting him. Of course it was pitch black and the area was not very healthy; bullets were hissing and

pinging around every few moments and we were glad when we saw the last of the boxes. We had carried 144 000 rounds. It was a fatigue that we will not readily forget.[348]

Not only does Corporal Fraser's diary entry provide a glimpse into the "rough" soldier humor that endures even through the toughest times, but it also touches on another feature of the build up for the Battle of Vimy Ridge. Since the Germans held the high ground they could see well into the Canadians' rear area, including the roads on which the Canadians brought up their supplies. For this reason most of the work, difficult as it already was because of the poor weather, had to be done under the cover of darkness. Canon Frederick Scott (1st Division) recalled the unpleasantness:

> The possession of the Ridge gave the Germans a great advantage, because it commanded a view of a very large piece of country and several main roads. Further up the road from Maison Blanche there was a place called Ariane Dump, where the Engineers had stored material in preparation for our attack. A long plank road connected it with the Anzin-St. Eloi Road. On a dark and rainy night that wooden track was an unpleasant place for a walk. Lorries, wagons, limbers, transports, horses and men crowded it, and the traffic every now and then would get blocked. No flashlights could be used, and it was hard to escape being run over. Yet to step off the boards meant to sink almost to your knees in mud. The language that one heard at such times in the darkness was not quite fit for ears polite. It is well that the horses were not able to understand the uncomplimentary speeches that were addressed to them.[349]

For the unfortunate horses, harsh language was the least of their difficulties. Cold weather and hard work took its toll on them. Canon Frederick Scott remembered:

> The winter rains had not improved the roads, but still day and night, through mud and water, a constant stream of vehicles of all descriptions passed up towards the front carrying ammunition. Ammunition was everywhere. At certain places it was stacked roads. The strain upon the horses was very great, and numbers of them died, and their bodies lay by the wayside for many days, no one having time to bury them.[350]

Nevertheless, the preparations had to go on for the offensive would be a failure if it was not properly supplied. Private James Johnston, with the transport for the 14th Machine Gun Company, described the long work days:

> The roads were plugged with all kinds of traffic imaginable. Horses, guns, trucks and troops going in all directions, but not too fast. The only time it seemed that we would move at all was when a big shell fell in the road, and then there would be a lot of rushing for a few minutes and then things would die down again. After a couple of hours of this it would be dark and things would get really con-

fusing. These trips, which we took almost each night until April 9, would last almost always from three to four in the afternoon until three or four next morning, and believe me that is a long time to stay in a saddle, if we had a team, or if we had a pack horse we would walk and ride the horse back.[351]

NAC-PA1229 – Bringing artillery ammunition forward to the guns by road during the preliminary bombardment. Note the mud and water.

While the Germans were never able to interrupt Canadian preparations, the continual work was still dangerous for those involved. The 13th Battalion (Royal Highlanders of Canada) War Diary entry for April 6 states:

> The roads were in a very bad condition with mud, and continued momentarily to become worse. On the road up towards MONTST ELOI, and also from there up to the various dumps, there was an incessant stream of traffic of all kinds, so thick, indeed, that it would have been difficult to plant a shell anywhere around the road without getting half a dozen limbers or transport wagons of some kind. One shell from an enemy gun, as a matter of fact, did land plump into the middle of a hut in one of the adjoining camps, and account for about 30 men, 13 of whom were killed outright, and the others nearly all seriously wounded.[352]

The days and nights leading up to the big attack were filled with exhausting labor. Roads and trenches were improved, ammunition brought forward and jumping-off positions prepared. While working mainly at night was difficult enough, the wet weather added a frustrating element to the men's labors as much work had to be re-done, for example, due to trench walls becoming water-logged and crumbling under a cool rain. German artillery activity made any work a potentially hazardous enterprise, but, despite their difficulties, the men endured and completed their preparations. The reward would be coming soon.

Sixteen

The German Response

What then of the Germans? As we saw in Part III, the Germans were active in conducting military operations in the Winter of 1917; albeit less aggressively than the Canadians. What were the Germans doing while the Canadians were preparing for their attack on Vimy Ridge?

Defending Vimy Ridge was *Gruppe* Vimy under the command of General Karl Ritter von Fasbender. Part of the German Sixth Army, *Gruppe* Vimy consisted of the 79th (Prussian) Reserve Division, 1st Bavarian Reserve Division and the 14th Bavarian Division. Both the Prussians and Bavarians earned reputations during the War as formidable soldiers and all three Divisions were veteran formations. Fasbender, who was very familiar with the defences of Vimy, was confident in the ability of his troops to repel any Allied assault on the Ridge.[353]

The 79th (Prussian) Reserve Division held most of Vimy Ridge, from Hill 145 to just north of Thelus and Hill 135. From there, part of the 1st Bavarian Reserve Division manned the defences from Thelus and Hill 135 to the Ridge's southern end. The remainder of the 1st Bavarian Reserve Division and the 14th Bavarian Division were located to the south of Vimy Ridge and would not be facing the Canadians' attack. Instead, they were to be attacked by men from Allenby's Third Army.

As may have been noticed, *Gruppe* Vimy did not defend all the area that the Canadians intended to attack, most notably the Pimple. To the north of *Gruppe* Vimy was *Gruppe* Souchez under General Wichura. *Gruppe* Souchez's 11th Bavarian Infantry Regiment from the 16th Bavarian Reserve Division was placed just to the north of Hill 145 with the Pimple being part of their defences. In all, there were about 10 000 men (including infantry, artillery and other units) manning the defences from the Pimple to Vimy Ridge's southern end.

239

Perhaps surprisingly, the Germans seemed quite complacent, enduring what the British and Canadians threw at them. On April 3, the War Diarist for the 9th Brigade CFA recorded:

> The enemy is apparently adopting a policy of "WATCHFUL WAITING" as outside of aerial activity, his visible activities have been nil of late.[354]

In terms of an artillery response to Canadian and British activity, the Germans' reply was rather feeble and ineffective. While there were periods of heavy German shelling, particularly on 4th Division's front around Hill 145, on the whole the Germans' retaliation to the preliminary bombardment was weak. For example, on April 2, on 2nd Division's front opposite Thelus, the British and Canadian artillery fired 12 562 rounds of all calibres, compared to only about 390 by the German artillery.[355] In early April the German artillery was so quiet that it lead the Canadian Corps High Command to suspect that the Germans might be planning a withdrawal from Vimy Ridge.

Consistent with their decreased artillery, German activity in No Man's Land also declined. Although the Germans were never as aggressive as the Canadians were at raiding, they still regularly conducted them in the Winter of 1917. However, this would come to a stop once the Canadians began preparations for their big offensive. The last German raid, albeit a successful one, was conducted on March 22. After that the Germans never ventured beyond their front line with aggressive intent. No Man's Land belonged to the Canadians.

Relevant to the Germans lack of response to Canadian preparations is the preliminary artillery bombardment and machine gun fire. Movement anywhere in German lines during the day was fraught with danger. Trenches were being systematically destroyed, villages were being bombarded and sniper guns were ready to fire on anyone who ventured overland. Night did not bring relief as the Canadians' night firing program for the artillery and Vickers machine gunners ensured a steady flow of projectiles into German lines. Reliefs for front line troops were interrupted and bringing forward rations and water to the front was a deadly job for German supply parties. After the Battle, the majority of prisoners captured said that they had been without food for two days, while some commented on the heavy casualties and disruption to rear area traffic wrought by the Canadian and British artillery.[356]

All the Germans could do was stay in their dugouts and endure, hoping the next shell would not entomb them. Waiting through an artillery bombardment was the most trying experience of the Great War; even more so than "going over the top" in an attack. Stuck in a dugout, with no where to go, no visible enemy to retaliate against and the constant threat of being buried alive, a human's natural "fight or flight" instinct was completely stifled. The stress of enduring these bombardments could drive some men to the breaking point.[357]

In terms of German morale amongst front line units, a worrying development occurred in the days prior to the attack. Five soldiers deserted to Canadian lines at the end of March. Of note is that at least four of them were Polish and all came from the 34th Reserve Infantry Regiment, which had only recently moved into the front line.[358] All desertions took place just north of Hill 145.

In response to this, the Canadians sent patrols out on April 3. The men carried messages written in Polish and Russian inviting desertion. There were six such messages, which were thrown into enemy lines when the patrol was about 15 yards away from a German sentry post.[359]

The messages had their desired effect as another German soldier deserted to the Canadians on April 6. Perhaps surprisingly, he was not from the 38th Reserve Infantry Regiment nor Polish like the earlier deserters. Instead, this man came from the 11th Bavarian Reserve Infantry Regiment, which had apparently relieved the 38th Reserve Infantry Regiment at or near the beginning of April. There seems to have been an odd calmness surrounding this man's desertion. It occurred at mid-day and, in full pack and carrying his rifle, he simply walked across No Man's Land and into a Canadian sap. No shots were fired by either side.[360]

It is clear that the Germans knew an attack was coming. The responses from prisoners captured before and during the Battle indicates that the massive artillery preparation suggested to them that an attack was pending, although they did not know when it would come. German reconnaissance aircraft were also active during the lead up to the Battle, including a number of low flights over Canadian artillery positions.[361] Adding to the aerial reconnaissance were observations from the high ground of Vimy Ridge.

Of particular note is a document prepared by General von Bachmeister, commanding 79th (Prussian) Reserve Division, circulated before the Battle within his Division. Von Bachmeister noticed Canadian preparations for an offensive. New British and Canadian artillery batteries had been located, there had been an increase in British and Canadian artillery activity and jumping-off trenches had been identified. The Germans knew that the Canadian Corps had shortened their frontage and that troops were massed behind Canadian lines. All signs were pointing to an imminent attack on Vimy Ridge.[362] On top of this, General von Bachmeister had a healthy respect for his opponents:

> The Canadians are known to be good troops and are, therefore, well suited for assaulting. There are no deserters to be found amongst the Canadians.[363]

Despite knowing that an attack was coming, the Germans did nothing to disrupt the Canadians' preparations. This complacency likely stems from past success. While success can breed confidence, it can also bring over-confidence. The Germans had twice in the past broken French assaults, both of which were larger in terms of manpower than the upcoming Canadian offensive. In the eyes of the German command, Vimy Ridge had already proved its impregnability. Now it would be time to demonstrate this to the Canadians.

Seventeen

April 8

Unlike much of the weather leading up to the Battle, April 8, Easter Sunday, was a beautiful spring day. Billy Bishop remembered:

> Easter Sunday was one of the most beautiful days I have ever seen, and we felt that at last the gods of the weather were going to smile on a British offensive. The sky was a wonderful blue, flecked only here and there with bits of floating white clouds. There was a warmth of spring sunshine that filled one with the joy of living.[364]

Originally, April 8 was slated to be the date for First and Third Army's offensive to open, but Third Army requested a one-day postponement, so the attack was set over to the 9th. The extra day was used by the Canadian Corps to ensure that all preparations for the assault were complete.

One such issue arose on the southern half of Vimy Ridge where the 10th (Canadians) Battalion were to attack the next day. The Battalion's assault frontage was one of the more difficult areas in the southern part of the Ridge as No Man's Land was heavily cratered. This resulted in most of the Battalion's frontage being impassable and the infantry would have to attack between the gaps in the large craters. Not surprisingly, the Germans had heavily wired these gaps.

For the 10th Battalion's attack to succeed, the barbed wire protecting these gaps would have to be dealt with. In the days leading up to the assault, this was a contentious issue. The artillery observers, positioned behind the Canadian forward trench system, were convinced that the wire protecting the gaps had been cut. However, the 10th Battalion's intelligence officers disagreed, believing that the wire had not been cut, rather, the artillery had merely buried it. Both sides were convinced that the other was wrong and the general commanding, General Currie of 1st Division, ordered a raid to settle the issue.

The last raid launched by the Canadians before the Battle took place at 4:30 a.m. on April 8. Under cover of a box barrage, 3 officers and 85 other ranks from the 10th Battalion, divided into two parties, crossed No Man's Land and entered the German forward defences. Resistance was met with, particularly from rifle fire, and 5 Canadians were killed with a further 13 wounded. In return, the Canadians took two prisoners, shot several other Germans and bombed three dugouts. Most important though, the raiders found that the German barbed wire was largely intact and remained an obstacle for the next day's assault. The raiders also noted that, while the German trenches had received some hits from shells, they were still in good condition. Thus, the 10th Battalion's intelligence officers were right and the artillery had to reduce the barbed wire and defences before the attack.[365] This the artillery did with great efficiency as those men who took part in the raid found the next day that they "could not recognize portions of the Enemy's defences" that they had raided and the wire "was almost entirely swept away by the Heavies."[366]

While the artillery were turning their attention to any defences that needed last minute reduction, the infantry were busy behind Canadian lines readying themselves for the great assault. Ammunition was doled out, equipment such as shovels and flares were picked up, weapons were checked and emergency rations given. Final conferences with officers and men were held and if there was any uncertainty in the men's minds as to their attack plan, these issues were dealt with. Captain Harold McGill (31st Alberta Battalion) sensed that:

> A spirit of quiet confidence pervaded the whole battalion. There were no signs of elation or excitement. The behaviour and demeanour of the men indicated that to them the storming of the hitherto impregnable Vimy Ridge was only something of a detail in a day's work and to be taken for granted.[367]

Turning to the infantry's plan of attack for the next day, the Divisions in the Canadian Corps were situated, from right to left (south to north), 1st, 2nd, 3rd and 4th Divisions. Major-General Arthur Currie's 1st Division was tasked with capturing the southern portion of Vimy Ridge, including Commandant's House. For the initial thrust against the Black and Red Lines the assault Brigades were the 2nd Brigade on the right (the far right for the entire Canadian Corps) with the 3rd Brigade to its left. Once these Lines were taken, the 1st Brigade would leap-frog through the 2nd and 3rd Brigades at the Red Line and advance to capture the Blue and Brown Lines.

To the left of the 1st Division was the 2nd Division under the command of Major-General Burstall. Its objectives included the Village of Thelus and the second highest point on Vimy Ridge, Hill 135. Attacking the Black and Red Lines were the 4th Brigade (right) and 5th Brigade (left). Passing through these Brigades on the Red Line were the 6th Brigade (right) and 13th (British) Brigade (left) attached from the 5th (British) Division.

The objectives for the 6th and 13th Brigades were the Blue Line and, for the 6th Brigade only, the Brown Line.

On 2nd Division's left was the 3rd Division commanded by Major-General Louis Lipsett. Located at the Crater Line, this Division's attack sector was shallower than that of 1st and 2nd Divisions, so there were only two lines to capture; the Black and Red Lines. To attack these were 8th Brigade on the right and 7th Brigade on the left.

Finally, Major-General Watson's 4th Division was located on 3rd Division's left and was the northernmost in the Corps. Its objectives included the highest point on Vimy Ridge, Hill 145, and the Pimple. Like the 3rd Division, the attack sector here was shallow and there were only the Black and Red Lines to take. The 11th Brigade, which was located on 4th Division's right, was to capture the Black and Red Lines on and around Hill 145, while the 12th Brigade was to attack to the left in the area between Hill 145 and the Pimple. The 10th Brigade was held in reserve for the attack on Vimy Ridge, but was tasked with assaulting the Pimple as soon as possible after the main assault on the Ridge.

Most of the Brigades attacked with three Battalions, each Battalion responsible for their immediate attack sector. The fourth Battalion in the Brigade was used as moppers-up or for reinforcements. For example, 2nd Brigade's assault was undertaken by 5th Battalion (Western Cavalry) on the right, 7th Battalion (1st British Columbia Regiment) in the centre and 10th (Canadians) Battalion on the left. The 8th Battalion (90th Winnipeg Rifles) were in support. Second Brigade had a battle strength of 3 269 all ranks; a bit higher than the Corps' average which was about 2 750 per Brigade.

There were exceptions to this three-battalion deployment, most notably in 4th Division. Both Brigades in this Division attacking on April 9 used all four of their Battalions to take the Brigade's objectives. Their support came from the Brigade tasked with attacking the Pimple next day, 10th Brigade, which supplied a Battalion each to 11th and 12th Brigades.

In all, about 30 000 infantry soldiers were readying themselves for the big attack the next day, faced by about 10 000 defenders (three attackers to one defender being a historically common ratio). It was, and still is, the largest single assault in Canadian history.

Part V

The Battle of Vimy Ridge

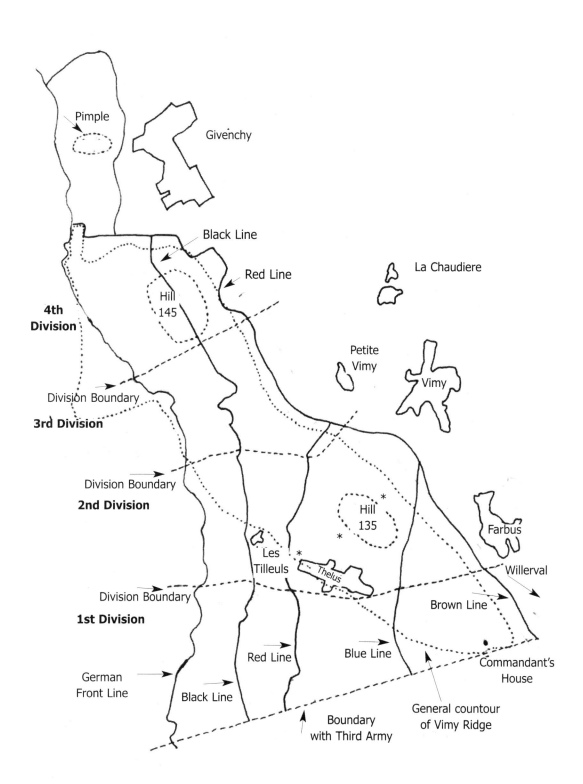

Pimple

Givenchy

Black Line

Red Line

La Chaudiere

Hill
145

**4th
Division**

Petite
Vimy

Vimy

Division Boundary

3rd Division

Division Boundary

2nd Division

Hill
135

Farbus

Les
Tilleuls

Thelus

Willerval

Division Boundary

Brown Line

1st Division

Red Line

Blue Line

Commandant's
House

German
Front Line

Black Line

Boundary
with Third Army

General countour
of Vimy Ridge

One

The Battle Begins

As April 8 turned into April 9, the Canadian lines below Vimy Ridge began to fill with assault troops. In most cases the men started from the rear area, using overland routes until they reached the relative safety of communication trenches or the complete protection of the underground Tunnels. From the communication trenches and Tunnels the men filtered into the jumping-off trenches, their last stop before they went "over the top."

Some of the troops received a spirited send off as they left the rear area for the front lines. The 27th (City of Winnipeg) Battalion's after-action report recorded:

> The Battalion bivouaced at Bois Des Arleux on the 8th inst. and spent the after-noon in being fully equipped with ammunition, bombs, flares and rations. The day was fine and all ranks were in excellent spirits. The Bands of all Battalions in the Brigade played throughout the afternoon and evening. At 9:20 P.M. the Battalion fell in under the trees and each Company was addressed separately by the Commanding Officer who pointed out the great work already done by the Battalion and what was expected in this attack. At 10 P.M. the Battalion moved off by Companies at 100 yards distance in the following order A. B. C. D., Hdqrs to the strain of the Regimental march. The details left behind lined the road and cheered each Company on passing.[368]

Many of the soldiers in the Canadian Corps were veterans and knew what the morning would bring. Nevertheless, even though April 9 would be the last day for many of them, the soldiers' morale going into the attack was high. The 73rd Battalion's (Royal Highlanders of Canada) War Diarist captured the spirit of the assault troops as they made their way down Coburg Tunnel to their jumping-off trenches:

> A striking feature of the occasion was that although the men had been in the line already for four days, they were cheerful and anxious for the Operation to

take place. It was an inspiring thing to move up and down the Tunnel among the men, and hear their cheerful remarks and songs.[369]

Also in a Tunnel, Grange Tunnel, were the Princess Patricia's Canadian Light Infantry. All ranks were ready for the assault and W. Miller recalled the varying ways that his comrades spent their time waiting for zero-hour:

> My Old Pal Don McDonald, Signal Section, he was always full of fun, just a real good Joe but not that night, sitting in a corner sobbing, eating his Emergency Ration, I said "Hey, Donald, you'll get hell for doing that." His answer was, "Bill I'm no comin back." He didn't. (sic)

> I'm sure there were many sad and true stories connected with this same operation. Some were trying to sing, some were playing cards, all milling around, smoking, wondering what time it was, and "How's The Weather?" you could hear in our Section, some trying to sleep, and for Sport, some trying to play with, or killing rats. I saw a guy picking lice. . . . We all had our own thoughts, waiting for that "Zero Hour."[370]

As the men filtered their way through the Canadian trench system to their jumping-off trenches, the Canadian and British artillery maintained a slow, but continuous bombardment, hoping to give the Germans the impression that nothing was out of the ordinary. Defensive patrols were in No Man's Land and on the alert, ready to deflect any curious Germans away from Canadian lines as the troops assembled for the attack.

The move to assembly positions was performed efficiently, but there still were some difficulties and casualties. In the south, where the 1st and 2nd Divisions attacked, some of the men did not move to assembly under the cover of the Tunnels. Their route through communication trenches was at times physically draining due to the poor condition of the trenches on account of the recent wet weather. Lieutenant Cyril Jones (16th Battalion Canadian Scottish) recalled that the "trenches were so wet and muddy that I had to take my platoon overland to reach the front line . . ."[371] Complicating matters was German artillery activity, including the use of some gas shells, that inflicted a few casualties as the men made their way forward through the muck.

Probably the most unlikely victims of this shelling were the cooks from the 13th Battalion (Royal Highlanders of Canada). After preparing the soup that was to be eaten by the troops once they were in the assembly trenches, three out of the four cook-houses in the Battalion were shelled. The Battalion cooks were killed and most of the soup was lost. Only one Company received hot soup before going "over the top."[372] The unfortunate men from the 13th Battalion aside, the assault troops had a warm meal and, if they chose, the rum ration.

While in the south the soldiers had to deal with German shelling, in the north below Hill 145 the Canadians faced a similar threat but from a different source. As the men from the 11th Brigade settled down in their jumping-off trenches they lost a few in their ranks from friendly fire as Canadian and British shells fell "short" hitting the Brigade's assembly area rather than the German trenches on Hill 145. Fortunately for the infantry, the artillery liaison officer with 11th Brigade was prompt to react to the friendly fire, phoned his artillery batteries and the guns adjusted their fire.[373]

The assembly was completed in the early hours of April 9. For those in the lead waves, their jumping-off trenches were as close as possible to the German front line. Around Hill 145, where No Man's Land was its widest, they were in advance of the Canadian front line and barbed wire. Elsewhere, they were mainly in and around the Canadian front line due to the nearness of the German positions. The men from the following waves assembled in jumping-off trenches behind. Silence and stealth were priorities as no one wanted to tip the Germans by a loud conversation or the sight of a cluster of lit cigarettes in advance of Canadian front lines.

Assisting the Canadians in concealing their assembly was the weather. While the weather had been fine on April 8, this changed by the early hours of the 9th, and a light, cold rain fell on the soldiers as they assembled for the attack. This misty rain, coupled with the early morning darkness, prevented the Germans from observing what otherwise could have been an obvious concentration of thousands of men in the Canadian front lines. However, the damp weather turned the ground "rather greasy."[374]

Once the soldiers were in position there was nothing to do but wait until zero-hour, 5:30 a.m. Corporal Donald Fraser (6th Machine Gun Company) recalled:

> There we lay shivering in the cold and wet. The weather was atrocious, alternating rain, sleet and snow which was driven by a chilling wind that cut to the bone and we became still and numb. It was a long, tedious wait as we moved up and down the trench trying to keep warm. There were no dug-outs and not such a thing as sleep.[375]

In his jumping-off position was Lieutenant E.L.M. Burns (11th Brigade Signal Section). He remembered his thoughts before the Battle:

> . . . I did not sleep much the night before the attack. Like nearly every other man who is to go into action, I was mainly thinking of whether I might be killed or wounded. A deeply religious person, I suppose, can get comfort by resigning his fate to God's will; nevertheless the various glands and organs in the complex human anatomy don't often respond to reason, will or faith in a high and just ruler of all things. However, before zero-hour I was in the proper place in the jumping off position, with my little groups of signallers, runners and carriers.[376]

Also in a jumping-off trench was Lieutenant R. Lewis from the 25th Battalion (Nova Scotia Rifles). In the hours before the attack his thoughts turned to home:

Zero hour had been set for 5:30 a.m., so we had two hours to wait, and a long two hours they were. Nobody can realize except those who have been through it the thoughts which pass through men's minds at such a time – thoughts of home and loved ones appear as a vision with a wonder as to whether you will ever see them again.[377]

The Princess Patricia's Canadian Light Infantry did their preliminary assembly in the complete safety of Grange Tunnel. Then, in the early hours of the 9th, the men filtered out of Grange Tunnel to their jumping-off trenches in No Man's Land from which they would attack. A.A. Bonar remembered:

Here we waited, our feet stuck in the gluey mud for zero time, when the order would be given to clamber over the top. Black clouds gathered and rain fell at intervals making the soil stickier than ever. A few enemy shells fell nearby, giving off their characteristic sweet pineapple odour. But no one paid attention to them.

Some men were leaning against the sides of the trench, others stooping or sitting in the mud on their bags of bombs. There was scarcely any conversation among that quiet crowd. Every man was alone with his own thoughts. In a short time he would face eternity. No matter whether one has been through bombardments before, few can face it again without realising how puny and impotent they are, and how absolutely necessary it is to pray for the strength to carry on, or for protection. Everyone becomes a child of faith again.[378]

As the minutes ticked by soldiers and officers checked their watches in anticipation of zero-hour. One of these men was Lieutenant Stuart Kirkland:

It was one o'clock in the morning before I had my platoon in position in the jumping off trench, and we stood there in mud to our waists all night waiting for the eventful hour. I can never describe my feelings as I stood there waiting for the moment to come. At a certain hour our artillery was to all open up on Fritz's front line and we were to jump out and advance as near as possible, ready to rush his front line when our artillery fire raised. After fifteen minutes before the time set, I took two-water bottles of rum and gave each of the men a good swallow, for it was bitter cold standing in the mud all night. Then I stood watch in hand, waiting, waiting! (underlined added)[379]

Thousands of men were crammed into the Canadian front lines, some only a few dozen yards away from their adversaries. Prayers were whispered, hands were shook, equipment was double checked and nerves were steeled. Lieutenant R. Lewis (25th Battalion Nova Scotia Rifles) remembered:

. . . two minutes before the time of advancing the word was passed from man to man to get ready and every man in those muddy trenches fixed his equipment, looked to the bombs and rifles and passed wishes of good luck to those nearest him, making a toe hold in the side of the trench to help himself up.[380]

Behind Canadian lines Canon Frederick Scott (1st Division) was an intensely interested spectator. He recalled the last moments:

> I watched the luminous hands of my watch get nearer and nearer to the fateful moment, for the barrage was to open at five-thirty. At five-fifteen the sky was getting lighter and already one could make out objects distinctly in the fields below. The long hand of my watch was five-twenty-five. The fields, the roads and the hedges were beginning to show the difference of colour in the early light. Five-twenty-seven! In three minutes the rain of death was to begin. In the awful silence around it seemed as if Nature were holding her breath in expectation of the staggering moment. Five-twenty-nine! God help our men! Five-thirty![381]

With the guns was Raymond Ives of the 13th Battery CFA. He described the final minutes and seconds before the artillery barrage began pulverizing the German trenches:

> During the last half hour a strange quiet filled the place. Broken only by the pattering of the rain which now began to fall in a steady stream.
>
> Are you ready number 1?
>
> Are you ready number 2?
>
> 5 minutes to go.
>
> 4 minutes to go.
>
> 3 minutes to go.
>
> 2 minutes to go.
>
> 1 minute to go.
>
> 10 seconds.
>
> 5 seconds. Whistle!
>
> We' er off.[382]

At 5:30 a.m. the thousand artillery pieces supporting the Canadian Corps opened fire "as one gun."[383] The War Diarist for the 5th Canadian Mounted Rifles recorded the moment:

> <u>Zero Hour</u> Intense artillery bombardment – one continuous roar. The ground trembled and there is mingled with the roar of the guns the swishing and screeching of the shell filled air . . . Smoke and debris thrown up by the bursting shells give the appearance of a solid wall (underlined in original).[384]

Attached to the 25th Battalion (Nova Scotia Rifles) was an artillery liaison officer, Lieutenant Purchas. To him, lying outside the parapet of his assembly trench with the infantry at zero-hour, "the Artillery seemed to open at practically the same moment and fell like a curtain in front of us."[385]

All along the Canadian lines the artillery roared to life at zero-hour. The 6th Brigade after-action report relates the scope of the barrage:

> The volume of our artillery fire was beyond description and the bursting shells all along the line as far as the eye could reach, was a sight to be remembered.[386]

The noise was tremendous. Private James Johnston was with the transport for the 14th Canadian Machine Gun Company. He remembered:

> It was terrific. It was the first all out barrage I had seen to date. I knew it was something extra, but did not know at the time that it was the heaviest concentrated fire since the first of the war. It was impossible to hear anyone talking and the whole front was lighted up as at a large fire.[387]

The barrage was so loud that, for the 3rd Battalion (Toronto Regiment), they could get no information from their observer in a post within Canadian lines as voices could not be heard over the telephone.[388]

Just in front of his Battalion's jumping-off trench, in an outpost on the Crater Line, was Private William Elder (Princess Patricia's Canadian Light Infantry). Being close to German lines, he felt the intensity of the opening barrage:

> A few minutes before the affair was to open three of us were sent to our outpost line to observe and report by telephone everything that was happening. In the first dawn of the morning the big guns opened fire on the enemy outpost line and front line. Standing near, I could feel every part of my body tingling. The air seemed charged with electricity. The snapping and crackling of the higher explosives added to the din of the crashing reports of the heavy shells. It was beautiful and magnificent, and yet how dreadful.[389]

For Signaller Wilfred Kerr (11th Battery CFA), what struck him was the smell of gunpowder:

> I had no special orders, and remained in bed until the firing began; then arose, watched the innumerable gun flashes, observed the long, low, grey cloud ahead of us on the ridge, which marked the progress of our barrage, and perceived a peculiar odour, that of the cordite from our own departing shells, which has become fixed in my mind as the especial smell of battle.[390]

Up in the air above the Battle, Billy Bishop had a unique, but dangerous, perspective from his aircraft:

The ground seemed to be one mass of bursting shells. Further back, where the guns were firing, the hot flames flashing from thousands of muzzles gave the impression of a long ribbon of incandescent lights. The air seemed shaken and literally full of shells on their mission of death and destruction. Over and over again one felt a sudden jerk under a wingtip and the machine would heave quickly. This meant a shell had passed within a few feet of you.[391]

The deafening noise, pounding of the shells and whizzing of the bullets seems to have inspired the Canadian infantry who had been waiting for the Battle to begin. Gus Sivertz (2nd Canadian Mounted Rifles) remembered:

> We were dancing a macabre dance as our nerves just vibrated to the thousands of shells and the millions of machine gun bullets that were whizzing over. And I felt that if I had put my finger up I should have touched a ceiling of sound because sound had acquired a new quality, the quality of solidity. It really was indescribable. It wiped out any fear in us.[392]

Almost immediately after the British and Canadian barrage began, the Germans lit the early morning sky with flares to signal their artillery to respond. In his assembly trench Corporal Donald Fraser (6th Machine Gun Company) was struck by the audio and visual display of the opening moments of the Battle:

> As the zero hour of 5:30 a.m. approached we came to life and gazed intently towards the German line. A terrific crash that resounded to the heavens heralded the attack. The barrage had begun. A constant stream of 18-pounder shells was sent pouring down on to the enemy front line amidst ear-splitting explosions and smashed and scattered the trench to the winds. Heavy shells would rock the earth and create enormous craters. The noise was bedlam. The Germans frantically fired their S.O.S. lights into the sky vainly calling to their guns for help. Lights of every hue in the rainbow flashed up from their line. Their trench and the vicinity was alive with fire and appeared a blazing inferno as the shell bursts spat out long tongues and jets of flame. It was a pretty although grim sight to watch a regular fireworks deluxe. Our eyes were glued in wonderment to the line and we felt that ungodly havoc was being wrought on the Hun. The shelling was so intense that the line was illuminated nearly all the time.[393]

It was not just the infantry who were struck by the spectacle. Even the gunners were impressed with the first minutes. From the 3rd Canadian Siege Battery War Diary:

> Promptly at 5:30 a.m. our artillery barrage opened up. It is the most appalling barrage that we have yet heard. The whole country in front of us was lit up with the flashes of field guns and beside us and behind us were the flashes of hundreds of siege and heavy guns. Immediately the barrage opened the enemy put up a most wonderful display of rockets and fireworks.[394]

Upon the barrage opening, the Canadian infantry made their move. A.A. Bonar (Princess Patricia's Canadian Light Infantry) remembered:

> A couple of minutes after the hurricane bombardment began to sweep over our heads, our platoon officer and sergeant were on top of the parapet, yelling orders and waving their arms as a signal to come along. It was impossible to hear any verbal orders. But we knew what was required.[395]

Thousands of men left their jumping-off trenches, picked their way through gaps cut in the Canadian barbed wire and made their way across No Man's Land toward German lines. It was no easy passage. The ground was horrible, broken up by the shelling from the past few weeks and sopping wet from the weather. The soldiers, weighted down with their weapons and equipment, pushed on, making good time despite the mud. They made for points close enough to the German front line so that they could rush the trench once the barrage lifted, yet far enough away that they would not be wiped out by friendly fire. Once there, no doubt with many of them breathless and with hearts pumping from the exertion of pulling themselves through the mud or the excitement and anxiety of the moment, the men formed into assault waves for the attack and waited for the barrage to lift from the German front line. The Battle of Vimy Ridge had begun.

Two

1st and 2nd Divisions

5:30 a.m. - 7:30 a.m.

The southern half of Vimy Ridge was the ultimate objective for the 1st and 2nd Divisions. Both Divisions had substantial territory to cross before they reached the Ridge, having to capture the Black Line, Red Line, Blue Line and then, finally, the Brown Line, before the Ridge would be in their hands. To allow these Divisions to attack so deep into German territory, they utilized leap-frog Brigades.

In 1st Division (the southernmost) the job of attacking the Black and Red Lines fell to the 2nd Brigade (on the right) and 3rd Brigade (left). Once the Red Line was captured, the 1st Brigade would leap-frog through and assault the Blue and Brown Lines, the taking of the last Line resulting in the capture of the Ridge in the 1st Division sector.

For 2nd Division, its 4th Brigade (on the right) and 5th Brigade (left) were to take the Black and Red Lines. As the 2nd Division's ultimate objectives on the Ridge were wider than those of 1st Division, the 2nd Division had two leap-frog Brigades. The 6th Brigade would leap-frog through the 4th Brigade and advance on the Blue and Brown Lines. Meanwhile, the 13th (British) Brigade would leap-frog through 5th Brigade and take the Blue Line (the Blue Line was east of the Ridge's crest here and, thus, no Brown Line for the 13th Brigade).

At zero-hour, as the British and Canadian artillery barrage roared, the assault troops made their way forward from their jumping-off trenches into No Man's Land, stopping once they were as close as safely possible to the shrapnel barrage that was exploding into the German front line. For this opening phase of the Battle, only the assault Brigades advanced, the leap-frog Brigades remaining in their assembly positions as their time was yet to come. Thus, from right to left (south to north), the men from 2nd, 3rd, 4th and 5th Brigades deployed for the attack.

The Canadians formed up in a wave formation, each man in the wave being about five yards apart. There were successive waves, between four to seven, depending on the Brigade. It would be inaccurate, though, to imagine all these waves of infantry lying out in No Man's Land waiting for the barrage to lift. Instead, only the first few waves were actually in waves, those behind being deployed in what was referred to as artillery formation.

The reason for this comes clear when one understands the nature of the defences the infantry from 1st and 2nd Divisions were attacking. Their objectives, the Black and Red Lines, contained the formidable German trench systems known as the *Stellung I* and *Swischen Stellung*. The area between the German front line and the Red Line was a veritable maze of trenches and defensive positions.

Starting with the defences up to the Black Line, the Canadians had to attack and capture the German front line, the support and then the Black Line (for some Battalions there was another trench before the Black Line). Beyond this, the Red Line contained the *Swischen Stellung*, itself a series of successive trenches. In between and connecting all these trenches were communication trenches, which could also provide defensive positions, particularly at trench junctions.

Since there were successive trenches to attack, successive waves were used. However, the rear waves could be vulnerable to German artillery if they began their advance from No Man's Land in a wave formation. Thus, they formed up and began their advance in artillery formation. This involved each platoon forming up like a diamond, with each section in the platoon being a corner of the diamond. It was used to reduce casualties from artillery fire. Each section would advance in single file taking advantage of passages through the shell craters and gaps in the German defensive barrage. Once the time came for the rear waves to carry forward the advance after the lead waves had done their jobs, the soldiers changed from artillery formation into wave formation.

Because of the difficult defences of the *Stellung I* and *Swischen Stellung*, the Canadians decided that successive assault waves would not be enough to completely suppress the German defenders. Interspersed between assault waves were moppers-up. These moppers-up were given the job of clearing the German trenches after they were captured by the assault waves. The Germans had many deep dugouts and underground tunnels built into their trench system and the fear was that once the assault waves captured a trench and carried on forward, German defenders would emerge from their deep dugouts and fire on the assault waves from the rear. To prevent this problem developing, the moppers-up would follow the assault waves into the German trenches and throw Mills

Bombs into the German dugouts, remaining in the area until all German soldiers were killed or captured.

Within three minutes of the British and Canadian barrage opening, the infantry were in position, formed up and ready to rush the German front line once the barrage lifted. Keeping close to the creeping barrage was vital to the success of the attack and had been strongly emphasised in the battle practices held during training.

The creeping barrage was to lift from the German front line at 5:33 a.m. and begin its advance through the German defensive system at a pace of 100 yards in three minutes. The creeping barrage, with its component rolling, standing, howitzer and machine gun barrages, was designed to protect the infantry through every successive trench they had to capture. For the 1st and 2nd Divisions' attack on the Black and Red Lines it was to lift from the front line at 5:33, from the support at 5:38 and from the Black Line at 6:02 a.m. A pause was then introduced into the barrage's advance, with it standing east of the Black Line until 6:45 a.m. During the pause the infantry were to complete the capture of the Black Line and re-organize so that rear waves could deploy for the attack on the Red Line. Throughout this period the standing barrage would prevent the Germans from counter-attacking the Canadians on the Black Line. Then, at 6:45 a.m., the barrage re-commenced creeping forward, lifting from the Red Line by 7:13 a.m., whereupon the infantry would storm the Red Line.

As the barrage lifted from the German front line and the lead Canadian infantry rushed it, the German artillery, responding to the frantic flares fired by their infantry, opened its defensive barrage. Fortunately for the assault waves, it fell mainly on Canadian lines and did not disrupt their attack.

While the German artillery was rather quick in responding to their infantry's SOS, the Canadian War Diaries are unanimous in describing the German artillery response as weak and erratic. The reason for this was the British and Canadian artillery's counter-battery work. At zero-hour, those heavy artillery pieces tasked with counter-battery work opened fire on all known German artillery batteries with a mixture of high explosive and gas shells. German artillery officers captured later in the Battle told their captors that "they got hell from our heavies."[396]

No doubt the Germans had pre-arranged SOS barrage lines upon which they expected to deluge any Canadian attack with shells while the infantry were still in Canadian lines and No Man's Land. However, between the counter-battery's high explosive shells exploding in and near the gun pits and the gas shells temporarily incapacitating (if not lethally poisoning) the gunners, the Germans were unable to put on a comprehensive and effective barrage. Some guns were able to fire, but most could not, so the planned intense defensive barrage instead was weak and seemingly erratic.

With the British and Canadian barrage moving forward ahead of them and the German defensive barrage falling behind them, the assault waves of 1st and 2nd Divisions pushed forward through the muddy and cratered ground, took the front line and pushed through the successive German trenches. Up in the air in his plane, Billy Bishop was struck by the spectacle:

> The waves of attacking infantry as they came out of their trenches and trudged forward behind the curtain of shells laid down by the artillery, were an amazing sight. The men seemed to wander across No Man's Land, and into the enemy trenches, as if the battle were a great bore to them. From the air it looked as though they did not realise that they were at war and were taking it all entirely too quietly. That is the way with clock-work warfare. These troops had been drilled to move forward at a given pace. They had been timed over and over again in marching a certain distance, and from this timing the "creeping," or rolling barrage which moved in front of them had been mathematically worked out.[397]

On the ground was Lieutenant Thomas Gordon Chisholm from the 15th Battalion (48th Highlanders of Canada). He recalled:

> When our time came, we climbed on the parapet and started over. Looking to either side one could see thousands of men walking slowly but none the less certainly into the German lines. Ahead of us the artillery cleared the way. When we reached the German lines we hardly recognized them. What had been trenches were only mere sunken lines. There was not a point in them that had not been touched. The ground between the trenches was so pitted with shell-holes that it resembled a gigantic honeycomb.[398]

Some of the assault Battalions were lead into the Battle by their pipers. This tradition of going into battle to the sound of bag-pipes, common to units with Scottish heritage throughout the armies of the British Empire, fascinated German soldiers in both World Wars. However, it is unlikely that many of the attacking Canadians heard the music. Lieutenant R. Lewis remembered his Battalion's pipers:

> The gallant pipers leading the 25th could be seen but it was impossible with the din to hear what they were playing. Gradually we advanced our ground – nothing but holes filled with mud and water to make the going very difficult.[399]

By about 6:30 a.m. it can be said that the Black Line was captured with the Red line falling about an hour later. That is, the objectives were taken on schedule with no need to deviate from the artillery's barrage plan. This does not mean that the Canadians had an easy time of it though.

Casualties were heavy in the Brigades that attacked the Black and Red Lines in the South, particularly in 1st Division. An average of 44 percent of the other ranks in the 1st Division's assault Battalions became casualties. Officer casualties were even heavier, as 56 percent of those engaged were killed or wounded.

The 10th (Canadians) Battalion was the hardest hit of all Battalions in 1st Division. Of the 22 officers and 741 other ranks that went into the assault, 8 officers and 72 other ranks were killed, with a further 9 officers and 298 other ranks wounded (a casualty rate of 77 percent for the officers and 50 percent for the other ranks). Many of these casualties occurred early in the attack. Even with the artillery clearing the last of the barbed wire the day before the Battle, the 10th Battalion had a particularly difficult area of No Man's Land to cross. Heavily cratered, the men had to advance between the huge craters, and the German defenders managed to mount their machine guns on their side of the crater lips before the Canadians were on them.

Enduring heavy machine gun and rifle fire, the Canadians were able to overcome the stiff German resistance, but the cost was high.[400] In one Company, they lost all their officers but one and over half of their men in the first 100 yards of their advance.[401] It was not just the lead waves that suffered, as the two Companies tasked with carrying the attack forward to the Red Line already had only one officer left between them by the time they reached the Black Line.[402] This before these Companies had even made their actual attack!

Some of the officers persisted, enduring their wounds and trying to lead. One of these men was Lieutenant Walter Stephenson Duncan, who, becoming wounded in the opening moments of the attack, continued with his men, despite having to crawl on his hands and knees.[403] Under these circumstances, the other ranks, drawing upon their battle training, took the initiative. One of these men was Private John Dunbar whose deeds were noted by his commanding officer:

> Private John C. Dunbar, on 9.4.17 at the Labyrinthe Sector, in the attack on the First Objective, displayed bravery and courage of the highest order. His platoon officer and N.C.O.'s being wounded, he organized his section, and charged in on the Enemy. 8 personally killed with the bayonet, and attacked a ninth German who shot him, but this soldier wounded him before dying.[404]

Encounters like these have almost an air of unreality when expressed in dry after-action reports. Nevertheless, in some the savagery of warfare still comes through:

> Private Ernest Bowering, on 9.4.17, in the Labyrinthe Sector, when in charge of a Lewis Gun, he did great execution, dealing many casualties to the enemy advancing with his Company and firing from the hip. When his ammunition supply became exhausted for the moment, he rushed a group of 4 Germans, using

his gun as a club, killing one of the enemy and causing the other three to sur-render.[405]

One wonders what was going through the three German soldiers' minds as Private Bowering bashed their comrade's head in right before their eyes.

NAC-PA1101 – Canadian soldiers with damaged German machine gun emplacement shortly after its capture.

Most of the opposition encountered by the 1st and 2nd Divisions came from posi-tions held by machine gunners, often with supporting riflemen. In many instances it is evi-dent that the Canadians used their training in the new platoon organization to good effect. For example, at Balloon Trench, a trench before their Black Line, the 19th (Central Ontario) Battalion was held up by a nest of machine guns. With the soldiers in front of the machine guns taking cover, others moved around the flanks and put the troublesome machine guns out of action within minutes by long range bombing with rifle grenades. The Canadians' advance quickly resumed.[406]

One of the more notable fights to overcome machine guns occurred to the 14th Battalion (Royal Montreal Regiment) as they attacked the *Eisner Kreuz Weg*; the last trench before the Battalion's Black Line. A severe fire-fight took place at this trench. In addition to the defenders at the *Eisner Kreuz Weg,* German machine gunners and rifle-men behind the *Weg* fired at the Canadians as they attacked. To counter this defensive fire, Canadian Lewis Gunners fired bursts over the heads of their advancing comrades. Under this covering fire, the Canadians closed in on the defenders of the *Eisner Kreuz Weg*, clearing the trench and taking out four German machine guns in close quarter fight-ing.

Two were dealt with by Mills Bomb hand grenades, while a lieutenant, after exchanging grenades with the crew of a third machine gun, finished the crew off with his revolver. The final machine gun was taken out in rather dramatic fashion with a company sergeant-major bayoneting the three man crew. While most of the defenders were killed, they had inflicted heavy casualties on the men of the 14th Battalion (Royal Montreal Regiment).[407]

Although 1st and 2nd Divisions' attack went according to schedule, this does not mean that in all instances it played out as if on the taped practice grounds. In some cases the Canadians had to deviate from their plans, take the initiative and overcome resistance by other means.

On the far right of the Canadian Corps' attack was the 5th Battalion (Western Cavalry). Their Black Line Objective was a trench called the *Zwolfer Graben*. On the 5th Battalion's approach to their Black Line the men were taking heavy machine gun and rifle fire from German defenders in trenches along a sunken road in front of the *Zwolfer Graben*. Adding to the maelstrom was defensive fire coming from near the junction of the *Berietschaft Stellung* and *Wittelsbacher Weg* trenches, located just behind the *Zwolfer Graben*.[408]

This defensive fire inflicted casualties across the 5th Battalion's advance and appears to have reached far enough to inflict casualties on the next battalion to the left, 7th Battalion (1st British Columbia Regiment). Despite their losses, the men from the 5th Battalion were able to overcome the resistance in the sunken road, taking out the machine guns from a distance with rifle grenades and clearing the defenders in the sunken road with the bayonet in hand-to-hand fighting.[409] The Black Line fell soon after.

However, there was a problem. It was at the *Zwolfer Graben* that the rear waves of 5th Battalion (Western Cavalry) were to pass through the lead waves and carry the attack forward to the Red Line. The difficulty lay in the fact that the German machine gunners and riflemen were still active from the *Berietschaft Stellung* and *Wittelsbacher Weg* trenches. They were pouring heavy fire onto the Canadians while they were on the Black Line, making any attempt to advance on the Red Line a potentially lethal undertaking.

Instead of blindly following orders and advancing overland to the Red Line in the face of withering fire, the officers and men from 5th Battalion improvised. The two Companies tasked with attacking the Red Line did so, but through a combination of overland movement and working their way down German communication trenches, thus avoiding much of the machine gun fire. Meanwhile, the two Companies that had already taken the Black Line (and, technically, were not supposed to attack any further, but dig in) moved down the *Wittelsbacher Weg,* drawing fire away from their comrades advancing on the Red Line.

Having made it into the *Wittelsbacher Weg* the Canadians moved east along the trench intent on taking out the defenders that were causing so much trouble. Through a combination of long range bombing with rifle grenades and close-quarters bombing with Mills Bombs, the men were successful in overcoming the German strong point, killing the garrison. From there they proceeded to bomb their way further down the *Wittelsbacher Weg,* linking up on the Red Line with their comrades who had advanced overland and down communication trenches. The Red Line was captured and the crisis overcome by some quick thinking and tough fighting by the officers and men of the 5th Battalion (Western Cavalry).[410]

It was the opinion of officers within 1st Division that the German machine gunners were elite soldiers, determined to hold on until the end.[411] While some of them did surrender when the Canadians closed in, the majority fought until they were killed. A good example of the stubborn resistance mounted by German machine gunners comes from the 7th Battalion (1st British Columbia Regiment) during their attack on the Red Line. The barrage had lifted and a group of 18 Germans hauled their machine gun from a deep dugout and took up a position in a small crater. From this spot they inflicted casualties on the attacking Canadians until all 18 machine gunners were killed, including three by the bayonet.[412]

While the German machine gunners were inclined to fight to the finish, the same cannot be said for the ordinary German infantryman. In many instances during the advance in 1st and 2nd Divisions' sectors, once the barrage lifted from a trench, those Germans left alive in their dugouts immediately surrendered to the Canadians. The 2nd Brigade commented after the battle on the varying levels of resistance offered, noting that while many machine gunners and snipers fought to the last, most of the ordinary infantrymen "surrendered freely."[413] The cause of this distinction is hard to find. While one Battalion was of the view that overall German morale was poor[414] and another found that those who "surrendered freely" were mainly older soldiers[415], the majority of after-action reports state that German morale was good.

It may be that the ordinary German infantrymen, worn out after enduring the day and night preliminary artillery bombardment, found themselves in an impossible position when the Canadian infantry rushed the trenches immediately after the creeping barrage lifted. Sometimes still in their dugouts when the barrage lifted, discretion may have been the better part of valor for these men.

The Canadians began capturing prisoners immediately after entering the German forward trenches. Upon surrendering, the prisoners were sent back to Canadian lines, often in small groups escorted by slightly wounded Canadians, but sometimes without any escort at all as the assault Battalions could not spare the men. Still in an assembly trench was Lieutenant Stuart Hopkins of the 6th Trench Mortar Battery; part of the leap-frog 6th

Brigade. Awaiting his time to go "over the top," he recalled his first view of prisoners making their way toward and into Canadian lines:

> We crouched low while the shells and bullets whistled overhead. I tried to keep the men down but even I could not resist taking periodic glimpses over the parapet. Suddenly over the low ridge, about 300 yards in front, I saw a disordered crowd of figures stumbling back into our lines. My heart was in my mouth; my first thought was "Our attack has failed; it is our men coming back." But as they got nearer and dropped into our lines, I saw they were Germans who had given themselves up. Apparently, they followed our communication trenches for some distance but as they came back a sentry turned them out and made them go overland. They came across our trenches in twos and threes, dirty, unkempt, pale and emaciated, the most pitiful sight I have seen, some of them wounded, stumbling along with the assistance of their comrades. Our men became wildly excited and would not keep down.[416]

NAC-PA1128 – The moment after surrender. German prisoners about to make their way back to Canadian lines. Note in the left of the photograph it apprears that words are being exchanged between captive and captor.

One of the more notable captures occurred in the Village of Les Tilleuls. The Village, included in the 21st (Eastern Ontario) Battalion's Red Line objective, had been taken and the soldiers went about mopping up any remaining defenders. A half hour into the job, a large underground cave was found beneath the Village. Inside were over a hundred German soldiers, including some from two battalion headquarters. At first they resisted capture, but the Canadians threw Mills Bombs into the cave. Recognizing their hopeless situation, the Germans surrendered.[417]

As the Canadians advanced into German lines, they saw up close the tremendous damage that the British and Canadian artillery had wrought on German defences during the preliminary bombardment. While there were some points where the defensive positions survived (such as at the *Eisner Kreuz Weg*), generally, the German trenches were badly damaged, sometimes with only outlines of the trenches remaining, and the barbed wire destroyed.[418] In fact, in 2nd Brigade, engineers carrying bangalore torpedoes accompanied the attacking infantry to explode their torpedoes against any remaining wire obstacles. As the barbed wire had been already obliterated by the artillery, the bangalore torpedoes were never used, the engineers setting them aside and carrying on with the infantry.[419]

NAC-PA1150 – German trench battered by the artillery as seen after its capture by the Canadians.

Although the German trenches and wire were badly damaged, the deep dugouts often remained. Only a direct hit by a heavy shell, or a hit that collapsed the dugout entrance entombing the garrison, could take out these deep dugouts. Complicating matters was that many dugouts had multiple entrances. It was from the dugouts that the Canadians met resistance; the garrison emerging after the barrage lifted to give battle.[420]

Once the Germans emerged from their dugouts, they did not have much time to get ready to receive the Canadian infantry's assault. The Canadians kept close to the barrage, sometimes relying on artillery liaison officers for advice as to the proper distance.[421] While the creeping barrage was excellent, being accurate and well-timed, there were still some casualties due to friendly fire; either from the infantry being too close to the shrapnel bursts, or the odd artillery piece firing "short."[422]

Those Germans who emerged from their dugouts to give battle met a highly motivated enemy. The Canadians had trained hard and were fully prepared for their task. This training, coupled with an eagerness to use it, resulted in the Germans having to face a formidable foe. The officer commanding 5th Battalion (Western Cavalry), Major Lorn Tudor, remarked:

> The initiative and resource of our men was never more noticeable than during this day's work, casualties among officers and N.C.O.'s were extremely heavy, but at no time were there wanting natural leaders among the men, to carry the work forward with speed to success.[423]

These comments were echoed by the officer commanding the 10th (Canadians) Battalion, Lt-Col. Daniel Ormond, who noted in his after-action report: "I cannot hope to have command, or be associated with officers or men with a higher standard of morale," comparing their spirit favorably to that of the original soldiers of 1915 (that is, the morale of those avid, but naive, men who had not yet been exposed to the rigors and horrors of warfare on the Western Front).[424]

The men of the 22nd (French Canadian) Battalion, in particular, appear to have been eager to take the fight to the Germans. These soldiers, given the job of moppers-up in 5th Brigade, went above and beyond. Tasked with clearing German trenches and dugouts once the assault waves moved on, the moppers-up did more, twice joining with the assault waves to outflank German strong points, capturing almost 400 prisoners.[425]

One of the more remarkable episodes occurred in 8th Battalion (90th Winnipeg Rifles). One of their Lewis Gunners, despite having one arm broken and the other wounded, still managed to fire bursts from his Gun by balancing it with its sling over his shoulder.[426] Unmotivated soldiers do not keep on fighting under such circumstances.

The Lewis Gunners were important to Canadian success in the South. Their portability allowed the Guns to be brought into the assault, providing important, immediate automatic fire. Not only did the Lewis Gunners give covering fire during the advance by firing from the hip at any Germans resisting, they were valuable assets once an objective was taken. Upon the Canadians capturing an objective, Lewis Gunners would quickly push forward, take a position with a good field of fire and shoot bursts at retreating Germans, usually inflicting casualties.[427]

During 1st and 2nd Divisions' attack on their Black and Red Lines, two out of the four Victoria Crosses awarded in the Battle were earned (the Victoria Cross being the British Empire's highest award for bravery in action). In 1st Division, Private William Milne and his comrades in 16th (Canadian Scottish) Battalion faced strong opposition as soon as the barrage lifted from the German front line. Like 10th (Canadians) Battalion, the men in 16th (Canadian Scottish) Battalion had to cross a heavily cratered No Man's Land, attacking through the gaps between the craters. The Germans were able to mount their machine guns on their side of the craters and delivered a withering fire into the advancing Canadians. The front line defenders were overcome through close quarter and long range bombing, but not before inflicting heavy casualties on the Canadians. German machine gunners were a menace throughout the rest of 16th Battalion's attack, whittling away at the Battalion's manpower all the way to the Red Line.[428]

It was at one of these difficult machine gun posts that Private William Milne earned his Victoria Cross. This particular machine gun was holding up the advance as it had repulsed several attempts to take it out and inflicted serious casualties on the attackers. Crawling on his hands and knees, Private Milne inched toward the German machine gun, bombing the machine gun and crew when he got close enough to throw his Mills bombs. With the position taken out, the Canadians' advance was able to resume due to Private Milne's actions. Unfortunately, his Victoria Cross was a posthumous award. William Milne was killed later that day, but not before putting another machine gun post out of commission.[429]

Second Division's Victoria Cross was earned by Lance-Sergeant Ellis Sifton from the 18th (Western Ontario) Battalion. Like the situation faced by Private Milne, Lance-Sergeant Sifton and the men from "C" Company were held up by a German machine gun. Working his way forward, Sifton was able to get close enough to the machine gun crew to rush it. Unbelievably, he managed to enter the German position and bayoneted the entire crew. If this were not already enough, Lance-Sergeant Sifton spotted more Germans coming down the trench to attack him. Still on his own, Sifton held them off, killing some with his bayonet and bludgeoned the rest using his rifle as a club. Like William Milne's award, Ellis Sifton's Victoria Cross was to be posthumous. After he had beaten the German attack and was joined by his comrades, one of the dying Germans took his revenge and shot Lance-Sergeant Sifton.[430]

While the Canadians were taking their objectives, it was necessary throughout the assault to ensure that the commanders in Canadian lines were advised on the progress being made. Communication was a difficult problem on Great War battlefields and the Canadians paid much attention to overcoming this at Vimy Ridge.

Within battalions information flowed from the individual soldier, to his section leader, to the officer in charge of the platoon, to the company commander and then to the officer leading the battalion's assault. While between the individual soldier and his section leader information could be exchanged by shouting, the ability for face-to-face communication disappeared the higher up the chain of command. A company commander and his men could be quite some distance away from the officer leading the battalion. Thus, runners were used, picking their way across the muddy, shell cratered terrain to deliver the messages.

This is only part of the communications story for the battalions had to communicate to their headquarters and the brigade commanders in Canadian lines. For this, the main means of communication was the telephone. Advancing with the assault were officers and soldiers tasked with running phone lines as they pushed forward and establishing communication report centres within German lines. From the report centres, so long as the lines were not cut by German shelling, telephone communication was possible to the commanders in Canadian lines. Generally, due to the weak German defensive barrage, the phone lines did survive unscathed, but where they did not, runners had to be used.

While telephones provided instant communication once they were set up, there would still be a gap in time between the arrival of the men tasked with establishing the report centre and the moment it became operational. To plug this gap, visual signalling equipment, such as signal flags, were also brought forward. Thus, once the men arrived at their destination, they would immediately use visual signals to communicate the attack's progress to the observers in Canadian lines, then turned their attention to establishing telephone communication.

Similar to that between the assault troops and their commanders in Canadian lines, were the lines of communication between the artillery's forward observation officers and the batteries in the rear. As they advanced, the Canadians wanted to ensure that the gunners were aware of the infantry's progress, as well as any targets that may arise during the course of the Battle, such as a German counter-attack. Thus, like the infantry, the artillery ran phone lines forward as well. Also like the infantry's experience, doing so was a hazardous undertaking. For example, 5th Brigade CFA's communication from the point of the attack was temporarily interrupted when the Brigade's forward observation officer was killed trying to establish the phone line ahead of the *Swischen Stellung*; two of his linesmen already being wounded.[431]

Back in Canadian lines, observation posts dotted the landscape. The men within were tasked with observing the Battle's progress and keeping a lookout for visual signals coming from the Canadians at the forefront of the attack. All were connected by telephone with headquarters (usually with the lines buried underground) and would immediately update the commanding officers when events could be observed and as information from the attack front was received. As can be imagined though, it was a difficult job for these observers, particularly since the battlefield was often shrouded by smoke shells (fired by the Canadians to cover their attacking troops) and precipitation.

To give one a sense of the type of information received during the Battle, the following is an excerpt from 4th Brigade's War Diary:

> 6:30 a.m.   Major Jennings reports our machine gun fire and barrage is very effective. The enemy are sending up golden showers and double green rockets from the THELUS Ridge. Major Jennings leaves

Lieut. Cockeram in charge of Bde Advanced R.C. while he moves forward to establish a new O.P. in order to obtain better observation.

6:35 a.m.   Prisoners are reported passing our advanced Bde Report Centre. Major Jennings reports the Black Objective appears to have been gained along the entire front. About 100 prisoners have passed 13th Battery O.P. They are BAVARIANS.

6:38 a.m.   5th C.I. Bde. report that their right Bn. is in the Black Objective and no word yet received from their left Bn. Visibility becoming very poor owing to mist. Very few wounded are coming back and the German barrage is very light.

6:40 a.m.   The 21st Bn. is now reported to be beyond the 18th Bn. Advanced Report Centre. German machine guns are sweeping the top of Phillip Crater. Division report that the right Bde. of the 1st Division are in the Black Objective and that the left Bde. is doing well.

6:42 a.m.   Division reports that 5th Bde. Bn. who are detailed to capture Red Objective has been seen going forward in good order. Instructions given to Divisional Signal Cable Burying Party to proceed forward.

6:50 a.m.   Enemy barrage is still on our original front line area. A German machine gun captured with its entire crew is reported passing Advanced Bde. R.C. carried by the Huns.

6:55 a.m.   Enemy barrage has dropped back to his original front line, not very heavy. Smoke interferes very badly with observation and more prisoners passing Bde. at Adv. R.C. 5th C.I. Bde. Report they are having very little opposition. 18th Bn. Very lights on their immediate front.[432]

From brigade headquarters the information received was then passed on to Division and then Corps through underground phone lines. Generally speaking, this system of communication from the forefront of the attack all the way to Corps Headquarters worked extremely well.

Supplementing communication on the ground was aerial observation. Two airplanes were designated "contact airplanes," tasked with observing the infantry's progress and communicating the information to Division and Corps headquarters. Flying at pre-arranged intervals throughout the attack, the infantry were aware of when the planes were flying overhead and fired ground flares visible to the aerial observers above, marking the infantry's progress. One contact plane was with 1st and 2nd Divisions, the other plane with 3rd and 4th Divisions. This system of communication worked well for 1st and 2nd

Divisions, but the contact plane with 3rd and 4th Divisions was shot down soon after zero-hour, apparently being hit by a "friendly shell"[433] (the two airmen were captured by the Germans and then re-captured by the Canadians on April 13).[434]

By 7:30 a.m., matters were well in hand in 1st and 2nd Divisions' sectors. Casualties were heavy, particularly in 1st Division, but all objectives were taken and on time. For 2nd, 3rd, 4th and 5th Brigades, their role in the attack had come to an end and the Battle would be carried forward to the Blue and Brown Lines by the leap-frog 1st, 6th and 13th (British) Brigades. However, before we turn to the next phase of the attack in the South, we will first examine how matters played out with 3rd and 4th Divisions from zero-hour to 7:30 a.m.

Three

3rd Division

5:30 a.m. - 7:30 a.m.

Third Division, located to the left of 2nd Division, held the infamous Crater Line. This was a particularly disorientating sector at Vimy Ridge as the opposing forces were very close, sometimes mere yards away. No Man's Land was full of old mine craters. Both sides sought to obtain the observation advantage that the crater lips gave over the opposing sides' trenches. Thus, the combatants placed observation posts on their respective crater lips, connected to their own front line by saps. With many craters in No Man's Land, the ground between the opposing front lines was a maze of deep craters, observation posts, saps and connecting trenches.

It was in 3rd Division's sector that the *Stellung I* and *Swischen Stellung* which, in the South were both well to the west of Vimy Ridge, came to be located on the western slope and crest of the Ridge. Since 3rd Division's front lines were relatively close to the crest and eastern slope, it had less distance over which to attack in order to capture all of Vimy Ridge in its sector than the Divisions had in the South. Rather than four Lines having to be seized, the 3rd Division had two; the Black and Red Lines. Due to this lesser depth in attack, 3rd Division would not employ leap-frog brigades. Instead, 8th Brigade (right-hand brigade) and 7th Brigade (left) would be responsible for taking both Lines. The 3rd Division's other brigade, 9th Brigade, was kept in reserve.

Even though there were less Lines to capture, those that had to be attacked were formidable nevertheless. Like the defences attacked by 1st and 2nd Divisions, those facing 3rd Division consisted of successive trenches with strong points, connected by communication trenches cutting the ground in different directions, along with deep dugouts and underground tunnels. For example, in the southern part of 7th Brigade's attack frontage, there were at least 10 trenches between the German front line and the Red Line, not counting the communication trenches. To overcome these defences 3rd Division used similar tactics as those used in the South; successive waves with accompanying moppers-up attacking successive trenches, all the while closely following the creeping barrage.

We saw in the South that when the Canadian and British barrage started at 5:30 a.m., the infantry began their advance on German lines. However, in 8th Brigade, the troops did not advance immediately upon the barrage commencing like the rest of their comrades in the Canadian Corps. The reason for this was that two communication trenches were to be blown in No Man's Land.

The reinforcement and supply of assault Battalions after they seize their objectives is an important consideration in any attack. To give protection to the reinforcements and carrying parties, the engineers from the British 172nd Tunnelling Company bored two tubes below the surface of the ground into No Man's Land. Packed with explosive ammonal, the tubes were blown 30 seconds after zero-hour creating "instant" communication trenches across No Man's Land and into German lines.[435] However, to avoid any casualties from the explosion of the ammonal tubes, the soldiers of 8th Brigade delayed their move from their jumping-off trenches.[436]

Just as in the South, once the British and Canadian barrage lifted from the German front line, the German artillery began its defensive barrage. With the 8th Brigade delaying their advance until after zero-hour, the defensive barrage fell on those soldiers who were still moving out of their jumping-off trenches. Fortunately for the Canadians, although some casualties were caused, the German barrage fell mainly on Canadian lines rather than No Man's Land, and was weak and scattered. Therefore, while there was the potential for disaster, it never happened due to the effective Canadian and British counter-battery work. The 1st Canadian Mounted Rifles' after-action report recorded the first moments of the attack in the early morning gloom:

> As soon as we had reached a point where the German lines were discernable, flares of all descriptions could be seen along the whole German front, evidently "S.O.S." Signals; and what barrage the enemy was able to put on came very quickly. The leading Company – "D" – had to pass through it before they were in the German front line. And each Company in turn had to go through it, and in doing so sustained rather a considerable number of casualties.
>
> D Company were not long in cleaning up the three front lines. Machine gun crews were immediately placed on the enemy's lip of the craters and as far as was necessary covered the advance of the front troops. The front lines were not strongly held but it is safe to say that not one of the enemy escaped from them . . . All were either killed or taken prisoners.[437]

The men of 7th Brigade had a bit easier time of it during their move from their jumping-off trenches. Here, instead of barraging the nearest German positions (the observation posts on the crater lips), the barrage fell just to the east. This allowed the soldiers in 7th Brigade to pick and crawl through the multitude of saps, posts, trenches and craters to creep as close as possible to German positions once the barrage lifted. For these men, when the German defensive barrage opened, it fell well to their rear and did not interfere at all with their rushing of the first German positions.[438]

A.A. Bonar of the Princess Patricia's Canadian Light Infantry described the advance across the Crater Line:

> One was conscious, however, on all sides of a surging mass carrying loads of bombs, ammunition, shovels, picks, rolls of barbwire and other materials for consolidating positions. They deployed from the narrow necks of ground between the craters. Up the lips of the craters they appeared, then disappeared with precipitous haste down the deep, yawning bowels, to clamber with effort over the opposite banks. Beyond the craters was a swarming, struggling host. Which recalled a colony of ants, whose hill had been disturbed, seeking in haste, each with a load, some new abode.
>
> Above a canopy of shells and bullets seemed to stretch across the sky. Beyond, the shells were exploding with thunderous crash, emitting fire and smoke, and throwing up spouts of brown earth and chalk. Close behind our protective barrage, muddy figures trudged over ground that had been ploughed and harrowed by countless shells.[439]

F.E. Conley (Princess Patricia's Canadian Light Infantry) was struck by the spectacle and power of the creeping barrage:

> A dancing wall of flame crept up the forward slope of the Ridge, lingered in terrible devastation over the German front line, and then moved slowly and inexorably on, blotting out support trenches and mauling communications. In its wake was stark havoc. The fortifications which had been considered almost impregnable were laid open to the advance of our infantry.[440]

Like the attack in the South, the Black and Red Lines were captured on schedule and without the need to deviate from the artillery fire-plan. In 3rd Division's sector, they were on the crest of Vimy Ridge and looking down on the Germans to the east by around 7:30 a.m.

The Black Line was the *Swischen Stellung*, expected to be a major hurdle in the Canadians' advance to the crest of the Ridge. It was not to be. The Canadians followed the barrage closely and immediately stormed the successive German lines, taking many prisoners in the process.

That they were able to keep close to the barrage was amazing considering the nature of the ground due to the shelling and wet weather. Shell craters and soft, muddy spots were everywhere, the soldiers having to carefully pick their way through.[441] A.A. Bonar remembered the mud:

> It was extremely heavy going. The soil was soft and sticky. It collected in large clumps on one's boots. Every time one tumbled, which was often, or climbed over shell holes, he carried away with him on his clothes a heavy coating of viscous mud. It was an effort to lift one's feet.[442]

Probably in an effort to keep up with the barrage, many of the soldiers ditched their picks and shovels to lighten their loads.[443]

The 1st Canadian Mounted Rifles' after-action report relates the ease in which the objectives were captured, but also some of the difficulties in getting there:

> C. B. and A. Companies immediately pressed through D Company and on toward the SWISCHEN STELLUNG. Very little opposition was encountered from this trench, which was supposed to be the enemy's strong line. The barrage was followed by the troops step by step until the trench was finally reached. As on the front line, the wire along the SWISCHEN STELLUNG had been completely cut by our artillery, and the trench itself had been knocked to pieces, and practically all the dugouts smashed in.
>
> One platoon of C. Company followed up the PRINZ ARNOLF GRABEN Tunnels for the purpose of cleaning up any of the dugouts which may have been left intact but they were found to be almost completely deserted and the entrances completely smashed in by our artillery. In fact, the whole ground was so completely smashed up that it was difficult to even follow the land marks and maintain proper direction.[444]

A.A. Bonar (Princess Patricia's Canadian Light Infantry) remembered the difficulty in keeping one's bearings:

> . . . it required tremendous effort of mind and body to keep up with the van guard, retain one's direction and not get mixed up with men from other companies. Positions and trenches, which were known on the map of the ground over which we advanced, had been obliterated. It was extremely difficult for companies to maintain their direction and distance and not lose contact with the battalions on their flanks. The heavy smoke contributed to this difficulty.[445]

One of the soldiers who became lost was Sergeant John C. Alvis from the 1st Canadian Mounted Rifles:

> In crossing an enemy trench, a cry for help came from a Lewis gun crew who was hopelessly mired in the mud of the trench, by the time I assisted the six

overloaded men out of the trench, my own comrades were nowhere in sight. In trying to find my way I wandered too far to the right and then to the left, machine gun
fire sent me to the shelter of a big shell hole. While there thoughts passed through
my mind of how best to get away from it. It lasted less than a minute, then a Major
CO, D Company appeared, he was looking for his own men. I told him I was lost, he
suggested as the next best thing that I follow him, shortly after I found my own platoon. When we reached our first objective, everything seemed mixed up for a while
as officers tried to locate their own men.[446]

This difficulty to keep one's bearings did result in some disorganization in 1st Canadian
Mounted Rifles' area. Being the southernmost battalion in 3rd Division, to their immediate
right were troops from 2nd Division. It appears that there was a tendency among 2nd Division
men to drift to their left, crossing into 1st Canadian Mounted Rifles' frontage. This resulted in
some confusion and over-crowding on the *Swischen Stellung.* Soldiers from the 22nd (French
Canadian), 24th (Victoria Rifles of Canada), 25th (Nova Scotia Rifles) and 26th (New
Brunswick) Battalions, plus the 13th (British) Brigade, were there; all in addition to its proper
occupants, the men from the 1st Canadian Mounted Rifles. There seems to have been only
one officer from the 2nd Division and he was lost. The mix-up was cleared up and, fortunately, does not appear to have caused the Canadians any unnecessary casualties.[447]

From this confusion came a unique event; Vickers machine-gunners leading the charge
on the Red Line. As we have already seen in the South, Lewis Guns were an important element to Canadian success, providing, among other things, immediate automatic fire to protect
objectives once captured. However, the Canadians were not willing to rely on the firepower
from their Lewis Guns alone. Instead, advancing with the rear waves of infantry were the
Vickers gunners, lugging their heavy machine guns, ammunition and equipment. Their princi-
ple role was to set up their machine guns on the objectives after they were captured and, with
the Lewis Gunners, protect the Canadians' conquests from German counter-attacks.

However, likely due to the mix-up on the *Swischen Stellung,* the Vickers machine-gunners attached to the 1st Canadian Mounted Rifles ended up in front of the infantry and were
the first to arrive on the Red Line overlooking the Ridge's eastern slope. They were positioned
at the top of the Bonval Ravine and from here the machine gunners observed about 300
Germans in the Ravine below. Quickly getting their four Vickers machine guns into action,
they opened fire on the Germans, inflicting casualties and forcing them to scatter into the safety of their deep dugouts excavated in the sides of the Ravine.

Taking the initiative, the lieutenant in command of the machine guns along with 8 other
ranks advanced on the deep dugouts, intent on bombing the Germans out. In one dugout
there was a fierce encounter, as a German officer threw a bomb at the Canadians as they tried
to enter, killing a sergeant and smashing the lieutenant's rifle. Drawing his revolver, the lieutenant proceeded to gun down the German officer and the officer's two comrades. While

between 150 to 200 Germans were captured from their deep dugouts, some did try to make a last minute escape from the dugouts' alternate exits. For these men there would be no safety though, as the Vickers machine guns positioned above the Ravine cut them down as they made their attempt.[448]

One of these groups of Germans trying to flee from the Canadians was the commander of a German battalion, his staff and about 20 men. Struggling through the mud, they were trying to make it to the *Stellung II*. It was a risky decision and there was a price to pay for this last second retreat. While the battalion commander survived, most of his staff and all of the men were left behind; dead or wounded by the Canadian Vickers gunners.[449]

Unlike 1st and 2nd Divisions' experience, German machine gunners were not as effective against 3rd Division. While the Royal Canadian Regiment did suffer heavy casualties from a machine gun on the Red Line, by in large, the German machine gunners were unable to bring their weapons into action. The Canadians kept close to the barrage and overwhelmed the machine gunners before they could offer significant resistance.[450]

A.A. Bonar (Princess Patricia's Canadian Light Infantry) recalled how he and his comrades overcame German defenders in the wooded area on their Red Line:

> Hidden behind these trees the enemy fired at us with rifles and machine guns. His shells too were now falling amongst us doing considerable damage. But our sections knew what to do in an instant. The bombers attacked a communication trench, which ran through the wood, which was strongly held. In this assault, Donnelly, our bombing corporal was killed. The rifle grenadiers started to drop their grenades beyond the bombers. The machine guns sprayed the wood. The little opposition from behind the trees didn't last long. Displaying splendid calm our officers led the way into the woods.[451]

While the relative ease in which the 3rd Division captured the Black and Red Lines has been emphasized, this does not mean that all went perfectly. We have already seen the confusion on the Division's right due to some intermingling of different Battalions at the *Swischen Stellung*. It was also on the 3rd Division's right that one of the Canadian Corps' greatest concerns almost became a reality.

The deep dugouts relied on by the Germans to garrison their troops was a worry. The fear was that the assault waves and moppers-up would miss a dugout, allowing the garrison to emerge behind the attacking Canadians and shoot at them from the rear.

On the far right of the 3rd Division, one Company from the 5th Canadian Mounted Rifles was tasked with supporting the 1st Canadian Mounted Rifles. When crossing the German front line at about 6:00 a.m., the Company came under fire from a group of about 40 Germans. As the Canadian assault Battalions were well forward, it is likely that these Germans emerged from deep dugouts along the Crater Line. Missed by the assault waves and their moppers-up, the Germans now prepared to give battle to the men of the support Company. The Canadians were alert though, and it was a short, but deadly, encounter, with 23 Germans surrendering only after the remainder of their group was killed.[452]

By 7:30 a.m., the men of 3rd Division were on Vimy Ridge, the first Canadians to do so. Having taken their objectives, the soldiers began to dig in, consolidating the Ridge into a fit state to repel any German counter-attacks, while carrying parties brought up ammunition and supplies. However, the soldiers on the extreme left of the 3rd Division, the 42nd Battalion (Royal Highlanders of Canada), were beginning to take rifle and machine gun fire from their left and rear. Something was going wrong with 4th Division.

Four

4th Division

5:30 a.m. - 7:30 a.m.

The most northern Division in the Canadian Corps was 4th Division. Its main objective for April 9 was Hill 145, the highest point on Vimy Ridge. Not only was Hill 145 the most heavily defended position on the Ridge, but its slope, which was relatively speaking the steepest any of the Canadian troops would face during the Battle, was a muddy wasteland, full of watery shell craters. To capture this commanding feature 4th Division used its 11th Brigade; the unit most familiar with the defences of the Hill. On 11th Brigade's left was 12th Brigade. The remaining brigade, 10th Brigade, was to provide a Battalion each to 11th and 12th Brigades as support, with its other two Battalions held back for the assault on the Pimple. This attack was planned to take place as soon as possible after the capture of Hill 145, likely on April 10.

11th Brigade was using all four assault Battalions to storm Hill 145. On the right, 102nd (North British Columbians) Battalion was to capture the Black Line, with 54th (Kootenay) Battalion passing through to take the Red Line. On the left, which included the highest point on Hill 145, the 87th Battalion (Canadian Grenadier Guards) would attack the Black Line and 75th (Mississauga) Battalion would pass through and capture the Red Line. Once the Red Line was taken, the Canadians would be at the foot of the eastern slope of the Hill.

12th Brigade had objectives of varying depth. To the left of Hill 145, 38th (Ottawa) Battalion was tasked with attacking the Black Line while the 78th Battalion (Winnipeg Grenadiers) would pass through to take the Red Line. To these Battalions' left the remaining two Battalions in 12th Brigade had the Black Line as their final objectives. The 72nd Battalion (Seaforth Highlanders of Canada) were to assault the German front line and the next trench beyond. On the left of the entire Canadian Corps' attack, 73rd Battalion (Royal Highlanders of Canada) were to capture the front line only. A unique aspect of 73rd Battalion's assault was that it was to be accompanied by the explosion of two underground mines beneath German lines at zero-hour.

Upon the British and Canadian barrage roaring to life at zero-hour and the two mines at the northern edge of the Canadians' attack exploding, the assault waves left their jumping-off trenches and made their way forward; prepared to rush the German front line upon the barrage lifting.

On the right and left of 4th Divisions attack, matters appeared to be going according to plan. On the right, observer's noted that 102nd (North British Columbians) Battalion "went over as one man and that their formation was perfect."[453] A strong point in the German front line was taken by an encircling movement and the 54th (Kootenay) Battalion, despite taking some initial casualties from firing on their left, passed through and were at the Red Line on schedule.[454] Lieutenant E.L.M. Burns (11th Brigade Signal Section) was with the advance and remembered the opening moments:

> As I recollect, when we started to plough across no man's land in the growing light of the dawn, my principal emotions were curiosity and a not unpleasant excitement. The noise of the barrage dominated all other impressions: imagine the loudest clap of thunder you ever heard, multiplied by two, and prolonged indefinitely. The sky was a cupola of lead, and the appalling uproar, reflected down from it, pressed on one like deep water. The shells burst only thirty rods ahead, but they were invisible, except for brief flames and showers of sparks. Our supporting machine guns poured forth their 800 shots a minute in insane stammering rhythm, just audible against the deep note of the artillery. No doubt all this noise had a stimulating psychological effect, and built up a sense of power in the attackers. I could identify no enemy reply; the barrage, on our immediate front at least, seemed fully effective.[455]

On the left, the Battalions of 12th Brigade were all able to capture the German front line with little opposition. As was the experience of the other Divisions in the Corps, the German defensive barrage fell mainly behind the attacking infantry, causing few casualties.

It was in front of Hill 145 that things went immediately wrong. Remarkably, the officer commanding 87th Battalion (Canadian Grenadier Guards), Major H. LeRoy Shaw, requested that the British and Canadian artillery avoid bombarding the German front line opposite the Battalion's right prior to the attack. This was the German front line ahead of the highest part of Hill 145. While not entirely clear, the reason for this request appears to be that Major Shaw wanted that portion of the front line preserved for ease in consolidation after the whole front line was captured. Possibly in deference to "the man on the spot," Generals Odlum (11th Brigade) and Watson (4th Division) acceded to the request.[456]

The failure to destroy the German front line was fatal. The men of 87th Battalion (Canadian Grenadier Guards) were raked by machine gun and rifle fire from the German front line, losing 60 percent of their men.[457] What appears to have happened is that the Canadians were not able to keep up with the creeping barrage on account of the terribly muddy and torn up ground.[458] Having lost the barrage, those Germans left unmolested in the front line had the time to emerge from their deep dugouts, man their defences and cut down the Canadians struggling across No Man's Land. With the Canadians stopped before the front line, the barrage moved on, lifting from German positions further up the western slope of Hill 145. This allowed the Germans garrisoning these positions to emerge and pour rifle and machine gun fire onto the Canadians below.

However, not all of the Canadians' attack was stopped in No Man's Land. As noted, it was only that portion of the German front line on the right of the 87th Battalion's attack that was left undamaged. On the left, the soldiers from the 87th Battalion and the supporting 75th (Mississauga) Battalion were able to cross No Man's Land and push beyond into German territory. However, they were taking heavy fire and began to take cover.

Turning back to 87th Battalion's right, those men still alive were forced to go to ground in front of the undamaged German front line and the remaining barbed wire. Behind them, soldiers from the 75th Battalion could not advance and were forced to take cover in the jumping-off trenches. With bullets zipping through the air from the German front line and positions further up the Hill, the attack was beginning to unravel before Hill 145.

Lieutenant E.L.M. Burns remembered the attack stalling:

Up to this point the action had been "according to plan"; now there was a sudden change. The barrage had moved some distance ahead and the surviving enemy now crawled out of their shelters and turned upon us. A machine gun fired a burst directly in front of us, less than 100 yards distant.

There is no more vicious noise than that of a machine gun trained directly at one: in the half light long streaks of flame reached out like adders' tongues. Fortunately, shell-holes were everywhere, rim to rim, and Hadow, the man who carried my telephone, and I took cover with one jump. As we did so I heard a faint clang from my tin hat and when well down in the hole, I removed it to find a neat longitudinal crease. The machine gunners had nearly scored.[459]

As for 12th Brigade, their difficulties began once the troops advanced beyond the German front line. While the muddy, shell cratered ground was an obstacle wherever the Canadians attacked, that in 12th Brigade's sector seems to have been particularly bad. It was a maze of shell holes, many partially filled with water. These water-filled shell holes were death traps as many Canadians who were wounded fell into them and drowned. Struggling through this muck, the soldiers in 12th Brigade lost the protection of the creeping barrage. Despite their extreme difficulties, the men carried on with the advance, taking their objectives including the Red Line, but casualties were severe from German defenders emerging from their dugouts after the barrage moved on.[460]

For 4th Division, the situation was insecure by 7:30 a.m. While the Battalions on the right and left of 4th Division had taken their objectives, casualties were heavy. At Hill 145 some men had penetrated the German front line, but most had not, leaving No Man's Land strewn with dead and wounded. Those who could desperately tried to find some cover, while soldiers from 75th (Mississauga) Battalion were pinned down in the jumping-off trenches.

Five

Summary at 7:30 a.m.

Before carrying on with the Battle Narrative, a moment will be taken to summarize the Canadians' progress by 7:30 a.m. First and 2nd Divisions had captured the Black and Red Lines, resulting in the capture of the entire *Stellung I* and virtually all of the *Swischen Stellung* in the southern sector. While the assault went according to plan and the troops benefited from keeping close to the creeping barrage, casualties were heavy. For the most part the German resistance in the South came from machine gun nests, in many cases the gunners having to be killed before the machine guns were silenced. Otherwise, the ordinary infantryman was inclined to surrender, rather than being wiped out by the advancing Canadians. Fortunately for the assault Brigades, the German artillery response, while prompt, was weak, mainly falling behind the waves of infantry.

In 3rd Division the attack went even more smoothly than in the South. The anticipated stiff resistance on the *Swischen Stellung* (Black Line) did not materialize and the Canadians followed the barrage closely, capturing Vimy Ridge in 3rd Division's sector by around 7:30 a.m. Prisoners were many and, excepting the early moments of 8th Brigade's attack, the German artillery did not interfere with the advance. There had been some confusion on the 3rd Division's right when 2nd Division men drifted into 3rd Division's sector, but this had been cleared up and the soldiers were consolidating their gains.

Unlike the rest of the Canadian Corps, the attack in the north was experiencing serious difficulties. While the right and left flanks of 4th Division were on their objectives by around 7:30 a.m., casualties had been severe. In 12th Brigade the troops lost the creeping barrage, allowing the Germans to man their defences and inflict casualties as the Canadians advanced. At Hill 145 the situation was even more dire. Although on the lower, southern half of Hill 145 11th Brigade soldiers were on their objectives and some men had made it into the German defences on the northern half, there was a dangerous gap in the advance directly in front of the highest point of the Hill. Here, much of the 87th Battalion

(Canadian Grenadier Guards) were lying on the ground (whether dead or alive) in front of a portion of the German front line that was left undamaged and from which the Germans were delivering a withering fire on any Canadian movement. Such was the intensity of the fire that many men from the 75th (Mississauga) Battalion could not advance and had to remain in the jumping-off trenches.

From here we will carry on with the story of 1st and 2nd Division's leap-frog Brigades from 7:30 a.m. to 11:00 a.m. We will then examine how 3rd and 4th Divisions fared during this time period, before a summary of the situation at 11:00.

Six

1st Division

7:30 a.m. - 11:00 a.m.

Following the capture of the Black and Red Lines by 2nd and 3rd Brigades in 1st Division, the creeping barrage paused a couple of hundred yards to the east, maintaining a standing barrage to prevent any German counter-attacks. Like the pause in the barrage between the capture of the Black and Red Lines, this allowed the men of 2nd and 3rd Brigades to mop up any remaining resistance points, re-organize and consolidate their newly won positions for defence. It was also during this time that the leap-frog Brigade, 1st Brigade, passed through and prepared to attack the remaining objectives for 1st Division.

As we have seen, the German artillery barrage did not interfere with the assault Brigades' advance or cause many casualties as the shells fell behind the attacking infantry. However, the area behind 2nd and 3rd Brigades was not empty space, as the men of 1st Brigade were following the advance. As these men moved to the Red Line to carry the attack forward they had to pass through the German barrage, which was falling between the Canadian front line and the Black Line. Fortunately though, due to the troops advancing in artillery formation and the effective British and Canadian counter-battery work, casualties were low.[461]

The first unit of 1st Brigade to leave their assembly trenches was 1st (Western Ontario) Battalion which advanced at zero-hour, following the soldiers from 2nd Brigade. The rest of 1st Brigade (2nd Eastern Ontario), 3rd (Toronto Regiment) and 4th (Central Ontario) Battalions did not depart until 7:30 a.m. The reason for the difference lay in the defences facing 1st Division beyond the Red Line.

NAC-PA1026 – April 9, 1917, the Battle of Vimy Ridge. In the foreground Canadian soldiers from the assault brigade finish "mopping up" the German trench. In the centre of the photograph are German prisoners with Canadian escort. Note in the background "leap-frog" units passing through to push the assault forward.

Everywhere else on the Canadian Corps' front, the Swischen Stellung fell within the Red Line. However, at the extreme southern end of 1st Division's sector, the Swischen Stellung angled away from the Red Line to the south-east. This portion of the Swischen Stellung was beyond the Red Line, but did not reach the Blue Line. Since it was a major German defence line, the decision was made that 1st (Western Ontario) Battalion would make a separate attack on the remaining portion of the Swischen Stellung before the assault on the Blue Line by the whole 1st Brigade. To allow the 1st (Western Ontario) Battalion to make its attack, the creeping barrage would re-commence its advance in the extreme south at 7:42 a.m., lead the infantry over the Swischen Stellung and then pause to form a standing barrage 200 yards east of the Stellung.

Following in 2nd Brigade's wake, it appears that the men of 1st (Western Ontario) Battalion were inspired to take the fight to the Germans early. While not part of orders, the soldiers of 1st Battalion helped out their comrades in 2nd Brigade, mopping up resistance points.[462] By the time the men had reached the Red Line and deployed into assault waves, their "blood was up."

Despite some barbed wire still protecting the *Swischen Stellung*, the soldiers of 1st (Western Ontario) Battalion kept close to the barrage and captured their objective. Resistance was encountered on the right, but with the troops on the left coming to assist, the defenders were overcome mainly by long range bombing with rifle grenades.[463]

As the soldiers consolidated their newly won gains, the rest of 1st Brigade came up and deployed into wave formation, along with the rear waves from 1st (Western Ontario) Battalion. For the men of the 4th (Central Ontario) Battalion, they received a spirited send-off as they passed through the Red Line. The pipers of 16th Battalion (Canadian Scottish), who had already piped their own men into battle at zero-hour, now gave the same inspiration to the 4th Battalion soldiers.[464] Once beyond the pipers, the men of 1st Brigade inched as near as possible to the barrage and were ready to advance on the Blue Line by 9:55 a.m.

Also advancing with the remainder of 1st Brigade were barrage Vickers machine gunners. Tasked with assisting the artillery in firing the creeping barrage, once the assault had reached the Red Line the machine gunners were losing the range. To continue providing the creeping barrage with machine gun fire, the machine gunners had to advance into captured German territory and set up their guns again to re-gain the range. They were in position in time to support the next phase of the attack, but had suffered during their advance. Like their comrades in 1st Brigade, the machine gunners had to advance through the German defensive artillery barrage. Despite the relative weakness of the German artillery, it was still able to cause some damage, killing 5 machine gunners, wounding 11 more and destroying 3 Vickers guns.[465]

NAC-PA1113 — In the foreground Canadian soldiers are consolidating. The line in front is perhaps telephone wire, but more likely is engineer's tape. The "dots" on the horizon are men from a "leap-frog" unit assaulting Blue Line positions. Shrapnel from the creeping barrage explodes ahead of them.

Turning to the assault on the Blue Line, due to the 1st (Western Ontario) Battalion's attack on the *Swischen Stellung*, the Canadian advance in the extreme south jutted further east than elsewhere in 1st Division. To coordinate the attack on the Blue Line, the rolling barrage would have a staggered advance, re-commencing its creep forward on the left first, followed by the centre, with the right joining in once the barrage met the standing barrage 200 yards east of the *Swischen Stellung*. With the infantry keeping up to the barrage, they were all in position to storm the next German defences when the barrage lifted simultaneously across the whole line of advance.

Now that the men of 1st Division were beyond the dense trench network of the *Stellung I* and *Swischen Stellung*, the German defences became more spread out. The Blue Line was a trench named the Island Traverse Trench and there was only one trench in front of this, although there were several major communication trenches running east-west. Perhaps for this reason, the Canadians found German resistance to be weak and the Blue Line was captured by around 11:00 a.m., with casualties not being heavy. From 1st Brigade observers timed 11:07 a.m.:

> Troops still advancing on Blue, but leading waves appear to have already reached there. They can be seen on sky line advancing and do not appear to be having much opposition. They advanced as if they were on parade.[466]

German machine gun fire was much less than that experienced during the Canadians' advance on the Black and Red Lines, while the German artillery continued to fire behind the assault waves. We saw earlier that 1st Division's assault Brigades suffered average casualties in the attacking Battalions of 56 percent in officers and 44 percent for other ranks. Reflecting the weaker opposition met by the leap-frog 1st Brigade, their casualties were much less by the end of the Battle. Officer casualties averaged 30 percent, while those suffered by the other ranks came to 17 percent of those engaged.

Following the attacking infantry was Signaller Wilfred Kerr (11th Battery CFA). Accompanying a forward artillery observation officer and two telephonists, Kerr and his small party were heading for the crest of Vimy Ridge. On the way to their destination Signaller Kerr got his first view of a Great War battlefield:

> We picked our way across the old German line. The ground was honeycombed with shell-holes; most of these filled with water, and in many the water was bloody. I saw corpses here and there, lying in strange attitudes; and I noticed the burial parties at work. To me it was new and sickening; but there was work to do, and I decided to try not to look at the corpses.[467]

Well behind was Canon Frederick Scott (1st Division). From his vantage point he was able to take in much of 1st Division's battlefield. He recalled:

The sight of the German trenches was something never to be forgotten. They had been strongly held and had been fortified with an immense maze of wire. But now they were ploughed and shattered by enormous shell holes. The wire was twisted and torn, and the whole of that region looked as if a volcanic upheaval had broken the crust of the earth. Hundreds of men were now walking over the open in all directions. German prisoners were being hurried back in scores. Wounded men, stretcher-bearers and men following up the advance were seen on all sides, and on the ground lay the bodies of friends and foes who had passed to the Great Beyond.[465]

By 11:00 a.m., 1st Division was steadily pushing forward. Resistance had been weaker on the Blue Line than at the previous Lines and the men of 1st Brigade were ready to carry on. Vimy Ridge in their sector was almost entirely in their hands.

NAC-PA1130 – Canadian troops dug in and holding captured German positions. Note the Canadian helmets "poking" above the ground. German prisoners in centre of photograph moving back toward Canadian lines, assisting a wounded Canadian.

Seven

2nd Division

7:30 a.m. - 11:00 a.m.

To the north of 1st Brigade was 6th Brigade, the right hand leap-frog brigade of 2nd Division. The three Battalions tasked with attacking the Blue Line, (31st (Alberta), 28th (Northwest) and 29th (Vancouver), left their assembly trenches at 8:05 a.m., making for a point just east of the Red Line, where they would deploy in waves for their attack.

Like their comrades to the south, the men of 6th Brigade had to pass through the German defensive barrage, which included some gas shells. Corporal Donald Fraser (6th Machine Gun Company) recalled:

> When in line with Neuville St. Vaast bordering Guillermot trench the enemy sent over a few shells bursting a hundred yards behind us. At first we took them for whiz-bangs on account of their rapid flight and did not pay much attention, but as the range was being lessened, the writer and a few others dropped into a shallow trench a little to our rear. Pausing there for a minute or two I was on the point of climbing out of the trench when a shell with a dull pop burst on the parapet almost in my face. My breathing stopped at once. With mouth open I could neither breathe in or out. Breathing was paralysed. It was a peculiar sensation. In a flash I knew it was a gas shell and it completely fouled the air. In a fraction of a second, in fact my quickness astonished me, I had my respirator on and was breathing freely, but not before I caught sight of Porter on my left, who looked as if he was a goner and had not the strength to do anything. He was on the elderly side and I thought should not have been in this action. However, we were signalled at the moment to advance on and I expected to hear later that Porter had breathed his last.[469]

The German barrage, while weak, did cause the leap-frogging Canadians some casualties. Captain Harold McGill (31st Alberta Battalion) remembered the Canadians pushing through the Germans' defensive fire that was falling near the old front line:

> As we proceeded I saw a shell burst in the centre of a group to our right, toward Zivy Cave. Two of the party crumpled up and fell; the survivors never missed a step nor even glanced at the fallen. That was the kind of discipline that made the taking of Vimy Ridge possible.[470]

NAC-PA1038 – Soldiers from a "leap-frog" brigade advancing in artillery formation toward photographer.

We have already seen that the Canadians brought Vickers machine guns forward with the attack to assist the Lewis Gunners in defending objectives once captured. To these were added Stokes trench mortars. The smallest calibre of trench mortar, their portability allowed them to be carried forward in the advance. With the 6th Trench Mortar Battery was Lieutenant Stuart Tompkins. He described the opening moments of his Battery's advance:

> At eight o'clock it came our turn to move, we climbed out of the trenches and formed up in artillery formation i.e. small columns in single file. I was busy picking out the weak spot in the German barrage; the horrible crumps they were throwing were very demoralizing so I edged over to the left towards the tanks. Soon we were in the barrage, making our way slowly forward. Big shells fell on both sides of us and we could see men falling around us, but gradually we drew clear without a single casualty. It was funny to go over our old front line. Things

look much different on top from what they do in the trenches. No man's land was easily negotiated. The wire was blown to smithereens. Then Fritz' front line, resting from time to time in shell holes. In fact that is about all there was.[471]

It was not a pleasant advance for these men, struggling through the mud, German shells falling around them and seeing those killed in the fighting for the Black and Red Lines. Corporal Fraser remembered moving up to pass through the assault Brigades:

At this stage the going was very difficult. The mud was thick and heavy, the shelling so severe that we began to scatter. Many were exhausted, but we could not halt, the shells were dropping and we were still within the portals of the barrage. The route lay between the wounded and the dead, and as we slowly dragged ourselves along our eyes rested on the fallen. Within a few hundred yards of the Lens-Arras Road the worst case was seen. A 5th Brigade man was struck on the head by a piece of shrapnel which knocked his brains out. They were lying two feet away and resembled the roes of a fish.[472]

Also with the machine gunners was Captain Claude Vivian Williams. He recalled the casualties he saw on his way across the battlefield:

Everywhere now dead Fritzes and our wounded, some limping out, dragging themselves along and some waiting in shell holes for the stretcher bearers to come up.[473]

NAC-PA1123 – Canadian soldiers from a "leap-frog" brigade advancing. Note the German prisoners moving back toward Canadian lines and the passing attention the Canadians show them.

The Blue Line objectives for 6th Brigade were the Village of Thelus, Hill 135 to its north-east and the trenches that protected both features. These defences caused the Canadians considerable concern. It was expected that Thelus would be a formidable objective to capture as the buildings, houses and cellars could provide the Germans with ideal defensive positions, not counting the trenches and dugouts in front of and within the Village. It was for this reason that Thelus was pounded prior to the attack by the heavy and super-heavy howitzers in their concentrated and systematic bombardments. As for Hill 135, being the second-highest point on Vimy Ridge, it provided the Germans with excellent observation over the Canadians' attack and Third Army's advance south of the Canadian Corps. It also gave the Germans the opportunity, not only to fire on 2nd Division's assault, but also on 1st Division's attack to the south.

By around 9:00 a.m., the leap-frogging Canadians had reached the Red Line, changed from artillery to wave formation and were preparing to carry the attack forward. The medical officer for the 31st Battalion, Captain Harold McGill, described the morale of the men:

> At 9 a.m. we reached the Red objective with A, the leading company, which at once went into extended order and formed up for the attack on the village. Everybody was in the highest spirits, and as each section came into the line, jokes and best wishes for continued good luck were shouted across from one to the other. The attack was evidently going – to use a hackneyed phrase of the time – "exactly according to plan."[474]

Not only was it evident that the assault Brigades had captured their objectives, but those men who had the opportunity to glance to the south during the move forward could see the soldiers from 1st Brigade taking the last of the *Swischen Stellung*. Captain McGill was struck by the sight:

> As far to the south as we could see, our barrage was sweeping like a storm over the Ridge, and the country behind seemed fairly crawling with troops advancing to the attack. A very high west wind, almost a gale, was now blowing, and this, driving the smoke of the bursting shells before it, made our advancing barrage resemble closely a blizzard on a Western Canadian prairie.[475]

At 9:25 a.m. the men from 6th Brigade were deployed and ready to attack, while the British and Canadian barrage increased its rate of fire in preparation for re-commencing creeping forward. Although the Canadians welcomed the effect this would have on the German defenders, they were not as enamored with the "shorts" that fell on 31st (Alberta) Battalion. These "shorts" caused some casualties, forcing the lead waves to withdraw further away from the barrage to avoid any more friendly fire.[476]

Despite the "shorts" and a brief interlude of snowfall, the Canadians followed the barrage when it advanced and pushed towards their objectives, capturing all of them by around 11:00 a.m. Perhaps surprisingly, bearing in mind the potential strength of the objectives, Canadian casualties were not heavy. Little opposition was met, with many of the casualties suffered by the Canadians being caused by "shorts" from their own barrage.[477]

NAC-PA1496 – An excellent demonstration of the scale of the Battle. Canadian soldiers advance past a tank. In the background, those dark "flecks" are more troops advancing in the distance.

That German resistance was found to be weak had much to do with the bombardments the British and Canadian heavy and super-heavy artillery had placed on Thelus before the Battle. From the 31st (Alberta) Battalion report:

> The damage to THELUS from our artillery fire is extraordinary. Buildings are demolished, trenches obliterated and wire smashed to atoms; there is hardly an inch but bears witness to the tremendous effect of our guns.[478]

Lieutenant Tompkins observed: "Houses, streets, dugouts, everything absolutely demolished, the earth a series of craters, here and there a vast hole made by our 12" and 15" howitzers."[479] Meanwhile, passing just to the north of Thelus, Corporal Fraser noticed that "Thelus was a village no longer, just a mere shell with scarcely the wall of a building standing higher than six feet."[480]

The destruction was not limited to Thelus. The 29th (Vancouver) Battalion was tasked with capturing that portion of Thelus Trench north of the Village and Hill 135 behind. Their War Diarist described the ease in which Thelus Trench was captured, along with its much weakened state:

> At 9:35 a.m. on the barrage moving forward, the Battalion followed through behind it, and captured THELUS LINE without opposition. A few Germans were seen running from THELUS TRENCH and every other man of the Front Wave advanced firing from the hip. Lewis Guns were also firing from the hip at these men. THELUS TRENCH was practically obliterated by our shell fire, and only one entrance to a dugout was found not to be blown in. Here eight prisoners were captured.[481]

As the prisoners appear to have been captured from the one remaining dugout, it is likely that the smashed-in dugouts contained entombed Germans.

Despite the pounding Thelus and area had received, some of the deep dugouts managed to survive intact. In fact, in one dugout, men from the 31st (Alberta) Battalion found a German officers' bar, fully stocked, with five waiters ready to serve their officers a meal on a set table. The waiters were promptly taken prisoner and the booze consumed by the unexpected "dinner guests."[482]

While 6th Brigade was able to capture the Blue Line with less fighting and casualties than that experienced by 4th Brigade at the Black and Red Lines, there still was some German resistance to eliminate. Lieutenant Tompkins (6th Trench Mortar Battery) related the effect his trench mortars had on a German machine gun crew:

> . . . one of our battalions was held up here by a machine gun. I found the gun and crew. They had succeeded in getting the gun over the parapet when the barrage lifted and rattling off a dozen or so belts before a shell put an end to gun crew and everything. They lay huddled up in all sorts of postures where they died.[483]

It will be recalled that the soldiers of 6th Brigade were to be supported by four tanks in their assault on Thelus. The lack of mention of the tanks so far is not due to oversight on the part of the writer, rather, it is because the tanks did not play any role in the attack. The muddy, cratered ground brought the tanks to a stop, none advancing beyond the Black Line. In the words of the 6th Brigade report:

> On the way forward to Advanced Headquarters four "TANKS," which had been detailed to accompany our attack on THELUS, were seen stranded about the vicinity of the German support trenches, in spite of the most strenuous efforts, these had been brought to a standstill by the exceedingly heavy going and deep mud which existed all over this vicinity.[484]

The only benefit the bogged down tanks gave to the Canadian advance was that they were enticing targets for the German artillery and seemed to be drawing away fire that would otherwise have fallen on the infantry.[485]

It was around this time that the German artillery made an effort at counter-battery work of their own, trying to take out the British and Canadian guns and gunners.[486] Unlike the British and Canadian counter-battery work, that of the Germans' was feeble, inaccurate and lasted for only a short time. At the guns was Sergeant Ernest Black. He remembered a German gun's attempt at counter-battery work:

> The first coal-box landed directly in line with our gun and some distance beyond our front aiming-post. The second was on the same line and landed between the two aiming-posts. The third one was half-way between our gun and the first aiming post. Another lift of the same distance would have put the fourth shell right on top of our gun. We knew, however, that that would not happen. The Germans were methodical gunners. When they started to shoot a pattern they carried it out to the end without variation. That was something that helped often to get us safely out of a shelled position. After the first three rounds you could tell exactly where the next shell would land. This time he was shooting what we called a sweep and walk. On that pattern three rounds were fired on one line at increasing ranges. Then the line was shifted to the gunner's right and three more rounds were fired at the ranges of the first three. This was repeated until the gun had fired twelve rounds on four lines; then the pattern was repeated. Long before the fourth shell landed we knew exactly where it would be.[487]

As the day before the German gunners had accurately found the range on Ernest Black's gun position, he was of the view that the Germans, under the stress and pressures of combat, had made a miscalculation:

> We were also lucky that the officer firing the German battery overlooked something. The day before we had been pinpointed and we should have been pinpointed again on that Easter Monday. Sunday had been bright, sunny and mild. Overnight the weather changed. There was a cold raw wind blowing straight toward the German battery and after the attack started there was snow. Before the day was over there was an inch of it. That change in atmospheric conditions was a handicap for the push but it was a godsend to us. There were several corrections to that pinpointing range that should have been made to allow for atmospheric change and the strong headwind and which, in the excitement of the attack, were apparently overlooked. If they had not been overlooked that German heavy would have been ploughing up our gun-pits for an hour or so that morning instead of ploughing up the area of our aiming posts.[488]

To the left of 6th Brigade were the men of 13th (British) Brigade of 5th (British) Division. The only British infantry involved in the attack on Vimy Ridge, they passed through the Canadians of 5th Brigade at the Red Line. Their final objective was the Blue Line, which they captured at the same time as the Canadians from 6th Brigade. Lieutenant Stuart Tompkins (6th Trench Mortar Battery) was impressed by their advance:

> . . . I shall never forget the sight of the division on our left slowly creeping up the slope as if on review with their barrage licking up the ground in front of them. It was magnificent.[489]

The 13th (British) Brigade's Blue Line included the eastern slope of the Ridge and this they secured, at the same time rushing German artillery positions in the *Bois du Goulot*.[490]

The failure of the tanks aside, by 11:00 a.m. the attack in 2nd Division's sector was unfolding according to plan. The 6th and 13th (British) Brigades had successfully leap-frogged through 4th and 5th Brigades and pushed the advance further, capturing the Blue Line, including the Village of Thelus and Hill 135. Only the Brown Line remained to be taken before success in 2nd Division's area would be complete.

Eight

3rd Division

7:30 a.m. - 11:00 a.m.

For 3rd Division, we have already seen that its assault had been a complete success, Vimy Ridge being in the hands of 7th and 8th Brigades by 7:30 a.m. For these men, their task changed from assault to defence, protecting what they had captured from possible German counter-attacks.

The Canadians immediately began consolidating their newly won gains, putting Vimy Ridge into a defensible state. Guarded by outposts and patrols, strong points were being constructed on and below the eastern slope to dominate the ground below Vimy Ridge. These strong points were ultimately to be garrisoned by machine guns and infantry. Behind the strong points a new trench was being dug just west of the Ridge's crest to act as the Canadians' new support line, while further back a German trench (Fickle Trench) was being reversed so that its defences now faced the Germans. Assisting the infantry in constructing their defences were the engineers. The 8th Field Company CRE's after-action report described how, with men from the 4th Canadian Mounted Rifles, the new support line was done:

> Lieut. Smith crossed road running along crest of Ridge and examined ground East of road to make sure of Location, then laid the trace of trench, and with the assistance of Lieut. Menzies, O.C. "C" Co., distributed men on this trace and carried on with the consolidation of the position, joining up with the RCR's on the left and 2nd CMR's on right.[491]

In some cases, German defences were put to new use. A.A. Bonar (Princess Patricia's Canadian Light Infantry) remembered the utility of a deep, rather extravagant, German dugout that had escaped the artillery fire:

The interior of the dugout was elaborately fitted out with mirrors, wash basins and chairs. Bottles of mineral water stood on the floor and wineglasses filled with liquor stood unfinished on the table when our men burst into the dugout. There were a number of bunks in this underground passage, and some of them were covered with fine, soft blankets. This place served as an improvised dressing station later.[492]

Not only were former German defences put to use by the Canadians, but German soldiers captured in the area were put to work by their captors in improving the Canadians' positions.[493]

The Canadians quickly took steps to take advantage of the observation the Ridge gave them to the east. By 7:30 a.m., the first artillery observation posts were established on the Ridge, with telephone communication with the guns still behind Canadian lines. From the Ridge, the forward observation officers could see German activity to the east and telephoned targets to the gunners.[494]

Consolidation was not easy nor safe for, although the Canadians had taken their objectives, there were still Germans in the vicinity. On and below the eastern slope of Vimy Ridge in 3rd Division's sector was the *Bois de la Folie*. This wooded area was still occupied by German soldiers, particularly snipers, who kept up a dangerous fire for the rest of the day. The snipers made the task of consolidation difficult, taking out any Canadians who exposed themselves for too long and forcing others to engage the hidden enemy.[495]

A.A. Bonar of the Princess Patricia's Canadian Light Infantry recalled the dangers these nearby German soldiers posed:

We kept a close watch lest the enemy hidden in the brushwood down the slope of the ridge should attempt to rush our position with a counter attack. Through the trees we could see the familiar potato-masher bomb being tossed, followed by the loud report of its explosion. But they didn't fall near enough to do any damage. We couldn't see any sign of the enemy, though he couldn't have been very far away. Snipers continued their work, and it was extremely dangerous to keep one's head above the shell hole where we lay.

In the meanwhile, the wiring party was busy putting up its fences. Suddenly I chanced to look back to see how they were getting on. The party had disappeared, several had been wounded. One poor fellow lay bent over his roll of wire, dead, with a large hole through his head.[496]

Compounding the Canadians' problems was the German artillery. At mid-morning German planes flew low over the northern half of Vimy Ridge, no doubt to locate the advanced Canadian positions for their artillery. Despite being fired on by Canadians on the ground, the planes appear to have completed their mission as the German artillery was active on the 3rd Division's front for the rest of the day, causing casualties.[497]

On the ground the Germans were not content to just snipe from the *Bois de la Folie*. Around 9:30 a.m. two counter-attacks were launched against the new Canadian positions. The one against the Princess Patricia's Canadian Light Infantry appears to have been small and easily repulsed, while a larger counter-attack hit the Royal Canadian Regiment who received assistance from men of the nearby 4th Canadian Mounted Rifles in beating it back. Even though their first attempt against the Canadians had been rebuffed, there were signs that the Germans were massing for another. Promptly, artillery assistance was asked for and received, breaking up the intended counter-attack before it developed.[498]

More troubling even than the snipers, artillery and counter-attacks was the situation on the 3rd Division's left. Here was located the 42nd Battalion (Royal Highlanders of Canada) and they were taking rifle and machine gun fire from Hill 145 to their left. While contact had been made on the Red Line with a few soldiers from the 54th (Kootenay) Battalion of 4th Division at around 8:00 a.m., matters were not going well for them. The men from the 54th Battalion were under heavy pressure from German snipers and machine gunners to their left. Through a combination of machine gun fire and long range bombing with rifle grenades, the Germans were pushed back, but their snipers still remained in the area. It was beginning to appear to the officers and soldiers of 42nd Battalion that the assault on Hill 145 had not gone well.

There was the real possibility that, with the 42nd Battalion all the way on the Red Line, the Germans could outflank the Battalion's left and rear from Hill 145. If this happened, not only might the 42nd Battalion be forced to fall back, it could be surrounded. Worse still, if the Battalion was pushed off its gains, this could put the entire 3rd Division's position on Vimy Ridge in jeopardy.

To deal with this crisis the 42nd Battalion soldiers created a defensive flank, all the way from their Red Line back to what had been the Canadian front line. With reinforcements and machine guns brought up the situation became stable, but not secure.[499] It was a tense time and the situation to their left on Hill 145 was obscure.

Nine

4th Division

7:30 a.m. - 11:00 a.m.

When we last looked at 4th Division's attack, the Canadians were on their objectives, except for the highest part of Hill 145. As we will see, the failure to seize the high ground caused 4th Division's attack to unravel by 11:00 a.m.

From Hill 145 the Germans were able to dominate the Canadian troops on the surrounding lower ground. They were able to keep men from 87th Battalion (Canadian Grenadier Guards) in No Man's Land and those from 75th (Mississauga) Battalion in the jumping-off trenches. The Germans delivered a withering fire, not only on the Canadians stopped before the undamaged portion of the German front line, but also on those to the right and left of the Hill. Adding to the Canadians' difficulties, since the creeping barrage had moved on, German defenders were able to emerge from their deep dugouts and counter-attack.

On the lower, southern half of Hill 145, the men from 54th (Kootenay) Battalion were at the Red Line on the eastern slope, but they were receiving machine gun and rifle fire from the higher ground to their left and casualties were heavy. Dangerously, Germans were emerging from their dugouts and counter-attacking. German soldiers began working around the Battalion's left flank, threatening encirclement. Low on manpower and uncertain about what happened to the Canadian attack on the high ground of Hill 145, the 54th Battalion was forced to withdraw, falling back to the Black Line.[500]

The Black Line was no sanctuary though. The 102nd (North British Columbians) Battalion was taking heavy casualties from the German defenders on Hill 145 too. By 8:00 a.m. there were no officers left unwounded and the men were under the command of a company sergeant-major. Within an hour the situation got even worse as the company sergeant-major became badly wounded in the stomach, hip and hand.

In an effort to take personal control of the situation, the officer commanding the 102nd Battalion, Major A.B. Carey, left Canadian lines and tried to make his way forward to his beleaguered men. It was a fruitless attempt, for within a few yards of the Canadian front line the sergeant accompanying Major Carey was killed and Carey never did reach his men, despite for three hours trying to get forward. He was not alone in his difficulties. So intense was the German fire from Hill 145 that a party from the 102nd Battalion sent forward as reinforcements had to make four separate efforts to reach the Black Line before they were successful in their mission.[501]

The officer commanding the 54th (Kootenay) Battalion, Lieutenant-Colonel Harvey, was also concerned about the lack of information coming back to his headquarters. He sent Lieutenant Alec Jack to ascertain the situation. Lieutenant Jack recalled that when he reached the Black Line:

> I found that the 54th and the 102nd, or the remnants of them, were all together. There were about 90 men of the 54th, and there were a few more of the 102nd; the 102nd, all of their officers were casualties and so were the 54th officers. So, as a young fellow of 25, I found myself in command of the remains of two battalions with our left flank up in the air and the Germans all around us at the back. I sent in a report on the situation and then I sorted out the men, getting the 54th to the exposed flank and the 102nd on our right.[502]

Pinned down just inside the German front line was Lieutenant Eedson L.M. Burns (11th Brigade Signal Section). He remembered a deadly exchange of rifle fire between the Canadians and the Germans:

> I was feeling rather pleased with my skill with the rifle when a shot struck the parapet a foot away, sending a shower of tiny stone splinters into my face, and making a most demoralizing crack. I was considerably shaken by this, and squatting down asked the man next to me anxiously if I had been hit. He inspected my face solemnly and reported only a few scratches.
>
> One of the other men, a smallish, red-haired intelligence observer, began staggering and making strange whistly noises. I held him up and saw he had been shot through the jugular vein, probably by the bullet which had just missed me. An inch and a quarter long split, purplish at the edges, sucked inwards at each pulsation of his heart and produced the queer whistle. I had a notion that if this gap could be closed he might live, and tried to do this with my fingers, but as I held him his face became scarlet, and then purple. Finally he ceased breathing. Possibly the bullet had gone on through the spine. He made no articulate sound

in dying. I laid him down at the side of the trench, and wiped my fingers on his jacket.[503]

While the Germans were able to inflict an intense fire on the Canadians, they were not unmolested on Hill 145. As we have already seen, some men from the 87th and 75th Battalions were able to advance into German territory on the Battalions' left. These soldiers were able to engage the German defenders on Hill 145. However, their situation was perilous.

Because of the dominating rifle and machine gun fire coming from the undamaged portion of the German front line and the defences on the slope above, those men who did enter German lines were cut off. No reinforcements could be sent across the bullet swept No Man's Land and communication was impossible. The Canadians in German lines formed pockets of resistance, combating the German defenders, but isolated from each other in the muddy, heavily cratered terrain. Worse, Germans emerged from their deep dugouts and counter-attacked the vulnerable groups of Canadians. Such was the intensity of these counter-attacks that one pocket of isolated men from the 75th (Mississauga) Battalion were forced to surrender.[504]

Eleventh Brigade's situation was chaotic. We saw previously that the Canadians had worked out plans to maintain communication from the point of attack back to commanders in the rear. In the South and with 3rd Division the system worked successfully, but this was not so with 11th Brigade.

The intense defensive fire the Germans were able to inflict on the Canadians from Hill 145 inhibited establishing any sort of communication; be it by phone, visual signals or runner. Very little information was coming back to the commanders and what made it through was vague and conflicting. In an attempt to obtain information from the assault Battalions, Brigadier-General Odlum (11th Brigade) sent out 30 scouts, but only one was able to return and what he told General Odlum did not clarify the situation. The rest of the scouts were either killed, wounded or pinned down by German fire.[505]

To the left of Hill 145, matters were not going any better for 12th Brigade. The Black and Red Lines had been captured by 38th (Ottawa) Battalion and 78th Battalion (Winnipeg Grenadiers) by 7:30 a.m., but casualties were heavy on account of the men losing the barrage in the sloppy terrain.

On the Black Line was Captain MacDowell commanding "B" Company in the 38th Battalion. The following is his message to his commanding officer timed 8:00 a.m. It is reproduced in full and, while lengthy, captures the confusion, conditions, casualties and courage of the moment:

> Objective reached but am afraid is not fully consolidated. The mud is very bad
> and our machine guns are filled with mud. I have about 15 men near here and

can see others around and am getting them in here slowly. Could "D" Company come up in support if they have stopped in the front line.

The runner with your message for "A" Company has just come in and says he cannot find any of the Company Officers. I don't know where my officers or men are but am getting them together. There is not an N.C.O. here. I have one machine gunner here but he has lost his cocking piece off the gun and the gun is covered with mud. The men's rifles are a mass of mud, but they are cleaning them. My two runners and I came to what I had selected previously as my Company H.Q. We chucked a few bombs down and then came down. The dugout is 75 feet down and is very large. We explored it and sent out 75 prisoners and two Officers. This is not exaggerated as I counted them myself. We had to send them out in batches of 12 so they could not see how few we were. I am afraid few of them got back as I caught one man shooting one of our men after he had given himself up. He did not last long and so am afraid we could not take any back except a few who were good dodgers, as the men chased them back with rifle shots. The dugout is a very large one and will hold a couple of hundred. The men were 11th Regiment R.I.R.

I cannot give an estimate of our casualties but believe they are severe. Will send back word as soon as possible. There is a field of fire of 400 yards or more and if there were a couple of Brigade Machine Guns could keep them back easily as the ground is almost impossible. Horrible mess. There are lots of dead Bosche and he evidently held well.

I can see 72nd men on our left. The 78th have gone through after we reached here. The barrage was good but the men did not keep close to it and held back. There are no shovels here found yet so will just get our rifles ready. No wire is here and cannot spare men to send out.

The line is obliterated, nothing but shell holes so wire would not be of much use. Men are pretty well under at present. There are no artillery officers here. His fire is very weak and suppose he is going back. This is all I can think of at present. Please excuse writing.[506]

For his actions in bluffing a much larger German force into surrender, Captain MacDowell was awarded the Victoria Cross.

As bad as the situation was for Capt. MacDowell on the 38th Battalion's left, it was worse on the Battalion's right; nearest Hill 145. This part of the Battalion's Black Line objective was a series of large craters from earlier underground mine explosions. While the 38th (Ottawa) Battalion did storm this portion of the Black Line in conjunction with the rest of the Line, the Battalion's hold on the position was insecure. The men had difficulty clearing the Germans from the Craters and the combatants lobbed hand grenades at each other in close quarters. By 8:00 a.m. the fight was still going on, placing the 38th Battalion's grasp on the Black Line in jeopardy.[507]

Ahead of the 38th Battalion, the water-logged ground was littered with the dead and wounded from the 78th Battalion (Winnipeg Grenadiers), the wounded being indicated by rifles sticking up in the mud.[508] Weakened by casualties, the remaining soldiers of the 78th Battalion were counter-attacked on the Red Line by German soldiers who emerged from their deep dugouts. After a desperate fight that resulted in the Red Line being strewn with Canadian and German dead, the remnants of the 78th Battalion withdrew, falling back to their comrades holding a trench in between the Red and Black Lines.

The Germans gave the Canadians no respite and pressed their counter-attack. However, the Canadians would retreat no further and their rifles and Lewis Guns took a heavy toll on the advancing Germans, forcing them to take cover in shell holes. After having done great damage to the 78th Battalion on the Red Line, the tables were now turned. The Germans were pinned down, unable to advance or retreat. They would spend the remainder of the morning and the afternoon stranded in front of the Canadians, their refuge being found in the water-filled craters they crouched within.[509]

Compounding difficulties was the lack of communication between the forward troops in German territory with the commanding officers in Canadian lines. Since the telephone lines run forward by the advancing infantry were being consistently cut by German shelling, the Canadians had to rely on runners.

Always a dangerous job, the runners in 12th Brigade had an especially hard time with the sloppy ground, it making any movement a slow and potentially lethal undertaking. A good example of how horrid the mud was comes from a wounded lieutenant in the 12th Canadian Machine Gun Company. Having been wounded in the head and body in German territory, he made his way back to Canadian lines, tearing his leg muscles as he struggled through the muck.[510]

For the runners trying to come from the Craters, the situation was even more lethal. With the Germans still holding the high ground of nearby Hill 145, they were able to snipe at the runners as they struggled back to Canadian lines and casualties to runners were severe. The result of the continual toll on runners was that the commanders in Canadian lines were without information as to what was going on with the 38th and 78th Battalions' right.[511]

The situation became critical as the morning wore on. Taking advantage of the breakdown of 11th Brigade's attack on Hill 145, the Germans began to filter down communication trenches reinforcing their soldiers in the Craters, making the 38th Battalion's hold on the Craters tenuous in the extreme. With the Canadians weakened by heavy casualties and scattered in groups in and around the Craters, it took all their energy just to hold on, let alone push the Germans out. Reinforcements, including two Vickers machine guns, were sent forward; stabilizing the situation, but unable to turn the tide.[512]

Adding to the confusion on 38th and 78th Battalions' right was the intermingling of these men with soldiers from the 11th Brigade. Those from 87th Battalion (Canadian Grenadier Guards) and 75th (Mississauga) Battalion who were able to advance at zero-hour took intense fire from the undamaged portion of the German front line at Hill 145 and positions on the slope above. In an effort to survive this withering fire, the men tended to drift to their left and move downhill, coming into 12th Brigade's sector and becoming mixed up. While these 11th Brigade men did assist their comrades, the intermingling of units complicated the already confusing situation in the Crater area.[513]

On the 12th Brigade's far left, the soldiers from 72nd (Seaforth Highlanders of Canada) and 73rd (Royal Highlanders of Canada) Battalions had captured their objectives by 7:30 a.m., but were sorely pressed. For the men of the 72nd Battalion, they had captured their final objective, Clutch Trench, but having lost the barrage casualties were severe from machine gun fire to their front and from the Pimple to their left. In fact, Clutch Trench had actually been taken by just one lieutenant and a few other ranks; all that remained of a platoon that numbered about 40 men going into the attack. Despite being outnumbered, these hardy few managed to clear the Trench by bombing ahead of them as they advanced down it. This forced the remaining defending Germans back, driving them into the British and Canadian artillery barrage and causing the Germans heavy casualties.[514]

Once their objectives were captured, the men had to hold onto their gains. In horrible conditions, with mud all around and the ground terribly cut up by shell-fire, the soldiers endured the shelling and bullets that the Germans fired at them. By the end of the day casualties were extreme. The 72nd Battalion, which went into the attack with 13 officers and 249 other ranks, had only one officer and 59 other ranks left standing at the end of the day.[515]

By 11:00 a.m., the 4th Division's attack was beginning to fall apart. While on the Division's far left the troops were able to retain all their captures, the failure to gain Hill 145 had serious consequences for the rest of the 4th Division. The stiff German defence had turned into counter-attack and, although the Canadians held, their assault was failing.

Ten

Summary at 11:00 a.m.

To recap the Canadian Corps' progress by 11:00 a.m., the Divisions had varying experiences by this point in the Battle. In the South, the leap-frog Brigades in 1st and 2nd Divisions had pushed the attack forward and captured the Blue Line, including the important Hill 135. Casualties were much less than suffered in the earlier advance on the Black and Red Lines. The anticipated stiff resistance at the Village of Thelus did not materialize as the German defences had already been effectively destroyed by the heavy and super-heavy howitzers during the preliminary bombardment. Indeed, the Village ceased to exist.

Third Division, having already captured all of its objectives by 7:30 a.m., turned its attention to defence, consolidating their sector of Vimy Ridge. Casualties were mounting though as the combination of sniping from the *Bois de la Folie*, German artillery shelling and local counter-attacks made the task of consolidation a dangerous operation.

In the north, 4th Division's failure to take Hill 145 had a ripple effect, unravelling what successes the Canadians had at 7:30 a.m. On the right of Hill 145, the troops on the Red Line were forced to fall back to the Black Line under heavy pressure. Once there, they continued to endure deadly fire from the Hill. So obscure was the situation that their 3rd Division neighbors to their right, (42nd Battalion Royal Highlanders of Canada), were compelled to form a defensive flank, protecting 3rd Division from any disaster that might afflict 4th Division.

At Hill 145 matters had not improved since 7:30 a.m. Soldiers were still stranded in No Man's Land and stuck in the jumping-off trenches. Those that had advanced into German territory were cut off from Canadian lines. In isolated groups, the Germans counter-attacked them, forcing one party of Canadians into surrendering. For these pockets of men, there was no question of advancing further. They had all they could handle just trying to survive.

To the left of Hill 145 the Germans counter-attacked the Canadians on the Red Line, pushing them back. Making a stand in a trench in front of the Black Line, the Canadians held, forcing the Germans to ground and pinning them down. Behind this trench, Germans from Hill 145 had filtered through communication trenches and reinforced their soldiers still holding out amongst the Craters on the Black Line. By 11:00 a.m., several of the Craters were still in German hands. While on 4th Division's far left their gains had been retained, there was the real possibility that the Division's failure to take Hill 145 would undo their entire attack.

Eleven

1st and 2nd Divisions

11:00 a.m. - 2:00 p.m.

The last major obstacles to Canadian possession of the entire Ridge in the South were a double row of thick barbed wire just below and on the Ridge's crest and the German artillery positions in wooded areas on and below the eastern slope. For this final objective 1st Division's 1st Brigade was using two Companies each from the 3rd Battalion (Toronto Regiment) and 4th (Central Ontario) Battalion. Second Division's 6th Brigade employed the 27th (City of Winnipeg) Battalion, plus one Company from 29th (Vancouver) Battalion.

By 11:30 a.m., the soldiers were deploying for their advance, protected by the artillery's standing barrage. For the men of 27th (City of Winnipeg) Battalion, who had not yet been involved in combat but had passed through the whole 2nd Division battlefield, there was a sense of calm confidence as they waited. The Battalion's after-action report noted that "All ranks were cool and collected and sat in shell holes, smoking and talking."[516] For others, it provided an opportunity to reflect on their battle practice. From "C" Company's report:

> The Bosche was sending over a little desultory shelling but it was hard to realize we were in the middle of an advance. Men and officers were strolling about getting into position and comparing the real thing with rehearsals.[517]

The double row of barbed wire facing the Canadians ran in a south-east direction, following the contours of Vimy Ridge. Up to this point, the advance in the South ran in generally a north-south direction. To coordinate the attack so that the infantry from both 1st Brigade and 6th Brigade attacked the Brown Line at the same time, the creeping barrage advanced in staggered lifts; from right to left. As the men from 6th Brigade waited for the barrage in front of them to creep forward, they had the chance to watch the 1st Brigade following the barrage to the south. Corporal Donald Fraser recalled:

> In extended order with few blanks they were following close behind a rolling barrage. The barrage showed up as a wall of smoke and so perfect were the shells laid down that there were no gaps and the line was kept as straight as a die, as the saying goes. It showed the artillery at its very best. The movable wall of bursting shells outlined by smoke was a pretty sight to watch.[518]

When the Canadians reached the double row of thick barbed wire they met an unwelcome sight. While, as we have seen, the artillery had been thorough in cutting the barbed wire elsewhere, this double row remained largely uncut. For 6th Brigade there were enough gaps that the men were able to pick their way through, but 1st Brigade soldiers in the south had a more difficult time. Here the infantry had to cut gaps themselves with wire cutters. Fortunately, between the creeping barrage and covering fire from Colt heavy machine guns brought with the advance, the soldiers successfully gapped the wire without any interference from the Germans.[519]

Once through the wire, the infantry attacked the German artillery positions upon the barrage lifting. The men in 6th Brigade found the Germans ready for them. The 6th Brigade's after action report relates the intensity of the German resistance and the spirit of the Canadians:

> Stiff opposition was met with from here on, as the German gunners held their ground and did the utmost to check our troops, by firing their guns point blank and using machine guns, rifles and revolvers.
>
> The machine guns were dealt with by the rifle grenadiers most successfully, and our troops of both Battalions, raising a loud cheer, charged for the final 50 yards, leaped down on to the German gunners in their gun pits and trenches. A stout fight was put up by these Germans, urged on by several Officers, but all were soon bayoneted or captured by our troops and their guns were in our hands. Capt. T.B. Lane and Sgt. Hodgson of "A" Company of the 27th were the first of that Battalion to get into the BROWN OBJECTIVE, leading on their men most gallantly. Sgt. Hodgson by quick action and great determination prevented the enemy from disabling three of his guns.[520]

Infantry attacking artillery and being fired on point blank was a rare event in the Great War. That the German artillery were fixed in place and not allowed to withdraw their guns before the infantry attack speaks well to the effectiveness of the British and Canadian counter-battery work. It is likely that the heavy artillery's gas and high explosive shells forced the Germans into taking cover, leaving their guns in their gun pits.

Then, pinned down by the creeping barrage, the German gunners were forced to defend their positions against the advancing Canadian infantry. Using the weapons at their immediate disposal, particularly long range bombing with rifle grenades, the Canadians were able to take out the German machine guns from a distance. This allowed the Canadians to close on the German defenders, overwhelm the position and capture prisoners and artillery pieces.

NAC-PA994 – German artillery emplacement in Farbus Wood after capture by the Canadians.

6th Brigade's success was mirrored by 1st Brigade to the south, which had met less resistance, so that by 2:00 p.m. the entire southern half of Vimy Ridge was in Canadian hands.[521] However, there was a worrying development to 1st Brigade's right. The Brigade's right flank was "in the air."

To understand the reason for this, we have to take a step back to the planning for the Battle. As noted earlier, Vimy Ridge was not an isolated battle. Instead, it was a supporting operation for the larger Third Army attack to the south around Arras. On 1st Division's right was 51st (Highland) Division, the northern most division in Third Army. The problem was that 51st (Highland) Division's attack, which had started well, began experiencing problems beyond their Red Line.

This was first noticed by the men of 1st (Western Ontario) Battalion after they captured that portion of the *Swischen Stellung* just beyond the Red Line. No Highlanders were seen to their right and a patrol sent out to find them returned having not come across any.[522] When 1st Brigade pushed on and captured the Blue Line, the Highlander's situation was still unknown and there were no 51st Division men on the Blue Line.[523]

To this point, the inability of the Highland Division to keep up with them caused the Canadians mainly uncertainty, but during the Canadian's advance to the Brown Line it took a toll in lives. While for the most part the men of 1st Brigade encountered less resistance at the Brown Line than their comrades in 6th Brigade, this was not true at the extreme south of Vimy Ridge. Here, German machine guns south of Vimy Ridge opened fire as the Canadians attacked. These machine guns were to have been taken out by the Highlanders, but, since the Highlanders' assault had stalled, the machine gunners were free to fire on the Canadians, causing casualties.[524]

The Canadians were still able to capture the Brown Line in the extreme south, but the Highlander's situation on their right was obscure. Therefore, like that which 3rd Division was forced to construct because of 4th Division's problems at Hill 145, the soldiers from 1st Division formed a defensive flank turning back near the Commandant's House.[525]

With the success of 1st and 2nd Divisions, all of Vimy Ridge was in Canadian hands by 2:00 p.m., with the exception of Hill 145. While the infantry on the Ridge mopped up the last remaining German defenders, the artillery placed a protective barrage just to the east of the Ridge. All was not secure though as the Canadians had to keep a sharp eye to their south, looking for the welcome sight of the Highlanders, or the feared spectre of a German counter-attack.

Twelve

1st, 2nd and 3rd Divisions Successful

The Canadian soldiers, be they from 1st, 2nd or 3rd Division, were amazed at the sight that lay before them when they reached the crest of Vimy Ridge. Their vision reached far to the east reinforcing the importance of the Ridge in their minds. Whereas for months all the Canadians saw was the squalor of No Man's Land and the formidable German defences behind, now their eyes cast on fields, woods and roads untouched by war.

Passing over his final objective was G.T. Hancox of the Princess Patricia's Canadian Light Infantry. He was able to see:

> Red brick mining villages among a score of slagheaps and pitheads. Liven, Avion, Mericourt and Lens itself and villages farther back. In the foreground were Vimy and Petit Vimy. All appeared to be untouched. The trees lining the Lens Arras road, ran straight as an arrow across the plain to Lens. In the foreground were the concrete gun emplacements of the German batteries. After months in the wilderness it was truly a glimpse of the promised land.[526]

Canon Frederick Scott (1st Division) recalled his first view of the ground to the east of Vimy Ridge:

> It was wonderful to look over the valley. I saw the villages of Willerval, Arleux and Bailleul-sur-Bertholt. They looked so peaceful in the green plain which had not been disturbed as yet by shells. The church spires stood up undamaged like those of some quiet hamlet in England.[527]

While the lion's share of Vimy Ridge was now in Canadian hands, those soldiers on Vimy Ridge could not relax. Instead, they immediately went to work consolidating the ground that they had captured. With the Ridge in 3rd Division's sector being in their possession since 7:30 a.m., their progress was already well in hand. For 1st and 2nd Divisions, they began constructing their defences in the afternoon. Connecting with 3rd Division on their left, the men in the South put in place successive defensive positions. In the woods at the bottom of the Ridge were placed outposts of Lewis Gunners, with a further line of outposts on the eastern slope of the Ridge. The main resistance line was constructed on the reverse (western) slope of Hill 135, buttressed by mutually supporting strong points behind. Further to the rear, the Canadians were also consolidating the Black and Red Lines. Thus, for the Canadians, who were already tired out by a morning of anxiety, excitement, cold weather, muddy ground and combat, the rest of the day would be filled with labor.

In the afternoon, Captain D.E. Macintyre (Brigade-Major of 4th Brigade) made his way forward through the 4th Brigade's battlefield towards the Ridge. He remembered:

> Our men swarmed everywhere. Telephone lines and light railways were being laid on, and I saw more than one battery blazing away in territory that had been enemy property only a few hours before. Everywhere I looked, men were digging and each one gave me a wide grin as I passed.[528]

NAC-PA1062 – Canadian soldiers consolidating their captured territory.

While most of the Canadians on Vimy Ridge were engaged in consolidation, others were scanning the ground to the east for targets. Once the Canadians crossed the Ridge an unfamiliar sight caught their gaze. German soldiers, artillery pieces and transport vehicles were all scrambling east, trying to get out of range of the Canadians on the Ridge. Canadian machine gunners took up positions to fire on these retreating parties, while forward artillery observers contacted their guns so that they could rain shells down on the fleeing Germans. Casualties were caused to the Germans making for the east, but, by and large, they were able to make a quick escape.

NAC-PA1079 – Canadian Vickers machine gunners digging in to protect the Canadians' gains.

The Canadians also pushed fighting patrols forward into the flat ground below Vimy Ridge, with the artillery's protective barrage dying down to allow the patrols to advance. These patrols maintained a defensive screen, tried to ascertain whether the Germans were constructing any new defensive lines and mopped up any remaining resistance points near the Ridge. Not only did patrols from the 4th (Central Ontario) Battalion encounter some resistance, they also received a welcome, if unintended, reward for a long day's work:

At this time our barrage lifted and the outpost platoons were able to enter FAR-BUS WOOD. The battery position was re-occupied, some Germans who had concealed themselves in the dugouts there being killed or taken prisoner, and patrols were pushed forward to beyond the Eastern edge of FARBUS WOOD, nothing being seen of the enemy as far as the railway.

The German retirement from this battery position was so hasty that the Officers lunch was left ready on the table in their dugout. It was of course promptly consumed.[529]

For the men of 1st, 2nd and 3rd Divisions, the remainder of the day was spent attending to the defence of their newly won gains. Defensive positions were established, lookout was kept on the Germans in the low ground to the east and patrols maintained a Canadian presence below Vimy Ridge. However, the fighting for Vimy Ridge was not over and we will now turn our attention north where Hill 145 remained a "thorn in the Canadians' side."

Thirteen

4th Division

11:00 a.m. - 5:00 p.m.

When we last looked at the struggle for Hill 145, the strong German defence of the Hill turned to counter-attack, resulting in the Canadians being forced from some of their gains. From 4th Division's nadir in the morning, its situation began to improve later in the day.

At noon the undamaged portion of the German front line on Hill 145 remained defiant. However, the threat it posed to 4th Division's advance was about to be eliminated. Around 1:00 p.m., two parties of Canadians had infiltrated the German front line under the cover of a Stokes trench mortar barrage. On the right, a lieutenant and 12 other ranks from the 75th (Mississauga) Battalion entered the front line while on the left entry was made by a sergeant and 12 other ranks from the 87th Battalion (Canadian Grenadier Guards). Upon entry, the parties moved down the trench towards each other, bombing the defenders with Mills bombs. It was a difficult and slow process and it was not until 3:00 p.m. that the German front line was cleared with some prisoners taken.[530]

From the newly captured German front line, a party from the 87th Battalion of about 20 men, commanded by a lieutenant and with four Lewis Guns, moved to the Craters where 38th (Ottawa) Battalion were and set up a strong point at a Crater.[531] This reinforcement was welcome. Although 12th Brigade had earlier sent reinforcements to the Craters, 38th Battalion was stalled, with the men in scattered groups throughout the Craters, and vulnerable to German counter-attacks.

While 4th Division's situation had improved, it still was not good. Behind the German front line on Hill 145 was Batter Trench. This was the 87th Battalion's (Canadian Grenadier Guards) original Black Line and from here the Germans were still able to dominate the Canadians below and to the right and left of Hill 145. By the afternoon the assault units of 4th Division were "used up," either being casualties or grimly holding on to what the Canadians had managed to capture. It would take "fresh blood" to re-start 4th Division's stalled attack.

Fourteen

The Cavalry

Before examining the Canadians' next attempt at Hill 145, we will briefly turn our attention back to the South as a rather remarkable event took place. As we have seen, once the Canadians captured Vimy Ridge, patrols were pushed forward to make contact with and ascertain the location and strength of German defences to the east of the Ridge. What was not mentioned earlier was that two of the patrols consisted of cavalry.

The retention of cavalry units on the Western Front in the Great War has become a controversial issue since. Long past the day when cavalry could charge with lances levelled, that cavalry units remained horsed has been seen as a waste of manpower, bearing in mind their vulnerability to machine gun and modern artillery fire. Countering this is the argument that there was no other mobile arm that could push an attack forward once the trench lines were crossed. We have already seen that the mobile arm of the future, the tank, was bogged down in the mud of Vimy Ridge. In any event, the importance of the debate may be exaggerated as cavalry units in the BEF were a very small minority within an increasingly modern army.

Within the Canadian Corps, there was only one unit of cavalry; the Canadian Light Horse. As the attack in the South was going according to plan, the Corps commander, Lieutenant-General Byng, ordered the Canadian Light Horse to push patrols into Willerval, a village to the east of 1st Division's sector of Vimy Ridge. If the situation allowed, they were to occupy and hold the Village, otherwise, they were to report on the state of the German defences. At around 4:30 p.m., the patrols left Vimy Ridge, one patrol to enter the Village from the south, the other from the north.

Neither patrol was very large and the one in the south was only six cavalrymen strong. Getting to within about 400 yards of Willerval, they came under fire from Germans in the Village and garrisoning its trenches. The effect on this small party was devastating as four men and all six horses were killed. The remaining two men (one of whom was wounded), took cover and managed to make their way back to Canadian lines by crawling from shell hole to shell hole.

NAC-PA1111 – The Canadian Light Horse advance.

The northern patrol of 13 all ranks was successful in entering Willerval. Upon reaching a cross-road in the middle of the Village, they noticed a group of about 10 Germans, including an officer. In a gallant move, yet seemingly out of place on a Great War battlefield, the cavalrymen drew their sabres and charged on horseback. The Germans, probably surprised by the sight of thundering horsemen surging at them, surrendered.

Now a surprise was in store for the cavalry as other Germans nearby had been in the process of setting up machine guns. They were in place just after the cavalry's old fashioned little charge and opened up on the Canadian horsemen. Completely outgunned, the cavalrymen abandoned their prisoners, tore up the road, reached the cross-road and rode for Canadian lines on Vimy Ridge. Their escape was not painless, for five of their number were hit. One of these casualties was the lieutenant leading the patrol, who, along with his horse, was shot just as he passed the cross-road. Badly wounded, he refused assistance from his sergeant, urging him to return to Canadian lines and report on what they had seen.[532]

In terms of cavalry on the Western Front, this was the limit of their usefulness. Too vulnerable to machine gun and artillery fire to be employed *en masse*, they could be used in small numbers to press an advance beyond the infantry, reconnoitring what was ahead. Even in this limited role they were large targets and casualties to patrols could be heavy, as was the case with the Canadian Light Horse at Willerval.

Fifteen

4th Division Secures its Black Line

While the undamaged portion of the German front line at Hill 145 was cleared of defenders, the Hill was still firmly in German hands by early evening on April 9. Their next defensive position, Batter Trench, was the Canadian's original Black Line in this area and it dominated any attack coming from the German front line. On the right of Hill 145 the Canadians were on the Black Line, but were facing defenders to their front and left. They were too depleted by casualties to re-gain the Red Line, or to clear the Germans from the troublesome Batter Trench. To the left of Hill 145 the Canadians were stalemated in the Craters, those to the north being in Canadian possession, but the Craters nearest the Hill were held by the Germans. Ahead of the Craters, the Canadians held an intermediate trench between the Craters and the Red Line, but there were Germans in front of them, still pinned down in shell holes after the failure of their earlier counter-attack.

The situation at Hill 145 and the Craters needed to be cleared up and the 4th Division turned to the men of the 46th (Saskatchewan) Battalion and 85th Battalion (Nova Scotia Highlanders) to do it. In terms of combat experience, these were two very different Battalions.

The 46th (Saskatchewan) Battalion was a veteran unit. Having come to the Western Front in the summer of 1916, it served in the Ypres Salient before moving south to the Somme. Once at the Somme, the Battalion saw action during the later stages of that Battle. At Vimy Ridge during the Winter of 1917, the 46th Battalion was an aggressive unit, undertaking a number of raids.

On the other hand, the 85th Battalion (Nova Scotia Highlanders) was not really a combat unit at all. New to the Western Front, it was used mainly for work parties in the Winter of 1917. The Battalion had never held a stretch of trench line itself. Its knowledge of trench warfare consisted solely of groups of officers and men being attached for experience to veteran units while the veteran units were in the line.

The men of two Companies from each Battalion assembled for their attack in the jumping-off trenches previously used by the assault forces at zero-hour. The 85th Battalion was on the right, tasked with capturing Batter Trench. To the left the 46th Battalion would take those Craters still in German hands, and link up with the men from the 85th Battalion at Batter Trench.[533]

The time set for the attack was 6:45 p.m. and as the seconds ticked by a change was made to the assault plan. At the last minute, it was decided by 11th Brigade that there would be no barrage supporting the attack. While the timing of this decision was inopportune, it was made to avoid friendly casualties. There still were pockets of Canadians in German lines, around Batter Trench and even behind it, and an artillery barrage just might wipe them all out.[534]

For the officer commanding 85th Battalion (Nova Scotia Highlanders), Lieutenant-Colonel A.H. Borden, he received this bit of news after his men had completed assembly and just before they were to jump-off. He was positioned behind the middle of his men and due to the nature of the ground and the winding jumping-off trench, he could not see or make contact with his Company commanders, each of whom was placed on the outer flanks of their respective Companies. Both Company commanders were still expecting there to be a supporting barrage, but there was no time to warn them of the change. With seconds until the assault, Lt-Col. Borden hoped that his men would attack without the barrage.[535]

At first Lieutenant-Colonel Borden's fears appeared to have come true. Six forty-five came and went and there was no movement in the 85th Battalion's jumping-off trenches. Then, about thirty tense seconds later, the soldiers began to move forward. Those on the left moved first, followed by the Company on the right. It is not known what triggered the men to advance, but it is possible that they looked to their left, saw the Companies from the veteran 46th (Saskatchewan) Battalion attacking despite there being no barrage and realized that they should do the same. On the other hand, they may have realized on their own that, barrage or no barrage, the attack had to go in.

The soldiers advanced slowly, the mud clinging to their feet. With no barrage the German defenders immediately opened up on the attackers with a withering machine gun and rifle fire. The Canadians responded, firing their Lewis Guns and rifles as they advanced. During this fire-fight the Canadians continued to push forward, foot by foot, closing the distance with their adversaries.[536]

Just as the Canadians reached their objectives, the tide turned. On Hill 145, the leading Canadians fired rifle grenades, taking out the German machine guns.[537] Then, as the Canadians crossed the remaining distance, those Germans still alive either surrendered to the attacking Canadians, or began to withdraw from Batter Trench and the Craters. With some men giving themselves up while others retreated, it is unlikely that the

German withdrawal was organized. Instead, it is more likely that it was a scramble for the safety of German lines to the east. In any war, the moment soldiers turn their backs on their enemy is a dangerous time. Vulnerable to being shot in the back and unable to effectively retaliate, casualties are often severe during a disorganized withdrawal. So it was on Hill 145 and at the Craters.

As the Germans withdrew from Batter Trench and the Craters, the attacking Canadians continued to fire on them, allowing no respite. However, it was not just their attackers that the German soldiers had to worry about. As the Germans tried to make their escape, all those Canadians in isolated groups spread across Hill 145 and the Craters joined in, adding a deadly Vickers machine gun, Lewis Gun and rifle fire to the maelstrom. Since many of these pockets of Canadians were on the flanks of the fleeing Germans, the Germans were receiving fire from behind and their flanks and casualties were heavy. The tables were turned on the defenders and the Canadians were able to take out their frustrations of the day on their recent tormentors.[538]

It was at this time that those Germans in front of the 78th Battalion (Winnipeg Grenadiers), who were hunkered down in water-filled shell holes ever since their failed counter-attack in the morning, decided to make their break for safety. Their effort was no more successful than that of their comrades at Hill 145 and the Craters. The Canadians were alert, spotted the movement and their Lewis Guns and rifles took a heavy toll on the retreating Germans.[539]

With the successful attack by the 85th Battalion (Nova Scotia Highlanders) and 46th (Saskatchewan) Battalion, the corpse strewn western slope of Hill 145 was in Canadian hands. The Germans had withdrawn to the eastern slope of the Hill, the Craters were cleared of defenders and contact was made with 78th Battalion (Winnipeg Grenadiers) in advance of the Craters. While 4th Division could take satisfaction in finally having captured Hill 145, the Battle still was not over. That which was gained on the 9th at Hill 145 represented the 11th Brigade's original Black Line. Their Red Line, Banff Trench on the Hill's eastern slope, was still defended in force. There would have to be a separate attack on April 10 before success would be complete at Hill 145.

Sixteen

The Artillery Advances

Infantry advances in the Great War were limited to the range of their supporting artillery. Once beyond that distance, the infantry were vulnerable to the defender's artillery and counter-attacks. In any offensive on the Western Front, it was important to bring the guns into forward positions as soon as possible to help the infantry defend what they had captured and to facilitate any further advance.

At Vimy Ridge, the Canadian and British artillery began their forward move on the first day of battle. The artillery's advance took place only in the South, where, due to the distance of the Ridge's crest from Canadian lines, the British and Canadian artillery that had fired the creeping barrage up to the Blue Line were now out of range of the attacking infantry. While these guns moved up, the forward batteries were able to carry the creeping barrage beyond the Blue Line and maintain a protective barrage just east of the Ridge after it was captured.

Some of the preparatory work for the guns' advance was done just after zero-hour. In 1st Division's sector, as soon as the infantry stormed the German front line, work parties of infantry and artillery moved into No Man's Land. Their job was to construct a road across No Man's Land to continue the existing one that lead from the artillery positions to the Canadian front line. Shell holes had to be filled in with earth and trenches had to be bridged so that the artillery could cross the Canadian trenches, make their way through No Man's Land, pass over the German forward trenches and take up positions in German lines.

We saw earlier that the German defensive barrage opened after the assault waves had passed the German front line. Missing the lead infantry, German shells exploded amongst the work parties struggling to construct the road in the muddy terrain of No Man's Land. Casualties were serious, but the men endured, and the road was ready for use close to noon.[540]

Some of the artillery pieces began their forward move in the latter half of April 9 and they found the going extremely difficult. For the 11th Battery CFA, despite the work done on No Man's Land, the guns could go no further than that. From the after-action report:

> At noon the battery took up a position near the 500 Crater in what had been No Man's Land. It had been found impossible to advance further as rain had made the sea of shell holes beyond the enemy's old front line utterly impossible.[541]

Although unable to go as far forward as planned, the Battery was still able to provide covering fire for the infantry as they consolidated their gains on Vimy Ridge.[542]

NAC-PA1073 – Canadian field artillery moving forward.

Also struggling forward on April 9 were the guns of the 1st Brigade CFA. They were able to penetrate beyond No Man's Land, establishing one battery between the Black and Red Lines. While an exceptional accomplishment under the conditions, the other three batteries in the Brigade were not so fortunate as all their guns were stuck in the mud.[543]

Adding to the gunners' difficulties was the weather. Poor throughout the day, by evening it began to snow, making the job of pulling the guns through the soggy, broken ground even more of an ordeal. Cold, wet and covered in mud, the men pushed on, but it was gruelling. For example, the men of 2nd Brigade CFA commenced their advance on the evening of April 9, but their guns were not in position until daylight on the 10th.[544]

While the infantry were busy consolidating their gains on Vimy Ridge, the gunners were busy too. Those not engaged in establishing a protective barrage to the east of Vimy Ridge or firing on any German movements to the east, were busy trying to move their artillery pieces forward through the battlefield squalor. Despite their best efforts, only some guns could be brought into position, with the others stretched out behind, bogged down in the cold mud.

Seventeen

Summary – April 9

As dusk fell on April 9, 1917, the Canadians could take stock of what they had accomplished. With the exception of the eastern slope of Hill 145, the entire Vimy Ridge was in Canadian hands.

In the South the attack had proceeded according to plan, with there being no need to deviate from the artillery barrage program. Casualties in taking the Black and Red Lines had been heavy, while the Blue Line, including the Village of Thelus, fell easier than expected. In the far south, 1st Division captured their Brown Line without much difficulty, however, Third Army's 51st (Highland) Division was not as successful, resulting in the Canadians having to form a defensive flank to protect their right. As for 2nd Division, they encountered stiff resistance at artillery positions below the eastern slope of the Ridge, but were able to overcome the German defenders. Thereafter, patrols, including some cavalry, pushed beyond the Ridge to discover the Germans' remaining defensive strength, while the remainder of the soldiers consolidated their gains.

The experience of 3rd Division was similar to that of their comrades in the South. The difference for these men was that they did not have Blue and Brown Lines to capture, Vimy Ridge being in their possession following the Red Line being taken at about 7:30 a.m. For 3rd Division, the rest of their day was spent in consolidation and patrols, but it was dangerous work. German sniping, shelling and counter-attacks resulted in the majority of 3rd Division's casualties being suffered after their objectives were taken. More troubling was the obscure situation to their north, forcing the construction of a defensive flank on the Division's left to protect it from being outflanked.

The reason for 3rd Division's concern was the situation at Hill 145. Here, 4th Division's initial thrust at the Hill failed with severe casualties, resulting in the 4th Division's entire attack being placed in jeopardy. The Division recovered though, taking the German front line at Hill 145 by mid-afternoon and using reserve Battalions to capture the Black Line in the early evening.

There was still the Red Line at Hill 145 to be taken and the follow up operation against the Pimple. Nevertheless, for the most part, the formidable German defences at Vimy Ridge fell to the Canadians in just one day.

Eighteen

Evening of the 9th and Day of the 10th

The night of April 9/10 was a hard one for the Canadian soldiers. The weather was bitterly cold, consolidation was difficult in the mud and there was the ever present fear of a German counter-attack. While in retrospect we know how ultimately successful the Canadians' attack was, the soldiers in their new defences on Vimy Ridge did not necessarily feel so secure.

On the evening of April 9, the weather took a turn for the worse. Snow began to fall and the soldiers, already wet and muddy, became chilled to the bone. While most of the men had some time to construct positions in which to "hunker down" for the night, those on Hill 145 were not so fortunate. For the soldiers of 85th Battalion (Nova Scotia Highlanders), after capturing the Black Line at Hill 145 in the early evening, they spent the night guarding their gains in shell holes, exposed to the falling snow and cold wind. Daylight brought little relief as it snowed again in the afternoon of the 10th, draining the soldiers' energy.[545]

Under these weather conditions, Brigadier-General Odlum, commanding the now depleted 11th Brigade, made an early morning reconnaissance on Hill 145. Establishing contact with his outposts, General Odlum realized that the actual crest of Hill 145 was deserted. He found no Canadians or Germans holding the crest and neither side seemed to realize this. Taking advantage of the situation, Odlum pushed his outposts forward, placing them in positions on and over the crest of the Hill.[546]

The snow that was falling did little to harden the ground. It was a wet snow, covering the ground during the cold darkness, but melting with the day's light. Once melted, it only added to the muck. On April 10 the 13th Battalion (Royal Highlanders of Canada) moved from what had formerly been German territory back to the old Canadian front line for a rest. Their War Diarist described the conditions:

Considerable difficulty was experienced in finding the different Dugouts, etc., to be used as Billets, owing to the terrible damage which had been done by the shell fire during the attack, for miles nothing could be seen but shell holes and damaged wire, trenches, etc. The trenches which were left more or less intact were nearly all flooded with water and deep with mud, even under these conditions the men were glad to reach their destinations, and have a chance of getting their equipment off.[547]

The gunners too were having difficulties, trying to pull their guns forward through the slop. We have already seen that some of the artillery batteries tried to move forward on the 9th, with little success. Those who began their advance on the 10th found the going no easier. By the end of the 10th, one-third of 5th Brigade CFA's guns were stuck in the mud of No Man's Land, while in 6th Brigade CFA, only one gun was able to make it half-way to its destination. So sticky was the ground that it was impossible to rescue some of the guns from it, and these pieces went into action where they were on April 12.[548]

Despite the difficulty in bringing the guns forward to the Ridge, the Canadians did receive some artillery reinforcement, albeit from an unlikely source. During the Battle, the Canadians captured 63 German artillery pieces.[549] Trained in the use of German artillery, 9 of these guns were in a fit condition to be used by the Canadians against their former owners by April 14.[550]

As hard as the weather conditions were for the men, they could be lethal for the horses. Motorized transport was impossible in the wake of a Western Front battle, so to bring forward supplies reliance was placed in the horse. Captain D.E. Macintyre recalled the plight a couple of horses suffered as he passed them on the way to the crest of Vimy Ridge:

> It was not long before we came upon a young transport driver in trouble. The faithful fellow had stayed beside his horse all night, trying in vain to extricate the poor pack animal from the mud in which it was buried to its belly. The horse was utterly exhausted and far beyond making any further effort and, as there was no hope of saving it, Consy drew his revolver and shot it. A little further on he had to shoot another.[551]

Adding to the Canadians' anxieties as they consolidated Vimy Ridge was German activity to the east. We have already seen how, when the Canadians captured the Ridge in the South, they were struck by the sight of German soldiers, artillery pieces and transport fleeing from the Ridge to the east. During the evening of the 9th, the Germans stopped retreating and instead began to reinforce their positions at the eastern foot of Vimy Ridge.

Below Vimy Ridge to the east was a railway line. Prior to the Battle the Germans had prepared this line for defence and these trenches represented the Germans' _Stellung_

II. With the Canadians on the Ridge above, it was not an ideal defensive position, but at this point the Germans were unsure whether they would make a stand on the *Stellung II* or further to the east on the *Stellung III*. Immediately after the Canadians' successful attack, the general commanding 6th Brigade, Brigadier-General Ketchen, wanted to attack the Railway Line, but was denied permission from 2nd Division on the grounds that the Railway Line was outside the range of the artillery's protective barrage.[552] Nevertheless, in the days following the capture of the Ridge, the Canadians put their minds to preparing an attack on the Railway Line in the near future.

The Canadian observers on Vimy Ridge kept a keen lookout to the east, remaining alert to any German movements. Vickers machine guns were brought up to the Ridge and set their sights, ready to shoot at any aggressive German moves. The British and Canadian artillery that had the range laid their guns on protective SOS lines just east of the Ridge, waiting for the flare signal from the men on the Ridge to deluge any counterattacking Germans with shell fire.

There were a couple of SOS's the night of April 9/10, the Canadians on these occasions flooding the darkness above Vimy Ridge with a quick succession of red flares. The most dangerous looking German movement in the evening was an advance of about 3 000 German soldiers from the east toward the southern part of Vimy Ridge. This force was intended to counter-attack the Canadians on Hill 135, but the Canadians responded to this movement like every other one, filling the area with shells and bullets. Unable to advance, the Germans reinforced their comrades on the Railway Line.[553]

Throughout the 10th the Germans continued their movement to the Railway Line, most of it being observed and fired on by the Canadians. Still, the Germans were able to keep up a harassing fire from the Railway Line, causing some casualties to the Canadians on Vimy Ridge.

This fire motivated the Canadians to push forward patrols to ascertain the German positions. Throughout the 10th, small parties of Canadians prodded the Railway Line and defences to the north in the *Bois de la Folie*, performing reconnaissance and exchanging shots and casualties with the Germans. One of the more intense encounters took place in the *Bois de la Folie* below 3rd Division's sector on Vimy Ridge.

Two platoons from the 49th Battalion (Edmonton Regiment), pushed ahead of their advanced outposts and worked toward the *Bois de la Folie*. Immediately receiving heavy machine gun fire from the woods, they were forced to fall back having suffered several casualties. However, the Germans were not content just to rebuff the Canadians, as about 60 Germans counter-attacked the Canadian patrol, throwing stick grenades while they advanced. Promptly, one of the Lewis Gunners in the patrol set up his Gun and covered his retreating comrades with bursts of automatic fire. This soldier managed to inflict about

25 casualties on the pursuing Germans, stopping the counter-attack and forcing the Germans back into the *Bois de la Folie*.[554]

While the 1st, 2nd and 3rd Divisions had achieved all their objectives by mid-afternoon on the first day of battle, the fighting did not automatically stop for these soldiers. They had to be alert to German reinforcements from the east and ready to repulse any counter-attack. From the Railway Line and the *Bois de la Folie* the Germans continued to harass the Canadians, while the German artillery added some shelling to the mix. The Canadians were active too, shooting at German movements, sending out patrols and bringing their artillery pieces forward from behind the Canadians' old front line. Through it all the weather continued to deteriorate, making any activity that much more difficult.

Nineteen

Hill 145 is Captured

Although the Canadians had taken the crest of Hill 145 on April 9, the Germans still held a strong line along the bottom of the Hill's eastern slope. This defensive position was based around Banff Trench and dugouts. It had been the 11th Brigade's Red Line, but remained uncaptured after the first day of the Battle. Now, on April 10, it was the last bit of Vimy Ridge still in German hands.

With the 11th Brigade weakened by exhaustion and depleted by casualties from the struggle on the first day of battle, the task of clearing the Germans completely off Hill 145 fell to the men of the 10th Brigade. The Battalions that made the attack were the 44th (Manitoba) and 50th (Calgary). To their left, soldiers from the 46th (Saskatchewan) Battalion and 87th Battalion (Canadian Grenadier Guards) established strong points to provide covering fire for the assault.

Advancing at noon in artillery formation from positions in the Canadian rear, the soldiers from the 44th (Manitoba) and 50th (Calgary) Battalions assembled for their attack in what had formerly been German trenches on Hill 145. Reaching their jumping-off positions by around 1:45 p.m., the men waited anxiously for the barrage to open at 3:04 p.m.; the signal for the infantry that the attack was to begin.

The artillery barrage opened right on time, the target being Banff Trench and nearby defences. It started as a slow barrage, but increased in intensity so that by 3:15 p.m. the gunners were firing at a rapid rate. While the gunners were blazing away, the infantry struggled through the mud, getting as close as possible to the barrage and deployed into their assault waves. There they waited for the barrage to lift off Banff Trench and begin its creep forward at 3:19 p.m.

The barrage lifted as planned and the infantry pushed forward, storming the German positions. It was not to be a one-sided affair though. Being the last defenders of Vimy Ridge, no doubt the Germans expected an attack and were ready for the Canadians.

Private Victor Wheeler (50th Battalion) recalled the stiff resistance they faced trying to reach Banff Trench:

> We took frightful punishment from the well-disciplined Brandenburgers, as score upon score of our men continued to disappear to the right and left of us; our ranks and those of the 44th Battalion were being steadily decimated. The distance between me and the next man, as we lurched forward, grew wider and wider every minute and left me with a sunken feeling of facing Heine and his guns alone.[555]

Despite their heavy losses, the Canadians pressed on, closing with the German defenders. That the men from the 50th (Calgary) Battalion were able to come to grips with their enemy had a lot to do with the actions of Private John Pattison. Faced with determined opposition from a German machine gun, the 50th Battalion's attack looked like it might be in jeopardy. However, Private Pattison got to within 30 yards of the machine gun by making short rushes from the cover of shell hole to shell hole. From this distance, Pattison was able to bomb the German machine gun with Mills bombs. Under the cover of these explosions, he rushed the position, bayoneting the crew. This action allowed the Canadians' advance to continue and lead to Private John Pattison receiving the Victoria Cross.[556]

The fighting was just as fierce for the rest of the Canadians. In one instance a lieutenant picked up a Lewis Gun and wiped out about 50 German defenders on his own.[557] Ahead of Banff Trench, a lieutenant and a small party of other ranks were later all found dead, surrounded by a larger number of killed Germans.[558]

Although the Germans put up a tough fight, the Canadians were too much for them and by around 3:45 p.m. the defenders of Banff Trench and vicinity had either been killed, had surrendered, or were retreating to the east. As we have seen elsewhere during the Battle of Vimy Ridge, attempting to retreat was a risky, often lethal, move. So it was on this day as the Canadians quickly positioned their Lewis Guns after capturing the German trenches and proceeded to gun down the fleeing Germans with bursts of automatic fire.[559]

While the Canadians were successful in their attack, the fighting did not immediately cease once the Canadians' objectives were seized. Just to the east was the *Bois de la Folie*. We have already seen that Germans in the *Bois de la Folie* continued to harass the Canadians of 3rd Division after they captured their sector of Vimy Ridge early on the 9th. It would be the same for the Canadians of 4th Division after they cleared Hill 145 on April 10. Private Victor Wheeler described the resistance the Canadian Lewis Gun outposts encountered and repulsed in the evening:

> We were preparing to establish ourselves on the line of our final objective   –
> the Givenchy Line – when Fritz suddenly appeared, snaking along one of those

deathly sunken roads to counter-attack. There was no time for Corporal Jock Galbraith's Lewis machine-gun crew to await an officer's order to fire. Without a moment's hesitation Corporal Galbraith sprang into action. He mounted the block in full view of the onrushing Fritzen, pulled his Lewis Gun up after him and in an instant the ammunition drum was spewing whizzing steel bullets into the oncoming enemy. Almost immediately, the fearless Corporal received a bullet through his skull.

One gunner after another took his fated place at the Lewis gun. Like the others before him had done, each triggered with great accuracy and bravery – until the last member of the indomitable crew crumbled in a heap alongside his still-warm buddies.[560]

With Hill 145 now completely in Canadian control, the Canadians could take satisfaction in their impressive achievement. However, any self-congratulations were tempered by the knowledge of the heavy losses suffered in the attack. Private Wheeler remembered the torment one of his comrades went through when he realized that he was the only survivor of the attack from his hometown of Okotoks:

> The sight of our decimated ranks, after the capture of Hill 145, almost tore the hearts out of us as we, who were still standing, looked around for our buddies and brothers – and saw them not. Runner Bob Forrest spoke with tears in his eyes. "I was the only one out of eighteen from Okotoks to come out alive. I knew we would not be back to cross the Ridge again, so I stopped a minute and took my steel helmet off in remembrance."

> We were relieved the same night by the 47th and moved back to Music Hall Line. Bob Forrest brooded. "Some of their mothers in Okotoks will ask me, if I get back home, how they got killed. How can I make them understand we all had to keep going no matter where and how our buddies fell!"[561]

The assault on Banff Trench completed the capture of Vimy Ridge. Only one matter was left undone; the attack on the Pimple. The Battle was not yet over and there was still more dying to come.

Twenty

April 11

April 11 was a "quiet" day, in terms of combat. While Canadian patrols and both sides' artillery were active, no assaults took place on this day. The weather, which as we have seen was poor ever since the 9th, began to deteriorate even more.

Moving forward to the new front line on the evening of the 11th were the men from the 60th Battalion (Victoria Rifles of Canada). Their War Diary captures how difficult the move was over the wet, shell-ravaged terrain:

> It had been snowing the 10th and 11th, and the trenches were in a terrible condition, as might be expected from those freshly dug. The ground also, between the craters and the ridge was churned up by the thousands of shells fired by the Canadian guns, during the ten days prior to the assault and during the actual assault. All calibres of guns from the eighteen pounder to our heaviest (15") guns were used and the result made the going, over what was previously enemy ground, exceedingly difficult, as it was necessary for the relieving troops to pick their way between the myriad of shell-holes, some of which were of gigantic proportions. The famous SWISCHEN STELLUNG was almost unrecognizable and had been converted into a muddy and irregular ditch. Everywhere, the entrances to dugouts, and dugouts themselves, were crumped to pieces.[562]

A welcome development for the Canadians on this day was that the 51st (Highland) Division was finally able to capture their Brown Line to the right of 1st Division.[563] With this, the Canadian right was secure. All that remained unfinished was the Pimple operation, to which we will turn our attention to next.

Twenty-One

The Pimple

The Pimple was a small hill separate from and located to the north-west of Vimy Ridge. While the Canadians were able to dominate the Pimple from Hill 145, it still was a dangerous position to allow to remain in German hands. From the Pimple the Germans would be able to harass the Canadians' left flank.

Originally, the Canadians intended to attack the Pimple on April 10. However, as we have seen, the 10th was used to clear out the last German defenders at Hill 145. Not only did the difficult battle for the Hill delay the Pimple operation, but it also resulted in the 44th (Manitoba) and 50th (Calgary) Battalions being thrown into the Battle early. The plan on April 8 was for the 44th and 50th Battalions alone to storm the Pimple. However, with the Battalions engaged on April 10 at Hill 145 and suffering casualties, two Companies from the 46th (Saskatchewan) Battalion were added to the Pimple assault. From north to south, the Battalions were deployed 46th (Saskatchewan), 50th (Calgary) and 44th (Manitoba). The 46th Battalion had the River Souchez to its left, while the Pimple itself fell within the 44th Battalion's sector.

Zero-hour for the attack on the Pimple was 5:00 a.m. on April 12. If the weather was bad for the operation on April 9, it was horrid on the 12th. Not only was the ground muddier due to the poor weather between the 9th to the 11th, but a blizzard set in during the early hours of the 12th. The 50th (Calgary) Battalion's report described the conditions:

> ZERO Hour was at 5:00 am, at which time a blinding snowstorm was raging, with a strong wind from the South-West. The ground was in the worst possible condition on account of the wet weather and the heavy shell fire. The mud in places was waist deep.[564]

Under this snowfall and through the mud, the assault troops moved into their jumping-off trenches in and around the Canadian front line. Unlike the assembly in the early hours of April 9th, the Germans detected the move. The men from the 46th (Saskatchewan) Battalion had to cross a stretch of ground overland rather than through communication trenches and they were spotted by the Germans, despite the snow and darkness. Immediately, flares were fired and the Germans opened up with machine guns and rifle fire. Quickly, the Canadians took cover in the watery shell-holes in the area. This, and the tendency of these Germans to shoot high, resulted in the German fire being ineffective. Once the shooting died down, the soldiers from the 46th Battalion were able to sneak forward to their jumping-off trenches.[565]

Like the attack on Vimy Ridge, the Canadians followed a creeping barrage that opened on the German front line at zero-hour. As with all previous barrages at Vimy, to the artillery was added a creeping Vickers machine gun barrage. The men firing the machine gun barrage at the Pimple, having already taken part in the earlier fighting, found that this last attack pushed their endurance to the limit. The War Diarist for the Borden Motor Machine Gun Battery recorded:

> This action commenced in a blinding Snow Storm, which raged throughout the operation and made it terribly trying for the Gunners who were working in mud and water, having no shelter and practically no sleep for 48 hours.[566]

Private Victor Wheeler of the 50th (Calgary) Battalion remembered the first moments of the attack:

> We jumped-off, the 46th on our left, the 44th on our right – blowing snow and Somme-like mud making our initial advance over treacherous ground very difficult. We were obliged, however, to maintain a pre-determined pace that was synchronized with our artillery's creeping barrage – every man's steel breast-plate; otherwise, we would have suffered disastrous casualties. Anyone who moved too fast forward would walk directly into line of our protective barrage; if too slowly he would expose himself to the enemy counter-fire. Discipline under fire proved much more important than bravery when facing our skilled enemy.

> We went forward with chronometer accuracy, virtually touching the steel edge of the beautiful creeping-barrage, always a few feet ahead of us, as it swished along, close to the ground, with the rhythm and rustle of a Victorian lady's taffeta skirt. The whipping, cutting sound of hard-steel fury was music to our ears, and the sight of German dugouts, parapets and machine-gun emplacements exploding skyward was pleasant to our eyes. Paradoxically, at one moment I was seized with stark fear, and the next instant I was inexplicably confident.[567]

Despite their best efforts, the muck was too much for the Canadians and they fell behind, losing the barrage.[568] Casualties began to mount as the Germans were able to man their defences and fire on the Canadians. Nevertheless, the Canadians pushed on and casualties could have been worse had it not been for the snow-storm. Due to the blizzard being blown into their faces, the Germans had difficulty seeing the advancing Canadians and firing accurately at them.[569]

Defending the area north of the Pimple was a Battalion from the 5th Prussian Grenadier Guards. Elite troops, they had only moved to the Pimple vicinity on April 10 in response to the Canadians' capture of Vimy Ridge. Being fresh, they appear to have been eager to take the fight to the Canadians. The night before, about 100 Guards left the Pimple and counter-attacked the 73rd Battalion (Royal Highlanders of Canada) on the left flank of 12th Brigade. Although repulsed by bursts of Lewis Gun fire, the incident does demonstrate the Guards' high morale, particularly bearing in mind that there was no way that this counter-attack could turn the tide at Vimy Ridge.[570]

Attacking north of the Pimple was the 46th (Saskatchewan) Battalion and they encountered Prussian Guards ahead of the German front line. It is likely that the Germans were garrisoning shell holes rather than the front line so as to avoid the artillery barrage, and an intense hand-to-hand struggle took place when the Canadians arrived. Despite the Canadians having already run the gauntlet of mud, the cold and bullets, they proved superior to the elite Prussian Grenadier Guards, killing them all.[571]

The fighting was just as intense elsewhere during the Pimple operation. Private Victor Wheeler (50th Battalion) recalled:

> The serious gaps in our ranks only sharpened our hatred for the Boche and heightened our determination to level every last one of the Crown Prince Rupprecht's 5th Prussian Grenadier Guards, his "Invincibles."
>
> Now driving forward in wretched weather, and heavily weighted down by cleaving clods of gumbo, we reacted more like enraged avengers than well-disciplined Canadian volunteer soldiers as we Mills-bombed, shot dead, bayoneted, grappled and rifle-butted the enemy to our maximum strength and ability. The fierceness of our onslaught, combined with the overwhelming impact of the avalanche of heavy shells pouring out of the skies on his already weakened positions, terrified the Deutschlanders. Les Allemands poured out of their deep dugouts like oil from gushing wells, singly and in small groups, with arms raised high above their heads, begging mercy, pleading, "Kamerad! Kamerad! Kamerad!"[572]

As the soldiers from the 44th (Manitoba) Battalion approached their final objective, the Quarries, they spotted a group of about 90 Germans trying to make an escape from their dugouts. Reacting quickly, the Canadian Lewis Gunners opened fire, striking the fleeing Germans with bursts of automatic fire. Bogged down in the same squalor that slowed down the Canadian advance, the retreating Germans were an easy target for the Lewis Gunners. Once the Canadians ceased fire, not one German was left alive.[573]

The poor ground, early morning darkness and snow caused some disorganization in the Canadians' advance. One of the 46th (Saskatchewan) Battalion's Companies, tasked with assaulting north of the Pimple, actually found themselves in the Quarries on the Pimple once they had finished their attack. Those troops from the 44th (Manitoba) Battalion who had the Quarries as their final objective and were supposed to be there were not. They had also become disoriented and ended up a few hundred yards east of the Quarries when their attack had reached its finale.

This resulted in those men from the 46th (Saskatchewan) Battalion on the far left of the assault being isolated from their comrades and vulnerable, despite the Canadians' success. The following is Lieutenant Johnson's message from his position on the Canadian far left in the early hours of April 13:

> Please send up rations and water. We have received none since coming in, and are badly in need of same. Also stretcher parties to carry out about 10 wounded, who have been here all yesterday. Some are serious cases. There are also a number of wounded men lying between here and jumping off trench still alive, who have not been attended to or carried in.
>
> Situation at present quiet.
>
> Men who are still at duty are quite exhausted, and I can give them no relief, as on account of lack of numbers every man is on duty all night. Some are also shell shocked a little.
>
> No M.G. magazines or Flare and S.O.S. pistols to hand yet, so I have no means of making usual signals.
>
> Have re-established block at old location, and do not intend to withdraw it unless shell fire forces me to do so.
>
> Could you possibly spare us about 15 fresh men tomorrow – unless it is intended to relieve us, which I think advisable, as the men are so exhausted.
>
> Your note re Artillery action at 4 A.M. acknowledged.
>
> Could you also send up some rum.[574]

Although Lieutenant Johnson and his men had to endure German shelling, machine gun fire and a small counter-attack on the 12th, overall, the confusion did not negatively impact the Pimple operation. Late on the 12th the disoriented men from the 46th and 44th Battalions made their way to their proper positions and the Pimple was secure.[575]

With the capture of the Pimple the Canadians had successfully completed all of their objectives. They had possession of the high ground at Vimy and now with the Pimple taken, their left was secure. Despite the formidable German defences, muddy ground and cold weather, the Canadians had triumphed.

Twenty-Two

The Cost

By April 13 the Battle of Vimy Ridge was over. The Ridge was taken, the defences on the Pimple had fallen and then, overnight on the 12th/13th, the Germans had withdrawn from the *Stellung II* to the *Stellung III*. In the days following the Canadians' capture of the Ridge, the Germans became of the opinion that their position on the *Stellung II* below Vimy Ridge was untenable, so they fell back to the safety of the *Stellung III*, about three miles away from the Ridge.[576] With this move, it became clear that the Germans had abandoned any hope of re-capturing Vimy Ridge and the Canadians' victory was complete.

The cost of this victory had been high. Canadian casualties between April 9 to 14 totalled 10 602.[577] The hardest hit Brigade, not surprisingly, was 11th Brigade, which suffered about 1 400 casualties in their struggle for Hill 145 on the 9th. It was 6th Brigade that came out of the Battle the least damaged, incurring about 450 casualties in their attack on Thelus, Hill 135 and, beyond the Ridge's crest, the artillery gun pits. Overall, an average of 32 percent casualties were suffered by the Brigades involved in the attack.

Out of the 10 602 Canadian casualties, 3 598 of these were men killed.[578] In a total war like the Great War, the deaths suffered in battle were not only felt at home when friends and family received news of their loss. With so many young Canadian men serving in France, it was not uncommon for friends and family to serve together. Being in such proximity, a soldier could know of his and his family's loss immediately. So it was with A. Farmer who saw his brother killed:

> My brother whom I lost at Vimy was just a very few feet from me when I lost him, actually. He was wounded first and I dropped into the shell hole to give him first-aid, and after giving him first-aid I left him. Of course I couldn't stay and apparently he raised up in the shell hole to watch me, see where I went and I heard the shot fired and heard it land and turned around to see him fall.[579]

As was the case with every Great War battle, the destructive power of the combatants' weapons could obliterated human beings. The medical officer for the 31st (Alberta) Battalion, Captain Harold McGill, recalled the sight that met his eyes:

> Just as we entered the barrage I came across a newly severed human foot lying on top of the mud directly in my path. It was cut off above the ankle as cleanly as though done with an axe. The boot and sock were completely stripped away, and the skin was as white and clean as if the owner had just come out of a bath. It was mute evidence that someone had been blown to pieces but a moment before.[580]

NAC-PA4388 – Canadian troops advancing past British tank. Dead Canadian soldier in foreground.

The remaining Canadian casualties were wounded as only a few Canadians were captured during the Battle. One of the many wounded men was Lieutenant Stuart Kirkland. He was hit early in the fight:

> . . . I jumped over the top and called to the boys to come on. I had gone about 15 yards when I felt a stinging sensation and looking down saw a trickle of blood on my left hand. A Heinie machine gun had got me. At the same time a sergeant

just to my right crumpled up in a heap riddled with machine gun bullets. How lucky I was![587]

So long as he was able to walk, the wounded soldier had to make the dangerous journey back across the muddy, projectile swept battlefield, into Canadian lines and then to a medical dressing station. As difficult as this was, many realized that their fate could have been much worse. Lieutenant Stuart Kirkland remembered the sights he saw in Canadian lines on the way to obtaining medical treatment:

> In one place where the trench had been blown in and it was very narrow I came on a poor fellow lying lengthwise of the trench and everyone had been tramping right over him til he was almost buried in the mud. Of course he was dead so I suppose it didn't inconvenience him any. But imagine the sensation of having to tramp on dead bodies. In another place I came on one of my <u>own</u> company lying with both legs blown off at the knees but still alive and conscious. I stopped and talked to him for a few moments. Scenes like these are not uncommon in war.[582] (underlined added)

As for those Canadians with more serious wounds, by and large, the evacuation of the wounded was efficient. Stretcher bearers were quick to follow the advance, often locating the wounded by their rifles sticking up in the mud, and carried the wounded back to Canadian lines for immediate treatment. From there, the wounded would be transported to the rear by trench railway or ambulance.[583] It was common for the bag-pipers, after piping their comrades "over the top," to act as stretcher bearers.

NAC-PA1021 – Wounded Canadian being taken to the rear by stretcher. Behind, a "walking wounded" Canadian is being assisted by German prisoners.

The ordinary soldier was warned against assisting his wounded comrades during the assault, instead, being told to leave the task to the stretcher bearers. This may seem harsh, but it was in the soldiers' best interest. If soldiers stopped their advance to assist the wounded, the attack would lose its strength, quite possibly resulting in the assault's failure. Not only would this leave the wounded and their helpers vulnerable to German defensive fire, but it would likely lead to a second attack on the position, causing further unnecessary casualties.

The stretcher bearers did receive a boost in manpower during the Battle as German prisoners were used (voluntarily or not) to help the stretcher bearers in their task. James F. Johnson recalled:

> The Germans worked hand in hand with us, dressing wounds, carrying stretchers over muddy, soaked ground. They were generally adept in first aid. The wounded were picked up as we found them, German or ours. The dead left until all the wounded were tended to.[584]

NAC-PA1034 – Canadian wounded waiting to be evacuated further to the rear by light railway.

While no doubt the wounded suffered during the Battle, having one's limbs smashed and lying in the cold mud waiting for assistance would be an extremely trying ordeal, but the Canadians did their best to minimize the time between the soldier getting wounded and his ability to receive treatment.

One of the notable exceptions to this overall efficient system was on 4th Division's attack front. Here, quick evacuation of the wounded at Hill 145 was largely impossible, the strong German defence during April 9 inhibiting any movement. From the Hill the Germans were also able to interrupt the rescue of the wounded to the right and left as well. This was particularly true near the Craters, as the 12th Brigade's after-action report remarked on the heavy toll taken on stretcher bearers due to German machine gun and rifle fire from Hill 145.[585]

Not all the wounded had physical wounds that required stretcher bearers. For some, the Battle scarred their minds. Corporal Fraser (6th Machine Gun Company) recalled the plight of one man:

> Casualties from the 27th were gathering around our quarter, most of them walk-ing cases. They were anxiously waiting for the shelling to cease so that they could get away. One poor fellow, a big chap, was crying like a baby with shell-shock. His nerves and control were absolutely gone and he was yelled at by everyone to shut up the moment he whimpered.[586]

While the soldiers' reaction to the shell-shocked man may seem insensitive, it is understandable bearing in mind that the soldiers had just been through an intense Battle themselves.

That Canadian casualties were heavy points to a larger fact about the Great War. The Battle of Vimy Ridge was a complete success and yet still about one in three of the attacking infantry involved became a casualty. While this ratio is less than that suffered in many attacks during the Battle of the Somme, it is consistent with most Great War bat-tles on the Western Front in 1917-1918. The point being that in any battle on the Western Front, casualties were going to be heavy due to the vast amount of firepower available to the combatants (a 30 percent casualty rate was also common in the American Civil War and Second World War too).

A good example of the heavy price even successful battles such as Vimy Ridge cost comes from Nurse Clare Gass who was overseas with the No. 3 Canadian General Hospital. From her April 15 and 16 diary entry:

> The casualties though reported as small from last week's action have simply filled all the hospitals hereabouts to over flowing. Robert O' Callahan who is at an English hospital in Wimereux says he never saw worse wounds than those they have & some of ours are heart breaking - Gas gangrene is very prevalent & we have lost several cases. We have had no hours off for a week & have been on duty late at night & are beginning to feel the effects of the extra work.[587]

Added to this, Clare Gass would soon learn that one of her brothers, Lieutenant Laurence Gass (165th Siege Battery), had died on April 8, while another brother, Lance Corporal Blanchard Gass in the 85th Battalion (Nova Scotia Highlanders), was killed at Hill 145 on April 9.[588]

Turning to the Germans, their casualties were around 10 000. This is a speculative conclusion and requires some explanation. Most of the German Great War records were destroyed during the Second World War resulting in the loss of the information contained therein. For those records that remain, direct comparison with British and Canadian official losses is difficult. This is so because the German Army did not consider those with slight wounds (able to remain at or quickly return to duty) as being officially wounded. The British and Canadians counted these men as wounded and they made up a significant number of those officially recorded as being wounded.[589]

Thus, to estimate German casualties, we should look at how many men were deployed for the Battle. In terms of infantry, six Regiments faced the Canadian Corps on April 9 (from north to south: 11th Bavarian, 261st Reserve, 262nd Reserve, 263rd Reserve, 3rd Bavarian Reserve and 1st Bavarian Reserve). Each Regiment had three Battalions; two in the Battle area forward of the *Stellung II*, with the other Battalion in reserve. The strength of each Battalion has been estimated at 600 all ranks.[590] (There was an exception to this deployment. The 3rd Bavarian Reserve Infantry Regiment had all three Battalions in the Battle area, but its average Battalion strength was only about 400 all ranks. Nevertheless, the 3rd Bavarian still had about 1 200 men in the Battle area, like the other Regiments.[591])

We saw in the Battle Narrative that the Canadians overwhelmed the *Stellung I* and *Swischen Stellung*, the main German defensive positions before the *Stellung II*. It is unlikely that the Germans holding these positions were able to withdraw unscathed, if at all. Between the Canadians following the creeping barrage closely, the depth of the creeping barrage overall and the quick work of Lewis Gunners in taking up positions after a trench was captured, escape to the rear for German soldiers was near impossible. For those men still garrisoning the German dugouts when the British and Canadian barrage lifted, it is likely that they were either killed or captured (with the prisoners including both wounded and unwounded) when the trench was stormed. Those few who tried to escape were either gunned down by the Lewis Gunners, or had to retreat into the British and Canadian barrage; a deadly option. It is probable that after the Battle the German Battalions that were holding positions forward of the *Stellung II* effectively ceased to exist as combat units; the vast majority of their ranks either killed or captured.

Assuming that the two forward German Battalions of each Regiment were destroyed, this would mean that German casualties would be about 7 200. This assumption is a bit absolute, however, it should be remembered that it was not the infantry alone who suffered in the Battle. Included in those taken prisoner by the Canadians were about 550 men from artillery, pioneer, trench mortar and work units.[592] No doubt these units also suffered casualties in dead and wounded. Thus, while some infantry from the forward German Battalions likely did escape, their survival would be off-set by casualties to the other units.

The figure of 7 200 only includes those Germans involved in the fighting up until the evening of April 9. The 5th Prussian Guards and 93rd Reserve Infantry Regiment each had one Battalion defending the Pimple on April 12 and they too were over-run. Drawing on the same assumptions as above, this would increase German casualties to 8 400.

Even then, casualties were inflicted on the reserve Battalions of each Regiment that ended up holding the *Stellung II* and German reinforcements received from the east. These reinforcements amounted to an additional seven German Battalions during April 9 and 10. Of these reinforcements, three Battalions were involved in the aborted counter-attack towards Hill 135 that was broken up by Canadian and British machine gun and artillery fire on the evening of April 9. Another Battalion, from the 14th Bavarian Infantry Regiment, launched a counter-attack around midnight toward Hill 145, but the Germans became bogged down in the mud and disoriented in the dark, and the counter-attack was repulsed with relative ease by a single Canadian Vickers machine gun.[593] On the 9th, a Battalion from the 118th Reserve Infantry Regiment arrived as reinforcement and became involved in the fighting for Banff Trench on April 10.

It was not just in attacks and counter-attacks that the reserve and reinforcing Battalions suffered casualties. We saw in the Battle Narrative that the Canadian and British artillery and machine gunners fired on any German movement from the east to reinforce the *Stellung II* on the evening of the 9th. This type of shooting continued from April 10 to 12, along with fighting patrols.

Bearing in mind the involvement of the reserve Battalions and reinforcing Battalions in the Battle, German casualties should be higher than 8 400. The writer is hesitant to add 2 500 to this number, just so as to make the estimate higher than Canadian casualties, but total German casualties from the period April 9 to 14 were likely around 10 000.[594] (It should be pointed out that some of this figure of 10 000 would include infantrymen holding positions forward of the *Stellung II* who were killed or wounded by the preliminary bombardment in the days immediately before the attack. It would not include infantry casualties caused by the preliminary bombardment before then, or to casualties to non-infantry units during the entire bombardment.)

The Brigade-Major for 4th Brigade, Captain D.E. Macintyre, recalled the sight of German dead as he made his way to the Ridge on the afternoon of the 9th:

> The first dead German I saw was spread-eagled against the parados, or back
> wall, of his trench, arms flung out as though crucified. Where his head had been

was a red pulp like a crushed strawberry. Many of the dead lay as though sleeping without a mark of disfigurement and I am certain felt no pain, but others were disembowelled or with limbs shattered and clothing torn from their bodies by the blast of high explosives. The water in the shell holes was stained blood red; altogether a horrible sight that I shall never forget, . . .[595]

In places it was possible to follow the course of the Battle by the bodies on the ground. This appears to have been the case in 3rd Brigade's area as Brigadier-General Tuxford described his tour of his Brigade's battlefield in his after-action report:

Some time after the capture of the RED LINE in the morning, I went forward as far as the EISNER KREUZ WEG, and our first dead casualty appeared in "No Man's Land." From there, our casualties were in evidence forward, but not a single Hun casualty until the old German support line was reached, from which line forward they were numerous, in places being 5 or 6 in a cluster. Our casualties were mostly S.A.A. (small arms ammunition).

Later in the day, about 3:30 p.m., I went forward as far as COMMANDANT'S HOUSE. There were some German dead between the LILLE - ARRAS Road, and the ZWOLFER WEG, after which, with the exception of bodies at the SWISCHEN STELLUNG, I saw no German dead. I saw very few of our dead between the LILLE - ARRAS Road and the SWISCHEN STELLUNG, and none in advance of that line. (parentheses added)[596]

Out of the total German casualties, 4 081 were prisoners (825 of which were wounded).[597] Bob Goddard from the 6th Trench Mortar Battery remembered capturing a group of German soldiers on the way to the Brown Line:

A machine gun commenced firing at us, so down our crew went into a shell hole and up went our gun and a few rounds silenced that machine gun; then forward again with the 27th. We struck a trench and worked our way down, for this was our objective. On the way we came to a large dugout, and it was full of Germans. As soon as we appeared at the entrance they started to holler, and one man tried to get out the other entrance, so our Sergeant shot him. We took the rest of them prisoners (about twenty altogether, officers and men) and we lined them up and went through their pockets. We took away their revolvers, badges, photos, and all sorts of things – in fact, we stripped them of everything but their lives and a few clothes and sent them back to our lines.[598]

The number of prisoners taken by the Canadians during the Battle could have been higher, but just because a German soldier surrendered did not mean that he survived the Battle. We have already seen that "friendly fire" was a factor in Canadian casualties, with men being killed or wounded either by moving too close to the barrage, or by "shorts" fired by the artillery. Friendly fire was dangerous for the Germans too. Once captured, the prisoners had to walk to Canadian lines (sometimes without Canadian guards). In doing so, they had to run the gauntlet of their own defensive barrage which, although weak, still caused casualties.

For example, the 72nd Battalion (Seaforth Highlanders of Canada) claimed to have captured 26 prisoners, but with the caveat that many of these men were reported to have been killed by shell-fire on their way to Canadian lines.[599] Lieutenant E.L.M. Burns (11th Brigade Signal Section), emerging from a captured German dugout, witnessed the effect German shelling had on a different group of prisoners:

> Suddenly someone shouted down the entrance: "Mr. Burns, Mr. Burns, quick! Fritz is counterattacking." I climbed the stairs, telling myself that I must appear less frightened than the men. On arrival in the trench I soon found the counter-attack to be nothing more than a dozen or so kamerads, nearly 300 yards away, making for our lines under escort. As we watched, one of their own five-nine shells dropped in their midst, and sent two or three flying through the air.[600]

There also was the inherent uncertainty associated with the moment of surrender. To put one's hands up is not a guarantee of mercy, especially when the man coming towards you has just lost his friends moments ago. Add the possibility that the man trying to surrender just killed the Canadian soldier's buddies, the chances of the German soldier being killed in "hot blood" increase. There also was the problem of German soldiers resisting after being captured which, in the heat of battle, is not going to be tolerated for very long. Having said this, there was nothing unique about such events occurring at Vimy Ridge as they happen in all wars and, in any event, were not widespread during the Battle. It is interesting to note that once the moment of surrender passed, prisoners were uniformly treated with care.

Reflecting the varying treatment German prisoners received at the point of the bayonet, was Sachimaro Moro-oka's experience. One of a significant number of soldiers in the 50th (Calgary) Battalion of Japanese heritage, he remembered capturing a German soldier during the fighting for the eastern slope of Hill 145 on April 10:

> During the battle a German charged me with a bayonet. I parried and went for his chest. I missed and the bayonet got him on the wrist. I was about to make my second thrust when I heard him cry, "Mother!" I thought of my aged mother in Japan and stopped. I made him my prisoner.[601]

For some men, the sight of surrendering Germans brought a sense of sympathy for what their enemy had just endured. A.A. Bonar (Princess Patricia's Canadian Light Infantry) remembered the plight of one German soldier:

> While we were crouching in this broken trench he [the German soldier] crawled up to us, on his knees, doing the best he could to keep his hands over his head. "Look out, Bill" someone called. I had my bayonet ready. Over the ground

towards the trench the grey clad figure with a large steel helmet crawled and jumped holding something in his hand, which I thought might be a bomb, hence, the proximity of my bayonet to his body.

Then when he tumbled into the trench and looked up from under the large flow-erpot helmet in which his whole head was almost encased, we saw he was only a boy of perhaps fifteen or sixteen. What might have been a bomb in his hand turned out to be his gas respirator which, unlike our, is in the shape of a tin box (sic).

He was trembling like a leaf with fright. His face was blanched. He uttered a few guttural sounds between gasps. Then we noticed that his left leg was broken at the ankle, such a pitiful specimen of abject fear and pain. We couldn't help but feel sorry for him, and I felt that I had scared him unduly perhaps, just when he had hopes of being captured, and released from the hell which he had escaped though injured. We showed him the way to our rear, hoping that he would reach it without further injury.[602]

NAC-PA1145 – German prisoners being marched away after the Battle.

As the Battle subsided, the burial parties went to work. While the Canadian dead were being buried as early as the 9th, some of the German dead had to wait longer. Victor Wheeler recalled the scene at Vimy Ridge after the Battle:

> As far as the eye could see, the Ridge was afire, with thousands of puffs of gaseous-white smoke spiralling upward. Swirling tufts of dirty-white smoke were rising from deep German dugouts that had once held the Kaiser's Elite. From end to end of Vimy Ridge plumes of smoke fluttered from the horribly battered dugouts still filled with allemand corpses, mercilessly blown to death by our bombs and hand grenades thrown down dugout entrances when the Squareheads refused, or were too frightened, to come out when we yelled, "Heraus mit dir!"
>
> Working-parties had gone the length and breadth of the Ridge shovelling great quantities of chaux vive (quicklime) in and over enemy dugouts as a means of burning up and destroying unburied bodies, that drew rats and flies and created an intolerable health hazard to the whole countryside. Bodies were also quicklimed atop the ground wherever Hell's fury had struck them in groups or in machine gun nests – for Time and Opportunity had denied them a decent burial. Hundreds of once brave soldaten of the Vaterland, piled like cordwood, were being cremated, and nauseating smoke rose from these funeral pyres with only the wind to scatter the ashes.[603]

Like all Great War battles, Vimy Ridge was costly in lives and limbs. Casualties were about equal, with each side suffering around 10 000. For the Canadians, this represented about one-third of the infantry assault force. As for the Germans, the majority of their casualties were incurred by those troops holding the line forward of the *Stellung II*. After the Battle, these German units effectively ceased to exist.

Twenty-Three

German Defensive Tactics

Before discussing the elements vital to success on the Canadian side, a moment should be taken to examine those decisions made by the German High Command before and during the Battle that impacted the way it unfolded. To ignore them is to assume that the Germans were a non-entity on the battlefield with no ability to influence events, a dangerous assumption to make as any battle is shaped by the enemy's decisions and deployments.

In the Battle Narrative, we have already seen how the Battle played out. The main resistance met by the Canadians was at the *Stellung I* and *Swischen Stellung*, represented by the Black and Red Lines. In the South, the stiffest resistance was met by and the heaviest casualties incurred by, the assault Brigades. The 3rd Division took significant casualties in their attack, which encompassed a Black and Red Line only, while 4th Division suffered severe casualties in assaulting Hill 145 and vicinity (4th Division's Black and Red Lines).

On the other hand, the attack on the Blue and Brown Lines, only necessary in the South, met with less resistance and Canadian casualties were reduced. While the average casualties in the assault Brigades of 1st and 2nd Divisions were about 900 men per Brigade, the average for the leap-frog Brigades' was half of that.

Indeed, in the South, the only significant resistance met beyond the Red Line was in the attack on the artillery positions at the Brown Line by the 27th (City of Winnipeg) Battalion, plus one Company from 29th (Vancouver) Battalion; both from 6th Brigade. It was here that the German gunners defended their position, even firing their artillery point-blank at the attacking Canadians. The Canadians overcame the defenders, but only after a tough fight, including hand-to-hand combat. Reflecting the stout defence at the gun pits, 27th Battalion suffered 206 casualties, compared to the average of around 80 casualties incurred by each of the other Battalions in the Brigade that attacked the Village of Thelus and Hill 135 (6th Brigade's Blue Line).

That the other Battalions in 6th Brigade suffered such comparatively light casualties in their assault on Thelus and Hill 135 had much to do with the artillery's preliminary bombardment; particularly the heavy and super-heavy howitzer's destruction of Thelus. There was an interesting contrast within 6th Brigade's attack. On the Blue Line it was the artillery that defeated the German infantry, while on the Brown Line it was infantry that beat German artillery.

What this analysis of how the Battle played out indicates is that on the first day of the Battle, the German defence of Vimy Ridge rested largely on the *Stellung I* and *Swischen Stellung*. Once the Canadians took these *Stellungs*, the Ridge was either in their hands (in the north), or there was no significant resistance to the Canadians' capturing the Ridge (in the South), with the exception of the gun pits.

Perhaps surprisingly, the next German resistance line, the *Stellung II*, was placed below Vimy Ridge along the Railway Line, the *Bois de la Folie* and east of Hill 145. Being so located, once the Canadians were on the Ridge they dominated it, allowing them to observe and direct artillery fire on the *Stellung II* and any moves to reinforce it. The Germans recognized the difficulties in holding the *Stellung II* and withdrew three miles east to the *Stellung III* on April 13. The distance from the *Stellung III* to Vimy Ridge was too great to allow the Germans to counter-attack, so this retreat signified the abandonment of Vimy Ridge by the Germans.

The Canadians were able to pick apart the German defences, defeating the *Stellung I, Swischen Stellung* and *Stellung II* in turn. However, it should be mentioned that the German method at Vimy Ridge of holding the *Stellung I* and *Swischen Stellung* strongly, with little behind to back these lines up, was at odds with current German defensive tactics.

The Germans too had learned lessons from the Battle of the Somme. In that Battle the Germans emphasized holding strong forward defensive lines based on trenches, refusing to yield any ground and immediately counter-attacking any breach in the line. This resulted in heavy German casualties, so the German High Command changed their defensive tactics to a flexible defence in depth.

With a flexible defence in depth, the German defences closest to Allied lines were to be weakly held in the expectation that they would be captured in an assault, although this area still contained some strong points to break up these assaults. Beyond this was an area garrisoned strongly; the battle zone. It was here that the Germans envisioned the main battle occurring, where strong, mutually supporting, non-linear German defences were supplemented by artillery support. Further back, outside the range of Allied artillery, were to be placed the German reserves of infantry, ready to smash any attackers who made it past the first German positions into the battle zone. These counter-attacks were not to be made reflexively as they were on the Somme, rather, counter-attacks were to be made at a time and over ground of the defender's choosing.[604]

Therefore, the Germans created a defensive system geared to allow the Allied attackers to make some headway into the German defences, but, once the attackers became worn down by exhaustion and casualties and were at the limit or beyond their artillery cover, the Germans would be ready to deliver a terrifying blow.

The lack of a flexible defence in depth at Vimy Ridge is evident as the Germans held the forward positions of the *Stellung I* and *Swischen Stellung* in strength. However, in defence of the local German commanders, the Ridge was not that suitable for a defence in depth system, especially on its northern half. Here, where 3rd and 4th Divisions attacked, the Canadian front line trenches were closer to their ultimate objectives than elsewhere on the Ridge. With the dominating crest, including Hill 145, being so close to Canadian lines, it would have been difficult, if not impossible, for the Germans to have used a spread out defence in depth.

In the South there was more space between the Canadian front lines and the Ridge's crest, opening the possibility of a more spread out defence. The Germans may have erred in having their defence in the South resting largely on the *Stellung I* and *Swischen Stellung*, with little between these *Stellungs* and the *Stellung II*. It also seems a bit odd that the *Stellung II* was located below the eastern slope of the Ridge, rather than on its reverse slope. If it had been so placed, it likely would have been a difficult target for the British and Canadian artillery to hit and could have been a more effective way to defend the crest. Instead, the *Stellung II* was untenable where located, the Germans retreating from it on the 13th.

Having said this, there is a strong argument that, no matter how the Germans positioned their defences, the Canadians would have captured them in any event. We have already seen the power that the creeping barrage, counter-battery work and infantry tactics had in overwhelming the strong defences of the *Stellung I* and *Swischen Stellung*. These same factors would have resulted in any strong defences between these *Stellungs* and the *Stellung II* falling in the same manner. Canadian casualties in the leap-frog Brigades would have been higher, but the defences would have fallen in any event.

Potentially more relevant was the placement of German reserves. Under the flexible defence in depth, these were to be positioned such that, once an attack was made, the reserves would be close on hand, available to make a well-placed and punishing counter-attack. At Vimy, the German immediate reserves were on the *Stellung III* three miles from the Ridge, while the counter-attack divisions were even further away. The German Sixth Army commander, General von Falkenhausen, had placed them there to avoid their being shelled by the Canadian and British artillery. He was confident that the defenders of Vimy Ridge could hold their positions for two days, allowing him plenty of time to bring forward his reserves and counter-attack divisions.[605] In the event, most of the defenders were over-run in a few hours and the reserves and counter-attack divisions were too far away to intervene in the Battle.

However, as with the placement of German defences on the Ridge, it is arguable that even if the Germans did counter-attack sooner and in greater force, they still would have been unable to push the Canadians back. The Canadian Corps was aware of the threat posed by immediate German counter-attacks and had planned to meet them. For this reason, the Canadians brought Vickers machine guns and Stokes trench mortars with the advance and quickly began consolidating the Ridge after their successful attack. On top of this, the artillery had pre-arranged protective barrages east of the Ridge, along with forward observation officers on the Ridge to direct artillery fire. Bearing this in mind, it is questionable whether any German counter-attack would have succeeded. If they had counter-attacked, the most likely consequence would have been to increase the casualties each side suffered during the Battle, without changing its result.

Therefore, while the defenders at Vimy had a defensive system quite at odds with current German thinking, this departure from convention may be less significant than it appears. Vimy Ridge itself was not suitable for a flexible defence in depth and, even if the Blue and Brown Lines were held in more strength, the Canadians would likely have still captured the Ridge. The placement of German reserves and counter-attack divisions too far from the Ridge prevented any large, immediate counter-attacks, however, the Canadians expected the Germans to counter-attack and were ready to repulse any attempt. While, from the German point of view, they may have made mistakes in deploying their forces, it probably would not have mattered anyways.

Twenty-Four

Keys to Canadian Success

How was it that the Canadians were able to take Vimy Ridge? The French tried twice in 1915 and failed. At the Somme in 1916, we saw how the British and Canadians fared on the offensive and the conclusion was that their attacks were, at best, inconsistent in their results. What were the keys to the Canadian Corps' complete victory at Vimy?

The starting point for this discussion has to begin with the artillery. Commencing March 20, the British and Canadian artillery comprehensively shattered the German defences. We have seen from anecdotes in the Battle Narrative that the artillery had done its job well. Trenches were reduced to muddy ditches, barbed wire was obliterated and many dugouts were smashed in. The large number of howitzers used wreaked havoc on German defences with their high explosive shells, while the new 106 fuze proved superior to past methods for destroying the protective wire.

Not only did this artillery fire wreck the defensive capacity of these physical obstacles, but it also caused suffering to the German garrison. Men were entombed in blown dugouts and any movement in German lines was fraught with danger. Added to this was the great mental strain the preliminary bombardment forced on the defenders. Hunkered down in dugouts, these soldiers had little to do but sit and wait, hoping the next shell would not smash in their dugout, yet not knowing when the pounding would end. Relief of front line units and their re-supply was hazardous, further weakening these men and isolating them from their comrades. It may be that the tendency of the ordinary infantryman to "readily surrender" to the attacking Canadians was due to the defenders being at the "end of their tether," unwilling or unable to hold out any longer.

This artillery fire did disclose to the Germans that an attack was in the offing. Interrogation of prisoners after the Battle showed that the Germans knew that the Canadians were going to attack. However, a wide range of suspected dates for the offensive were given to their captors, indicating that, while they knew an attack was coming, the Germans had no idea when it would take place. The Canadians had achieved tactical surprise.

It is possible that the feint barrages fired by the British and Canadian artillery prior to the Battle added to the Germans' confusion. Replicas of the actual creeping barrage, but only being fired up to the Black Line, these may have dulled the Germans within their dugouts into believing that when the barrage opened at 5:30 a.m. on April 9, it was just another feint.

When the real creeping barrage came, it met all expectations. Accurate and synchronized with the infantry's advance, the barrage protected the soldiers throughout the Battle. The component rolling barrage, standing barrage, machine gun barrage and, behind that, howitzer barrage, covered the battlefield, inflicting casualties on any Germans who were above ground and keeping those alive underground. While there were some friendly casualties, overall, the creeping barrage was vital to Canadian success.

Firing deeper than the creeping barrage, those artillery pieces tasked with counter-battery work flooded the German gunners and their guns with high explosive and gas shells. Having located most of the German artillery positions before the Battle, the British and Canadian fire was accurate, incapacitating the majority of the German artillery. For this reason, when the German defensive barrage opened early in the Battle it was weak and seemingly erratic, and remained so, failing to disrupt the Canadian infantry attack or the move of leap-frog units, reinforcements and supplies later on.

Turning to the infantry, the keys to their success were sown before the Battle began. From the battle practices held before the attack, all ranks were thoroughly familiar with the defences they would face, the operation of the creeping barrage and their role in the Battle. Having turned their minds to the inevitability of casualties, less than ideal scenarios were practised, such as the removal of officers from mock attacks and dealing with resistance points. With officer casualties in the Battle being higher, relatively speaking, to those suffered by the other ranks, the value of the training becomes evident in that in many cases the other ranks carried the attack forward without their officers.

Crucial to the realistic training and effective artillery bombardment and barrage fire was the prior observation and reconnaissance that the Canadians did before the Battle. A feature of trench life during the Winter of 1917, the accumulated knowledge from that period was supplemented with intelligence gathered from March 20 onwards. The comprehensive knowledge that the Canadians had of the German defences was of great importance to the Canadians in devising their Battle plan. It is no accident that in their after-action reports completed after the Battle, the officers commanding the Canadian Battalions praised the Corps' intelligence gathering.

Important in the pre-Battle training was practising the new platoon organization. Developed from lessons learned in the Battle of the Somme, the infantry platoon went from a largely rifle armed unit, to one including rifle grenades, Mills Bomb hand-grenades, Lewis Guns and rifles; all useful weapons in trench warfare. Having all these weapons within a small, 40 man unit allowed great flexibility in the attack as a given resistance point could be reduced by the infantry with the weapons they had on hand. This flexibility was increased when one bears in mind that the individual Canadian soldier was trained in all weapons within the platoon, not just his own.

In their after-action reports, the officers commanding the Canadian Battalions were virtually unanimous in their praise of the new platoon organization. We have seen from some of the anecdotes in the Battle Narrative how effective the new organization was. When resistance points were encountered, the Canadians would close in on, or outflank, the Germans under the covering fire of Lewis Guns and/or rifle grenades. If the defenders were not already eliminated from a distance, the covering fire allowed the Canadians to bomb, shoot or bayonet any Germans left at close range.

NAC-PA1086 – Classic photograph from the Battle of Vimy Ridge. Men from the 29th (Vancouver) Battalion advancing in artillery formation. Note the soldier in the centre with the "fat" gun over his shoulder. He is a Lewis Gunner.

During the Battle the most useful weapon was the Lewis Gun. Fired from the hip during the advance at any Germans who emerged from their dugouts to man their defences, the Lewis Guns provided important covering fire for the initial rush once the creeping barrage lifted. The Lewis Gunners assisted in reducing resistance points, as described in the paragraph above, and quickly took positions with good fields of fire once the defences were captured. From here they could defend the newly won position and shoot at any Germans trying to withdraw. As we have seen from anecdotes in the Battle

Narrative, trying to escape in the face of Canadian Lewis Gunners was a lethal move for the Germans.

Rifle grenades were not used as extensively as was thought necessary before the Battle. This does not mean that they were not useful, for we have seen from Battle anecdotes that rifle grenades were, in fact, used to suppress and eliminate German defensive positions. However, in many places on the battlefield the Canadians were able to quickly capture a trench upon the barrage lifting, resulting in it being unnecessary to deluge the defenders with rifle grenades.

The same holds true for the hand-grenade; the Mills Bomb. However, the Mills bombs did have another purpose once a defensive position was stormed. With German defences manned by garrisons in deep dugouts, Mills bombs were used to bomb the dugouts, killing any Germans within, or motivating them to come out and surrender.

The thorough training and expertise developed in using the platoon weapons seems to have bred confidence within Canadian ranks. Confident in themselves, the Canadians were motivated to use their skills and win the Battle. Perhaps surprisingly, there were a significant number of hand-to-hand encounters during the Battle. In these the Canadians were undoubtedly superior, wiping out the German defenders in some instances. A skilled, confident and motivated group, the Canadians were a formidable foe for the Germans.

The new offensive tactics, developed from lessons learned in the Battle of the Somme, proved their worth at the Battle of Vimy Ridge. At its most fundamental level, these tactics were the close cooperation between the artillery and infantry. The artillery knew the infantry's assault plan and the infantry understood the operation of the creeping barrage. With this understanding, the infantry were able to keep close to the barrage allowing each successive German defensive position to be stormed after each barrage lift. Once Germans were encountered, the Canadians drew upon their training and utilized the variety of weapons in the new platoon organization to maximum effect. All resistance was overcome.

Seen in this light, the ostensibly "simple" frontal assault at Vimy Ridge was a complex affair. Coordinating and synchronizing the artillery and infantry, accurate shooting by the artillery and the use of the new platoon organization, while simple to discuss, were difficult to implement. Exchanging knowledge and realistic training were necessary for this system to work and it was accomplished by the Canadian Corps. That, in retrospect, the attack seemed "simple" has much to do with the thought and energy put into the Canadians' plan. This planning, along with the Canadians' motivation and skills to carry it out, were the keys to Canadian success.

Twenty-Five

The Breakthrough Illusion

The completeness of the Canadians' victory at Vimy Ridge is highlighted by bearing in mind the Canadians' initial intentions. The Battle was planned, at the outset, as a supporting operation for Third Army's attack around Arras which, in turn, was a diversion for the larger French offensive to commence later in April. The goal of the Canadians' operation was always tactical, that is, the capture of Vimy Ridge.

The Canadians planned and executed a "bite and hold" operation. Their objective was a limited one; seizing the dominating Vimy Ridge. Once captured, their immediate concern was to consolidate their gains and protect them from counter-attack, rather than pushing on and trying to create a breakthrough. No reinforcements were readied before the Battle to push beyond the Ridge, rather, the Allies' manpower reserves were earmarked for supporting the larger British attack at Arras and the main French offensive on the Chemin des Dames. It is within this context of a limited "bite and hold" operation that the Battle must be viewed and it was a total success.

Some have seen the Germans fleeing from the Ridge in the afternoon on April 9 as a lost opportunity to convert the capture of Vimy Ridge into a larger breakthrough of the German defences on the Western Front; possibly winning the War. This view does not seem to accord with the reality on the ground.

To begin with, once the Canadians' were beyond the eastern slope of the Ridge, they were at the limit of their supporting creeping barrage. We have already seen that the general commanding 6th Brigade, Brigadier-General Ketchen, wanted to push on from the Ridge and take the Railway Line, but was denied permission due to this objective being outside the range of the creeping barrage. For any advance from the Ridge to be successful, it would have to be supported by the artillery.

In order to provide the necessary artillery support for any further advance the guns would have to be brought forward. At Vimy, this was easier said than done. The ground between Canadian lines and the crest of the Ridge had been shattered by the artillery shelling and was soaked by the wet weather. It was hard enough for the infantry to pick their way through the passable spots, and it was virtually impossible for the artillery. We have seen in anecdotes from the Battle Narrative that many of the Canadian artillery pieces got bogged down in the mud trying to move forward between April 9 to 11. The situation on April 12 was the same as recorded by the 2nd Canadian Divisional Artillery's War Diarist:

> With help of infantry, I and J groups got one third of their guns into action. The NEUVILLE ST. VAAST - LES TILLEULS road is not to be used until repaired, so all ammunition must be packed across country. This is almost impossible owing to mud and shell holes. It is clear that unless adequate provision is made for clearing and repairing roads and laying light railways, it is impossible to get field guns forward across a heavily shelled area and keep up ammunition supply. It still will be several days before the heavies can come up.[606]

Operating under such impediments, any quick advance aimed at a breakthrough was impossible.

By April 13, much of the Canadian field artillery had actually dragged themselves through the mud and were ready for action. However, by then the Germans had with-drawn, falling back to the *Stellung III* three miles away. The guns were out of range again.

The existence of the *Stellung III* points to another fact that made a breakthrough from Vimy Ridge impossible. Even if the Canadians planned a breakthrough (and the weather allowed), there still was the *Stellung III* blocking the way. The situation on the afternoon of April 9 was not that the Canadians had taken Vimy Ridge and the way east was open to them. Instead, in reality, the Germans fleeing east were making for their next defensive line; the *Stellung III.*

If the Canadians had planned to turn Vimy Ridge into a breakthrough, they would have to bring up their artillery to support an attack on the *Stellung III*; a slow and diffi-cult operation in the Great War under ideal weather conditions. There was time for the Germans to move reinforcements by road and rail to the *Stellung III* and prepare a strong defence.

First of all there was the *Stellung II* below the Ridge that had to be dealt with. While many Germans initially fled when the Canadians took the Ridge, many others did not, and we have already seen the casualties these remaining German soldiers caused to the Canadians, particularly in 3rd Division, after they captured the Ridge. By early evening the German reserve Battalions were being used to hold the *Stellung II.* In addition to this,

German reinforcements began arriving as early as mid-day on April 9, consisting of a Battalion each from the 56th Infantry Division and 80th Reserve Infantry Division.[607] Further reinforcements arrived as the day drew on. Bearing in mind the firepower available in the Great War, it is highly unlikely that the Canadian infantry would have been successful immediately rushing the *Stellung II* without the support of the artillery's creeping barrage.

Assuming ideal weather conditions, even if the artillery could have somehow been brought forward quickly and the Canadians attacked and captured the *Stellung II* late on the 9th, more German reinforcements were on the way. Throughout April 10 those divisions earmarked as counter-attack divisions before the Battle were arriving and were being used to garrison the *Stellung III* and reinforce the *Stellung II*.[608] Therefore, already on April 10 (if not before), the *Stellung III* was gaining strength.

By the time the Canadians would have got into a position to attack the *Stellung III*, they would have to make a set piece assault on it, much like they just did at Vimy Ridge. Even then, the Germans had a fall back position for the *Stellung III*; the *Wotan Stellung*.[609] Taking the *Stellung III* would still not lead to a breakthrough.

Making the potential for a breakthrough even more unrealistic were Canadian casualties. Thirty percent of the infantry involved in the Battle became casualties. The Canadian Corps had only one reserve Division, the 5th (British) Division, and it had already supplied one of its three brigades for 2nd Division's attack. It would be asking a lot for the Canadians to take the Ridge and the *Stellung II* on the 9th, with a further assault on the *Stellung III* in the days following.

To appreciate the Canadians' achievement, it must be seen in its proper context. There never was an intention to turn the Battle into a larger breakthrough. It was a limited, "bite and hold" operation, designed to capture the tactically important Vimy Ridge. In this, the Canadians were completely successful. In the event, it was sensible that the Canadians limited their planning to only attacking the Ridge. The weather, ground conditions and existence of the *Stellung III* to the east made any breakthrough impossible.

Twenty-Six

A Model Assault

In terms of attacks made during the years of trench warfare in the Great War, the Canadian assault at Vimy was a model for others to follow. It represented the successful application of all that had been learned in warfare on the Western Front to that date. The ostensibly "simple" frontal assault, was actually a complex affair.

Extensive use was made of aerial and ground observation and reconnaissance to inform the Canadians as to the defences they faced. With this knowledge, a comprehensive and effective artillery program was developed, including the preliminary bombardment, creeping barrage and counter-battery fire. Drawing on the same intelligence, the Canadian infantry practised their assault plans on accurate taped training grounds.

Since the artillery and infantry worked together prior to the Battle, the artillery was able to create a creeping barrage that conformed with the infantry's advance and the infantry was aware of how the barrage operated. With cooperation achieved, synchronization was realized by the officers synchronizing their watches. In a war in which the infantry was so dependant on the artillery to protect them, cooperation and synchronization with each other were important for any attack to succeed. When the attack came, the close work between the artillery and infantry were evident. The creeping barrage was accurate and well-timed, leading the infantry onto their objectives.

Important for allowing the infantry to follow the creeping barrage was the British and Canadian counter-battery work. Utilizing scientific techniques such as flash spotting and sound ranging to locate German artillery pieces before the Battle, the British and Canadian gunners effectively neutralized their German counterparts with high explosive and gas shells after zero-hour. With most of the German guns and gunners incapacitated, their defensive barrage was weak and seemingly erratic, failing to disrupt the Canadian infantry attack.

As much as the assault relied on accurate and well-timed shooting by the artillery, the shells could not kill all the German defenders. Once the barrage lifted, there would still be fighting to do. It was at this point that the role of the "intelligent soldier" became paramount. At Vimy Ridge, success ultimately depended on the smallest units in the army; the platoon, section and individual soldier. Thoroughly trained in their tasks and able to draw on a variety of weapons within the new platoon organization, the Canadians were able to successfully overcome all German defences on the Ridge, even when casualties were high. This says much for the morale and training of the individual Canadian soldier who, sometimes without his officers, took the initiative and completed his mission. In a war in which casualties, particularly to officers, were often severe, a flexible, heavily armed, tactical formation at the lowest level, along with a knowledgeable and motivated soldiery, were vital to success.

Canadian casualties were heavy, but they were heavy in any Great War operation. As dangerous as it was for the attacking Canadians, incurring one casualty for every three men engaged, the casualties were heavier for the defending Germans. While there were less Germans defending the Ridge than Canadians attacking (thus, overall, Canadian casualties were a bit higher than German), those who were manning their defences were overwhelmed by the Canadians, being either killed or captured.

Once the Ridge was taken, the Canadians quickly began consolidation, putting it into a defensible state. While the artillery had difficulty moving forward, the ground just to the east of Vimy Ridge was still within their range, allowing the Canadians a measure of protection while they dug in. In the event, the Germans withdrew further east and did not try to re-take Vimy Ridge, leaving it safely in Canadian hands. Success was complete. The sound and comprehensive planning, intensive training, close cooperation between artillery and infantry and effective use of the new counter-battery techniques and platoon organization were models for others to follow.

Part VI

Conclusion

One

Nivelle's Spring Offensive

Before discussing the larger significance of the Battle of Vimy Ridge, it is appropriate to first turn our attention briefly to how the Spring Offensive fared elsewhere. As already mentioned, the Canadian assault at Vimy Ridge was part of a larger British attack at Arras, undertaken by the Third Army under General Allenby, itself a diversion for a larger French offensive further south.

Like the Canadian attack on Vimy Ridge, the British assault at Arras was preceded by an intense preliminary bombardment and commenced at 5:30 a.m. on April 9. The ten British Divisions of General Allenby's Third Army went "over the top" on a ten mile front, attacking in wave formation, using the new platoon organization, supported by some tanks and following a creeping barrage. Bearing in mind that the Canadian Corps and Third Army held a continuous front, the whole area from Vimy Ridge to south of Arras erupted in battle at 5:30 a.m. on the 9th.

We have already seen in the Battle Narrative of Vimy Ridge that on the Canadians' right, the 51st (Highland) Division ran into problems, not reaching its final objective on the first day of battle. However, the Highlanders' difficulties were atypical of the Third Army's experience on the whole. Elsewhere, British success was spectacular as they penetrated the German defences to a depth of three and a half miles on April 9; the greatest advance by any combatant since the dawn of trench warfare. We saw earlier that the Canadians used leap-frog brigades to push their attack forward. The British did the same, but also used leap-frog divisions, giving them the manpower to advance over three miles into German territory. About 11 000 German soldiers were taken prisoner and 100 artillery pieces captured.[610] It was only in the far south and 51st (Highland) Division's sector in the north that success was incomplete, but this should not detract from the Third Army's achievement.

However, as the British soldiers consolidated their gains on the evening of the 9th, the weather turned against them. As was the Canadians' experience, the weather remained miserable for the next three days. With the ground torn by shellfire and now covered in wet snow, the British artillery could only be brought forward to assist the infantry with the greatest of effort. This inability to move the artillery would detrimentally affect subsequent British efforts at Arras.[611]

Attacks at Arras resumed on April 11, including a supporting assault further south at Bullecourt by the Australians in General Gough's Fifth Army. Without sufficient artillery support, the Australians' attack was a costly failure, while the British advance at Arras began to slow down. German reinforcements had arrived and, while some objectives were captured on the 11th, most remained in German hands. Fighting carried on at Arras into the 14th as Allenby ordered renewed efforts to push deeper into German lines. Like the attacks on April 11, artillery preparation and support was ineffective, the German defenders had recovered from their defeat on the 9th and the attacks resulted in failures.

One such costly failure involved the unfortunate Newfoundland Battalion. We saw earlier that this Battalion was destroyed on the first day of the Battle of the Somme. Rebuilt after that disastrous day, the Newfoundlanders with the 1st Essex Battalion attacked on April 14 and captured their objective, but were in a dangerous position. At the forefront of the British attack, but with no support behind them, they formed an island of British held ground within German territory. Taking advantage of this weakness, the Germans counter-attacked, surrounding the Newfoundlanders and 1st Essex and forced them to surrender. The Newfoundlanders lost 17 officers and 468 other ranks and the 1st Essex 17 officers and 585 other ranks; almost the entire force that went into the attack.[612]

Despite their reverses after the 9th, the British had achieved much with the operation at Arras. They had taken ground of tactical importance and had drawn in German reinforcements to stem further British assaults. Being a diversion, the operation's objectives had been achieved. With the French offensive set to commence any day, the attacks on the 14th should have ended the Battle of Arras as a major offensive. The Battle's objectives had been realized and further advances were losing momentum due to the inability to bring forward heavy artillery, poor weather and the arrival of German reinforcements.

As complete as success was for the Canadians at Vimy and as well as the British had done at Arras, the fate of the 1917 Spring Offensive rested on Nivelle's self proclaimed "war winning" attack on the Chemin des Dames. Sixty-eight French infantry divisions were assembled for the offensive, with 49 of these divisions earmarked for the main attack. The infantry were supported by 5 300 French artillery pieces, of which 1 900 were heavy calibres. It was the most formidable accumulation of artillery firepower the French had ever used to support an assault. The 1917 Spring Offensive would also see the French deploy

128 tanks, the first time they had used tanks in the War. In addition, five cavalry divisions were assembled to take advantage of any breakthrough.[613]

Nivelle's plan rested on three elements; surprise, overwhelming force and speed. Essentially, the French preliminary bombardment would pound the German positions into oblivion and on the day of the assault the infantry would rush forward through the German defences behind the protection of the artillery's creeping barrage. All divisions were exhorted by Nivelle to push on through the German lines in an all out effort until they had reached the end of their tether, rather than stopping to consolidate gains won and allow other formations to pass through to the next objective. Combining speed with surprise and brute force, Nivelle expected to breakthrough the German lines in 48 hours.[614]

Ostensibly the most powerful thrust of the Spring Offensive, its effectiveness was undercut in the days leading up to the April 16 attack. Nivelle's problems started early when the Germans retreated to the Hindenburg Line in mid-March. While no withdrawal occurred opposite the main offensive at the Chemin des Dames, the Germans did retreat away from the French diversionary attack on the River Oise, leaving devastation in their wake. It was impossible for the French to quickly re-organize their attack on this shattered ground, so the diversion was cancelled. Not only did the German's withdrawal lead to the abandonment of the French diversionary attack, but it also freed reserves to deal with the main attack at the Chemin des Dames.

The Germans also knew the French were coming. The French were sloppy in keeping their upcoming attack a secret and much of the blame for this rests with Nivelle himself. Nivelle spoke openly about the upcoming attack to the extent that it was common knowledge in the French government and press where and when their Army would strike.[615] In addition to obtaining information generated from Nivelle's "loose lips," the Germans gained intelligence from captured sources. Prior to the French offensive the Germans conducted raids on French lines which resulted in the capture of key documents, including some French battle plans.[616] Unlike at Vimy, there would be no tactical surprise attack by the French on the Chemin des Dames; the Germans were ready for it.

The French opened their offensive with a massive 14 day preliminary artillery bombardment. However, while the German first line was shattered by shellfire, the further into German held territory, the less effective the bombardment was. Nivelle's offensive was suffering from similar problems encountered by Haig on the Somme. French objectives were too ambitious, over-stretching the artillery. Although the artillery could smash the German forward positions, there were not enough guns to comprehensively destroy the entire German defensive system. The problem was made worse for the French because the Germans were using their new flexible defence in depth at the Chemin des Dames. Bearing this in mind, those forward defensive positions that the French artillery destroyed were only lightly garrisoned, with the main defence situated further back, remaining operational.

So fixated was Nivelle on the simplicity of his plan that he failed to heed factors that militated against success. One of these factors was the terrain. The Chemin des Dames was not an ideal location for a large scale attack. It was a long ridge about 200 yards high, steep on the side facing the French, and consisting of slopes, plateaux, thickets and woods; all ideal natural features for the Germans to take advantage of for defence. It was also fronted by the Aisne River. On the French left their line was to the east of the river with it to their backs, but on the French right they were facing the river and would have to cross it in their assault. To add to the difficulties on the French right, the ground leading to the Chemin des Dames from the Aisne River was flat and marshy; difficult terrain for attackers to pass through. Therefore, even though the French creeping barrage would advance at a similar rate as that used by the Canadians and British, the terrain of the Chemin des Dames, coupled with the poor weather and broken ground, made maintaining speed very difficult.[617]

Nivelle was untroubled by any potential difficulties that might stand in his way. There were, however, reservations expressed by others within the French Army as to the soundness of Nivelle's plan. One of the most influential voices, General Henri Petain the hero of Verdun, believed that Nivelle was overly optimistic in what he sought to achieve. While the German positions could be taken, Petain was of the opinion that it should be done by limited "bite and hold" attacks, rather than by undefined, unlimited and unsupported thrusts into German held territory.[618]

Even the commander of the upcoming assault, General Micheler, was sceptical of success. He feared that the recent German retreat to the Hindenburg Line freed German reserves to deal with the French offensive. Micheler also noticed that the Germans had been fortifying the area around the Chemin des Dames, a fact that did not influence Nivelle to change his plans.[619]

These doubts within the French Army were such that the French Minister of War, Paul Painleve, summoned a council of war attended by the senior French generals, including Nivelle. Faced with the doubts of his fellow generals, Nivelle threatened to resign if he did not get his way. The French government, reluctant to replace Nivelle so soon after he assumed command, relented to his threat, although did gain the concession from Nivelle that if the attack did not succeed within 48 hours, he would not persist and perpetuate failure.[620]

The infantry assault, twice postponed on account of heavy rains, proceeded on April 16. It began at 6:00 a.m. in weather that was cloudy and foggy with the ground wet from the previous night's rain. Almost immediately the French soldiers ran into trouble. The ground, muddy and shell-torn, was difficult to tread and made all the more so on the

Chemin des Dames by the uphill climb through broken wire obstacles. Speed was impossible to maintain. The French advanced slowly, picking their way through the German first line, purposely defended lightly by the Germans. Following the capture of the first line, the French infantry crested the Chemin des Dames, passed from view from the French lines and headed towards the German second line.

It was at the second line, the Germans' battle zone, that the French attack was crushed. Defended in more strength than the first line, it was protected by machine gun posts located in fortified positions, shell holes and the entrances to dug-outs and caves (with some machine gun posts hidden underground to "pop up" amongst the French). Protected from the preliminary bombardment by deep caves, dugouts and galleries, and expecting a French assault, the machine gunners were plentiful and on the alert. The French attack became held up, particularly in places where the German barbed wire remained uncut. Casualties steadily mounted.

With the French infantry checked before the German second line, the artillery fire plan fell apart. Pinned down before German machine guns, the infantry could only look on hopelessly as the creeping barrage moved ahead. Adding to French difficulties was that German reserve formations, located beyond the range of the French artillery and thus safe from the preliminary bombardment, began to move forward to engage the French on the second line.

As the battle developed on the German second line, French supporting troops, expecting to easily follow the leading units through the German defences, instead encountered resistance on the second line and added their bodies to those already collecting on the Chemin des Dames. Dangerously, further supporting troops also began to clog up the French front lines, waiting for their turn to move up. Probably the only fortuitous event for the French on this day, the German artillery did not take advantage of the target presented by these French soldiers crammed together in their front-line.

By the end of the day it became clear that Nivelle's great offensive had utterly failed. All along the Chemin des Dames lay dead and wounded French soldiers, not far from where their assault had originated. Rather than sweeping through the German defences, the German battle zone halted French progress. Where there was penetration into the German second line, most of these gains were subsequently lost in German counter-attacks. The "war winning" offensive fell far short of what was anticipated by Nivelle prior to the Battle.

Two

Consequences of Failure

Contrary to his promise made at the council of war before the Spring Offensive, Nivelle decided to continue the struggle on the Chemin des Dames. This, in spite of the weather, which remained wet, hampering the effectiveness of the French artillery. The attack turned into small, but fierce, struggles for communication trenches and individual strong points, a far cry from the dramatic advance envisioned before the battle. The weather, poor state of the ground and stiff German resistance and counter-attacks made any breakthrough impossible. Nevertheless, Nivelle persisted.

It was only on April 20 that General Nivelle called a halt to the Offensive, after the French had suffered about 130 000 casualties.[621] With their hopes raised before the Battle to expect a stunning success, the French soldiers' spirits correspondingly sunk once it was realized that there would be no breakthrough. The high casualties, poor weather, difficulties bringing food and supplies to the front and inability of the French medical service to adequately deal with the wounded, lead to a breakdown in French morale. After years of suffering through failed French offensives and being promised by their commander that it would not happen again, the 1917 Spring Offensive was the "straw that broke the camel's back."

The French Army mutinied. Largely involving those infantry soldiers who had taken part in the Spring Offensive, the men objected to further wasteful bloodshed. It was not a violent or co-ordinated revolt, and it may be inaccurate to call it a mutiny at all. Rather, it was more like collective indiscipline. Beginning on April 17, with peaks in May/June and ending in the autumn, about half of the French Army was affected with this indiscipline.

Soldiers refused to go to the front, made angry demonstrations and occasionally committed acts of vandalism. It was a statement against the French Army. Not really politically motivated (although some did exhort their comrades to form soldiers' soviets), it was more a protest against the soldiers' situation. Unlike the BEF, in the French Army leave was irregular, the food was poor and the medical service inadequate. The men wanted better living conditions, regular leave, better treatment for soldiers' families and an end to wasteful offensives. There were some demands that peace be made but, by in large, the soldiers were still willing to defend France, just not willing to make further pointless sacrifices on the German side of No Man's Land.

Interestingly, there were virtually no acts of violence against the French officers, although one French general was shouted at, had stones thrown at him and his rank badges ripped off his uniform.[622] Among the junior officers in particular, there was sympathy for the plight of the other ranks, with the soldiers' anger more directed towards the French High Command. In many cases, the junior officers tried to act as intermediaries between the soldiers and their generals.

As the French Army's morale crumbled, General Nivelle's star faded. The French president, Poincare, forbid Nivelle from launching any further attacks on the Chemin des Dames.[623] Despite this, Nivelle was still hoping to continue with the offensive in May, but there was resistance to renewed attacks within the French High Command as well. The commander of the offensive, General Micheler, advised against any further large scale actions on the grounds of lack of fresh units and ammunition and the strength of the German defences in the area.[624]

Wary of Nivelle's future plans, the French government appointed General Petain, the antithesis of Nivelle, as his chief of staff. Soon after Nivelle was asked to resign, but he refused. Finally, on May 15, Nivelle was relieved of his command with Petain appointed in his place. Even then Nivelle refused to leave and following some acrimonious encounters, he finally departed on May 19.[625] Initially, Nivelle was posted to command the northern group of Armies, but he did not last long there as Petain soon placed him on the inactive list. It was not until December of 1917 that Nivelle received a new command, in North Africa, far away from the Western Front where he could do no damage.[626]

It was left to General Petain to sort out the mess that Nivelle had left the French Army in. Fortunately for the French soldiers, Petain was sympathetic to the plight of his men and cautious in battle. There were to be no more large scale offensives until the American Army arrived in force.

Petain was also firm, but reasonable, in how he handled the mutiny. In terms of punishment, some soldiers were arrested with 499 sentenced to death by court-martial. Of these, only 27 were actually executed. The rest joined the approximately 3 000 who were sentenced to forced labor (for periods varying from one year to life) or to prison (for terms from 15 days to 15 years).[627]

Punishment was not Petain's only response to the mutiny as he made changes within the French Army to accommodate the soldiers' demands. Incompetent officers were removed, all officers were reminded of their obligations towards the welfare of their men, front line conditions were improved, better food provided and leave was made regular (7 to 10 days leave every four months).[628] These measures ensured that discipline returned to the French Army and it was able to function for the rest of the War.

The immediate result of the mutiny for the British was that, against their wishes, the offensive at Arras had to continue. Pressure had to be maintained on the Germans to divert attention from Britain's wounded ally. What resulted were two further major offensives by the British on April 23 and May 3 at Arras. The objectives for these offensives were more limited than those of April 9, but the returns were much less.

Fresh German reserves had arrived on the Arras battlefield to counter the tired British divisions. This, along with insufficient British artillery support, hasty planning and the lack of any element of surprise, lead to the two major attacks at Arras failing to achieve their objectives by and large. Nevertheless, some satisfaction could be taken in that German attention was drawn away from the French. On the First Army front, the Canadian Corps was engaged and secured two of the rare successes; taking Arleux on April 28 and Fresnoy in early May. With heavy fighting dying down at Arras, the Battle officially ended on May 17. British casualties totalled about 150 000 and German 120 000.

Looking beyond the Spring Offensive, the Offensive and its resultant mutiny had a lasting effect on the French Army and how the French contributed to the fighting for remainder of the War. It marked a turning point in the War, at least to the extent of how it was prosecuted on the Allied side. Prior to the spring of 1917, the main burden of fighting lay on the French. Following Arras and the Chemin des Dames this would change. It would be the BEF that shouldered the burden for the rest of the War, even with the appointment of the French Field Marshal Ferdinand Foch as Allied Commander-in-Chief in 1918, and the arrival of the American Army.

Three

A Building Block for Success

What then of Vimy? It was the "shining star" of the 1917 Spring Offensive. However, what lasting impact could a tactical success have within a larger strategic disaster?

The most immediate impact of the Battle was that it demonstrated the effective application of all the BEF had learned in trench warfare to date. The cooperation between infantry and artillery, the comprehensive artillery program, realistic infantry training and effective use of the new platoon organization were models for others to follow. The Battle was the first completely successful offensive operation up to that point in the War and was celebrated as such at the time.

This is not to say that Vimy Ridge was the apex of Great War battle tactics. Instead, it provided a strong base for future improvements. We have already seen how the preliminary artillery bombardment put the Germans on notice that an offensive was coming. It also shattered the ground so badly that it was difficult for the infantry to advance and almost impossible for the gunners to pull their artillery pieces through the mud. Had the Battle been planned as a breakthrough, it is likely that the Canadians would have had to stop at the Ridge in any event, so hard was forward movement. Indeed, after the Battle First Army's commander, General Horne, was of the view that, due to the extensive artillery preparation now employed by the BEF, the actual assault was the easier part of an operation, with the advance through the battlefield to take on the next German position being the most problematic.[629]

By late 1917, the BEF was in a position to deal with this problem. The artillery had developed methods to calibrate their guns behind the lines and to pre-register their guns by shooting off map references. This dispensed with the need to calibrate the guns and register shots on a target before a battle through aerial and ground observation. Not only did this allow the BEF to prevent disclosing their guns before an attack, it also lead to a reduction in scale of the preliminary bombardment. No longer would the Germans be given a week or more to realize that an attack was coming. Instead, the artillery would open fire at zero-hour, taking the Germans by complete surprise and the infantry could advance over a battlefield less destroyed than that encountered at Vimy Ridge.[630]

There would be changes to the platoon organization too. By 1918, instead of a rifle, rifle-grenade, Mills bomb and Lewis Gun section, there would be two sections of rifles/rifle-grenadiers and two based around Lewis Guns.[631] These changes retained the flexibility of the 1917 version, but increased the platoon's fire-power.

An important element of Canadian success was the close cooperation between the artillery and infantry. Not only would this cooperation be maintained for the rest of the War, but tanks and ground attack aircraft were added to the mix. By 1918 the BEF engaged in an all-arms battle, relying on the close cooperation of infantry, artillery, tanks and aircraft. It was a formula that the Germans did not achieve in their own offensives and could not repel when they were attacked.

Seen in this light, the Battle of Vimy Ridge was an important "building block" for the BEF on the Western Front. Drawing on past experience, the British and Canadians devised an effective plan for overcoming, what was thought to be, an impossible Ridge. Having demonstrated the effectiveness of their methods in the Battle, how the Canadian Corps won their victory became a model for future operations within the BEF. Upon this were added new developments as the War went on, ultimately leading to the successful all-arms offensives that won the War.

Four

An Elite Corps

If the importance of Vimy Ridge relied solely on tactical innovations, one may be forgiven for thinking that this is not enough to distinguish it from other battles. As we have seen, the British Third Army was very successful in the opening of the Battle of Arras, using similar methods as the Canadians did at Vimy. Part of Vimy Ridge's significance lay in the effect the victory had on the Canadian Corps itself.

Vimy Ridge was the first battle in which all Canadian Divisions fought together. Soon after the Battle, General Julian Byng was promoted to command Third Army, while a Canadian, General Arthur Currie, took over the Canadian Corps. By summer 1917, Canadians were at all levels of the Corps' command.

Following Vimy, the Canadian Corps went from victory to victory. In August of 1917, the Canadians successfully fought the Battle of Lens, a diversion for the larger Battle of Third Ypres (also known as Passchendaele) taking place at the same time in Belgian Flanders. The Passchendaele Battle was a drawn out, bloody affair, and by the autumn of 1917 it was the Canadians' turn to take part in the offensive. Despite appallingly muddy conditions (worse than at Vimy), the Canadians succeeded in capturing the Village of Passchendaele in November and ending the Battle.

In 1918, the Canadian Corps played a key role in the offensives that won the War in the summer and fall of that year. At Amiens in August the Canadians, with the Australians and supported by the mass deployment of British tanks, spear-headed a devastating surprise assault on the Germans, helping to turn the tide of the War. From there the Canadians took on the vaunted Hindenburg Line. Breaking through its northern end near Arras in a series of successful battles from late August to early October 1918, they effectively outflanked the entire Line, while Australian and British forces pushed through the Line to the south, as the French and Americans kept pressure on the Germans south of the BEF. The Corps ended the War in Mons, Belgium, the very place the BEF fought its first battle in 1914.

The Canadian Corps was an elite formation; second to none in the Great War, indeed, in any war. With all four Canadian Divisions fighting together from the beginning of 1917 until the end of the War, an *espirit de corps* developed, as the soldiers took pride in their accomplishments and those of the Corps. As important, the permanent structure of the Canadian Corps allowed the creation of a highly effective fighting force from the top down. While British divisions were transferred from corps to corps, the Canadian Divisions always fought together. With central authority resting in General Currie, the permanent composition of the Corps greatly facilitated the exchange of knowledge and expertise among all the Canadian units. This, with a constant focus on training, placed the Canadians always on the "cutting edge" in terms of battle skills.

That matters developed this way points back to the Battle of Vimy Ridge. We have already seen that both the Germans and the French considered the capture of the Ridge to be an impossibility. A point of pride for the Canadians after the Battle was that they had accomplished what others believed could not be done. Since for the remainder of the War the Canadian Corps was stationed around Vimy Ridge (with notable exceptions such as the Battles of Passchendaele and Amiens), the Ridge was a visible symbol of this pride; both for veterans of the Battle and new recruits who had not been there.

Vimy set a high standard for subsequent Canadian operations. The Canadians built on this bedrock of impossible victory, going from success to success, all the while improving their skills and increasing their morale. Had Vimy Ridge not been captured, it is questionable whether the Canadian Corps would have developed as it did. Success breeds confidence and further success, and this appears to have been particularly true with the Canadians in the Great War.

Seen in this light, the Battle of Vimy Ridge was a turning point for the Canadian military in the Great War. While the Canadians had performed well in the fighting of 1915-1916, Vimy Ridge was the springboard for later accomplishments. The Canadians went from a group of four good Divisions to a powerful, elite, assault Corps that contributed greatly to Allied victory.

Five

Canadian National Identity

Effectively entering the Great War as a British colony, without any say in foreign policy and seen by the outside world as only one part of Britain's vast Empire, Canada emerged from the War as a nation of its own on the world stage. The Great War was the defining moment for Canada as a nation separate from the Empire. That this transformation took place owes much to the Canadian Corps.

Although in terms of military organization the Canadian Corps was only a corps within a much larger BEF, to Canadians it became a *de facto* national army. This nationalistic element influenced how and when the Canadians deployed for battle after Vimy Ridge.

For example, when the Canadians moved to Passchendaele in October of 1917 to take part in that Battle, General Currie did so, but with the express reservation that the Corps not serve under General Gough, commander of Fifth Army. The Canadians, much like other Dominion troops such as the Australians, lost confidence in Gough and did not want to waste lives under his command. Not only did Currie receive his request, but Haig also allowed him to plan and execute the attack on Passchendaele on his terms.

The most extreme test to the idea of the Canadian Corps being a national army came in the spring of 1918. At this time the Germans had launched a massive offensive aimed at the BEF in the hope of winning the War. The attacks placed great pressure on the BEF and Haig wanted to break up the Canadian Corps, using the individual Canadian Divisions to plug gaps in the British line. Currie refused to allow this, believing that the Canadians fought best when together. While this caused some strain in Currie's relationship with Haig at the time, Haig relented and the Corps was not broken up.

That the British held the Canadians in high regard and took their suggestions seriously has much to do with the performance of the Canadian Corps on the battlefield. If the Canadians were not as successful on the battlefield as they were, it is questionable whether Currie would have had as much influence as he did. A defeated general leading a weak force does not garner much respect. For Haig and the British High Command the Canadian Corps was a valuable asset and they were willing to accede to Currie's requests.

At the same time, the pride that the soldiers felt in the Canadian Corps was reflected in Canadian society. Although the Corps had become a professional fighting force, it was still a citizen's army, drawn almost entirely from civilian ranks. There were few back in Canada who did not know someone serving overseas. The natural affection the people of Canada had for their soldiers was reinforced with pride as the Corps went from victory to victory in 1917-1918. It could be seen what Canadians could accomplish on the world stage. Although for some it is an uncomfortable truth, the Canadian Corps played a major role in Canadian nation building.

This shared experience distinguishes the Great War from other events in Canada's history (with some notable exceptions, such as the Depression and Second World War). Canada as a nation was directly involved on a daily basis in the War. Be it soldiers at the front, workers in the war effort (male and female) or family and friends anxiously waiting at home for loved ones, virtually all Canadians had a stake in the Great War.

Tying these threads together, by November 11, 1918, the Canadian Corps had proved itself as an elite force. Their string of victories gave confidence to those within the Corps and brought respect from their British comrades. Back home, the Canadian public looked on with pride at what "their boys" had achieved in the greatest crisis the world had yet faced. These are powerful emotions and, more importantly, were backed up by actions.

Drawing on this impressive performance, the Canadians were able to assert themselves, taking greater control of their troops as the War went on. By the end of the War, it was felt that the Canadians deserved to be seen as a nation on their own; separate from the larger British Empire. This was accomplished as the British and Americans acceded to the Canadians' request to have their own seat at the Paris Peace Conference and in the League of Nations. Canada was a nation and would control its own destiny from that time forward.

Once again, the Battle of Vimy Ridge was the springboard. It was the first time that the Canadians had all served together. The Canadians demonstrated what they could do when they captured the impossible Ridge. From Vimy, the Canadian Corps and Canada as a nation, took the path toward true nationhood.

Six

The Battle of Vimy Ridge

There are layers of significance to the Battle of Vimy Ridge. There is the long term impact the Battle had in developing a Canadian national identity on the world stage, but also immediate effects on how the BEF would conduct future offensives on the Western Front. In between, the Battle was the bedrock for the development of the Canadian Corps into a premiere fighting formation.

The Battle of Vimy Ridge would not have had such influence had it not been a complete success under difficult circumstances. The Ridge was seen by both the Germans and the French as an impregnable position, the most difficult to attack on the Western Front. Two French offensives in 1915 had failed to capture the Ridge, both suffering heavy casualties.

Relevant too was the Allies' experience on the offensive prior to 1917. Attacks in the early years of the War were bedevilled by a lack of sufficient weapons and ammunition, resulting in assault after assault failing before the devastating firepower available to the defence. By 1916, weapons and ammunition were available in the necessary quantities, but the experience in using them was lacking. Thus, during the Battle of the Somme mistakes were made, leading to a Battle characterized by inconsistency in methods and results. Nevertheless, the British and Canadians were learning and were intent on improving their performance in the future.

In the spring of 1917 at Vimy Ridge, the Canadians demonstrated what could be done. Honing their skills during the Winter of 1917, they devised an effective assault plan for taking the impossible Ridge. Drawing on developments from the Battle of the Somme, such as the creeping barrage and powerful new platoon organization, and basing their plan on prior observation and intelligence, the Canadian Corps created an efficient offensive scheme.

Key to Canadian success was the cooperation between artillery and infantry. The artillery comprehensively destroyed German defences during the preliminary bombardment and formulated a barrage that effectively supported the infantry during their advance. As for the infantry, training was realistic, focussing on potential problems that might be encountered, with emphasis on utilizing the weapons at the soldiers' immediate disposal and keeping to the artillery barrage. At the heart of this training was the "intelligent soldier"; aware of what was expected of him, how the attack would operate, the means at his disposal and how he could accomplish his task. That the preparation was so thorough, and demonstrated to all ranks as being so, helped motivate the soldiers to complete the job when the day came to put all their practice into effect.

While not an easy Battle, for casualties were heavy and there were some moments of crisis, it was a complete victory, with Vimy Ridge being wholly in Canadian hands at the end of the Battle. That it turned out this way owed much to the pre-Battle planning and training, along with skilful execution, demonstrating that an offensive could be successful on the Western Front. While not glamorous, the Canadians' methods were intelligent and effective. It was "sophisticated simplicity."

The Battle, and the methods employed for victory at Vimy, were stepping stones, leading to the all-arms offensives that won the Great War, the development of the Canadian Corps as an elite formation and, from this development, a new sense of Canadian nationhood.

Bibliography

Adamson, Agar, *The Letters of Agar Adamson*, (Nepean: CEF Books) (1997).

Astore, William J. and Showalter, Dennis E., *Hindenburg: Icon of German Militarism*, (Dulles: Potomac Books, Inc.) (2005).

Bagnall, Fred, *Not Mentioned in Despatches*, (Ottawa: CEF Books) (2005).

Barker, Ralph, *The Royal Flying Corps in World War I*, (London: Constable & Robinson Ltd.) (2002).

Barron Norris, Marjorie (ed), *Medicine and Duty: The World War I Memoir of Captain Harold W. McGill, Medical Officer, 31st Battalion C.E.F.*, (Calgary: University of Calgary Press) (2007).

Barton, Peter, Doyle, Peter and Vandewalle, Johan, *Beneath Flanders Fields: The Tunnellers' War 1914-18*, (Montreal: McGill-Queen's University Press) (2004).

Beattie, Kim, *48th Highlanders of Canada*, (Toronto: Southam Press Toronto Limited) (1932).

Beckett, Ian F.W. and Corvi, Steven J. (eds.), *Haig's Generals*, (Barnsley: Pen & Sword Books Ltd.) (2006).

Bennett, S.G., *The 4th Canadian Mounted Rifles 1914-1919*, (Toronto: Murray Printing Company Limited) (1926).

Beresford Topp, C., *The 42nd Battalion CEF Royal Highlanders of Canada*, (Montreal: Gaxette Printing Co., Limited) (1931).

Berton, Pierre, *Marching as to War: Canada's Turbulent Years 1899-1953*, (Doubleday Canada) (2001).

Berton, Pierre, *Vimy*, (Anchor Canada) (1986).

Bidwell, Shelford & Graham, Dominick, *Fire-Power: The British Army Weapons & Theories of War 1904-1945*, (Barnsley: Pen & Sword Books Limited) (2004).

Bird, William R., *Ghosts Have Warm Hands*, (Ottawa: CEF Books).

Bishop, William Avery, *Winged Warfare*, (Manchester: Crecy Publishing) (2002).

Black, Ernest G., *I Want One Volunteer*, (Toronto: The Ryerson Press) (1965).

Bond, Brian and Cave, Nigel (eds.), *Haig: A Reappraisal 70 Years On*, (Barnsley: Pen & Sword Books Ltd.) (1999).

Brown, Malcolm, *1918: Year of Victory*, (London: Pan Macmillan Ltd.) (1999).

Brown, Malcolm, *The Somme*, (London: Pan Macmillan Ltd.) (2002).

Brown, Malcolm, *The Western Front*, (London: Pan Macmillan Ltd.) (2001).

Brown, Malcolm, *Verdun 1916,* (Stroud: Tempus Publishing Limited) (2003).

Buffetaut, Yves, *The 1917 Spring Offensives,* (Paris: Histoire & Collections) (1997).

Burns, E.L.M., *General Mud,* (Toronto: Clarke, Irwin & Company Limited) (1970).

Canadian Broadcasting Corporation, *Flanders' Fields,* (DVD Series).

Cassar, George H., *Kitchener's War: British Strategy from 1914 to 1916,* (Dulles: Brassey's, Inc.) (2004).

Cave, Nigel, *Vimy Ridge,* (Barnsley: Pen & Sword Books Limited) (1996).

Clayton, Anthony, *Paths of Glory: The French Army 1914-18,* (London: Cassell) (2003).

Cobb, Paul, *Fromelles: 1916,* (Stroud: Tempus Publishing Limited) (2007).

Cook, Tim, *At the Sharp End: Canadians Fighting the Great War 1914-1916,* (Toronto: Viking Canada) (2007).

Corrigall, D.J., *The History of the Twentieth Canadian Battalion,* (Toronto: Stone & Cox Limited) (1935).

Corrigan, Gordon, *Mud, Blood and Poppycock,* (London: Cassell) (2003).

Cowley, Deborah (ed.), *Georges Vanier: Soldier, The Wartime Letters and Diaries, 1915-19,* (Toronto: Dundurn Press) (2000).

Dancocks, Daniel G., *Gallant Canadians: The Story of the Tenth Canadian Infantry Battalion 1914-1919,* (Calgary: The Calgary Highlanders Regimental Funds Foundation) (1990).

Davies, Frank and Maddocks, Graham, *Bloody Red Tabs: General Officer Casualties of the Great War, 1914-1918,* (London: Leo Cooper) (1995).

Dempsey, James L., *Warriors of the King,* (Regina: Canadian Plains Research Center) (1999).

Diary of the Eleventh: Being a Record of the XIth Canadian Field Ambulance (publisher not indicated).

Dieterich, Alfred, "The German 79th Reserve Infantry Division in the Battle of Vimy Ridge, April 1917", *Canadian Military History,* Vol. 15 No. 1 pages 69-85.

Dixon, John, *Magnificent But Not War: The Second Battle of Ypres 1915,* (Barnsley: Pen & Sword Books Limited) (2003).

Doughty, Robert A., *Pyrrhic Victory: French Strategy and Operations in the Great War,* (Cambridge: The Belknap Press of Harvard University Press) (2005).

Duffy, Christopher, *through German eyes: the British & the Somme 1916,* (London: Weidenfeld & Nicolson) (2006).

Ellis, John, *Eye-Deep in Hell,* (Baltimore: The Johns Hopkins University Press) (1989).

Facey-Crowther, David R. (ed.), *Lieutenant Owen William Steele of the Newfoundland Regiment,* (Montreal & Kingston: McGill-Queen's University Press) (2002).

Farr, Don, *The Silent General: Horne of the First Army,* (Solihull: Helion & Company Limited) (2007).

Fetherstonaugh, R.C., *The 13th Battalion Royal Highlanders of Canada 1914-1919,* (The 13th Battalion, Royal Highlanders of Canada) (1925).

Fetherstonaugh, R.C., *The 24th Battalion, CEF, Victoria Rifles of Canada 1914-1919,* (Montreal: Gazette Printing Company) (1930).

Fetherstonaugh, R.C., *The Royal Canadian Regiment 1883-1933,* (Fredericton: Centennial Print & Litho Ltd.) (1981).

Fetherstonaugh, R.C., *The Royal Montreal Regiment,* (Montreal: The Gazette Printing Co. Limited) (1927).

Fortescue Duguid, A., *History of the Canadian Grenadier Guards,* (Montreal: Gazette Printing Company (Limited)) (1965).

Foster, Charles Lyons and Duthie, William Smith (eds.), *Letters from the Front Vol. 1* (CIBC) (1920).

Fraser, Donald, *The Journal of Private Fraser,* (Nepean: CEF Books) (1998).

Freeman, Bill and Nielsen, Richard, *Far From Home,* (Toronto: McGraw-Hill Ryerson) (1999).

Fromkin, David, *Europe's Last Summer,* (New York: Vintage Books) (2005).

Gagne, Lucie E., *Pounding the Enemy: Diary of the 13th Battery, C.F.A. 1914-1918,* (Ottawa: CEF Books) (2006).

Gilbert, Martin, *The Battle of the Somme,* (Toronto: McClelland & Stewart Ltd.) (2006).

Girardet, Jean-Marie, Jacques, Alain and Duclos, Jean-Luc Letho, *Somewhere on the Western Front,* (Arras: Documents d' Archeologie et d' Histoire du XX Siecle – No. 8) (2003).

Goodspeed, D.J., *Battle Royal: A History of the Royal Regiment of Canada 1862-1962,* (The Royal Regiment of Canada Association) (1962).

Grafton, C.S., *The Canadian "Emma Gees",* (London: Hunter Printing Company) (1938).

Granatstein, J.L., *Canada's Army,* (Toronto: University of Toronto Press) (2002).

Granatstein, J.L. and Morton, Desmond, *Canada and the Two World Wars,* (Toronto: Key Porter Books Limited) (2003).

Granatstein, J.L., *Hell's Corner,* (Vancouver: Douglas & McIntyre Ltd.) (2004).

Greenfield, Nathan M., *Baptism of Fire: The Second Battle of Ypres and the Forging of Canada, April 1915,* (Toronto: HarperCollins Publishers Ltd.) (2007).

Grescoe, Audrey and Paul (eds.), *The Book of War Letters,* (Toronto: McClelland & Stewart Ltd.) (2003).

Griffith, Paddy, *Battle Tactics of the Western Front: The British Army's Art of Attack 1916-18,* (New Haven: Yale University Press) (1994).

Griffith, Paddy, *Fortifications of the Western Front,* (Oxford: Osprey Publishing Ltd.) (2004).

Groom, Winston, *A Storm in Flanders,* (New York: Atlantic Monthly Press) (2002).

Gudmundsson, Bruce I., *Stormtroop Tactics: Innovation in the German Army, 1914-1918,* (Westport: Praeger Publishers) (1989).

Hamilton, Richard F. and Herwig, Holger H., *Decisions for War, 1914-1917,* (Cambridge: Cambridge University Press) (2004).

Harris, J.P., *Amiens to the Armistice,* (London: Brassey's) (1998).

Hart, Peter, *Bloody April: Slaughter in the Skies over Arras, 1917,* (London: Cassell) (2006).

Hart, Peter, *The Somme,* (London: Weidenfeld & Nicolson) (2005).

Hayes, Joseph, *The Eighty-Fifth in France and Flanders,* (Halifax: Royal Print & Litho Limited) (1920).

Hewitt, G.E., *The Story of the Twenty-Eight (North-West) Battalion 1914-1917,* (London: Canadian War Records Office).

Hodder-Williams, Ralph, *Princess Patricia's Canadian Light Infantry,* (Toronto: Hodder and Stoughton Limited) (1923).

Holland, J.A., *The Story of the Tenth Canadian Battalion 1914-1917,* (London: Charles and Son).

Hogg, Ian, *Allied Artillery of World War One,* (Ramsbury: The Crowood Press Ltd.) (1999).

Holmes, Richard, *The Little Field Marshall: A Life of Sir John French,* (London: Cassell) (2005).

Horne, Alistair, *The Price of Glory: Verdun 1916,* (London: Penguin Books Ltd.) (1993).

Howard, Gordon S., *The Memoires of a Citizen Soldier 1914-1945,* (publisher not indicated).

Hull, Isabel V., *Absolute Destruction: Military Culture and the Practices of War in Imperial Germany,* (Ithaca: Cornell University Press) (2005).

Hyatt, A.M.J., *General Sir Arthur Currie: A Military Biography,* (Toronto: University of Toronto Press) (1987).

Ito, Roy, *We Went to War,* (Stittsville: Canada's Wings, Inc.) (1984).

Jager, Herbert, *German Artillery of World War One,* (Ramsbury: The Crowood Press Ltd.) (2001).

Johnston, James Robert, *Riding Into War,* (Fredericton: Goose Lane Editions) (2004).

Junger, Ernst, *Storm of Steel,* (New York: Penguin Books) (2003).

Keegan, John, *The Face of Battle,* (London: Pimlico) (1991).

Keegan, John, *The First World War,* (Toronto: Random House of Canada Limited) (2000).

Kerr, Wilfred, *Shrieks and Crashes,* (Ottawa: CEF Books) (2005).

Kitchen, Martin, *The German Offensives of 1918,* (Stroud: Tempus Publishing Limited) (2005).

Liddle, Peter H. (ed.), *Passchendaele in Perspective,* (Barnsley: Pen & Sword Books Ltd.) (1997).

Lee, John, *The Warlords: Hindenburg and Ludendorff,* (London: Weidenfeld & Nicolson) (2005).

Lewis, R., *Over the Top with the 25th,* (Halifax: H.H. Marshall, Limited) (1918).

Macdonald, Lyn, *1915: The Death of Innocence,* (London: Penguin Books Ltd.) (1997).

Macdonald, Lyn, *Somme,* (London: Penguin Books Ltd.) (1993).

Macdonald, Lyn, *They Called it Passchendaele,* (London: Penguin Books Ltd.) (1993).

Macintyre, D.E., *Canada at Vimy,* (Toronto: Peter Martin Associates Limited) (1967).

MacPherson, Donald Stuart, *A Soldier's Diary,* (St. Catherines: Vanwell Publishing Limited) (2001).

Mann, Susan (ed.), *The War Diary of Clare Gass 1915-1918,* (Montreal & Kingston: McGill-Queen's University Press) (2000).

Mathieson, William D., *My Grandfather's War,* (Toronto: MacMillan of Canada) (1981).

McClare, Dale (ed.), *The Letters of a Young Canadian Soldier During World War 1,* (Dartmouth: Brook House Press) (2000).

McEvoy, Bernard and Finlay, A.H., *History of the 72nd Canadian Infantry Battalion Seaforth Highlanders of Canada,* (Vancouver: Cowan & Brookhouse) (1920).

McKean, George B., *Scouting Thrills,* (Ottawa: CEF Books) (2007).

McLeod Gould, L., *From B.C. to Baisieux,* (Victoria: Thos. R. Cusack Presses) (1919).

McWilliams, James and Steel, R. James, *Amiens: Dawn of Victory,* (Toronto: Dundurn Press) (2001).

McWilliams J. and Steel, R.J., *Gas! The Battle for Ypres, 1915,* (St. Catharines: Vanwell Publishing Limited) (1985).

McWilliams, James L. and Steel, James R., *The Suicide Battalion,* (St. Catherines: Vanwell Publishing Limited) (1990).

Middlebrook, Martin, *The First Day on the Somme,* (London: Penguin Books Ltd.) (1971).

Murray, W.W., *The History of the 2nd Canadian Battalion,* (Ottawa: Mortimer Ltd.) (1947).

Lord Moran, *The Anatomy of Courage: The Classic WWI Account of the Psychological Effects of War,* (New York: Carroll & Graf Publishers) (2007).

Neiberg, Michael S., *Foch: Supreme Allied Commander in the Great War,* (Washington: Brassey's, Inc.) (2003).

Neiberg, Michael S., *The Second Battle of the Marne,* (Bloomington: Indiana University Press) (2008).

Neillands, Robin, *The Death of Glory,* (London: John Murray) (2006).

Nicholls, Jonathan, *Cheerful Sacrifice: The Battle of Arras 1917,* (Barnsley: Pen & Sword Books Limited) (2003).

Nicholson, G.W.L., *Canadian Expeditionary Force 1914-1919,* (Ottawa: Queen's Printer) (1964).

O'Brien, Jack, *Into the Jaws of Death,* (Cornwall: Diggory Press Ltd.) (2008).

Passingham, Ian, *All the Kaiser's Men: The Life and Death of the German Army on the Western Front 1914-1918,* (Stroud: Sutton Publishing Limited) (2003).

Passingham, Ian, *Pillars of Fire: The Battle of Messines Ridge June 1917,* (Stroud: Sutton Publishing Limited) (2004).

Pieroth, Doris H., *A Canadian's Road to Russia,* (Edmonton: The University of Alberta Press) (1989).

Pimm, Gordon, *Leo's War: From Gaspe to Vimy,* (Ottawa: Partnership Publishers) (2007).

Prior, Robin & Wilson, Trevor, *Command on the Western Front: The Military Career of Sir Henry Rawlinson 1914-1918,* (Barnsley: Pen & Sword Books Limited) (2004).

Prior, Robin & Wilson, Trevor, *Passchendaele: The Untold Story,* (New Haven: Yale University Press) (2002).

Prior, Robin & Wilson, Trevor, *The Somme,* (New Haven: Yale University Press) (2005).

Rawling, Bill, *Surviving Trench Warfare: Technology and the Canadian Corps, 1914-1918,* (Toronto: University of Toronto Press) (1992).

Robbins, Simon, *British Generalship on the Western Front 1914-1918: Defeat into Victory,* (Oxon: Routledge) (2005).

Robertshaw, Andrew, *Somme 1 July 1916: Tragedy and Triumph,* (Oxford: Osprey Publishing) (2006).

Rommel, Erwin, *Attacks,* (Provo: Athena Press, Inc.) (1979).

Schreiber, Shane B., *Shock Army of the British Empire: The Canadian Corps in the Last 100 Days of the Great War,* (St. Catherines: Vanwell Publishing Limited) (2004).

Scott Calder, D.G. (ed.), *The History of the 28th (Northwest) Battalion, CEF,* (publisher not indicated).

Scott, Frederick G., *The Great War As I Saw It,* (Ottawa: CEF Books) (2000).

Sheffield, Gary and Todman, Dan (eds.), *Command and Control on the Western Front: The British Army's Experience 1914-18,* (Staplehurst: Spellmount Limited) (2004).

Sheffield, Gary and Bourne, John (eds.), *Douglas Haig War Diaries and Letters 1914-1918,* (London: Weidenfeld & Nicolson) (2005).

Sheffield, Gary, *Forgotten Victory: The First World War: Myths and Realities,* (London: Headline Book Publishing) (2002).

Sheffield, Gary, *The Somme,* (London: Cassell) (2003).

Sheffield, Gary (ed.), *War on the Western Front: In the Trenches of World War I,* (Oxford: Osprey Publishing Ltd.) (2007).

Simkins, Peter, Jukes, Geoffrey & Hicky, Michael, *The First World War: The War to End All Wars,* (Oxford: Osprey Publishing) (2003).

Singer, Horace C., *History of the 31st Canadian Infantry Battalion C.E.F.,* (Calgary: Detselig Enterprises Ltd.) (2006).

Steel, Nigel and Hart, Peter, *Passchendaele: The Sacrificial Ground,* (London: Cassell & Co.) (2001).

Swanson, Victor N., *Who Said War is Hell!,* (Saskatoon: Modern Press) (1983).

Swettenham, John, *McNaughton Vol. 1 1887-1939,* (Toronto: The Ryerson Press) (1968).

Swettenham, John (ed.), *Valiant Men,* (Toronto: A.M. Hakkert Ltd.) (1983).

Terraine, John, *The Smoke and the Fire: Myths & Anti-Myths of War 1861-1945,* (Barnsley: Pen & Sword Books Limited) (1992).

Terraine, John, *To Win a War: 1918 The Year of Victory,* (London: Cassell & Co.) (2000).

The Canadian Images and Letters Project. (website)

Todman, Dan, *The Great War: Myth and Memory,* (London: Hambledon and London) (2005).

Travers, Tim, *How The War Was Won: Factors that Led to Victory in World War One,* (Barnsley: Pen & Sword Books Limited) (2005).

Travers, Tim, *The Killing Ground: The British Army, the Western Front & the Emergence of Modern War 1900-1918,* (Barnsley: Pen & Sword Books Limited) (2003).

Tuchman, Barbara W., *The Guns of August,* (New York: Ballantine Books) (1994).

Turner, Alexander, *Cambrai 1917: The birth of armoured warfare,* (Oxford: Osprey Publishing) (2007).

Turner, Alexander, *Vimy Ridge 1917: Byng's Canadians Triumph at Arras,* (Oxford: Osprey Publishing) (2005).

Urquhart, H.M., *The History of the 16th Battalion (The Canadian Scottish),* (Toronto: The MacMillan Company of Canada, Limited) (1932).

Walker, Jonathan, *The Blood Tub: General Gough and the Battle of Bullecourt, 1917,* (Staplehurst: Spellmount) (2000).

Walsh, Milly and Callan, John (eds.), *We're Not Dead Yet,* (St. Catharines: Vanwell Publishing Limited) (2004).

War Diaries of the Canadian Corps (National Archives of Canada) for the Winter of 1917, including: Corps, Corps Artillery, Divisions, Divisional Artilleries, Divisional Trench Mortar Groups, Divisional Engineers, Brigades, Field Artillery Brigades, Battalions, Machine Gun Companies, Field Companies CRE, Motor Machine Gun Brigade, Motor Machine Gun Batteries and Canadian Light Horse.

War Diaries of the Canadian Corps (National Archives of Canada) for the months of March and April 1917, including: First Army, Corps, Corps Artillery, Corps Heavy Artillery, Corps Chief Engineer, Corps Deputy Director Medical Services, Divisions, Divisional Artilleries, Divisional Trench Mortar Groups, Divisional Engineers, Brigades, Field Artillery Brigades, Garrison Artillery Brigades, Battalions, Siege and Heavy Batteries, Machine Gun Companies, Field Companies CRE, Motor Machine Gun Brigade, Motor Machine Gun Batteries and Canadian Light Horse.

Watson, Alexander, *Enduring the Great War: Combat, Morale and Collapse in the German and British Armies, 1914-1918,* (Cambridge: Cambridge University Press) (2008).

Weatherbe, K., *From the Rideau to the Rhine and Back,* (Toronto: The Hunter-Rose Co., Limited) (1928).

Wheeler, Victor W., *The 50th Battalion in No Man's Land,* (Ottawa: CEF Books) (2000).

Wiest, Andrew A., *Haig,* (Washington: Potomac Books, Inc.) (2005).

Williams, Jeffrey, *Byng of Vimy,* (London: Leo Cooper) (1983).

Zubkowski, Robert F., *As Long as Faith and Freedom Last,* (Calgary: Bunker to Bunker Books)(2003).

Zuckerman, Larry, *The Rape of Belgium: The Untold Story of World War 1,* (New York: New York University Press) (2004).

Endnotes

[1]G.W.L. Nicholson, *Canadian Expeditionary Force 1914-1919,* (Ottawa: Queen's Printer) (1964) at 523-524.

[2]Adv. Canadian Corps to 2nd Canadian Division dated March 30, 1917, attached to 26th Battalion April 1917 War Diary.

[3]Letter from Ernest Mosley Taylor to Annie (sister), March 24, 1916, The Canadian Letters and Images Project.

[4]Charles Henry Savage, Memoir, The Canadian Letters and Images Project.

[5]George B. McKean, *Scouting Thrills,* (Ottawa: CEF Books)(2007) at 16.

[6]Donald Fraser, *The Journal of Private Fraser,* (Nepean: CEF Books)(1998) at 55.

[7]The Journal of Private Fraser at 75-76.

[8]Gordon Corrigan, *Mud, Blood and Poppycock,* (London: Cassell) (2003) at 89.

[9]Letter from Ernest Mosley Taylor to Annie (sister), December 4, 1915.

[10]Bill Rawling, *Surviving Trench Warfare: Technology and the Canadian Corps, 1914-1918,* (Toronto: University of Toronto Press) (1992) at 50.

[11]Flanders' Fields, Chapter 6: A World of Stealth, CBC (DVD Series).

[12]The Journal of Private Fraser at 48.

[13]William R. Bird, *Ghosts Have Warm Hands,* (Ottawa: CEF Books) at 19.

[14]Charles Henry Savage, Memoir, The Canadian Letters and Images Project.

[15]Jack O'Brien, *Into the Jaws of Death,* (Cornwall: Diggory Press Ltd.) (2008) at 28.

[16]Ghosts Have Warm Hands at 13.

[17]Victor W. Wheeler, *The 50th Battalion in No Man's Land,* (Ottawa: CEF Books) (2000) at 57.

[18]The Journal of Private Fraser at 53.

[19]Charles Lyons Foster and William Smith Duthie (eds.), Letters from the Front Vol. 1 (CIBC) (1920) at 13.

[20]The 50th Battalion in No Man's Land at 60.

[21]Deborah Cowley (ed.), *Georges Vanier: Soldier, The Wartime Letters and Diaries, 1915-19,* (Toronto: Dundurn Press) (2000) at 83.

[22]Georges Vanier: Soldier, The Wartime Letters and Diaries, 1915-19, at 85.

[23]CBC, Baptism of Fire.

[24]Mud, Blood and Poppycock at 85-98.

[25]John Ellis, *Eye-Deep in Hell,* (Baltimore: The Johns Hopkins University Press) (1989) at 137-138.

[26]Mud, Blood and Poppycock at 96-97 and J.L. Granastein and Desmond Morton, *Canada and the Two World Wars,* (Toronto: Key Porter Books Limited)(2003) at 38.

[27]Gordon Pimm, *Leo's War: From Gaspe to Vimy,* (Ottawa: Partnership Publishers) (2007) at 102.

[28]The Journal of Private Fraser at 79.

[29]Agar Adamson, *The Letters of Agar Adamson,* (Nepean: CEF Books)(1997) at 59.

[30] Ian Hogg, *Allied Artillery of World War One,* (Ramsbury: The Crowood Press Ltd.) (1999) at 23-24.

[31]Mud, Blood and Poppycock at 121.

[32]The Journal of Private Fraser at 36-37.

[33]Letters from the Front at 146.

[34]Leo's War at 78.

[35]Paddy Griffith, *Battle Tactics of the Western Front: The British Army's Art of Attack 1916-18,* (New Haven: Yale University Press) (1994) at 136.

[36]Frederick G. Scott, *The Great War As I Saw It,* (Ottawa: CEF Books) (2000) at 33.

[37]Gary Sheffield, *Forgotten Victory: The First World War: Myths and Realities,* (London: Headline Book Publishing) (2002) at 110 and 111 and Battle Tactics of the Western Front at 137.

[38]Surviving Trench Warfare at 178.

[39]Battle Tactics of the Western Front at 135-137.

[40]The Journal of Private Fraser at 15-16.

[41]CBC, Apprentices at Arms.

[42]Alfred Andrews Diary, The Canadian Letters and Images Project.

[43]Letters of Agar Adamson at 63.

[44]Georges Vanier: Soldier The Wartime Letters and Diaries 1915-1919 at 67.

[45]CBC, Apprentices at Arms.

[46]Letters from the Front at 64.

[47]Gordon S. Howard, *The Memoires of a Citizen Soldier 1914-1945,* (publisher not indicated) at 13.

[48]Forgotten Victory at 111.

[49]Charles Henry Savage, Memoir, The Canadian Letters and Images Project.

[50]Surviving Trench Warfare at 178.

[51]Surviving Trench Warfare at 154.

[52]Mud, Blood and Poppycock at 129.

[53]Surviving Trench Warfare at 129.

[54]Mud, Blood and Poppycock at 129.

[55]Shelford Bidwell & Dominick Graham, *Fire-Power: The British Army Weapons & Theories of War 1904-1945,* (Barnsley: Pen & Sword Books Limited) (2004) at 28-29 and Mud, Blood and Poppycock at 129-131.

[56] Mud, Blood and Poppycock at 132.

[57] Surviving Trench Warfare at 72 and 124 and Battle Tactics of the Western Front at 130.

[58] Battle Tactics of the Western Front at 134 and Bruce I. Gudmundsson, *Stormtroop Tactics: Innovation in the German Army, 1914-1918,* (Westport: Praeger Publishers) (1989) at 148.

[59] Surviving Trench Warfare at 38.

[60] John P. Sudbury "Down Memory Lane"(1958-59), The Canadian Letters and Images Project.

[61] Forgotten Victory at 111.

[62] Mud, Blood and Poppycock at 115.

[63] Robert F. Zubkowski, *As Long as Faith and Freedom Last,* (Calgary: Bunker to Bunker Books)(2003) at 86.

[64] Surviving Trench Warfare at 65.

[65] The Journal of Private Fraser at 26.

[66] Eye-Deep in Hell at 77-78.

[67] Eye-Deep in Hell at 78.

[68] Surviving Trench Warfare at 57-58.

[69] Surviving Trench Warfare at 50-51.

[70] Battle Tactics of the Western Front at 115.

[71] Surviving Trench Warfare at 51.

[72] Charles Henry Savage, Memoir, The Canadian Letters and Images Project.

[73] The 50th Battalion in No Man's Land at 8-9.

[74] The 50th Battalion in No Man's Land at 56.

[75] Mud, Blood and Poppycock at 166-170.

[76] The 50th Battalion in No Man's Land at 108.

[77] Mud, Blood and Poppycock at 166-171.

[78] The Great War as I Saw it at 107.

[79] Alfred Andrews Diary, The Canadian Images and Letters Project.

[80] Mud, Blood and Poppycock at 173.

[81] Forgotten Victory at 177 and Mud, Blood and Poppycock at 291.

[82] Letters of Agar Adamson at 220.

[83] The Journal of Private Fraser at 207-208.

[84] Forgotten Victory at 143-145.

[85] The Great War as I Saw it at 99-100.

[86] The Journal of Private Fraser at 150-151.

[87] Charles Henry Savage, Memoir, The Canadian Letters and Images Project.

[88] The Journal of Private Fraser at 204-205.

[89] As Long as Faith and Freedom Last at 88-89.

[90] The Journal of Private Fraser at 207.

[91] The Journal of Private Fraser at 111.

[92] The Journal of Private Fraser at 121.

[93] Into the Jaws of Death at 84-85.

[94] Alfred Andrews Diary, The Canadian Images and Letters Project.

[95] CBC, The Somme.

[96] Marjorie Norris Barron (ed), *Medicine and Duty: The World War I Memoir of Captain Harold W. McGill, Medical Officer, 31st Battalion C.E.F.,* (Calgary: University of Calgary Press) (2007) at 172.

[97] The Journal of Private Fraser at 113-114.

[98] Charles Henry Savage, Memoir, The Canadian Letters and Images Project.

[99] CBC, The Second Battle of Ypres.

[100] The 50th Battalion in No Man's Land at 30.

[107] R. Lewis, *Over the Top with the 25th,* (Halifax: H.H. Marshall, Limited) (1918) at 32.

[102] As Long as Faith and Freedom Last at 223.

[103] As Long as Faith and Freedom Last at 180.

[104] As Long as Faith and Freedom Last at 185.

[105] McGill at 183.

[106] McGill at 182.

[107] The Great War as I Saw it at 95-96.

[108] Robin Prior & Trevor Wilson, *Command on the Western Front: The Military Career of Sir Henry Rawlinson 1914-1918,* (Barnsley: Pen & Sword Books Limited) (2004) at 23-24.

[109] Robert A. Doughty, *Pyrrhic Victory,* (Cambridge: The Belknap Press of Harvard University Press)(2005) at 115.

[110] Barbara W. Tuchman, *The Guns of August,* (New York: Ballantine Books) (1994) at 225-226.

[111] See Larry Zuckerman, *The Rape of Belgium,* (New York: New York University Press)(2004).

[112] Isabel V. Hull, *Absolute Destruction,* (Ithaca: Cornell University Press)(2005) at 248-257.

[113] Anthony Clayton, *Paths of Glory: The French Army 1914-18,* (London: Cassell) (2003) at 41.

[114] Peter Simkins, Geoffrey Jukes & Michael Hicky, *The First World War: The War to End All Wars,* (Oxford: Osprey Publishing) (2003) at 27-31.

[115] Forgotten Victory at 115-117.

[116] The First World War at 190 and Paths of Glory at 66.

[117] Paths of Glory at 36 to 38.

[118] Tim Travers, *The Killing Ground* (Barnsley: Pen & Sword Books Ltd.)(2003) at 38.

[119] Paths of Glory at 30.

[120] The First World War at 54 and Paths of Glory at 70.

[121] Pyrrhic Victory at 201.

[122] Forgotten Victory at 125.

[123] CEF at 81.

[124] Tim Cook, *At the Sharp End,* (Toronto: Viking Canada) (2007) at 304 and 347-348.

[125] CEF at 128.

[126] J.L. Granatstein, *Canada's Army,* (Toronto: University of Toronto Press) (2002) at 88.

[127] Letter to Sir Sam Hughes from Sir Charles Ross, dated June 23, 1915, Canadian Archives.

[128] Surviving Trench Warfare at 63-65.

[129] CEF at 134-137.

[130] Mud, Blood and Poppycock at 259.

[131] Gary Sheffield, *The Somme* (Cassell: London)(2003) at 36.

[132] John Keegan, *The Face of Battle, 15th ed. (Pimlico: London)(2001) at 231 and Martin Middlebrook, The First Day on the Somme,* (London: Penguin Books Ltd.) (1971) at 87.

[133] Gary Sheffield, The Somme at 36.

[134] Mud, Blood and Poppycock at 261.

[135] The First Day on the Somme at 76 and 90 and Forgotten Victory at 166-167.

[136] The Killing Ground at 142-143.

[137] The Killing Ground at 132-133.

[138] Battle Tactics of the Western Front at 56-57.

[139] Forgotten Victory at 167.

[140] The First Day on the Somme at 82.

[141] Mud, Blood and Poppycock at 262-263.

[142] The Face of Battle at 247-248.

[143] Robin Prior and Trevor Wilson, *The Somme* (Yale University Press: New Haven and London)(2005) at 116.

[144] David R. Facey-Crowther (ed.), Lieutenant Owen William Steele of the Newfoundland Regiment, (Montreal & Kingston: McGill-Queen's University Press) (2002) at 192.

[145] The First Day on the Somme at 187-190.

[146] The First Day on the Somme at 332.

[147] Malcolm Brown, *The Somme (*Pan Books: London)(2002) at 72.

[148] Forgotten Victory at 165.

[149] The Killing Ground at 161-164.

[150] The Face of Battle at 247.

[151] Prior and Wilson, The Somme at 64.

[152] The First Day on the Somme at 88.

[153] Battle Tactics of the Western Front at 172.

[154] Ian Passingham, *All the Kaiser's Men: The Life and Death of the German Army on the Western Front 1914-1918,* (Stroud: Sutton Publishing Limited) (2003) at 104.

[155] All the Kaiser's Men at 98-102.

[156] The First World War at 83.

[157] The Killing Ground at 166.

[158] Prior and Wilson, The Somme at 187.

[159] John Terraine, *The Smoke and the Fire,* (Leo Cooper: London)(1990) at 124.

[160] Jonathan Walker, *The Blood Tub,* (Spellmount Limited: Kent)(2000) at 10-11.

[161] The Blood Tub at 2.

[162] The Killing Ground at 178.

[163] Surviving Trench Warfare at 73-74 and J.L Granatstein, *Hell's Corner,* (Vancouver: Douglas & McIntyre Ltd.) (2004).

[164] CEF at 153.

[165] CEF at 153.

[166] CEF at 153-154.

[167] Gary Sheffield, The Somme at 122-124.

[168] Forgotten Victory at 177.

[169] CEF at 151-152.

[170] Gary Sheffield, The Somme at 132-133.

[171] CEF at 156-158.

[172] CEF at 158-159 and Gary Sheffield, The Somme at 132-133.

[173] CEF at 160-164.

[174] CEF at 164.

[175] The First World War, at 90.

[176] The Killing Ground at 183-185.

[177] CEF at 166-170.

[178] The Killing Ground at 187-189.

[179] Gary Sheffield, The Somme at 141-142.

[180] Gary Sheffield, The Somme at 144.

[181] Gary Sheffield, The Somme at 150.

[182] CEF at 171-173.

[183] CEF at 174.

[184] All the Kaiser's men at 123-125.

[185] Donald Stuart MacPherson, *A Soldier's Diary* (St. Catherines: Vanwell Publishing Limited)(2001) at 45-46.

[186] As Long as Faith and Freedom Last at 264.

[187] Ghosts Have Warm Hands at 9.

[188] The Journal of Private Fraser at 235-236.

[189] The Letters of Agar Adamson at 233.

[190] Lt. Col. D.E. Macintyre, *Canada at Vimy,* (Toronto: Peter Martin Associates Limited)(1967) at 64-65.

[191] Letters of Agar Adamson at 229.

[192] Ghosts Have Warm Hands at 10.

[193] Peter Hart, Bloody April, (London: Cassell)(2005) at 132.

[194] Royal Canadian Regiment January 2, 1917, War Diary Entry.

[195] January 2 Summary of Intelligence (attached to 3rd Division January 1917 War Diary).

[196] 7th Brigade (CFA) January 29, 1917, War Diary Entry.

[197] Ghosts Have Warm Hands at 10.

[198] Letters from the Front at 191.

[199] Mud, Blood and Poppycock at 111.

[200] National Archives of Canada - Order of Battle of the Canadian Corps and Attached Troops, 9th April, 1917.

[201] Mud, Blood and Poppycock at 140.

[202] Nikolas Gardner, "Julian Byng" in Ian F.W. Beckett and Steven J. Corvi (eds.), *Haig's Generals,* (Barnsley: Pen & Sword Books Ltd.) (2006) at 54.

[203] Jeffrey Williams, *Byng of Vimy,* (London: Leo Cooper) (1983).

[204] Letters of Agar Adamson at 254.

[205] "Julian Byng" in Haig's Generals at 54-74.

[206] Canada's Army at 58 and Pierre Berton, *Vimy,* (Anchor Canada) (1986) at 100.

[207] Surviving Trench Warfare at 90-93 and Canada's Army at 110-111 and 97.

[208] Canada's Army at 58, 81 and 118.

[209] Canada's Army at 98.

[210] See also A.M.J. Hyatt, *General Sir Arthur Currie: A Military Biography,* (Toronto: University of Toronto Press)(1987).

[211] Vimy at 99-100 and Canada's Army at 91.

[212] Vimy at 99 and Canada's Army at 94.

[213] Vimy at 99.

[214] Vimy at 98-99 and Canada's Army at 93.

[215] Frank Davies and Graham Maddocks, Bloody Red Tabs, (London: Leo Cooper)(1995) at 22.

[216] Bloody Red Tabs at 33-35.

[217] Bloody Red Tabs at 95.

[218] Bloody Red Tabs at 204-205.

[219] Bloody Red Tabs at 82.

[220]Bloody Red Tabs at 24.

[221]Bloody Red Tabs at 6.

[222]Canada's Army at 75, Canada and the Two World Wars at 87 and Bill Freeman and Richard Nielsen *Far From Home*, (Toronto: McGraw-Hill Ryerson) (1999) at 94.

[223]Georges Vanier: Soldier at 64.

[224]Wilfred Kerr, *Shrieks and Crashes,* (Ottawa: CEF Books)(2005) at 28-29.

[225]The 50th Battalion in No Man's Land at 74.

[226]Surviving Trench Warfare at 27-28 and Bloody April at 25-26.

[227]William Avery *"Billy" Bishop, Winged Warfare* (Manchester: Crecy Publishing)(2002) at 23.

[228]John Swettenham, McNaughton Vol. 1 1887-1939, (Toronto: The Ryerson Press) (1968) at 139-140.

[229]See, for example, Summary of Operations attached to the 1st Division February 1917 War Diary and RCR February 1, 1917 War Diary entry.

[230]See Operation Order No. 65 attached to the 3rd Canadian Divisional Artillery February 1917 War Diary.

[231]See 19th Battalion January 17, 1917, War Diary entry and 19th Battalion Operation Order dated January 14, 1917 (attached to 19th Battalion January War Diary).

[232]See January 25, 1917, Intelligence Summary attached to the 4th Division January 1917 War Diary.

[233]See January 3 and 5 entries in the 46th Battalion's January 1917 War Diary.

[234]See January 5 and 11 entries in 73rd Battalion January 1917 War Diary and January 11 entry in 78th Battalion January War Diary.

[235]See January 3 and 5 entries in 46th Battalion January 1917 War Diary.

[236]Ghosts Have Warm Hands at 12-13.

[237]The Journal of Private Fraser at 251.

[238]January 18, 1917, 3rd Division Intelligence Summary (attached to 3rd Division January 1917 War Diary).

[239]Ghosts Have Warm Hands at 21-22.

[240]The 50th Battalion in No Man's Land at 82.

[241]The 50th Battalion in No Man's Land at 241.

[242]Scouting Thrills at 25-26.

[243]Scouting Thrills at 24-25.

[244]See 4th Division Report on Operations for Week Ending January 4, 1917 (attached to 4th Division January 1917, War Diary).

[245]Bloody April at 24-25.

[246]Bloody April at 47.

[247]Bloody April at 78.

[248]Surviving Trench Warfare at 101.

[249]See 42nd Battalion Jan 1, 1917, War Diary entry and Jan 3, 1917, 3rd Division Summary of Intelligence.

[250]See 42nd Battalion Jan 1, 1917, War Diary entry.

[251]See Raids Carried out by the Canadian Corps dated January 4, 1917 (attached to 6th Brigade January 1917 War Diary).

[252]See 7th Brigade Report to 3rd Division, 42nd Battalion O.C.'s Report, "D" Battery Report on effect of Artillery Barrage (attached to 3rd Division February 1917, War Diary), Left Group 3rd C.D.A. Intelligence Report dated February 13-14, 1917, (attached to 3rd C.D.A. February 1917, War Diary), 7th Brigade February 13, 1917, War Diary entry and 42nd Battalion February 13, 1917, War Diary entry.

[253]StormTroop Tactics at 84.

[254]See 3rd Division Report to Canadian Corps and 3rd Division February 10 and 11, 1917, Summaries of Intelligence (attached to 3rd Division February 1917, War Diary) and 60th Battalion February 9, 1917, War Diary entry.

[255]See 2nd Division January 17 and 19 Daily Intelligence Summaries (attached to 2nd Division January 1917, War Diary).

[256]See Preliminary Report on Raid Carried out by 10th Canadian Infantry Brigade on Night 12th - 13th February, 1917, by Officer Commanding Raiding Parties, Full Report on Raid Carried out by 10th Canadian Infantry Brigade on Night 12th - 13th February, 1917, by Officer Commanding Raiding Parties, Officer Commanding 10th Field Company (CRE) Report to HQ 10th Brigade, 4th Division Summary of Intelligence dated February 14 and 15, 1917 (all attached to 4th Division February 1917 War Diary), 10th Brigade Operation Orders dated February 8, 9, 10 and 12, 1917 (attached to 10th Brigade February 1917 War Diary), 10th Brigade Operation Order dated February 8 and 11, 1917, and 10th Field Co. CRE Report to 4th Division (all attached to 10th Field Co. CRE February 1917 War Diary) and February 5-13 entries to 10th Field Co. CRE February 1917 War Diary, February 13 entry to 44th Battalion February 1917 War Diary, February 13 entry to 46th Battalion February 1917 War Diary, 47th Battalion Operation Order dated February 10, 1917 (attached to 47th Battalion February 1917 War Diary) and February 13 entry to 47th Battalion February 1917 War Diary and February 14 entry to 50th Battalion February 1917 War Diary.

[257]Report on Operations of Canadian Corps against Vimy Ridge at 1.

[258]Pyrrhic Victory at 309.

[259]Mud, Blood and Poppycock at 334.

[260]Mud, Blood and Poppycock at 321.

[261]Yves Buffetaut, *The 1917 Spring Offensives,* (Paris: Histoire & Collections)(1997) at 7.

[262]The 1917 Spring Offensives at 102-103.

[263]Mud, Blood and Poppycock at 320-321

[264]Forgotten Victory at 54-57.

[265]Mud, Blood and Poppycock at 322.

[266]Mud, Blood and Poppycock at 322.

[267]CEF at 216-221.

[268]The 1917 Spring Offensives at 7.

[269]Jonathan Nicholls, *Cheerful Sacrifice: The Battle of Arras 1917,* (Barnsley: Pen & Sword Books Limited) (2003) at 27 and 32.

[270]Gary Sheffield and John Bourne (editors), *Douglas Haig: War Diaries and Letters 1914-1918*, (Weidenfeld and Nicolson: London)(2005) at 270-271 and Alexander Turner, *Vimy Ridge 1917,* (Osprey Publishing Ltd.: Oxford)(2005) at 13.

[271]See Report - Canadian Corps Operation - Vimy at 2.

[272]See Canadian Corps Artillery Instructions for the Capture of Vimy Ridge at 46-47 (attached to GOC RA Canadian Corps April 1917 War Diary), Appendix III dated April 7, 1917 (attached to 2nd Brigade CFA April 1917 War Diary), Operation Order No. 114 dated April 6, 1917 (attached to 2nd CDA April 1917 War Diary), Appendix IV dated April 2, 1917 (attached to 6th Brigade CFA April 1917 War Diary) and Operation Order No. 75 dated April 3, 1917 (attached to 3rd CDA April 1917 War Diary).

[273]See Canadian Corps Additional Instructions with regard to Machine Gun Organization, Barrages and Supporting Fire dated March 1917 (attached to Yukon Motor M.G. Battery April 1917 War Diary and 1st Canadian Motor M.G. Brigade March 1917 War Diary), Instructions for the Offensive No. 1 dated March 27, 1917 (attached 5th Machine Gun Company March 1917 War Diary) and Instructions for the Offensive No. 2 dated February 27, 1917 attached to (2nd Division February 1917 War Diary).

[274]Battle Tactics of the Western Front at 124.

[275]Surviving Trench Warfare at 91 and Battle Tactics of the Western Front at 77.

[276]See 1st Division Platoon Organization and Organization of a Company dated February 23, 1917 (attached to 2nd Brigade February 1917 War Diary).

[277]See January 4 entry to 13th Battalion January 1917 War Diary.

[278]Canada at Vimy at 84-85.

[279]The 50th Battalion in No Man's Land at 81.

[280]CBC, The Battle of Vimy Ridge.

[281]The Journal of Private Fraser at 261.

[282]CBC, The Battle of Vimy Ridge.

[283]See, for example, Appendix A attached to 25th Battalion April 1917 War Diary.

[284]See, for example, March 22 entry to 31st Battalion March 1917 War Diary and 1st Division Platoon Organization dated February 23, 1917 (attached to 2nd Brigade February 1917 War Diary).

[285]See, for example, March 9-13 entries to 5th Battalion March 1917 War Diary and March 1-17 entries to 8th Machine Gun Company March 1917 War Diary.

[286]April 3 entry to 13th Battalion April 1917 War Diary.

[287]See, for example, April 2 entry to 5th Battalion April 1917 War Diary and April 2 entry to 26th Battalion April 1917 War Diary.

[288] CBC, The Battle of Vimy Ridge.

[289] As Long as Faith and Freedom Last at 251-252.

[290] First Army Report on Vimy (Vimy Operation) at 3.

[291] Canadian Corps Artillery Instructions for the Capture of Vimy Ridge Appendix "A" attached to GOC RA Canadian Corps April 1917 War Diary.

[292] Mud, Blood and Poppycock at 86.

[293] First Army Report on Vimy (The Artillery Preparation for the Attack on the Vimy Ridge by First Army) at 1.

[294] First Army Report on Vimy (Vimy Operation).

[295] Prior and Wilson, The Somme, at 52-56.

[296] First Army Report on Vimy (Vimy Operation) at 3.

[297] Allied Artillery of World War One at 27 and 76.

[298] Canadian Corps Artillery Instructions for the Capture of Vimy Ridge at 41, 44, 48 and 49 (attached to GOC RA Canadian Corps April 1917, War Diary).

[299] See, for example, 2nd Division Instructions for the Offensive No. 3 "Action of Artillery" at 2 (attached to 19th Battalion April 1917 War Diary).

[300] See, for example, Eaton's Group 3rd CDA Operation Order No. 2 dated March 27, 1917 (attached to 8th Brigade CFA March 1917 War Diary).

[301] Forgotten Victory at 141-142.

[302] Canadian Corps Artillery Instructions for the Capture of Vimy Ridge at 42 (attached to GOC RA Canadian Corps April 1917, War Diary).

[303] See April 6 entry to 5th Brigade CFA April 1917 War Diary.

[304] See March 28 and 31 entries to 1st Divisional Trench Mortar Group March 1917 War Diary and April 1 to 9 entries in 1st Divisional Trench Mortar Group April 1917 War Diary.

[305] See April 5 to 7 entries to 5th Brigade CFA April 1917 War Diary, April 7 entry to 6th Brigade CFA April 1917 War Diary and 26th Battalion Wire Cutting Report to 5th Brigade dated April 6, 1917 (attached to 26th Battalion April 1917 War Diary).

[306] See 4th Division Report (attached to 4th Division April 1917 War Diary) and General Alfred Dieterich, "The German 79th Reserve Infantry Division in the Battle of Vimy Ridge, April 1917, Canadian Military History Vol. 15 No. 1 pgs 69-85, at 74.

[307] See Canadian Corps Scheme of Operations (attached to Canadian Corps March 1917 War Diary).

[308] See, for example, Eaton's Group 3rd CDA Operation Order No. 6 dated April 2, 1917 (attached to 8th Brigade CFA April 1917 War Diary).

[309] Allied Artillery of World War One at 86-87.

[310] Canadian Corps Artillery Instructions for the Capture of Vimy Ridge at 44 and GOC RA Canadian Corps Artillery Instructions No. 2 dated April 1, 1917 (both attached to GOC RA Canadian Corps April 1917, War Diary).

[311] Canadian Corps Artillery Instructions for the Capture of Vimy Ridge at 44-45 (attached to GOC RA Canadian Corps April 1917, War Diary).

[312] See, for example, 3rd CDA March 31 Intelligence Report (attached to 3rd CDA March 1917 War Diary) and Operation Order No. 4 dated March 21 (attached to 4th Brigade CFA March 1917 War Diary).

[313] Command on the Western Front at 293-294.

[314] McNaughton at 19 and 66-97.

[315] See, for example, 2nd Canadian Siege Battery April 2-7 entries to April 1917, War Diary and 5th Canadian Siege Battery April 1, 3, 4, 6 and 8 entries to April 1917 War Diary.

[316] April 1 entry to 3rd Canadian Siege Battery April 1917 War Diary.

[317] Canadian Corps Artillery Instructions for the Capture of Vimy Ridge at 41-43.

[318] See March 31 entry to 2nd CDA March 1917, War Diary.

[319] Turner, Vimy Ridge 1917 at 48.

[320] See First Army - Report - Vimy.

[321] GOC RA Canadian Corps Artillery Instructions No. 8 dated April 6, 1917 (attached to GOC RA Canadian Corps April 1917 War Diary).

[322] Canadian Corps Artillery Instructions for the Capture of Vimy Ridge at 47 and 51 and First Army Report - Vimy Operation.

[323] Canadian Corps Artillery Instructions for the Capture of Vimy Ridge at 44-45.

[324] McGill at 264.

[325] April 5 and 7 entries to 3rd Canadian Siege Battery April 1917 War Diary and April 4 and 6 entries to 1st Brigade Canadian Garrison Artillery April 1917 War Diary.

[326] Canadian Corps Artillery Instructions for the Capture of Vimy Ridge at 44-45.

[327] Bloody April at 31, 42 and 43 and Ralph Barker, The Royal Flying Corps in World War I, (London: Constable & Robinson Ltd.) (2002) at 280.

[328] A Brief History of the Royal Flying Corps in World War I at 87.

[329] A Brief History of the Royal Flying Corps in World War I at 254.

[330] Into the Jaws of Death at 97.

[331] A Brief History of the Royal Flying Corps in World War I at 260.

[332] See Preparations under supervision of Chief Engineer at 30-36 (attached to Chief Engineer Canadian Corps April 1917 War Diary).

[333] Notes on Conference held at Canadian Corps HQ on 30 March 1917 (attached to 26th Battalion April 1917 War Diary).

[334] See April 5 entry to 2nd Battalion April 1917 War Diary and April 4 entry to 1st Brigade April 1917 War Diary.

[335] April 5 entry to 2nd Battalion April 1917 War Diary and April 5 entry to 1st Brigade April 1917 War Diary.

[336] April 4 entry to 1st Battalion April 1917 War Diary.

[337] Attachment to 31st Battalion Report to 6th Brigade (attached to 6th Brigade March 1917 War Diary).

[338] CEF at 212.

[339] 19th Battalion Instructions for the Offensive No. 7 attached to 19th Battalion April 1917 War Diary and 29th Battalion Instructions for the Attack attached to 29th Battalion April 1917 War Diary.

[340] Bloody April at 118.

[341] See Notes on Conference Held at Canadian Corps HQ on March 30, 1917, attached to 26th Battalion April 1917 War Diary and 13th (Imperial) Brigade Preliminary Order No. 2 dated April 4, 1917, attached to 4th Brigade April 1917 War Diary.

[342] See Instructions for the Offensive dated April 5, 1917, attached to 5th Brigade April 1917 War Diary.

[343] Report on Operations Carried out by 12th Canadian Infantry Brigade (In Conjunction with 11th Canadian Infantry Brigade) on 1st March 1917 (attached to 4th Division March 1917 War Diary).

[344] Canadian Corps Artillery Instructions for the Capture of Vimy Ridge at 47-48 (attached to GOC RA Canadian Corps April 1917 War Diary).

[345] Shrieks and Crashes at 21.

[346] Letters from the Front at 201.

[347] Robert Gordon Brown Diary, The Canadian Letters and Images Project.

[348] The Journal of Private Fraser at 256-257.

[349] The Great War as I Saw it at 114.

[350] The Great War as I Saw it at 113.

[351] James Robert Johnston, *Riding into War*, (Fredericton: Goose Lane Editions)(2004) at 37.

[352] See April 6 entry to 13th Battalion April 1917 War Diary.

[353] Cheerful Sacrifice at 39.

[354] April 3 entry to 9th Brigade CFA April 1917 War Diary.

[355] 2nd Division Daily Intelligence Summary for April 2, 1917 (attached to 2nd Division April 1917 War Diary).

[356] See First Army Intelligence Summary dated April 10 (attached to 27th Battalion April 1917 War Diary) and April 9 entry to 1st Brigade April 1917 War Diary.

[357] Alexander Watson, *Enduring the Great War*, (Cambridge: Cambridge University Press)(2008) at 26 to 31.

[358] 4th Division March 22, 1917 Summary of Intelligence, Weekly Summary of Operations March 22 to 29, 1917 (attached to 4th Division March 1917 War Diary) and Weekly Summary of Operations March 29 to April 5, 1917 (attached to 4th Division April 1917 War Diary).

[359] April 3 entry to 72nd Battalion April 1917 War Diary.

[360] April 6 entry to 38th Battalion April 1917 War Diary.

[361]See, for example, March 24 3rd CDA Intelligence Report (attached to 3rd CDA March 1917 War Diary) and March 24 entry to 5th Brigade CFA March 1917 War Diary.

[362]See April 12 Intelligence Summary (attached to Canadian Corps April 1917 War Diary).

[363]See April 12 Intelligence Summary (attached to Canadian Corps April 1917 War Diary).

[364]Winged Warfare at 65.

[365]See April 8 entry to 2nd Brigade April 1917 War Diary, 2nd Brigade Report on Raid Carried out by 10th Battalion (attached to 2nd Brigade April 1917 War Diary) and Daniel G. Dancocks, *Gallant Canadians: The Story of the Tenth Canadian Infantry Battalion 1914-1919,* (Calgary: The Calgary Highlanders Regimental Funds Foundation) (1990) at 108-109.

[366]See Report on Operations, 9th / 20th April 1917 (attached to 10th Battalion April 1917 War Diary).

[367]McGill at 266-267.

[368]Narrative of Offensive 9.4.17. attached to 27th Battalion April 1917 War Diary.

[369]April 9 entry to 73rd Battalion April 1917 War Diary.

[370]As Long as Faith and Freedom Last at 262.

[371]Letters from the Front at 201.

[372]April 9 entry to 13th Battalion April 1917 War Diary.

[373]April 9 entry to 102nd Battalion April 1917 War Diary and April 9 entry to 11th Brigade April 1917 War Diary.

[374]1st Battalion Report to 1st Brigade (attached to 1st Battalion April 1917 War Diary).

[375]The Journal of Private Fraser at 262.

[376]Lt. Gen. E.L.M. Burns, *General Mud,* (Toronto: Clarke, Irwin & Company Limited)(1970) at 42.

[377]Over the Top with the 25th at 53.

[378]As Long as Faith and Freedom Last at 263.

[379]Stuart Kirkland, The Canadian Images and Letters Project.

[380]Over the Top with the 25th at 53.

[381]The Great War As I Saw It at 116.

[382]Raymond Ives, The Canadian Letters and Images Project.

[383]April 9 entry to 2nd Brigade CFA April 1917 War Diary.

[384]April 9 entry to 5th CMR April 1917 War Diary.

[385]Report on Artillery in Attack on April 9th 1917 (attached to 5th Brigade CFA April 1917 War Diary).

[386]Narrative of Offensive Operations on 9th and 10th April 1917 (attached to 6th Brigade April 1917 War Diary).

[387]Riding into War at 46.

[388]See "B" Narrative attached to 3rd Battalion April 1917 War Diary.

[389]William Elder Letter, from the Canadian Great War Project (originally published in the Huntington Gleaner, Huntington, Quebec, May 24, 1917).

[390]Shrieks and Crashes at 23.

[391]Winged Warfare at 72.

[392]CBC, The Battle of Vimy Ridge.

[393]The Journal of Private Fraser at 262-263.

[394]See April 9 entry to 3rd Canadian Siege Battery April 1917 War Diary.

[395]As Long as Faith and Freedom Last at 265.

[396]See Information from FOO's and Liason Officers 2nd CDA at 18 (attached to 2nd CDA April 1917 War Diary).

[397]Winged Warfare at 72-73.

[398]Letters from the Front at 206.

[399]Over the Top with the 25th at 54.

[400]Gallant Canadians at 110-115.

[401]See Appendix "C" to Operations on the 9th of April 1917 (attached to 10th Battalion April 1917 War Diary).

[402]Appendix "C" to Operations on the 9th April 1917 (attached to 10th Battalion April 1917 War Diary).

[403]See Appendix "C" to Operations on the 9th April 1917 (attached to 10th Battalion April 1917 War Diary).

[404]Appendix "C" to Operations on the 9th April 1917 (attached to 10th Battalion April 1917 War Diary).

[405]Appendix "C" to Operations on the 9th April 1917 (attached to 10th Battalion April 1917 War Diary).

[406]See April 9 entry to 4th Brigade April 1917 War Diary and Major D.J. Corrigall, *The History of the Twentieth Canadian Battalion,* (Toronto: Stone & Cox Limited)(1935) at 107-122.

[407]See 14th Battalion April 12 1917 Report to 3rd Brigade (attached to 14th Battalion April 1917 War Diary).

[408]See Appendix to Summary of Operations on April 9th, 1917 (attached to 5th Battalion April 1917 War Diary).

[409]See Appendix to Summary of Operations on April 9th, 1917 (attached to 5th Battalion April 1917 War Diary).

[410]See Appendix to Summary of Operations on April 9th, 1917 (attached to 5th Battalion April 1917 War Diary).

[411]See, for example, 14th Battalion Report to 3rd Brigade dated April 25, 1917 (attached to 14th Battalion April 1917 War Diary) and Report on Operations 9th / 20th April 1917 (attached to 10th Battalion April 1917 War Diary).

[412]See April 9 entry to 2nd Brigade April 1917 War Diary.

[413] Report of 2nd Canadian Infantry Brigade dated May 2, 1917 (attached to 2nd Brigade April 1917 War Diary).

[414] See April 9 entry to 21st Battalion April 1917 War Diary.

[415] See Report on Operations 9th / 20th April 1917 (attached to 10th Battalion April 1917 War Diary).

[416] Doris H. Pieroth, *A Canadian's Road to Russia,* (Edmonton: The University of Alberta Press) (1989) at 313-314.

[417] See 21st Battalion Report (attached to 21st Battalion April 1917 War Diary) and CEF at 232.

[418] See, for example, April 9 entry to 21st Battalion April 1917 War Diary and 3rd Brigade Report to 1st Division (attached to 2nd Brigade April 1917 War Diary).

[419] See Summary of Operations 9th and 10th April, 1917 (attached to 2nd FC CRE April 1917 War Diary).

[420] See, for example, April 9 entry to 2nd Brigade April 1917 Wasr Diary and 3rd Brigade Report to 1st Division (attached to 3rd Brigade April 1917 War Diary).

[421] See Report on Artillery in Attack on April 9th 1917 (attached to 5th Brigade CFA April 1917 War Diary).

[422] See, for example, Report on Operations 9th / 20th April 1917 (attached to 10th Battalion April 1917 War Diary).

[423] See Appendix to Summary of Operations on April 9, 1917 (attached to 5th Battalion April 1917 War Diary).

[424] See Report on Operations, 9th / 20th April 1917 (attached to 10th Battalion April 1917 War Diary).

[425] See Summary of Operations 8th April to 18th April, 1917 (attached to 5th Brigade April 1917 War Diary) and April 9 entry to 22nd Battalion April 1917 War Diary.

[426] Notes on Points of Interest (attached to 2nd Brigade April 1917 War Diary).

[427] See, for example, 14th Battalion Report to 3rd Brigade dated April 25th, 1917 (attached to 14th Battalion April 1917 War Diary) and Appendix "C" to Operations on the 9th April 1917 (attached to 10th Battalion April 1917 War Diary).

[428] H.M. Urquhart, *The History of the 16th Battalion (The Canadian Scottish),* (Toronto: The MacMillan Company of Canada, Limited)(1932) at 210-219.

[429] John Swettenham ed., *Valiant Men,* (Toronto: A.M. Hakkert Ltd.)(1983) at 51.

[430] *Valiant Men* at 53.

[431] See April 9 entry to 5th Brigade CFA April 1917 War Diary.

[432] See April 9 entry to 4th Brigade April 1917 War Diary.

[433] See April 9 entry to 9th Field Company CRE April 1917 War Diary.

[434] See April 13 entry to 4th Division April 1917 War Diary.

[435]See April 4 entry to 5th CMR April 1917 War Diary and April 4 entry to 9th FC CRE April 1917 War Diary.

[436]See Operation Order No. 82 dated April 7, 1917 (attached to 8th Brigade April 1917 War Diary).

[437]See Report on Operations Carried out by the 1st CMR on the 9th April 1917 (attached to 1st CMR April 1917 War Diary).

[438]See 7th Brigade Report to 3rd Division dated April 16, 1917 (attached to 7th Brigade April 1917 War Diary).

[439]As Long as Faith and Freedom Last at 266.

[440]As Long as Faith and Freedom Last at 264-265.

[441]See Report on Operations Carried out by the 1st CMR on the 9th April 1917 (attached to 1st CMR April 1917 War Diary).

[442]As Long as Faith and Freedom Last at 266-267.

[443]See 7th Brigade Report to 3rd Division dated April 16, 1917 (attached to 7th Brigade April 1917 War Diary).

[444]See Report on Operations Carried out by the 1st CMR on the 9th April 1917 (attached to 1st CMR April 1917 War Diary).

[445]As Long as Faith and Freedom Last at 267.

[446]Victor N. Swanson, *Who Said War is Hell!,* (Saskatoon: Modern Press)(1983) at 41.

[447]See Report of Operations on 9th, 10th and 11th April 1917 and Report on Operations Carried out by the 1st CMR Battalion on the 9th April 1917 (attached to 1st CMR April 1917 War Diary), April 9 entry to 5th CMR April 1917 War Diary and Report on No. 2 Section 8th Field Company Canadian Engineers, in conjunction with 1st CMR Batt'n (attached to 8th FC CRE April 1917 War Diary).

[448]See Report by Lieut Morgan commanding 4 guns attached to 1st CMR Bn (attached to 8th Canadian Machine Gun Company April 1917 War Diary) and Lt. Col. C.S. Grafton, The Canadian "Emma Gees", (London: Hunter Printing Company)(1938) at 68.

[449]CEF at 233.

[450]See Summary of Operations (attached to RCR April 1917 War Diary) and Operations Against Vimy Ridge (attached to 2nd CMR April 1917 War Diary).

[451]As Long as Faith and Freedom Last at 269.

[452]See April 9 entry to 5th CMR April 1917 War Diary.

[453]See April 9 entry to 102nd Battalion April 1917 War Diary.

[454]See April 9 entries to 102nd Battalion and 54th Battalion April 1917 War Diaries.

[455]General Mud at 43.

[456]See 4th Canadian Division Report at 4 (attached to 4th Division April 1917 War Diary).

[457]See 4th Division Report at 6 (attached to 4th Division April 1917 War Diary).

[458] Duguid A. Fortescue, *History of the Canadian Grenadier Guards,* (Montreal: Gazette Printing Company (Limited) (1965).

[459] General Mud at 43.

[460] See Report on Operations on Vimy Ridge between 9th and 13th April 1917 (attached to 12th Brigade April 1917 War Diary).

[461] See 1st Battalion Report to 1st Brigade (attached to 1st Battalion April 1917 War Diary), 2nd Battalion Report to 1st Brigade (attached to 2nd Battalion April 1917 War Diary) and 3rd Battalion Report (attached to 3rd Battalion April 1917 War Diary).

[462] See Report on Operations 9th to 16th April 1917 (attached to 7th Battalion April 1917 War Diary).

[463] See 1st Battalion Report to 1st Brigade (attached to 1st Battalion April 1917 War Diary).

[464] See April 9 entry to 16th Battalion April 1917 War Diary and 4th Battalion Report to 1st Brigade (attached to 4th Battalion April 1917 War Diary).

[465] See April 9 entry to 13th Machine Gun Company April 1917 War Diary.

[466] See April 9 entry to 1st Brigade April 1917 War Diary.

[467] Shrieks and Crashes at 24.

[468] The Great War as I Saw it at 117.

[469] The Journal of Private Fraser at 263.

[470] McGill at 268.

[471] A Canadian's Road to Russia at 314.

[472] The Journal of Private Fraser at 264.

[473] Audrey and Paul Grescoe eds., The Book of War Letters, (Toronto: McClelland & Stewart Ltd.)(2003) at 144.

[474] McGill at 268-269.

[475] McGill at 268.

[476] See 31st Battalion Report to 6th Brigade (attached to 31st Battalion April 1917 War Diary).

[477] See April 9 entry to 29th Battalion April 1917 War Diary.

[478] See 31st Battalion Report to 6th Brigade (attached to 31st Battalion April 1917 War Diary).

[479] A Canadian's Road to Russia at 314-315.

[480] The Journal of Private Fraser at 264.

[481] See April 9 entry to 29th Battalion April 1917 War Diary.

[482] Major Horace C. Singer, History of the 31st Canadian Infantry Battalion C.E.F., (Calgary: Detselig Enterprises Ltd.)(2006) at 210.

[483] A Canadian's Road to Russia at 314.

[484] See Narrative of Offensive Operations on 9th and 10th April 1917 (attached to 6th Brigade April 1917 War Diary).

[485] See April 9 entry to 27th Battalion April 1917 War Diary.

[486] See Information from F.O.O.'s and Liaison Officers 2nd CDA at 39 (attached to 2nd CDA April 1917 War Diary) and Chronological Report of Attack (attached to 3rd CDA April 1917 War Diary).

[487] Ernest G. Black, *I Want One Volunteer,* (Toronto: The Ryerson Press)(1965) at 60.

[488] I Want One Volunteer at 60-61.

[489] A Canadian's Road to Russia at 314.

[490] Byng of Vimy at 159 and Turner, Vimy Ridge at 74-75.

[491] See Report of No. 1 Section, 8th Field Company Canadian Engineers, in conjunction with 4th CMR Batt'n (attached to 8th FC CRE April 1917 War Diary).

[492] As Long as Faith and Freedom Last at 272.

[493] See Narrative of Part Played by the Engineers of the 3rd Canadian Division (attached to 3rd Division CRE April 1917 War Diary).

[494] See April 9 entry to 3rd CDA April 1917 War Diary.

[495] See Summary of Operations (attached to RCR April 1917 War Diary), R.C. Fetherstonaugh, *The Royal Canadian Regiment 1883-1933,* (Fredericton: Centennial Print & Litho Ltd.)(1981) at 281, Captain S.G. Bennett, *The 4th Canadian Mounted Rifles 1914-1919,* (Toronto: Murray Printing Company Limited)(1926) at 44-57 and Ralph Hodder-Williams, *Princess Patricia's Canadian Light Infantry,* (Toronto: Hodder and Stoughton Limited)(1923) at 213-234.

[496] As Long as Faith and Freedom Last at 270.

[497] See Narrative of Operations (attached to PPCLI April 1917 War Diary), Operations Against Vimy Ridge (attached to 2nd CMR April 1917 War Diary) and Report by Lieut. Dickinson (attached to 8th MG Co. April 1917 War Diary).

[498] See Summary of Operations (attached to RCR April 1917 War Diary), Report on Action of 4th CMR Battalion on Assault and Capture of Vimy Ridge (attached to 4th CMR April 1917 War Diary), 7th Brigade Report to 3rd Division (attached to 7th Brigade April 1917 War Diary) and Hodder-Williams, Princess Patricia's Canadian Light Infantry.

[499] See April 9 entry to 42nd Battalion April 1917 War Diary and Lt. Col. C. Beresford Topp, *The 42nd Battalion CEF Royal Highlanders of Canada*, (Montreal: Gazette Printing Co., Limited)(1931) at 117-132.

[500] See April 9 entry to 54th Battalion April 1917 War Diary.

[501] See April 9 entry to 102nd Battalion April 1917 War Diary.

[502] CBC, The Battle of Vimy Ridge.

[503] General Mud at 46-47.

[504] See April 9 entry to 11th Brigade April 1917 War Diary, Report on Operations from April 9th to 13th (attached to 78th Battalion April 1917 War Diary), April 9 entry to 11th FC CRE April 1917 War Diary, Appendix "A" covering operations 8-4-17 to 14-4-17 (attached to 85th Battalion

April 1917 War Diary), April 9 entry to 4th Division April 1917 War Diary and Communications Report (attached to 4th Division April 1917 War Diary).

[505] CBC, The Battle of Vimy Ridge.

[506] Capt. MacDowell's Report to OC 38th Battalion 8 am April 9 (attached to 12th Brigade April 1917 War Diary).

[507] See Appendix 1 to Report on Operations on Vimy Ridge between 9th and 13th April 1917 (attached to 12th Brigade April 1917 War Diary).

[508] See Capt. MacDowell's Report to OC 38th Battalion 10:30 am April 9 (attached to 12th Brigade April 1917 War Diary).

[509] See Report of Operations from April 9th to 13th (attached to 78th Battalion April 1917 War Diary) and Report on Operations on Vimy Ridge between 9th and 13th April 1917 (attached to 12th Brigade April 1917 War Diary).

[510] See Report on Recent Operations (attached to 12th MG Co. April 1917 War Diary).

[511] See Report on Operations on Vimy Ridge between 9th and 13th April 1917 (attached to 12th Brigade April 1917 War Diary).

[512] See Report on Operations April 9th to 13th 1917 (attached to 38th Battalion April 1917 War Diary) and Report on Operations on Vimy Ridge between 9th and 13th April 1917 (attached to 12th Brigade April 1917 War Diary).

[513] See Report on Operations on Vimy Ridge between 9th and 13th April 1917 (attached to 12th Brigade April 1917 War Diary), Report on Operations from April 9th to 13th (attached to 78th Battalion April 1917 War Diary) and April 9 entry to 87th Battalion April 1917 War Diary.

[514] See Report on Operations on Vimy Ridge Between 9th and 13th April 1917 (attached to 12th Brigade April 1917 War Diary) and Bernard McEvoy and Capt. A.H. Finlay, History of the 72nd Canadian Infantry Battalion Seaforth Highlanders of Canada, (Vancouver: Cowan & Brookhouse)(1920) at 49.

[515] See Preliminary Report of Operations of 9/4/17 (attached to 72nd Battalion April 1917 War Diary).

[516] See Narrative of Offensive 9.4.17. (attached to 27th Battalion April 1917 War Diary).

[517] C Company Narrative (attached to 27th Battalion April 1917 War Diary).

[518] See the Journal of Private Fraser at 264-265.

[519] See Narrative of Operations on 9th and 10th April 1917 (attached to 6th Brigade April 1917 War Diary) and 4th Battalion Report to 1st Brigade (attached to 4th Battalion April 1917 War Diary).

[520] See Narrative of Offensive Operations on 9th and 10th April 1917 (attached to 6th Brigade April 1917 War Diary).

[521] See 4th Battalion Report to 1st Brigade (attached to 4th Battalion April 1917 War Diary).

[522] See 1st Battalion Report to 1st Brigade (attached to 1st Battalion April 1917 War Diary).

[523] See April 9 entry to 1st Brigade April 1917 War Diary.

[523]See Report (attached to 3rd Battalion April 1917 War Diary).

[525]Major D.J. Goodspeed, Battle Royal: A History of the Royal Regiment of Canada 1862-1962, (Canada: he Royal Regiment of Canada Association)(1962) at 181.

[526]As Long as Faith and Freedom Last at 271.

[527]The Great War As I Saw It at 118.

[528]Canada at Vimy at 111.

[529]See 4th Battalion Report to 1st Brigade (attached to 4th Battalion April 1917 War Diary).

[530]See April 9 entry to 11th Brigade April 1917 War Diary, April 9 entry to 87th Battalion War Diary and April 9 entry to 75th Battalion War Diary.

[531]See April 9 entry to 87th Battalion April 1917 War Diary.

[532]See Report of Patrols sent to Willerval 9th April, 1917 and OC's Report (both attached to Canadian Light Horse April 1917 War Diary) and April 9 entry to Canadian Light Horse April 1917 War Diary.

[533]See Appendix "A" covering operations 8-4-17 to 14-4-17 (attached to 85th Battalion April 1917 War Diary), Report on Operations April 9th to April 13th 1917 (attached to 46th Battalion April 1917 War Diary) and Diary. First Army (attached to 12th Brigade April 1917 War Diary).

[534]See April 9 entry to 4th Division April 1917 War Diary.

[535]See Appendix "A" covering operations 8-4-17 to 14-4-17 (attached to 85th Battalion April 1917 War Diary).

[536]See Appendix "A" covering operations 8-4-17 to 14-4-17 (attached to 85th Battalion April 1917 War Diary) and Lt. Col. Joseph Hayes, The Eighty-Fifth in France and Flanders, (Halifax: Royal Print & Litho Limited)(1920) at 53-54.

[537]CBC, The Battle of Vimy Ridge.

[538]See Appendix "A" covering operations 8-4-17 to 14-4-17 (attached to 85th Battalion April 1917 War Diary), Report on Operations on Vimy Ridge Between 9th and 13th April 1917 and Diary. First Army (both attached to 12th Brigade April 1917 War Diary) and April 9 entry to 87th Battalion April 1917 War Diary.

[539]See Report of Operations from April 9th to 13th (attached to 78th Battalion April 1917 War Diary) and Report on Operations on Vimy Ridge Between 9th and 13th April 1917 (attached to 12th Brigade April 1917 War Diary).

[540]See 9th, 10th, 11th and 12th Battery's CFA Records of Events from a Period of Preparation for the Attack on Vimy Ridge up to September 7th 1917 (attached to 3rd Brigade CFA April 1917 War Diary).

[541]See Record for the 11th Battery CFA of Events from the Period of Preparation for the Attack on Vimy Ridge up to September 7th 1917 (attached to 3rd Brigade CFA April 1917 War Diary).

[542]See Record for the 11th Battery CFA of Events from the Period of Preparation for the Attack on Vimy Ridge up to September 7th 1917 (attached to 3rd Brigade CFA April 1917 War Diary).

[543] See April 9 entry to 1st Brigade CFA April 1917 War Diary and April 9 entry to 1st CDA April 1917 War Diary.

[544] See April 9 entry to 2nd Brigade CFA April 1917 War Diary and April 9 entry to 1st CDA April 1917 War Diary.

[545] See Appendix "A" covering operations 8-4-17 to 14-4-17 (attached to 85th Battalion April 1917 War Diary).

[546] CBC, The Battle of Vimy Ridge.

[547] See April 10 entry to 13th Battalion April 1917 War Diary.

[548] See April 10, 11 and 12 entries to 6th Brigade CFA April 1917 War Diary, April 10 and 11 entries to 5th Brigade CFA April 1917 War Diary and April 10, 11 and 12 entries to 2nd CDA April 1917 War Diary.

[549] See Report - Canadian Corps Operation - Vimy at 31.

[550] Report - Canadian Corps Operation - Vimy at 29 and McNaughton at 91.

[551] Canada at Vimy at 115.

[552] See April 9 entry to 6th Brigade April 1917 War Diary and Narrative of Offensive Operations on 9th and 10th April 1917 (attached to 6th Brigade April 1917 War Diary).

[553] See April 9 entry to 2nd CDA April 1917 War Diary, 4th Battalion Report to 1st Brigade (attached to 4th Battalion April 1917 War Diary), April 9 entry to 13th Canadian Machine Gun Company April 1917 War Diary, Report (attached to 1st Canadian Machine Gun Company April 1917 War Diary), Turner, Vimy Ridge at 78-79 and General Alfred Dieterich at 80-82.

[554] See 49th Battalion Report to 7th Brigade (attached to 49th Battalion April 1917 War Diary) and Sub-Appendixes 55 and 56 (attached to 3rd Division April 1917 War Diary).

[555] The 50th Battalion in No Man's Land at 95.

[556] Valiant Men at 55.

[557] See Report on Attack Carried out by the 50th Battalion on Hill 145, April 10, 1917 (attached to 10th Brigade April 1917 War Diary).

[558] See Report on Attack Carried out by the 50th Battalion on Hill 145, April 10, 1917 (attached to 10th Brigade April 1917 War Diary).

[559] See Report on Attack on Hill 145 by 44th and 50th Canadian Infantry, April 10, 1917 (attached to 10th Brigade April 1917 War Diary).

[560] The 50th Battalion in No Man's Land at 97.

[561] The 50th Battalion in No Man's Land at 97-98.

[562] See Report (attached to 60th Battalion April 1917 War Diary).

[563] See April 11 entry to 1st Brigade April 1917 War Diary.

[564] See Report on Attack Carried Out by the 50th Battalion on the "Pimple", April 12, 1917 (attached to 10th Brigade April 1917 War Diary).

[565] James L. McWilliams and R. James Steel, *The Suicide Battalion,* (St. Catherines: Vanwell Publishing Limited) at 83 and Report on Attack on "Pimple", 46th Battalion, April 11th to 13th, 1917 (attached to 10th Brigade April 1917 War Diary).

[566] See April 9 entry to Borden Motor Machine Gun Battery April 1917 War Diary.

[567] The 50th Battalion in No Man's Land at 98-99.

[568] See Report of Attack on "Pimple" by 44th Battalion, April 12, 1917, Report on Attack Carried out by the 50th Battalion, on the "Pimple", April 12, 1917 and Report on Attack on "Pimple", 46th Battalion, April 11th to 13th, 1917 (all attached to 10th Brigade April 1917 War Diary).

[569] See April 12 entry to 50th Battalion April 1917 War Diary and The Suicide Battalion at 83.

[570] See April 9 entry to 73rd Battalion April 1917 War Diary and Report on Operations on Vimy Ridge Between 9th and 13th April 1917 (attached to 12th Brigade April 1917 War Diary).

[571] See 4th Division Report at 8 (attached to 4th Division April 1917 War Diary).

[572] The 50th Battalion in No Man's Land at 100.

[573] See Report on Attack on "Pimple" by 44th Battalion, April 12, 1917 (attached to 10th Brigade April 1917 War Diary).

[574] See Messages and Signals Appendix 21 (attached to 46th Battalion April 1917 War Diary).

[575] See Report on Attack on "Pimple", 46th Battalion, April 11th to 13th, 1917 and Report on Attack on "Pimple" by 44th Battalion, April 12, 1917 (both attached to 10th Brigade April 1917 War Diary) and Messages and Signals Appendix 21 (attached to 46th Battalion April 1917 War Diary).

[576] Turner, Vimy Ridge at 30.

[577] CEF at 241.

[578] CEF at 241.

[579] CBC, The Battle of Vimy Ridge.

[580] McGill at 268.

[581] Stuart Kirkland Letter, The Canadian Letters & Images Project (originally published in May 10, 1917, Dutton Advance, Dutton, Ontario).

[582] Stuart Kirkland Letter.

[583] See Report on the Collection and Evacuation of Wounded (attached to Deputy Director Medical Services Canadian Corps April 1917 War Diary).

[584] William D. Mathieson, *My Grandfather's War,* (Toronto: MacMillan of Canada) (1981) at 119.

[585] See Report on Operations on Vimy Ridge Between 9th and 13th April 1917 (attached to 12th Brigade April 1917 War Diary).

[586] The Journal of Private Fraser at 268.

[587] Susan Mann (ed.), *The War Diary of Clare Gass 1915-1918,* (Montreal & Kingston: McGill-Queen's University Press) (2000) at 165.

[588] Clare Gass at 287-288.

[589] See 3rd Brigade Report to 1st Division (attached to 3rd Brigade April 1917 War Diary).

[590]See Turner, Vimy Ridge at 21-22.

[591]See April 10 Intelligence Summary (attached to Canadian Corps April 1917 War Diary).

[592]See April 15 Intelligence Summary (attached to Canadian Corps April 1917 War Diary).

[593]Turner, Vimy Ridge at 79 and CEF at 237.

[594]Turner, Vimy Ridge at 22 and Canadian Corps Intelligence Summaries dated April 9 and 10, 1917 and First Army Intelligence Summary dated April 10, 1917 (all attached to 27th Battalion April 1917 War Diary).

[595]Canada at Vimy at 112.

[596]See 3rd Brigade Report to 1st Division (attached to 3rd Brigade April 1917 War Diary).

[597]See Report on Operations of Canadian Corps against Vimy Ridge at 31.

[598]Into the Jaws of Death at 98.

[599]See Preliminary Report of Operation of 9/4/17 (attached to 72nd Battalion April 1917 War Diary).

[600]General Mud at 46.

[601]Roy Ito, *We Went to War,* (Stittsville: Canada's Wings, Inc.)(1984) at 57.

[602]As Long as Faith and Freedom Last at 268.

[603]The 50th Battalion in No Man's Land at 106-107.

[604]CEF at 216-217 and Paths of Glory at 127.

[605]CEF at 244.

[606]See April 12 entry to 2nd CDA April 1917 War Diary.

[607]Turner, Vimy Ridge at 78 and Alfred Dieterich at 80.

[608]Turner, Vimy Ridge at 82-83.

[609]Turner, Vimy Ridge at 90.

[610]The 1917 Spring Offensives at 56.

[611]Cheerful Sacrifice at 135.

[612]Cheerful Sacrifice at 165-166.

[613]Mud, Blood and Poppycock at 334.

[614]The 1917 Spring Offensives at 102.

[615]The 1917 Spring Offensive at 116.

[616]The 1917 Spring Offensive at 116.

[617]Paths of Glory at 127.

[618]The 1917 Spring Offensive at 102.

[619]The First World War at 119.

[620]Mud, Blood and Poppycock at 335-336.

[621]Paths of Glory at 129.

[622]Paths of Glory at 133.

[623]Paths of Glory at 129.

[624] The 1917 Spring Offensives at 174.

[625] Paths of Glory at 130.

[626] The 1917 Spring Offensives at 177.

[627] Paths of Glory at 134.

[628] Paths of Glory at 134-135.

[629] Douglas Haig: War Diaries and Letters 1914-1918 at 281.

[630] Forgotten Victory at 217-218.

[631] Surviving Trench Warfare at 175-176.

Index